D0857649

Fifty Years of
Personality Psychology

A Continuation Order Plan is available for this series. A continuation order will bring delivery of each new volume immediately upon publication. Volumes are billed only upon actual shipment. For further information please contact the publisher.

Fifty Years of Personality Psychology

Edited by

Kenneth H. Craik

University of California
Berkeley, California

Robert Hogan

University of Tulsa
Tulsa, Oklahoma

and

Raymond N. Wolfe

State University of New York
Geneseo, New York

PLENUM PRESS • NEW YORK AND LONDON

Library of Congress Cataloging-in-Publication Data

Fifty years of personality psychology / edited by Kenneth H. Craik,
Robert Hogan, and Raymond N. Wolfe.
    p.   cm. -- (Perspectives on individual differences)
    A comparative analysis of the 1937 textbooks Personality by Gordon
W. Allport and Psychology of personality by Ross Stagner.
    Includes bibliographical references and index.
    ISBN 0-306-44291-4
    1. Personality--History. 2. Allport, Gordon W. (Gordon Willard),
1897-1967. Personality. 3. Stagner, Ross, 1909-   Psychology of
personality.   I. Craik, Kenneth H. II. Hogan, Robert, 1937-   .
III. Wolfe, Raymond N. IV. Allport, Gordon W. (Gordon Willard),
1897-1967. Personality. V. V. Stagner, Ross, 1909-   Psychology of
personality. VI. Series.
    [DNLM: 1. Allport, Gordon W. (Gordon Willard), 1897-1967.
2. Stagner, Ross, 1909-   . 3. Personality--congresses.
4. Personality Assessment--congresses. 5. Psychological Theory-
-congresses.   BF 698 F469]
BF698.F525 1993
155.2'09'04--dc20
DNLM/DLC
for Library of Congress   92-48903
                                                               CIP

ISBN 0-306-44291-4

Printed in the United States of America

To GORDON W. ALLPORT AND ROSS STAGNER
in celebration of their contributions
to personality psychology

Contributors

Irving E. Alexander, Department of Psychology, Duke University, Durham, North Carolina 27706

Roy F. Baumeister, Department of Psychology, Case Western Reserve University, Cleveland, Ohio 44106

Peter Borkenau, Department of Psychology, University of Bielefeld, N-4800 Bielefeld 1, Germany

Bertram J. Cohler, Committee on Human Development, University of Chicago, Chicago, Illinois 60637

Kenneth H. Craik, Institute of Personality and Social Research, University of California, Berkeley, California 94720

Bella M. DePaulo, Department of Psychology, University of Virginia, Charlottesville, Virginia 22903

Alan C. Elms, Department of Psychology, University of California, Davis, California 95616

Robert A. Emmons, Department of Psychology, University of California, Davis, California 95616

Garth J. O. Fletcher, Department of Psychology, University of Canterbury, Christchurch 1, New Zealand

David C. Funder, Department of Psychology, University of California, Riverside, California 92521

Robert Hogan, Department of Psychology, University of Tulsa, Tulsa, Oklahoma 74104

Oliver P. John, Department of Psychology, University of California, Berkeley, California 94720

Salvatore R. Maddi, School of Social Ecology, University of California, Irvine, California 92717

Gerald A. Mendelsohn, Institute of Personality and Social Research, Berkeley, California 94720

Lawrence A. Pervin, Department of Psychology, Rutgers University, New Brunswick, New Jersey 08903

Richard W. Robins, Department of Psychology, University of California, Berkeley, California 94720

M. Brewster Smith, Board of Studies in Psychology, University of California, Santa Cruz, California 95064

Ross Stagner, Department of Psychology, Wayne State University, Detroit, Michigan 48202

David G. Winter, Department of Psychology, University of Michigan, Ann Arbor, Michigan 48109

Raymond N. Wolfe, Department of Psychology, State University of New York, Geneseo, New York, 14454

Lawrence S. Wrightsman, Department of Psychology, University of Kansas, Lawrence, Kansas 66045

Preface

This volume celebrates the textbooks *Personality: A Psychological Interpretation* by Gordon W. Allport and *Psychology of Personality* by Ross Stagner, both first published in 1937. In 1987, several occasions were held to mark the fiftieth anniversary of the publication of the two volumes and to acknowledge their role in defining and establishing the identity of personality psychology as a distinctive field of scientific inquiry within the United States.

At any given time, the textbooks of a science offer revealing information about its intellectual structure and research program. Even more so, its "founding" textbooks provide a temporal anchor for gaining a historical perspective on the field and a source of insights concerning its subsequent development and current situation.

In spring 1987, at the University of California's Institute of Personality Assessment and Research (IPAR) (now the Institute of Personality and Social Research) in Berkeley, Ross Stagner was invited to offer his personal perspective on these two textbooks and the subsequent development of personality psychology. In addition, a special symposium was devoted to an appreciation of the life and works of Gordon W. Allport. In a third series of talks, invited speakers offered commentaries on issues that were central to personality psychology in 1937 and that continue to warrant our attention today. As part of its annual meetings in August 1987, the American Psychological Association's Division of Personality and Social Psychology held a special marathon four-hour symposium that was an expanded version of IPAR's celebrations.

In this volume, we offer highlights of these occasions as well as additional contributions developed especially for this publication. The book is organized into four sections. First, the introductory chapter presents a comparative analysis of the 1937 textbooks by Allport and Stagner and then uses this context to describe the origins and conceptualization of our volume and to give a detailed account of its organization and contents. The second section of the volume includes three chapters dealing with the historical and personal background of the two textbooks. The third section groups three chapters concerning the current state of personality psychology and its contemporary textbooks. In the fourth section, we devote twelve chapters to gaining a present-day perspective on such abiding issues in personality psychology as the individual and the single case, motives and the self, judging persons, and personality assessment and prediction. Finally, the epilogue offers an optimistic view of the future of our field.

This volume has three aims. First, we see it as a contribution to our ongoing task of gaining a historical perspective on the development of personality psychology as a scientific endeavor. Beyond its intellectual importance, such collective remembering holds the promise of serving valuable social functions for a community of researchers. For example, narrative accounts of a community's origins can generate vivid reminders of its members' shared aspirations. Second, we hope that the volume will bring about more explicit and concerted discussion of the possible forms and substance of contemporary textbooks in personality psychology. Many pertinent issues have been raised in rather fragmented fashion over the years in textbook reviews published in *Contemporary Psychology* and elsewhere. This volume constitutes a beginning forum for reflecting on and joining opposing views on these matters. The third aim of the volume is to employ a historical vantage point as one means of gaining a comprehensive overview of our current research agenda in personality psychology. Has a particular research topic now perceived as "trendy" in fact been an enduring concern of our field from the outset? Have some topics and methods fallen by the wayside that should not have been abandoned after all? The comparative analysis of textbooks over time can afford us a broad picture of such continuities and discontinuities in our field's research directions.

Given these purposes, we have been remarkably fortunate in gaining the cooperation of an array of contributors who are authorities in the fields of their individual assignments. We greatly appreciate their willingness to take time away from their own research programs to aid in this effort at historical perspective taking. The logistics of assembling papers delivered at several different gatherings and arranging for additional new works for the volume have combined with our own geographical separation to cause some delays in publication. At times we feared that the materials for this book would themselves have become "historic" by the time of their publication. We appreciate the patience and goodwill of our contributors in this regard. We also want to acknowledge the dispatch with which publication has been facilitated once the final manuscripts became available—thanks are due here to Eliot Werner and Patrick Connolly and their colleagues at Plenum and to Robert Brown and Cecil Reynolds, coeditors of Plenum's series Perspectives on Individual Differences. Finally, we salute the sustaining interest and support of Ross Stagner throughout this project.

Editing a volume can sometimes turn into a bit of a chore, but not so in this case. We have been happy to serve as agents of a scientific community delighted in sharing a worthy and inspiring heritage. That community encompasses our contributors, our symposia audiences, and now—we trust—the readers of this volume as well.

KENNETH H. CRAIK
ROBERT HOGAN
RAYMOND N. WOLFE

Contents

PART III. CURRENT STATE OF PERSONALITY PSYCHOLOGY AND ITS TEXTS

PART IV. PRESENT-DAY PERSPECTIVES ON BASIC ISSUES

PART V. EPILOGUE

PART ONE

INTRODUCTION

CHAPTER ONE

The 1937 Allport and Stagner Texts in Personality Psychology

KENNETH H. CRAIK

In August 1937, Gordon W. Allport and Ross Stagner completed and dated the prefaces to their distinctive new textbooks. Allport's textbook was entitled *Personality: A Psychological Interpretation* and was published by Henry Holt in New York, with a later English edition by Constable & Company issued in London in 1949. Stagner's textbook was entitled *Psychology of Personality* and was published in New York and London by McGraw-Hill. In 1961, Allport prepared a revision that preserved the overall structure of his 1937 volume but with major rewriting and a new title: *Pattern and Growth in Personality*. Stagner's textbook continued steadily through four editions (1937, 1948, 1961, 1974) with substantial revisions, especially between the first and second editions.

The identity of personality psychology as an empirically based scientific field was heralded by the appearance of these two textbooks. Each in its own way brought the considerable body of pertinent research from the pre-1937 era together into the formulation of a coherent field of inquiry (Craik, 1986). The present volume derives from celebrations of the golden anniversary of the publication of these two books and offers a set of commentaries on their origins, distinctive themes, and topical contents. Before describing the development and

KENNETH H. CRAIK • Institute of Personality and Social Research, University of California at Berkeley, Berkeley, California 94720.

Fifty Years of Personality Psychology, edited by Kenneth H. Craik *et al.* Plenum Press, New York, 1993.

organization of this volume, it is helpful to reintroduce briefly these original textbooks of personality psychology to modern readers.

ALLPORT AND STAGNER:
PERSONAL BACKGROUNDS AND INTENTIONS

In the 1920s and 1930s, an increasingly vigorous, empirically oriented research program addressing issues of personality was emerging in the United States and Europe. Allport (1968) suggests that his 1924 course at Harvard University, "Personality: Its Psychological and Social Aspects," may have been the first undergraduate personality course in the United States. In any case, offerings of personality courses were becoming widespread during the subsequent decade and the need for adequate textbooks was evident by the mid-1930s.

Allport later recalled that from the time he completed his Ph.D. dissertation at Harvard in 1922 on traits of personality he had been "haunted with the idea that I should write a general book on personality" (Allport, 1968, p. 392). The project began to take form during his four years on the faculty at Dartmouth College (1926–1930). Support from Richard Cabot, a Boston Brahmin philanthropist and professor of social ethics at Harvard, provided Allport with a semester of free time in 1936 to complete *Personality: A Psychological Interpretation.* Allport recalls that "I did not write the book for any particular audience. I wrote it simply because I felt I had to define the new field of the psychology of personality as I saw it" (1968, p. 394). When he completed his textbook, Allport was almost 40 years old (born November 11, 1897), 15 years beyond his Ph.D. degree, and an associate professor at Harvard University.

Ross Stagner received his Ph.D. from the University of Wisconsin in 1932, with a dissertation in which he demonstrated that the relation between academic aptitude and achievement is moderated by personality traits (Stagner, 1933). As he reports in his contribution to this volume, Stagner's final commitment to write a textbook came when he was teaching the course on personality psychology during his first full-time appointment in 1935 at the University of Akron: "Seeking a possible text, I found that none was available, and decided to write my own" (Stagner, Chapter 2, this volume). The project enjoyed the encouragement of a McGraw-Hill publisher's representative and drew upon materials Stagner had already gathered in 1932–1933 when he had been awarded a Social Science Research Council fellowship at the University of Wisconsin (Stagner, 1937, p. ix). When he completed his textbook,

Stagner was 28 years old (born June 15, 1909), five years beyond his Ph.D. degree, and an assistant professor at the University of Akron.

Allport maintained his association with Harvard University until his death in 1967. Stagner's academic career also took him to Dartmouth College, then to the University of Illinois, and finally to Wayne State University, where he is professor emeritus. As we well know, both Allport and Stagner subsequently enjoyed eminent scientific careers: Allport in personality psychology and social psychology, Stagner in personality psychology and industrial–social psychology. For example, Allport was elected president of the American Psychological Association (1939–1940) and Stagner was elected president of APA's Division of Personality and Social Psychology (1960–1961) as well as its Division of Industrial (now Industrial–Organizational) Psychology (1965–1966).

ALLPORT AND STAGNER:
CONVERGENCES AND DIVERGENCES

Although generated independently, these two pioneering textbooks in personality psychology display a number of important similarities, as well as certain noteworthy differences. The most important shared characteristic of the two volumes is their authors' self-assured formulation of personality psychology as a coherent and distinctive field of inquiry. Allport sets out "to gather into a single comprehensive survey the most important fruits of the psychological study of personality" and "to supply new coordinating concepts and theories" (1937, p. ix) for this purpose. Stagner presents "a systematic set of concepts on which to hang the framework of trait psychology, measurement procedures, etc." (1937, p. viii).

Just five years earlier, Gardner Murphy and Friedrich Jensen (1932) had published a volume entitled *Approaches to Personality: Some Contemporary Conceptions Used in Psychology and Psychiatry.* In it, they offered an eclectic assortment of points of view, drawing upon Gestalt and behaviorist psychology, psychoanalysis, analytic (Jungian) and individual (Adlerian) psychology, and genetic–developmental notions from the field of child guidance. Murphy and Jensen make explicit their orienting conclusion that "The confusion in the contemporary psychology of personality is considerable" (p. vi) and assert that "We do not believe that anyone today can seriously undertake to say that he knows what personality is" (p. x).

In contrast, Allport (1937) moves decisively through an array of 49 definitions of personality and confidently introduces his own, now well-known version. And Stagner (1937) opens his preface by claiming that "The material which may legitimately be included in a treatment of the psychology of personality has grown too large to be brought within the compass of a single volume of reasonable size" (p. vii) and then proceeds briskly to list the principles of exclusion and inclusion for his textbook. Given these aims, Allport and Stagner generated organizations for their textbooks that embody their 1937 identifications of the inherent structure and fundamental issues of the field of personality psychology.

Allport's volume consists of five major parts. Part I deals with his approach to personality and includes chapters on (1) psychology and the study of individuality, (2) defining personality, and (3) a brief history of characterology. Part II covers the development of personality, with chapters on (1) foundations of personality, (2) basic aspects of growth, (3) the self and its constraints, (4) the transformation of motives, and (5) the mature personality. Part III focuses on the structure of personality, with chapters on (1) the search for elements, (2) the theory of identical elements, (3) the theory of traits, (4) the nature of traits, and (5) the unity of personality. Part IV, on the analysis of personality, brings together chapters on (1) a survey of methods, (2) common traits: psychography, (3) analysis by ratings, tests, experiments, and (4) expressive behavior. The concluding Part V, on understanding personality, consists of chapters on (1) the ability to judge people, (2) inference and intuition, and (3) the person in psychology.

Stagner's book consists of four sections. Section I, the introduction, also includes two chapters on methods, one dealing with analytic approaches, including behavior observations, ratings, free associations and scales, and one dealing with the study of the total personality, including clinical formulations, life histories, and sociocultural contexts. Section II addresses the descriptive psychology of personality and includes chapters on (1) the nature of personality structure, (2) basic reactions: feelings and emotions, (3) personality acquisition: simpler forms of learning, (4) personality acquisition: complex forms of learning, (5) implicit traits of personality, (6) character, (7) attitudes and values, (8) the overt level of personality structure, and (9) type theories of personality. Section III treats the dynamics of personality, with chapters on (1) appetites and aversions, (2) theories of dynamics: Freud, Adler, Lewin, and (3) a cultural interpretation of motivation. The final section contains eight chapters that review factors that shape personality: (1) biological determinants of personality, (2) social determinants of personality: the family (i), (3) social determinants of personality; the family (ii), (4) play and recreation relationships, (5) personality and the school system, (6) economic conditions affecting personality, (7) personality and patterns of culture (a chapter contributed by Abraham H. Maslow), and (8) the personality and social values.

The basic organization of these two textbooks was continued in their subsequent editions. In *Pattern and Growth in Personality*, Allport (1961) retains five major parts: I. An approach to personality; II. Development of personality; III. Structure of personality; IV. Assessment of personality; and V. Understanding personality. Some minor changes occur at the chapter level; for example, the addition of a chapter on culture, situation, and role. In his third edition, Stagner followed Allport by adding a fifth section on development, through some reassignment of chapters: I. Introduction; II. Development; III. Description; IV. Dynamics; and V. Determinants.

Thus, the 1937 Allport and Stagner textbooks both embody an assurance regarding what the field of personality is all about. Furthermore, both authors organized their textbooks according to their own personal and comprehensive formulation of the intellectual structure of the field and its array of fundamental issues. Finally, in light of present-day trends in the merchandising of textbooks, it is worth noting that both authors risked a high level of difficulty in the expositions presented in their books. Allport recalled his "desire to avoid jargon and try to express my thoughts in proper and felicitous English. The result was that some readers regarded the book as difficult and pretentious," but he also notes that others labeled it as "classic" (Allport, 1968, p. 394). In his preface, Stagner (1937) warns the reader that he had set out to offer a coherent point of view on the field and "I accepted, in doing so, the danger of making the book too difficult" (p. viii).

CROSS-GENERATIONAL DIFFERENCES IN VANTAGE POINTS

Perhaps it is indicative of the then early stage of personality psychology's development that both Allport and Stagner began to consider writing a textbook so soon after receiving their doctoral degrees. Allport was thinking about the textbook project in 1922, at age 24; Stagner set about the task in 1935, at age 26, and worked more rapidly on it.

Hints of a generational difference in their perspectives and aims can be discerned in the volumes they produced in 1937. Allport approached the task as a first-generation pioneer with the goal of justifying the new field's existence. As a second-generation personality psychologist, Stagner could take the field's existence as a given and set about fashioning a textbook in more standard form.

The tone of Allport's preface is that of a founding member of a new field. After all, he had quite likely completed the first empirical American dissertation on the component traits of personality in 1922 and probably had offered the first undergraduate course in the field in 1924. Within the context of academic psychology of that time, Allport considered his person-centered formulation of a new field as "thoroughly radical" (1937, p. 549). As a pioneer, he had to ask himself: "But did I have enough courage and ability to develop my deviant interests?" (1968, p. 385). Thus, here was Allport, with over a decade of experience observing the field as it emerged in the 1920s, setting out to write, as an early explorer, "a guide book that will *define* the new field of study—one that will articulate its objectives, formulate its standards, and test the progress made thus far" (p. vii; italics in the original).

In doing so, Allport was particularly dedicated to establishing the distinctiveness of the field within a broad historical, interdisciplinary, and scholarly context. One problem to which Allport appears to have been responding was highlighted by A. A. Roback's *A Bibliography of Character and Personality* (1927). In this comprehensive, 340-page compendium, Roback emphasizes the breadth and diversity of then available approaches to the study of personality, ranging from anthropology, biography, history, and literature to philosophy, psychoanalysis, psychiatry, religion, and sociology. Thus, it is no accident that Allport added the subtitle, *A Psychological Interpretation*, to qualify his primary title, *Personality*. To a significant degree, he saw his mission as one of making a persuasive case for the intellectual and scientific distinctiveness of the psychology of personality.

Eleven years younger and coming on the scene a decade later, Stagner appears to have found the field of personality psychology as much more of a given, even though proper textbooks were still needed for the courses being widely offered by the mid-1930s. In his preface, Stagner (1937) explicitly takes on the task of differentiating a proper textbook in the psychology of personality from an array of textbooklike competitors. In stating his basis for selecting material for his volume, he announces that he had "in almost all cases eliminated consideration of therapeutic techniques, suggestions for self-improvement, hints to parents and other aspects of what might be considered 'the applied psychology of personality' " (p. vii).

Early examples of this self-help tradition include William M.

Thayer's *Tact, Push, and Principle* (1885), whose organization is forecast in its title. Under "tact," Thayer presents separate chapters on thoroughness, singleness of purpose, and observation (a combination of social insight and practical intelligence); under "push," separate chapters on decision and energy, perseverance, industry, economy of time and effort, punctuality, and order; and under "principle," chapters on character, conscience, honesty, benevolence, the Bible, and religion in business. The volume is affectionately dedicated to its intended readership: "To the young men of the United States, facing difficulties, subject to reverses, unassisted by influence or capital, the brave and hopeful of success." A later, assessment-oriented volume along similar lines is John T. Miller's (1922) *Applied Character Analysis in Human Conservation*, dealing with vocational types, guided primarily by phrenological theory, and dedicated to "All who use the true science of mind in human improvement, physically, socially, intellectually, morally and spiritually."

Volumes published closer in time to the appearance of the 1937 Allport and Stagner textbooks often stressed philosophical or spiritual issues (Brown, 1927), ways to deal with or avoid the development of abnormalities in personality (Bagby, 1928; Gordon, 1928), and issues concerning character and personality in such fields as child guidance, education, and mental hygiene (Betts, 1937; Thorpe, 1938; Valentine, 1927). Some of the latter genre, such as Thorpe's *Psychological Foundations of Personality: A Guide for Students and Teachers* (1938), drew on much of the same research literature as did Allport and Stagner, but possessed a practical rather than scientific orientation and were primarily addressed to educators of our youth and students of education rather than to students of psychology itself.

In summary, Allport's 1937 volume can be seen retrospectively as a textbook and at the same time as more than a textbook. Allport sought to articulate and justify the identity of a new field of scientific inquiry and to establish the nature of its basic concepts and issues (Pettigrew, 1990). This latter characteristic may primarily account for the volume's continuing high frequency of citation. Stagner's more classroom-oriented volume also considered the person within a social framework, in contrast to Allport's treatment of the individual transcendent. A perusal of most present-day personality textbooks as well as the research literature of our field strongly suggests that, in seeking to place the person within a cultural, institutional, and societal context, Stagner was going against the grain of personality psychology, at least as it has emerged in this country.

A MAJOR CONTRAST: AN ANALYSIS OF THE INDIVIDUAL PER SE VERSUS THE INDIVIDUAL IN SOCIETY

A basic divergence in the formulations guiding the 1937 Allport and Stagner textbooks occurs in their treatment of the individual in context. Allport was strongly committed to establishing personality psychology as an intellectually and epistemologically distinct field of inquiry. Perhaps for this reason, he concentrated on making a case for the study of the individual as a primary scientific unit of analysis and indeed, for personality psychology, as *the* fundamental unit of analysis. Taking a different approach, Stagner devoted over a third of his textbook to the task of understanding the individual within a societal context. This emphasis distinguishes his volume not only from Allport's but also from those of his contemporary "pre-textbook" competitors. While some volumes may have highlighted such social factors as the family, the school, or the general culture, none appear to have offered the broad-based social institutional framework for the study of individual personality that is advanced by Stagner.

This contrast between the two textbooks is clearly illustrated by their treatment of the upheavals associated with the Great Depression, at its worst depths when these volumes were being completed. Reading Stagner today, one gets a vivid sense of this catastrophe's impact on individuals in the United States and Europe. A chapter reviewing economic conditions affecting personality deals explicitly with such topics as the effects of unemployment on workers' morale, the influences of parents' economic uncertainty on children and child rearing, and the role of such "economic hazards" in the incidence of juvenile delinquency. In his preface, Allport acknowledges at the outset that he anticipates being criticized for neglecting the important relationships between personality and culture. Furthermore, in the one reference to these wider events of his own times, Allport puts an individualistic twist on the issue. He asks: "Why is it that in our times, when Western culture is sadly disorganized, our personalities are not correspondingly disorganized?" Allport concludes that "Cultural determinism is one of the monosymptomatic approaches; it has a blind spot for the internal balancing factors and structural tenacity within personality" (1937, pp. viii–ix).

Allport makes a well-substantiated claim that he provides a valuable historical orientation for the varied formulations concerning personality that have been advanced over the course of Western culture. However, because of their differing approaches toward analyzing the person within society, it is the Stagner volume that provides the present-day reader with a sense of the historical context of the volumes themselves. In contrast, Allport's textbook is written with a generality of tone that affords it a timeless, or at least ahistorical, aura.

Conceptually, Allport and Stagner take a similar stance in distinguishing between psychological and sociological levels of analysis. For Allport, culture is important only to the extent that "it has become *interiorized* within the person as a set of personal ideals, attitudes, and traits. Likewise, culture conflict must become *inner* conflict before it can have any significance for personality" (1937, p. viii). On this point, Stagner concurs, asserting that "The object of our study is a single human being. . . . Social systems, cultures, etc., have psychological reality as, and only as, habits and beliefs of specific human beings" (1937, pp. viii–ix). Nevertheless, they differ markedly in how central a place they assign to the analysis of interactions between persons and their society.

ALLPORT: THE INDIVIDUAL TRANSCENDENT

Allport, while not denying their role, narrowly circumscribed his own treatment of societal factors influencing personality, for "the interest of psychology is not in the factors *shaping* personality, rather in personality *itself* as a developing structure" (1937, p. viii). Allport's conceptual contributions were aimed at appreciating this relatively enduring and unique organization and bringing it under appropriate scientific analysis. First, his neuropsychic formulation of traits emphasized their status as "internally generalized, flexible, interdependent dispositions" (pp. 559–560). Second, he distinguished between the concept of individual traits and that of common traits; a common trait provides a basis for comparison among persons but never "corresponds exactly to the neuropsychic dispositions of individuals" (p. 300). Third, he dealt thoroughly with the multiplicity of traits and motives of any individual, in part as a means of highlighting the complex organization specifically entailed by the structure of any individual's personality (p. 560). Fourth, he developed the concept of the functional autonomy of motives as a device for analyzing the high degree of differentiation and specific multiplicity to be found in the adult personality structure of an individual (p. 207). Fifth, he isolated the psychological study of an individual's personality from any analysis of the person's social stimulus value (May, 1932) and reputation in society at large. Sixth, he granted primary emphasis to the task of understanding the unity of personality. In his revised textbook, Allport (1961) still viewed the problem of the organization of personality as our field's greatest conceptual challenge and continued to address it, notably through his notions of the morphogenetic analysis of personal dispositions (p. 358) and the propriate functions of personality.

Allport was explicit and almost provocative in eschewing systematic treatment of sociocultural factors (Allport, 1937, pp. viii–ix; Smith, Chapter 4, this volume). He appears to have made a strategic decision that his efforts to focus the spotlight on the study of the individual and the analysis of personality organization could be best realized by a deliberate neglect of the relations between persons and their society. A secondary factor may have been Allport's initial tendency to view any attention to this issue as entailing a position of cultural determinism versus individualism; he gives little attention to the possibility of an interactional model. The result of his strategy is a ringing declaration of the integrity of each individual, at the expense of presenting a severely decontextualized formulation of personality. This depiction is attenuated somewhat in his 1961 volume, where he adds a chapter taking note of cultural context, social role, and situation and the distinction between individual and collective structures.

Given Allport's important contributions to both personality psychology and social psychology, one might hypothesize that perhaps Allport conceptually split his scientific identities—attending to the individual as a personality psychologist and to the social environment as a social psychologist. However, Allport's contributions to social psychology have been identified from some theoretical perspectives as excessively individualistic. For example, his conception of attitudes in traitlike fashion can be contrasted to their formulation as more collective, social representations (Farr, 1981; Moscovici, 1984). In this sense, Allport's basic credo pervaded his scientific orientation:

> Thus, there are many ways to study man psychologically. Yet to study him most fully is to take him as an individual. He is more than a bundle of habits; more than a nexus of abstract dimensions; more too than a representative of his species. He is more than a citizen of the state, and more than a mere incident in the gigantic movements of mankind. He transcends them all. (1937, pp. 566–567)

STAGNER: THE INDIVIDUAL IN SOCIETY

Stagner's commitment to a contextual perspective on personality is evident in the organization and context of his textbook. Eight of its twenty-three chapters are devoted to sociocultural factors. One of the three chapters of the third section, on the dynamics of personality, deals with a cultural interpretation of motivation. In this exposition, Stagner rejects a generalized energy conception of drive in favor of a more particularistic formulation of individual motivational patterns as sensitive to cultural and other environmental influences. He cites cross-cultural and historical variations in the manifestations of sexuality, will-to-power, acquisitiveness, and social approval in support of this framework.

The fourth and longest section of the volume examines the determinants of personality. In this way, Stagner incorporates questions regarding the *shaping* of personality that Allport had explicitly rejected from consideration. One of its eight chapters reviews biological determinants and the remaining seven address an array of sociocultural determinants.

The family as an institution is covered in two chapters. The first focuses on child rearing as influenced by parental affection, quarrels and jealousy, problems of discipline, sibling relationships, parent substitutes, and adolescent concerns regarding dependence–independence. The second deals with the adults of the family, examining the role of personality in marital satisfaction and conflict, mate similarity, illness and drinking as escapes from marital conflict, and the relation of personality to parenting styles. The social context of play and recreation are highlighted as important extrafamilial settings for competition in the realms of physical prowess, sociability, and sexual attractiveness as well as settings for cooperation through team play and membership in gangs and cliques. The role of reading and the movies in identity formation is also discussed as well as the increasing commercialization of recreation. A chapter on the school system covers the topics of personality and academic achievement, the role of teachers' personalities, and the influence of the school on economic and social attitudes through the curriculum, and more indirectly through power relations and the way in which controversial issues of the day are handled. We have already noted the extent to which a chapter on the impact of economic conditions on personality reflected the urgent effects of the Great Depression. Maslow's chapter on culture and personality stresses the point of cultural relativism in part as a counter to ethnocentric biases in conceptions of personality and also offers a review of cultural implications for the concepts of abnormal personality and adjustment and a brief interpretation of psychotherapy as social philosophy.

Stagner's final chapter on personality and social values is of particular interest for a present-day reader. He addresses the issue of levels of analysis and offers an interactional model of the individual and society. In this framework, he argues that individual personalities are shaped more or less equally by sociocultural factors, on the one hand, and individual factors (e.g., biological, hereditary, specific biographical events) on the other. Sociocultural systems are shaped predominantly by other sociocultural forces (e.g., the effect of political change on economic functioning) but also to some important extent by actions of individual personalities (Stagner, 1937, pp. 431–434 and Fig. 24). This model permits Stagner to incorporate systematic treatment of sociocultural influences on personality in his textbook without being committed to the unidirectional cultural determinism that so concerned Allport. At the same time, it permits Stagner to incorporate a consideration of the impact of individual actions on the sociocultural system. He cites the "Russian experiment," with its combination of political dictatorship and rejection of capitalism, as an instance of dramatic change brought about in a social system.

Stagner is explicit about his interactional formulation:

> Our purpose throughout has been to depict the development of the human organism with its inherent tendencies and equipment, struggling through an environment of things and people, trying, failing, learning, viewing situations from successively different angles; the description of a personality and its determination by cultural influences has been sketched. We should now . . . see the beginning of a new cycle in which the personality tries various ways of modifying the environment. (1937, pp. 443–444)

Thus, the model encompasses processes by which the individual emerges as an agent within the societal context. Specifically, when an individual becomes conscious of his system of values, then

> it becomes possible for him to achieve a certain psychological distance from his social setting and attempt to evaluate it without confusion from his own set of pre-existing biases and prejudices. He may then be able to see clearly its own virtues and vices, and then decide calmly whether or not it should be preserved, reformed or remade. (p. 443)

This interaction model is formulated primarily at the institutional level and thus remains largely within the tradition of personality system–social system analysis (Smelser & Smelser, 1964) rather than within the more recent framework of efforts to analyze everyday person–environment interactions (Walsh *et al.*, 1992). Nevertheless, Stagner's textbook had a modern interactive and contextual sound.

PLANNING AND ORGANIZATION OF THIS VOLUME

In 1987, several celebrations of the golden anniversary of the 1937 Allport and Stagner textbooks took place. At the University of California in Berkeley, the Institute of Personality Assessment and Research (IPAR)* organized a special colloquium series commemorating the occasion. Ross Stagner took part in this series, delivering an address on "Fifty Years of Development in the Psychology of Personality." Other speakers in this series included Irving E. Alexander, Bertram J. Cohler, Lewis R. Goldberg, Ravenna Helson, Robert Hogan, Salvatore R. Maddi, Lawrence A. Pervin, and Paul Wink. In addition, a special session was devoted to Allport and his textbook. In this context, Allan C. Elms presented a talk on "Allport's *Personality* and Allport's Personality," which was followed by a roundtable discussion by five former graduate students at Harvard during Allport's tenure there. The discussants (with the year of their Ph.D.) included the late Sheldon J. Korchin (1946), Gardner Lindzey (1949), Pavel Machotka (1962), R. Nevitt Sanford (1934), and M. Brewster Smith (1947), with Ernest R. Hilgard (Yale, 1930) moderating.

Subsequently, Robert Hogan and I decided to take a modified version of this successful "show" to Broadway, as the annual meetings of the American Psychological Association were scheduled to take place in New York City in August. Division 1 (Division of General Psychology) generously afforded us the opportunity to organize two consecutive two-hour sessions, which were heavily attended. For this occasion, Alan Elms presented a modified version of his talk on "Allport's *Personality* and Allport's Personality," Salvatore Maddi spoke on "The Continuing Relevance of Personality Theory," and Lawrence A. Pervin reviewed "Current Trends in Personality Theory." The remainder of the two sessions was organized around five topics suggested by the contents of Allport's 1937 textbook. On the topic of the self, Stephen R. Briggs spoke on "Constructing the Self" and Anthony G. Greenwald on "How Shall the Self Be Conceived?" On the topic of the single case, Irv Alexander dealt with "Science and the Single Case," and Lawrence S. Wrightman with "Allport's Personal Documents: Then and Now." On the issue of psychological maturity, Roy F. Baumeister addressed "Modern Conceptions of Identity" and Ravenna Helson addressed "Allport's Conception of Maturity." On motivation, Robert A. Emmons reviewed the "Current Status of the Motive Concept" while Christopher Langston and Nancy Cantor analyzed "Life Tasks and Motivation." Finally, on the issue of judging other persons, David C. Funder spoke on "Judg-

---

* In conjunction with the expansion of its research program to encompass the study of persons within their cultural, institutional, organizational, and societal contexts, this institute was renamed in 1992 as the Institute of Personality and Social Research (IPSR).

ments of Personality" and Bella M. DePaulo on "The Ability to Judge Others."

In developing this book, we were able to enlist the editorial collaboration of Raymond N. Wolfe and contributions from most of the participants in the APA symposia. Due to prior commitments, we lost the involvement of Cantor and Langston, Greenwald and Helson. However, relevant contributions from Peter Borkenau, Bertram J. Cohler, Garth J. O. Fletcher, Oliver P. John, Richard W. Robins, Gerald A. Mendelsohn, M. Brewster Smith, David G. Winter, and Ray Wolfe have served wonderfully to augment the materials from the APA sessions.

CONTENTS

The volume is organized around three major themes. First, the personal and historical contexts of the 1937 Allport and Stagner textbooks are addressed in contributions by Ross Stagner, Alan C. Elms, and M. Brewster Smith. Stagner provides his own perspective on his and Allport's textbooks gained from over 50 years of personal experience in the field. Elms relates the structure and emphases of Allport's textbook to characteristics of his background and personality. Through notes taken from meetings in 1946–1947 at Harvard, Brewster Smith offers a glimpse of Allport's personal and theoretical relations with a colleague who also contributed an important volume to personality psychology in the late 1930s: Henry A. Murray, who, with his research team, had published *Explorations in Personality* in 1938.

Second, analysis of the current state of personality psychology and its textbooks is offered by Lawrence A. Pervin, Salvatore R. Maddi, and Gerald A. Mendelsohn. In his stocktaking essay, Pervin selects the central issues of the pattern and organization of personality as a framework for examining current trends and prospects for our field. He also notes how Stagner's conceptual orientation in the subsequent editions of his textbook was influenced by his close reading of Kurt Lewin's *Dynamic Theory of Personality*, which had been published in 1935. Maddi presents a spirited argument in favor of comprehensive theorizing in personality psychology. Specifically, he continues the textbook theme of our volume by advocating a model of the personality textbook that emphasizes the integrative function of comparative analysis of alternative grand theories. His position appears to be: Preach what personality psychology might ideally become, not the fragmented manner in which it is now practiced. In contrast, Mendelsohn discerns a serious gap between these grand theories of personality and the nature of contemporary personality research. He opts instead for a textbook format exemplified by the 1937 Allport and Stagner textbooks, which is organized around basic topics and fundamental issues in personality psychology, such as units of analysis, methods, development, determinants, and dynamics. In opposition to Maddi, Mendelsohn's position is explicitly asserted: Preach what you practice.

The third theme of our volume constitutes a present-day perspective on some of the basic issues in personality psychology, as suggested by the themes and organization of Allport's 1937 textbook:

1. *The individual and the single case.* In this section, Alexander deals with the scientific issues of single-case analysis and offers a succinct historical perspective on the fate of this issue over the past five decades of personality research. Cohler presents a review of current work on the description and understanding of individual lives as it bears on Allport's formulations. Drawing on biographical information regarding the relations between Allport and "Jenny," Winter suggests new interpretations of his major single-case analysis, the *Letters from Jenny* (Allport, 1965; Anonymous, 1946). Finally, Wrightsman provides a general summary of Allport's work on the analysis of personal documents and reviews current research activities using this method.

2. *Motives and the self.* Baumeister places Allport's views on the self in the perspective of current formulations regarding the natural self (the knower and the body), the conceptual self (self-representations and identity), and the action self (self-referenced motives). Emmons historically traces analyses of the concept of motive from its treatment in the 1937 Allport and Stagner textbooks to its present revival in personality psychology.

3. *Judging persons.* DePaulo and Funder revisit Allport's analysis of expressive behavior and the ability to judge others. DePaulo discusses recent work on un-self-conscious expressive behavior and the issue of deception. During the 1960s and 1970s, psychologists seemed to be discouraged about the prospects of examining the ability to judge others because of the difficulties encountered in establishing criteria regarding the target persons. Funder offers encouragement that convergently valid criteria can indeed serve as a basis for studying the accuracy of individuals' judgments of the personalities of other persons.

4. *Personality assessment and prediction.* The 1937 Allport and Stagner textbooks both highlighted the importance of trait concepts and their measurement. In this section, John and Robins place the 1936 Allport–Odbert psycho-lexical study of trait names (Allport & Odbert,

1936) in the context of subsequent research on trait taxonomies derived from the ordinary language of personality description. In so doing, they advance a clarifying distinction between the empirically derived "big five" factor structure of personality descriptions, on the one hand, and a theoretical "Five-Factor Model" of personality traits and personality structure that is increasingly being used as a conceptual guide for organizing research in personality, on the other.

Borkenau relates Allport's 1937 treatment of the consistency-specificity controversy, raised by Hartshorne and May (1928, 1929) and Hartshorne, May, and Shuttleworth (1930) to the ways in which it has been addressed more recently in the form of the person–situation controversy. Fletcher examines Allport's stance on naive "heuristic realism" regarding the nature of traits. He locates the issue within more recent and broader discussion concerning the relevance that studying laypersons as naive scientists may hold for the more formal process of personality and cognitive social theorizing. In formulating the field of personality psychology, Allport noted that "I have tried to make a special ally of common sense" (Allport, 1937, p. viii); and the same spirit imbues his approach to trait concepts and methods of assessment. Wolfe identifies an emerging common-sense orientation in the construction and interpretation of self-report scales for assessing trait concepts and discusses the extent and limits of this current trend in personality measurement.

Finally, in the epilogue, Hogan offers a closing perspective on the current state of personality psychology as a scientific enterprise.

In hindsight, it now strikes us that by planning the third section of this volume around the themes and organization of Allport's 1937 textbook, we have continued an unduly narrow orientation, through placing greater emphasis on the individual as transcendent than on the individual in societal context. But our goal has not been to review the past 50 years of personality research; comprehensive handbooks in personality psychology are more appropriate to that task (Briggs et al., forthcoming; Pervin, 1990). Instead, our intention is to foster a greater appreciation of our field's past and trends in its development. We will consider this volume a success if it enhances recognition of the impact of these pioneering personality textbooks and sustains the respect and gratitude that our field has already bestowed on their authors, highlights the usefulness of systematic discussion concerning the nature and influence of contemporary textbooks in personality psychology, and encourages greater historical perspective on the development of personality psychology as a field of inquiry.

ACKNOWLEDGMENTS. I wish to thank R. T. Hogan, O. P. John, G. A. Mendelsohn, R. W. Robins, W. M. Runyan, and R. N. Wolfe for their helpful comments on earlier drafts of this chapter.

REFERENCES

Allport, G. W. (1937). *Personality: A psychological interpretation.* New York: Holt.

Allport, G. W. (1961). *Pattern and growth in personality.* New York: Holt, Rinehart and Winston.

Allport, G. W. (1965). *Letters from Jenny.* New York: Harcourt, Brace and World.

Allport, G. W. (1968). An autobiography. In G. W. Allport, *The person in psychology: Selected essays by Gordon W. Allport* (pp. 376–409). Boston: Beacon Press.

Allport, G. W., & Odbert, H. S. (1936). Trait-names: A psycho-lexical study. *Psychological Monographs, 47* (Whole No. 211).

Anonymous (1946). Letters from Jenny. *Journal of Abnormal and Social Psychology, 41,* 315–350, 449–480.

Bagby, E. (1928). *The psychology of personality: An analysis of common emotional disorders.* New York: Holt.

Betts, G. H. (1937). *Foundations of character and personality: An introduction to the psychology of social adjustment.* New York: Bobbs-Merrill.

Briggs, S. R., Hogan, R. T., & Jones, W. (forthcoming). *Handbook of personality psychology.* New York: Academic Press.

Brown, W. (1927). *Mind and personality: An essay in psychology and philosophy.* New York: Putman's.

Craik, K. H. (1986). Personality research methods: An historical perspective. *Journal of Personality, 54,* 18–51.

Farr, R. M. (1981). On the nature of human nature and the science of behavior. In P. Heelas & A. Lock (Eds). *Indigenous psychologies: The anthropology of the self* (pp. 303–317). New York: Academic Press.

Gordon, R. G. (1928). *Personality.* London: Kegan Paul, Trench, Trubner.

Hartshorne, H., & May, M. A. (1928). *Studies in the nature of character: Volume 1. Studies in deceit.* New York: Macmillan.

Hartshorne, H., & May, M. A. (1929). *Studies in the nature of character: Volume 2. Studies in service and self-control.* New York: Macmillan.

Hartshorne, H., May, M. A., & Shuttleworth, F. K. (1930). *Studies in the nature of character: Studies in the organization of character.* New York: Macmillan.

Lewin, K. (1935). *A dynamic theory of personality.* New York: McGraw-Hill.

May, M. A. (1932). The foundations of personality. In P. S. Achilles (Ed.), *Psychology at work* (pp. 81–101). New York: McGraw-Hill.

Miller, J. T. (1922). *Applied character analysis in human conservation.* Boston: Gorham Press.

Moscovici, S. (1984). The phenomenon of social representation. In R. M. Farr & S. Moscovici (Eds.), *Social representation* (pp. 3–69). Cambridge: Cambridge University Press.

Murphy, G., & Jensen, F. (1932). *Approaches to personality: Some contemporary conceptions used in psychology and psychiatry.* New York: Coward-McCann.

Murray, H. A. (1938). *Explorations of personality.* New York: Oxford University Press.

Pervin, L. A. (1990). *Handbook of personality: Theory and research.* New York: Guilford Press.

Pettigrew, T. F. (1990). A bold stroke for personality a half-century ago. *Contemporary Psychology, 35,* 533–536.

Roback, A. A. (1927). *A bibliography of character and personality.* Cambridge, MA: Sci-Art.

Smelser, N. J., & Smelser, W. T. (1964). Analyzing personality and social systems. In N. J. Smelser & W. T. Smelser (Eds.), *Personality and social systems* (pp. 1–18). New York: Wiley.

Stagner, R. (1933). Relation of personality to academic aptitude and achievement. *Journal of Educational Research, 26,* 648–660.

Stagner, R. (1937). *Psychology of personality.* New York: McGraw-Hill.

Thayer, W. M. (1885). *Tact, push, and principle.* Boston: Earle.

Thorpe, L. P. (1938). *Psychological foundations of personality: A guide for students and teachers.* New York : McGraw-Hill.

Valentine, P. F. (1927). *The psychology of personality.* New York: Appleton.

Walsh, W. B., Craik, K. H., & Price, R. H. (Eds.) (1992). *Person–environment psychology.* Hillsdale, NJ: Erlbaum.

PART TWO

HISTORICAL AND PERSONAL BACKGROUND OF THE 1937 TEXTS

CHAPTER TWO

Fifty Years of the Psychology of Personality
Reminiscences

ROSS STAGNER

As we are fond of saying about psychology in general, the study of personality has a long past but only a short history. The proposal to specify 1937 as the date of origin for modern personality psychology has a certain plausibility: Gordon Allport and I both published formal textbooks on personality in that year, giving shape and academic respectability to the field; and Henry Murray's *Explorations in Personality* (1938) came out less than 12 months later. It seems proper, therefore, to designate 1987 as the 50th year of the psychology of personality.

We have a recent precedent for doing this. The American Psychological Association declared the year 1879 as the birth date of scientific psychology. At once, of course, critics noted the importance of various contributions prior to that date; and the same is possible with regard to the study of personality. The prehistory, or archaeology, of personality study goes back to Galen and Plutarch. In 1927, A. A. Roback assembled a bibliography of over 2200 titles dealing with personality; however, most of these were literary or speculative. Few could be called empirical investigations (although case studies were common), and

ROSS STAGNER • Department of Psychology, Wayne State University, Detroit, Michigan 48202.

Fifty Years of Personality Psychology, edited by Kenneth H. Craik *et al.* Plenum Press, New York, 1993.

even fewer had any firm anchoring in the mainstream of psychological science. Of the sources Roback catalogued, writings by Freud, Jung, and Adler stand out as the works that are still viewed as important.

Another set of important ancestral influences is found in the writings of Charcot and Janet, psychiatrists who sought to explain suggestibility, dissociation, and symptom formation. By contrast, the German experimentalists we celebrated in 1979 (Wundt, Stumpf, Külpe, Ebbinghaus, and others) ignored the phenomena nowadays labeled as personality. We note, of course, the disagreement between Wundt and J. M. Cattell over the place of individual differences in a scientific psychology; and it is appropriate to mention Hermann Rorschach, whose inkblot test was designed to exclude meaning from the measurement of personality—an effort stimulated by Wundt's distinction between experience and meaning. And it seems only fair to mention the feeble gesture of E. B. Titchener, that advocate of research on the "mind-in-general," who included in one edition of his introductory textbook a page dealing with the topic of temperament, using Galen's scheme of the four humors. Titchener suggested a relationship between these and such phenomena as speed of association and intensity of affect; however, he quickly dropped the subject and never returned to it.

It is also proper to mention the speculation of William James, who could hardly ignore a phenomenon as ubiquitous as personality. Adopting an environmentalist stance, he speculated about the importance of the social context in shaping emotions and social interactions. James wrote

> ...at the age of 25 you see the professional mannerism settling down on the young commercial traveler, on the young doctor, on the young minister...you see the little lines of cleavage running through the character, the tricks of thought, the prejudices... by the age of 30, the character has set like plaster, and will never soften again. (1890, pp. 121–122)

I regret to have to add that James considered this molding of personality a fine idea because "it keeps different social strata from mixing." It is surprisingly difficult to write about personality without revealing your personal prejudices.

James acknowledged the influence of Charcot and Janet on his thinking, but his emphasis on social determinants links him to sociological theorists such as George Herbert Mead and Charles Horton Cooley. On the subject of the self, James seems to have embraced the concept of "social stimulus value" while oscillating between emphasis on unity of the self and dissociation of role-related selves.

> Properly speaking, a man has as many social selves as there are individuals who recognize him and carry an image of him in their mind. But . . . we may practically say that he has as many different social selves as there are distinct groups of persons about whose opinions he cares (1890, p. 294)

In this statement James anticipates the views of Walter Mischel and others to the effect that the self is no more than a response to a social context (and its associated reinforcements), and Kurt Lewin's treatment of the subjective personality as a kind of internalization of group memberships.

I want to mention one other pre-1937 book because of its relevance to a contemporary theoretical debate. English Bagby's *Psychology of Personality*, published in 1928, reflected some psychoanalytic and some behavioristic leanings. While its focus was on counseling, it raises issues of general importance. The following case summary illustrates some theoretical problems:

> The patient, a university sophomore, sought assistance in connection with a strong impulse to gnaw the back of his right hand. The tendency had existed for a period of two months and already a large callous area had developed. The patient appeared to be quite ashamed of his inability to secure control of this habit, and said that he had been wearing a glove to conceal the scar, although the weather had not been cold. (Acid was applied to his hand so that a bitter taste would result when it was placed in his mouth.)
>
> On the third day the young man reported that the inclination to bite his hand was no longer troubling him. However, he called attention to a new symptom. He found himself almost constantly beset by moral worries. (These were illustrated by trifling points such as choice of neckties, walking with friends on the campus, etc., over which he had worried to excess.)
>
> The condition of moral uncertainty persisted for several days, Finally, however, the patient came to report that his distressing condition had completely disappeared and that he was once again serene. But, in the course of the conversation, it was noted that he repeatedly bit his *left* hand. Thus, a modified form of the original impulsive habit had developed, and, when the fact was called to his attention, he gave unmistakable evidence of surprise and chagrin. (1928, p. 7)

I cite this early instance of an attempt at behavior modification to point up some recurring themes in the psychology of personality. (1) There has been a tendency to focus on distinctive or unusual behavior, or on unique personality characteristics. (2) The behavior of interest is often performed unconsciously. (3) There is a presumed underlying phenomenon—a trait perhaps, or some specifiable personality dynamics—that can trigger alternative behaviors. One task for the personality theorist is to identify this underlying process.

The foregoing illustration suggests that the psychology of personality has its roots in clinical psychology and of course there is some truth in this statement. However, the outstanding aspect of the publications of 1937 and 1938, cited as the emergent manifestations of the new psychological specialty, is that the clinical approach is a minor feature, at least as regards the contribution of Allport and Stagner; and even of Murray's work it can be said that it is closer to "pure" scientific psychology than to clinical practicalities.

Another differentiating feature of the new approaches to personality was the concern for individual differences. Allport had already collaborated with his brother Floyd on a scale for measuring the traits of ascendance and submission; and with Philip Vernon on the Study of Values, each devised to obtain quantitative indices of hypothesized personal attributes. Murray and his students also attempted to derive quantitative indices of various behavioral tendencies. My own experience included extensive work with personality inventories, the development of a Thurstone-type scale for attitude to parents, and the first "fascist attitude" scale for American populations. Thus McKeen Cattell's (1886) concern with individual differences was deeply embedded in the formation of the new specialization within psychology.

SOME PERSONAL BACKGROUNDS

It is inevitable that one's position regarding the psychology of personality will be affected by one's personality. This need not lead to esoteric psychoanalytic speculations; in many instances the relevant information is empirical and indeed obvious.

Let me illustrate this generalization with the case of Gordon Allport. In his autobiography (Allport, 1967), he conceded that he had experienced some sibling rivalry with his older brother, Floyd. Floyd received his Ph.D. from Harvard in 1919, the same year in which Gordon completed his B.A. Although Gordon did not try to conceal their rivalry, it was most clearly expressed in an anecdote by Floyd in his autobiography (Allport, 1974). His description of a family incident is quite revealing:

> Not long ago my brother Gordon was visiting us in California. At the breakfast table my wife took the occasion to recount to him what she considered to be certain of my "fine qualities." After her

lengthy eulogistic recital my brother looked up and without a moment's hesitation added: "And is he still stubborn, lazy, and procrastinating?" Aside from the fact that they were delivered by a master of the science of personality traits, what startled and dismayed me most about these words was the glibness with which he uttered them, not needing to pause for a moment's thought or recollection. (1974, p. 5)

Floyd did not raise the possible issue of sibling rivalry, but this would seem to be the appropriate rubric under which to file this incident.

The father of Floyd and Gordon was a physician who was financially able to send both of his sons to Harvard. Henry Murray also came from a well-to-do family and got his education at preparatory schools, followed by a B.A. at Harvard and a medical degree at Columbia. Like Sigmund Freud, he spent several years in what would be considered "pure" research (on embryonic development in chickens); this ultimately led to his receipt of a Ph.D. degree in biochemistry from Cambridge University in England.

Murray's transition from biochemistry to psychology almost had the quality of a conversion. In 1923, he read C. G. Jung's *Psychological Types*, which fascinated him; and in 1925 he spent three weeks with Jung in what seems to have been a therapeutic relationship. He abandoned his work in biochemistry and decided on a career that would combine medical and academic psychology. His earliest studies in personality were experimental tests of Jungian concepts.

Murray's career at Harvard throws light on some of the more obscure features of academia, particularly in the early part of this century. The psychiatrist Morton Prince offered Harvard a gift of $80,000 (an impressive sum in 1927) to establish a psychological clinic. Over the bitter opposition of the psychology staff, the gift was accepted and the clinic established. Prince was appointed director of the clinic, with Murray as his assistant; when Prince died in 1928, Murray was promoted to the position of director, but with only a three-year term as an assistant professor. In 1931, his reappointment was opposed by Harvard's experimental psychologists. At this point, Gordon Allport rallied support from other departments and saved Murray from being dropped from the faculty.

It is interesting to note that while Murray freely acknowledged his indebtedness to Allport for this, the two nevertheless continued a low-temperature feud over the relevance of psychoanalytic theory to research on personality. Of the three of us (Allport, Murray, and myself), Murray looked most favorably upon the potential usefulness of psychoanalytic concepts.

As I was much younger than either Allport or Murray, there is less to be said about my training and career up to 1937. Unlike them, I was born into a poor Texas family with few books or other stimuli toward intellectual development. Neither of my parents attended high school. My early behavior must have puzzled them. My mother used to tell with amusement of her surprise when, after my first day in the first grade, I could read the first two pages in my primer. She was even more astonished when she found that I could read the text just as well upside down. I had simply memorized the words and recited them in perfect sequence without using any visual cues. (This quasi-eidetic memory served me well in graduate school, where it was a real advantage to be able to recall many details of procedure and results of the experiments being discussed.)

My father died in 1923, when I was 14. My mother, no doubt puzzled as to what to do with this "duckling," took me to a newly established child guidance clinic in Dallas. A social worker there, Mrs. F. T. Buss, was an alumna of Washington University in St. Louis, and she contrived to obtain a tuition scholarship for me at that school. I worked for my expenses—as a printer in downtown St. Louis and later on campus. My first major was English literature, and I looked forward to a career of teaching and writing. However, by what was probably good fortune, Marion Bunch wanted to offer a course in the psychology of learning and needed one more enrollee to have the course offered. He saw me in the corridor and urged me to elect it (he had been impressed by my performance in his introductory class). The learning course involved laboratory research with human subjects. This fascinated me, and I promptly changed my major from English to psychology.

Bunch not only gave me a good introduction to research methods; he also arranged for me to enter graduate training at Wisconsin and to work there as an assistant to Clark Hull. Regrettably (from my point of view), Hull moved to Yale before I moved to Madison. Hull's aura, however, continued to dominate the graduate program. Of those who influenced me, Norman Cameron is the first to come to mind; a brilliant lecturer, he taught the course on theories of psychology. W. H. Sheldon was another dynamic teacher, deeply committed to behaviorism but a bit more systematic than John B. Watson. Richard Husband and Harry Harlow came to Madison directly from Stanford and espoused generally a moderate, functionalist–behaviorist view. Kimball Young, another significant influence, adopted what might be called a functionalist position when he dealt with purely psychological issues as opposed to sociological matters. Hulsey Cason, who joined the Wisconsin faculty just before I finished, could be characterized as a functionalist in the Thorndike–Woodworth tradition. I have often wondered how Abe Maslow (who studied with these same teachers) developed his strong humanistic streak. Perhaps most graduate students are like B. F. Skinner, who once wrote of his graduate work at Harvard that "in graduate school I had the advantage of scarcely being taught at all" (1983, p. 25). At any rate, I cannot blame my graduate professors for any more than the strong behavioristic bias in the first edition of my book. Later editions made more use of Gestalt and phenomenological frameworks.

My resistance to indoctrination by the faculty was shown in my selection of a master's thesis topic. Despite the behavioristic atmosphere, I proposed a Gestalt-based study on the role of absolute versus relative differences in a visual discrimination task, designed to test Kenneth Spence's theory regarding relational learning. This was progressing well until an epidemic wiped out my cat colony.

Feeling financial pressure, I wanted to get my M.A. and earn some money right away. I hastily devised a project using human subjects and a theoretical issue derived from psychoanalysis. Essentially, what I demonstrated was that high scorers on the Woodworth Personal Data Sheet ("neurotic" personalities) remembered unpleasant words in a laboratory task better than they recalled pleasant words while the "nonneurotic" subjects remembered more of the pleasant words.

I taught one semester at Gustavus Adolphus College. While there I followed up my master's project with one on the forgetting of details of pleasant and unpleasant experiences from real life. Back in Madison, I next chose to study whether personality test scores could enhance the prediction of college grades from aptitude test scores.

Nominally, my doctoral advisor was V. A. C. Henmon, who was well known for his work in intelligence testing in World War I. Regrettably, he was chronically ill during my years at Wisconsin, and while he approved my plans for a dissertation, he was not in a position to provide regular guidance as it progressed. It focused on an interaction hypothesis; that a student's use of his or her aptitude was moderated by personality traits. This was one of the earliest moderator variable studies (although unfortunately I did not label it as such). My population was the entire freshman class enrolling at the University of Wisconsin in September 1931. They took the Bernreuter Personality Inventory during registration. In June, their aptitude scores were correlated with their grade-point averages for the first year of college work. The results were most gratifying: Subgroups scoring high on a given trait-measure differed from corresponding subgroups of low scorers on the same trait-measure in terms of the ability–achievement correlation. For example, in a group of high-dominance males, the ability–

achievement correlation was .71, whereas among low-dominance males
this correlation was only .44 (Stagner, 1933).

When I received my doctorate in 1932, the nation was in the grip
of a severe economic recession. Luckily I received a Social Science
Research Council (SSRC) fellowship grant to continue my work on personality. With this support, I investigated some of the relationships
between family characteristics and children's personalities; the findings
showed clearly that poverty was detrimental to desirable personality
development (Stagner, 1935).

The rise of fascism was another prominent feature of the 1930s. It
seemed to me that psychology should be capable of providing some
insights into that phenomenon. I culled from the German and Italian
reports some policy statements that could be recast in the American
context and presented to subjects in the form of propositions or
attitude statements to be endorsed or not. The source of the statement
was not given and the word "fascism" was never used. The resulting
scale was thus able to tap the susceptibility of Americans to fascist
attitudes. Articles on the use of this scale (Stagner, 1936a,b) started a
series of studies that culminated in the "authoritarian personality"
project at Berkeley (Adorno et al., 1950).

Another aspect of the personality–politics relationship that ap-
pealed to me was the extent to which young people from fairly secure,
well-to-do homes espoused radical doctrines. In collaboration with my
friend Maurice Krout, I collected some autobiographical data from hundreds of Chicago youths and separated them into conservative, Stalin-
ist, and Trotskyist groups. In general, our findings supported the thesis
that rebellious adolescents were often expressing their hostility against
their parents in their political activities.

In 1935, I got my first full-time teaching appointment, at the University of Akron. There I was asked to offer a course in the psychology
of personality. Seeking a possible text, I found that none was available,
and decided to write my own. Allport was engaged in a parallel project
at the time, but I knew nothing of this. I was, of course, familiar with
his work on the ascendance–submission scale and on expressive movements (Allport & Vernon, 1933). As he often remarked, his course at
Harvard was the first on personality in the United States; I am sure
this is correct, but my own offering developed quite independently.

My book was finished in 1936, and I began talking to publishers'
representatives about it. I was lucky to mention it to the McGraw-Hill
representative, Ed Booher, and he negotiated a contract for publication. An interesting consequence of this occurred in 1974, on the occasion of the fourth edition. Booher had by now attained the presidency

of McGraw-Hill and was about to retire. As a memento of his first acquisition for the company, he had two copies of the fourth edition bound handsomely in leather, one for himself, the other a gift for me.

As I look back at 1937–1938, I am pleased to note that the three books under discussion (Allport's, Murray's, and mine) represented the three major currents in systematic psychology of that period. Allport wrote in a broadly humanistic tradition with attention to phenomenology; Murray emphasized psychoanalytic hypotheses; and I built an interpretation of major phenomena involved in "personality" as behavioristic. I believe it is fair to say that these are still the major perspectives characterizing European and American theorizing about personality. Parenthetically, I regret the ethnocentrically American approach of most recent writings in this field. But this is no place to introduce a detailed discussion of European viewpoints.

Allport, of course, fought against this "isolationist" trend in American psychology. He praised Wilhelm Stern's "Verstehen" psychology, and included in his text brief discussions of traditional philosophical issues, many of which were, in my opinion, beside the point and/or potentially confusing to the student. Gordon's approach was one of emphasizing what he considered to be the important issues and deleting those that did not seem worth special attention. This extended to the American tradition of reviewing all kinds of historical material that might be relevant to a theoretical or empirical issue. Once I casually mentioned to him that he had completely ignored a certain empirical study; cheerfully, he asserted of his book that "There isn't a fact in it." This was not true, but it does illustrate Gordon's preference for a coherent treatment of an issue as against piling up mountains of empirical studies that defy integration.

I often thought of this dictum and decided that what Gordon preferred was fitting "facts" into a theoretical framework, not simply cataloging the literature. Of course, this approach was used in my book, too, and in Murray's (1938) volume. No one can review all the directly or tangentially relevant literature on a significant topic. Murray, for example, always considered—and usually found—a psychoanalytic interpretation for his empirical data. Similarly, in my 1937 book, I always looked for, and usually offered, a Hullian or Watsonian model for my findings. A point that does intrigue me in this connection is that the three dominant currents in psychology—phenomenology, behaviorism, and psychoanalysis—were so visible in the foundation of a "psychology of personality."

Of the three textbooks that we have identified as proof of the viability of this new specialty within psychology, Allport's was the first to appear. It was, deservedly, a tremendous success, and it no doubt contributed importantly to his election as president of the American Psychological Association in 1939. I got no such "immediate" reinforcement, but after the second edition of my book appeared in 1948, I was elected president of Division 8 (Personality and Social Psychology) of APA. Murray's academic honors, though delayed even longer, included APA's Distinguished Scientific Contribution Award in 1961 and awards from the Society for Projective Techniques, the American Psychoanalytic Association, and the American Psychosomatic Society. He was chosen president of Division 8 in 1962.

In my personal contacts with Allport, he impressed me with his easygoing, confident manner. I think he must have resembled William James, whom I never met. I recall with pleasure a conversation I had with Allport shortly after the 1948 revision of my book appeared. Gordon congratulated me, and then suggested—no doubt with tongue firmly in cheek—that I should now revise his 1937 volume. "But Gordon," I protested, "I've already revised your book—right into mine!" There was a lot of truth in my statement, and he accepted it as a compliment rather than an admission of piracy.

My theoretical orientation evolved over time. Starting in 1937 as a Hullian behaviorist, by 1948 I had shifted to a cognitive emphasis influenced by Allport and Lewin. At this time I was also collaborating with T. F. Karwoski on some work on homeostasis and applied this approach to personality (Stagner, 1951, 1977).

In 1939, I moved to Dartmouth, where I taught introductory psychology and some specialized courses in world politics and in industrial conflict. I was pleased to fancy that I was a replacement for Allport, who had taught at Dartmouth from 1926 to 1930. I was also astonished to learn (from faculty gossip) why he had returned to Harvard in 1930. It seems that in 1929, the Dartmouth administration informed the psychology staff that one faculty member could be awarded tenure; the department voted to grant tenure to Edwin M. Bailor rather than to Allport. Not surprisingly, Gordon wrote some letters and got an invitation to rejoin Harvard, where he remained for the rest of his life.

This experience at Dartmouth may well have been an important factor in Allport's considerable efforts, soon after he joined the Harvard faculty, to improve Murray's prospects for receiving tenure. Many faculty members, including such influential figures as Edward G. Boring and Karl S. Lashley, were opposed to tenure for Murray. Gordon rather uncharacteristically mounted a vigorous campaign on Murray's behalf, collecting endorsements of Murray from distinguished psychologists around the country. The campaign succeeded, but only to a limited extent: Murray's appointment was renewed, but he was not granted permanent tenure. In fact, he did not achieve tenure until 1947, and was not promoted to the rank of professor until 1951.

Psychologists who believe in the validity of human judgments of the abilities of others will perhaps be baffled by the treatment of Allport at Dartmouth and of Murray at Harvard. Certainly, if we are going to use psychological assessments of persons to predict their future performance, we ought to be able to achieve higher validity than these two cases indicate. And the judges in both instances were professional psychologists!

I do not know enough about the Dartmouth matter to offer an explanation. However, in the Harvard situation, strong professional biases were operative. Boring and Lashley led a faction seeking to assert the "scientific" status of "pure" psychology. Because Murray often espoused a psychoanalytic approach, they rejected his claim to belong in a scientific department that aspired to parity with, or at least acceptance by, such disciplines as physics and chemistry. Many of today's psychologists are unaware of the schism within the American Psychological Association in 1935, when clinical and industrial psychologists broke away from the "scientific" establishment and set up the American Association of Applied Psychology. This was followed, in 1936, by the organization of the Society for the Psychological Study of Social Issues when the officers of APA refused to take stands on fascism and other burning public issues. (We now witness a reversal of the 1935 fission; the "applied" psychologists seem to have taken over APA and "scientific" psychologists transfer into the American Psychological Society.)

From the perspective of 1993, it seems strange that Boring and Lashley, two devotees of objectivity in psychology, fought so vigorously against Murray's promotion. He was, after all, a physician and a biochemist, eminently qualified by the criteria of the "established" sciences. The explanation lies in academic politics. Boring and Lashley wanted psychology to be accepted as a science; they feared loss of status if they were identified with the ambiguities of psychoanalysis.

PERSONALITY AND PSYCHOANALYSIS

I have referred to the hostility expressed by my instructors at Wisconsin to psychoanalytic theories. Much of this was, as I see now, due to a confusion of some highly imaginative writings with the solid clinical observations that underlie most of Freud's generalizations. As I read Murray, he was critical of psychoanalytic fantasies but not of the better-founded components of the doctrine.

Not having been psychoanalyzed, I refrain from offering any psychodiagnosis of my inner dynamics. As I have noted, in terms of instructional influence, I should have been biased against Freudian theory. At least two of the professors I admired (Cameron and Sheldon) were vigorous critics of psychoanalysis. Yet I remained friendly, or at least tolerant, with regard to this approach to personality. Maybe the relationship between student and teacher is as often dialectic as it is imitative. Perhaps B. F. Skinner spoke for many graduate students when he wrote of his Harvard Ph.D., "I had the advantage of scarcely being taught at all" (1983, p. 25). Perhaps our future theoretical predilections are laid down in early childhood, as Freud speculated. At any rate, I tried to integrate Freud into my behavioristic frame of reference, and I believe that I succeeded, at least in later years. One relevant bit of evidence is a study I did with another graduate student, Neal Drought (Stagner & Drought, 1935), utilizing a Thurstone scaling technique to measure students' attitudes toward their parents. This study was mentioned in the *Time* magazine roundup of items dealing with psychology from 1923 to 1988 (Gerow, 1988, pp. 21–22).

VIEWS ON METHODOLOGY

It is not likely that Gordon Allport's most enthusiastic admirers would describe him as an expert on methodology. His approach would have to be characterized as thoughtful and occasionally inspired, but not emphasizing precision or elaborate experimental controls. On the other hand, he liked to push at the boundaries of accepted methodologies—as can be seen in H. S. Odbert's dissertation, *Trait-names: A Psycholexical Study* (Allport & Odbert, 1936). To Gordon, language and culture were instrumental in shaping individuals' personalities.

Allport also advocated the use of autobiographies and other personal documents as ways of studying personality. A major problem here, as he probably would have been the first to admit, is the tendency to distort reporting in such a way as to improve the self-image. B. F. Skinner's writings (1976, 1979) provide a case in point. In the first volume of his autobiography, Skinner described himself, during graduate school at least, as a creature of strict routine with tight time schedules governing his daily activities:

> I would rise at six, study until breakfast, go to classes, laboratories,
> and libraries with no more than fifteen minutes unscheduled during

the day, study until exactly nine o'clock at night and go to bed. I saw no movies or plays, seldom went to concerts, had scarcely any dates and read nothing but psychology and physiology. (1976, p. 398).

This passage delighted me because it seemed to confirm Allport's theory about the unity of personality, tying in so well with Skinner's concern with uniformities of behavior, schedules of reinforcement, and stimulus control of behavior. My enthusiasm was dashed when, in a second volume of autobiography that appeared three years later, Skinner dismissed the earlier description of his graduate school years as pure fiction: "I was recalling a pose rather than the life I actually led" (1979, p. 5).

Allport might have defended his faith in autobiographies by noting that scholars can search for just such contradictions or revisions of the writer's past. To me, the excerpts from Skinner's accounts suggest that we ought to defer to the historians and political scientists, who have for centuries warned us about the weaknesses of autobiographies as sources of reliable data about past events.

As a matter of fact (fact as I see it), Allport was not seriously interested in methodological questions. He sympathized with Wilhelm Stern's psychology of understanding *(Verstehen)* and subordinated "objectivity" to a highly subjective empathy. Even so, Allport deserves credit for an important methodological formulation: the idiographic hypothesis. He proposed that instead of studying frequencies of responses across a universe of persons (the traditional research practice), we could study patterns within the universe of actions by a single individual.

Murray's interest in methodology was much stronger than Allport's. At least two of Murray's innovations met with wide acceptance: the Thematic Apperception Test (TAT) (now a basic clinical tool) and team assessment. During World War II, he headed a group of psychologists (OSS Assessment Staff, 1948) that administered performance tasks under stressful conditions. The OSS staff were seeking to predict behavior in actual high-stress circumstances, such as those encountered by parachutists on a sabotage mission when dropped behind enemy lines. Variations on OSS procedures for assessing complex personal attributes became quite popular in industrial psychology during the 1960s and 1970s; the selection decisions made at these assessment centers tended to be valid. The relative success of team assessment (in contrast to the errors noted above in the Allport and Murray tenure decisions) may have been partly due to the fact that observers were trained specifically to avoid biases in judgment.

As for myself, I cannot claim any innovative contributions to method-ology. The "fascist attitude" studies did set in motion a train of re-searches on the "authoritarian personality" and later on dogmatism and rigidity. My interests in these topics, and the organization of the Soci-ety for the Psychological Study of Social Issues in 1936, in which I was actively involved, led me to deal with linkages between personality and political behavior in my 1937 book. Allport and Murray were both drawn into applied aspects of psychology during the war, Allport mak-ing contributions to rumor analysis and Murray, of course, in combat-related selection procedures. I took a defense-related job in industrial personnel work, and this played a large part in my subsequent focus on industrial psychology. However, I found plenty of personality problems among industrial personnel, and often obtained insights from my work in industry that were useful in the study of personality. So I feel that I have had not two separate careers in psychology, but one—it merely moved from academic to industrial settings.

I would like to add one note with respect to methods in the study of personality. In a recent review, Craik (1986) analyzed this field thor-oughly, and what struck me about his paper was that, of the seven classes of procedures he identified, every one is mentioned in the three books that we have taken as our starting point in this review of the psychology of personality.

RETROSPECTIONS

As I look back at 50 years of psychological research on and specu-lation about personality, I find myself uncertain as to how much prog-ress we have made. We have certainly increased the reliability of our methods, but a parallel increase in validity is hard to find. Murray's introduction of the team assessment format has been widely imitated and seems to have been of some utility in industrial work. On the other hand, I have noted the low validity of judgments made by professional psychologists (with Allport at Dartmouth and Murray at Harvard), which casts doubt on the validity of the team approach to assess-ment. Similarly, Allport's reliance on autobiographical data is under-mined by the frequency with which individuals publish reports about themselves that are full of distortions and inaccuracies. Personality in-ventories are susceptible to faking and even indirect measures such as the Rorschach inkblots and the TAT pictures can be faked without much trouble.

Although these last 50 years have certainly been eventful, we have not yet arrived at a consensus on just what we mean by personality nor on the optimal procedures for studying it. Nevertheless, the search has been fun.

ACKNOWLEDGMENTS: I wish to acknowledge the valuable assistance of Dr. Sheldon J. Lachman in verifying some items of information cited here. My thanks also go to Dr. M. Brewster Smith for valuable comments on an earlier draft of this chapter.

REFERENCES

Adorno, T. W., Frenkel-Brunswik, E., Levinson, D. J., & Sanford, R. N. (1950). *The authoritarian personality*. New York: Harper & Row.

Allport, F. H. (1974). Autobiography. In G. Lindzey (Ed.), *A history of psychology in autobiography* (Vol. VI, pp. 3–29). Englewood Cliffs, NJ: Prentice-Hall.

Allport, G. W. (1937). *Personality: A psychological interpretation*. New York: Holt.

Allport, G. W. (1967). Gordon W. Allport. In E. G. Boring (Ed.), *A history of psychology in autobiography* (Vol. V, pp. 3–25). New York: Appleton-Century-Crofts.

Allport, G. W., & Odbert, H. S. (1936). Trait-names: A psycholexical study. *Psychological Monographs, 47* (1, whole No. 211).

Allport, G. W., & Vernon, P. E. (1933). *Studies in expressive movement*. New York: Macmillan.

Bagby, E. (1928). *Psychology of personality*. New York: Holt.

Cattell, J. M. (1886). Psychometrische Untersuchungen. *Philosophische Studien, 3,* 305–355.

Craik, K. H. (1986). Personality research methods in historical perspective. *Journal of Personality, 54,* 18–51.

Gerow, J. R. (Ed.) (1988). Psychology 1923–1988 (Special Issue of *Time*). New York: Time.

James, W. (1890). *Principles of psychology* (Vol. 1). New York: Holt.

Murray, H. A. (1938). *Explorations in personality: A clinical and experimental study of fifty men of college age*. New York: Oxford University Press.

OSS Assessment Staff (1948). *Assessment of men*. New York: Rinehart.

Roback, A. A. (1927). *Personality, character, and temperament: A bibliography*. Cambridge, MA: Sci-Art.

Skinner, B. F. (1976). *Particulars of my life*. New York: Knopf.

Skinner, B. F. (1979). *The shaping of a behaviorist*. New York: Knopf.

Skinner, B. F. (1983). Interview. *Psychology Today, 17, 25ff.*

Stagner, R. (1933). Relation of personality to academic aptitude and achievement. *Journal of Educational Research, 26,* 648–660.

Stagner, R. (1935). Economic status and personality. *School and society, 42,* 551–552.

Stagner, R. (1936a). Fascist attitudes: An exploratory study. *Journal of Social Psychology, 7,* 309–319.

Stagner, R. (1936b). Fascist attitudes: Their determining conditions. *Journal of Social Psychology, 7,* 438–454.

Stagner, R. (1937). *Psychology of personality. New York: McGraw-Hill.*

Stagner, R. (1951). Homeostasis as a unifying concept in personality theory. *Psychological Review, 58,* 5–17.

Stagner, R. (1977). Homeostasis, discrepancy, dissonance: A theory of motives and motivation. *Motivation and Emotion, 1,* 103–138.

Stagner, R., & Drought, N. (1935). Measuring children's attitudes toward their parents. *Journal of Educational Psychology, 26,* 169–176.

CHAPTER THREE

Allport's *Personality* and Allport's Personality

ALAN C. ELMS

INTRODUCTION

In Gordon Allport's (1967) brief autobiography, written a year before he died, he asked the question repeatedly: "How shall a psychological life history be written?" It was a question he had asked recently about another life, in preparing for book publication the *Letters from Jenny* (1965). It was a question he had asked more broadly a quarter-century earlier, in writing his monograph on *The Use of Personal Documents in Psychological Science* (1942). It was a question he had asked quite early in his career, in a paper on a confessional work titled *The Locomotive God* (1929). Indeed, Allport said that even his doctoral dissertation, *An Experimental Study of the Traits of Personality* (1922a), "was an early formulation of the riddle: How shall a psychological life history be written?" (1967, p. 7).

I did not begin as early and I have not persisted for nearly as long as Allport, but for over 15 years I have been asking the same question, "How shall a psychological life history be written?" Among a variety of psychobiographical subjects, I have asked the question most often about personality theorists, ranging from Freud and Jung to Skinner and Murray. My first published attempt to answer the question was a five-

ALAN C. ELMS • Department of Psychology, University of California, Davis, California 95616.

Fifty Years of Personality Psychology, edited by Kenneth H. Craik *et al*. Plenum Press, New York, 1993.

page paper on Gordon Allport, which appeared in 1972. I felt rather more nervous than usual about the publication of that paper. It suggested an interpretation of Allport's personality and a set of connections between his life and his work for which I had little hard evidence. I had never met Allport; I had not discussed him in detail with anyone who had known him well; and I was advancing a psychoanalytically tinged account of the core theoretical concepts of a man who had been a career-long critic of psychoanalysis.

Fortunately for my own budding career as a psychobiographer, reactions to my paper on Allport—or at any rate the reactions I heard about—were generally favorable. Several friends and colleagues of his told me I had done a pretty good job, at least in so brief a space and for someone who didn't know him. Most offered additional information to support my hypotheses. I felt encouraged enough by these reactions to move on to psychobiographical studies of other theorists. I also began to think about writing a book that would combine my studies of a number of theorists, including Allport. So I have continued to read his work and to collect information about him, rather sporadically, through interviews with additional colleagues of his and through occasional examination of archival materials. The larger part of my attention in recent years has been directed toward more provocative subjects, especially Sigmund Freud and Henry Murray, among psychologists, plus such bizarre personalities as Elvis Presley and Alexander Haig in other areas of endeavor. However, I keep returning, now and then, to the quiet but firm person of Gordon Willard Allport.

ALLPORT'S ENCOUNTER WITH FREUD

My first paper on Allport focused on his one and only meeting with Sigmund Freud. It was a story that Allport told often—so often that the several surviving versions of it in his own words are almost identical, sentence for sentence. It was the single personal anecdote included in his *New York Times* obituary (October 10, 1967). The version below has not been previously published, but it will sound familiar to the many people who heard the story from Allport himself:

> So, in my callow youth—this story is very much at my own expense—in my callow youth, I wrote Freud a note, announcing that I was in Vienna and no doubt he would be glad to see me. I received a reply in his own handwriting inviting me to come to his office, at a certain time and place. I went there, to the famous red burlap room with pictures of dreams on the wall. He opened the

door and invited me into the inner sanctum, and sat there silent. You may not believe this possible, but I was not prepared for silence. It occurred to me it was up to me to say something, so I fished around in my mind and I told him about an episode on the tram car coming out. I had seen a little boy about four years old and the little boy obviously was developing a real dirt phobia. His mother was with him. She was a starched Hausfrau, terribly clean and purposive looking. And the little boy was saying: "I don't want to sit *there*! Don't let *him* sit near me, *he's* dirty." He kept this up all the time, and I thought it might interest Freud how early a phobia of dirt can get set. He listened, and fixed his therapeutic eye upon me and said "Was that little boy you?" Honestly, it wasn't, but I felt guilty. (Allport, 1962, p. 2)

Allport's adjectives describing the boy's mother vary slightly from version to version: "excessively clean and well starched ... domineering in manner" (Allport, 1958, p. 2); "a well-starched *Hausfrau*, so dominant and purposive looking that I thought the cause and effect apparent" (Allport, 1967, p. 8); "well starched and very prim" (quoted by Evans, 1970, p. 4). The little boy is described in 1958 as looking "excessively clean and well starched" like his mother; in the 1967 account, Allport says that to the little boy "everything was *schmutzig*" (p. 8); otherwise the little boy's description remains the same in each telling. The story's punchline ("Was that little boy you?" or "And was that little boy you?") is always followed by Allport's denial: "It wasn't. (But I felt almost guilty!)" (Allport, 1958, p. 2); "It was not, honestly, but I felt guilty" (1964 filmed interview, slightly reworded in Evans, 1970, p. 4); "Flabbergasted and feeling a bit guilty, I contrived to change the subject. While Freud's misunderstanding of my motivation was amusing...." (Allport, 1967, p. 8).

As Allport indicates here, he told his story both as a kind of joke on Freud and as a joke on the young Gordon Allport. However, he also made clear that the incident was ultimately no joke for him. He referred to it variously as "profoundly revealing" about Freud in ways he had thought back on "many times since becoming a professional psychologist myself" (1958, p. 2), as "a very important experience to me" (1962, p. 2), and as "an event of pungent significance ... [having] the character of a traumatic developmental episode" (1967, p. 7). Allport described his reaction following the meeting in this way:

But thinking that little episode over, it grew in importance to me, because the fact is that Freud, with his tendency to see pathological trains, and most of his people who came to see him were patients, of course, it was natural he should break through my defenses and get down to business, you see. But actually, he mistook my motives. If he had said, "Well, here is a brassy young American youth, a tourist who is imposing on my good nature and time," he would have been somewhere near correct, I think. But to ascribe my motivation to the unconscious in this case was definitely wrong. (1964 filmed interview, somewhat reworded in Evans, 1970, pp. 4–5)

In his autobiography, Allport summarized the Freud incident's longer-term professional effects on him:

> This experience taught me that depth psychology, for all its merits, may plunge too deep, and that psychologists would do well to give full recognition to manifest motives before probing the unconscious. Although I never regarded myself as anti-Freudian, I have been critical of psychoanalytic excesses. A later paper entitled "The Trend in Motivational Theory" (1953) is a direct reflection of this episode and has been reprinted, I believe, more frequently than any other of my articles. (1967, p. 8)

ALLPORT'S THEORY OF THE CLEAN PERSONALITY

Allport's vigorous and repeated denial that he was the little boy with the dirt phobia intrigued me as it has intrigued others (e.g., Faber, 1970; Morey, 1987). I do not consistently practice what Erikson (1969, p. 98) calls "originology," the strategy of attempting to explain adult psychological patterns always by reference to their earliest and most primitive form. But it seemed to me that if Allport insisted so strenuously on denying his resemblance to the clean little boy on the tramcar, we should at least find out what sort of little boy Allport himself had been.

In looking for such information, I quickly struck pay dirt. In his autobiography, Allport described his childhood in only one cautiously phrased paragraph. That paragraph, however, appeared to explain a great deal about his reaction to the Freud encounter. Allport's paragraph is worth repeating in full:

> Our home life was marked by plain Protestant piety and hard work. My mother had been a school teacher and brought to her sons an eager sense of philosophical questing and the importance of searching for ultimate religious answers. Since my father [a physician] lacked adequate hospital facilities for his patients, our household for several years included both patients and nurses. Tending office, washing bottles, and dealing with patients were important aspects of my early training. Along with his general practice my

father engaged in many enterprises: founding a cooperative drug company, building and renting apartments, and finally developing a new specialty of building and supervising hospitals. I mention his versatility simply to underscore the fact that his four sons were trained in the practical urgencies of life as well as in a broad humanitarian outlook. Dad was no believer in vacations. He followed rather his own rule of life, which he expressed as follows: "If every person worked as hard as he could and took only the minimum financial return required by his family's needs, then there would be just enough wealth to go around." Thus it was hard work tempered by trust and affection that marked the home environment. (Allport, 1967, pp. 4–5)

Largely on the basis of that passage, I drew several connections between Allport's early history and his later career. They key paragraphs in my 1972 paper were these:

We may now wonder whether Freud's question was received so traumatically ... because unconsciously he [Allport] was still carrying within him the super-clean little boy whose schoolteacher mother stressed to her children the importance of "plain Protestant piety," philosophical questions, and "ultimate religious answers"; whose physician father had no time for play but transmitted to the children his concern with hard work and tight money; and who himself spent much of his childhood living in the abnormally clean environment of a home–hospital, washing bottles and coping with patients who must either be kept from infection ... or be avoided as infectious. ...

Not only might such an early history have made the adult Allport peculiarly sensitive to small boys with dirt phobias; it may also have been translated into Allport's expressive movements, into a "prim" and "well starched" pattern of gesture, dress, and speech ... that would have been Freud's only other clue besides the story itself to Allport's presence. Allport later in his life proposed ... that the *"style of execution"* of a person's behavior "is always guided directly and without interference by deep and lasting personal dispositions" [1937, p. 466]. Freud is reported to have been particularly adept at reading such nonverbal cues. ...

If our inferences are reasonably accurate, then the apparent force of this brief encounter with Freud becomes more understandable. It was [not merely] one misguided comment by Freud ... that set Allport upon a career of discounting unconscious forces. Allport's reaction can instead be viewed as compatible with his developmental history. The high-minded and clean little boy had become a high-minded and clean young man, unwilling to examine any "dirty" foundations for his choice of conversational gambit, for his "flabbergasted" reaction to Freud's question, or for his behavior in general. This high-minded young man eventually became an important psychological theorist who promulgated a view perhaps appropriately described as [a theory of] "The Clean Personality." He argued against digging into the unconscious except in unusual cases.... He rarely discussed sexual motivation except to protest Freud's emphasis upon it.... He rejected psychological data on such unsavory creatures as rats, children, and neurotics as being largely irrelevant to an understanding of the mature personality. His key motivational concept was *functional autonomy*, the proposition that most adult motives become somehow totally independent of their baser origins. He saw the ultimate criterion of the mature personality as a unifying philosophy of life, perhaps ideally a religious one. Allport appears to have recognized a certain degree of continuity between his [positive] adult theory-building activities and his parents' "plain Protestant piety"; but it may have been precisely [the same] early training in piety, cleanliness, and order that led him to reject the importance of unconscious and infantile motives to the normal adult personality. (Elms, 1972, pp. 629–631)

I cautiously noted, at the end of my paper, that "Our knowledge of Allport's childhood is so slight that we must not push our speculations further." I also pointed out that "Allport's theoretical formulations are clearly the immediate product of much intellectual effort of the highest quality" (p. 631). Nonetheless, it seemed clear to me that Allport's early training in cleanliness and virtue had left him with an unusual sensitivity to certain aspects of personality that other people, including Freud, tended to overlook; and with a distinct insensitivity to, or avoidance of, certain aspects of personality and life to which Freud was particularly sensitive.

I have subsequently obtained other information that supports this interpretation. For instance, the Allport Papers at Harvard contain a letter from Henry Murray to Allport's widow, describing various aspects of his friendship with Gordon:

This brings me once more to that old unresolved question... Freud's reason for asking: "Was that little boy you?" Gordon (and you) seemed to think that Freud had gained the (mistaken) impression that Gordon was (unconsciously) seeking therapeutic relief in visiting the Master. Is that right? But suppose that Freud made no such mistake (having frequently been visited by similar seer-hunters): he simply noted a certain psychological similarity between (i) Gordon's perfect neatness and cleanliness of body and clothes as well as his perfect gentility of speech and (ii) the little boy's obsessional determination to keep free from dirt (a similarity which would account for Gordon's special attention to the boy's behavior), and then Freud, not without a touch of malice, asked his question, as if to say: "Were you not, at one time, as intent as that little boy to avoid dirt (dirty words)?" (Murray, 1972)

Dan Ogilvie, at one time a student of Allport's, has recalled an occasion in 1964 on which Allport asked him to retrieve some copies of Allport's first book from a dusty storage space. Allport handed Ogilvie a clean rag to wipe the dust from his hands while Allport autographed a copy of the book for him.

> In the meantime I had removed the dust, but he insisted I use the rag anyway. I did that and seeing that the rag was in no worse shape than when it had been handed to me, I refolded it and placed it on the corner of his desk. With an expression of disgust, he gingerly deposited the rag in a waste basket. Suddenly I was glued to the floor with the realization that in a critical way the little boy [of the Freud anecdote] ... *did* represent an important aspect of Professor Allport after all. (Ogilvie, 1984, p. 13)

Another of Allport's graduate students has described Allport to me as "extremely orderly," as a man who often referred to "buttoning up things," and who indeed described himself as "buttoning up his life" during the final months of his fatal illness (Thomas Pettigrew, personal communication, 11 August 1977)—an image of precise control reminiscent of that well-starched Viennese hausfrau whom Allport was so fond of characterizing.

In my original paper, I did not speculate on toilet-training history or anal personality traits as sources of Allport's later responses, because I had no specific information on such matters and because I did not wish to be so crudely reductionistic. Both Thomas Pettigrew (personal communication, 30 September 1988) and Robert Allport, Gordon's son (personal communication, 26 October 1988), have suggested to me that describing Allport's personality solely in terms of dirt avoidance and orderliness would leave a distorted picture of a complex man. Allport's heavy smoking habit, which probably contributed to his death from lung cancer, also appears inconsistent with impressions of a compulsively clean and totally self-controlled individual. Nonetheless, the evidence for his strong cleanliness concerns and for his reluctance to acknowledge them is substantial. Further evidence may be found in Allport's only detailed written description of the rest of his encounter with Freud, previously unpublished:

> After this opening episode [ending with Freud's question] I realized that my attitude was too much that of a "tourist" and that

Dr. Freud had been expecting a professional consultation. I then brought out a more personal idiosyncrasy: my dislike of cooked raisins. I told him I thought it due to the fact that at the age of three, a nurse had told me they were "bugs." Freud asked, "When you recalled this episode, did your dislike vanish?" I said, "No." He replied, "Then you are not at the bottom of it." . . .

I then spoke of a common sexual problem of youthful males of my age. [Here Allport may have been referring to anxieties about masturbation or wet dreams; "self-pollution" was a popular term for such matters in those days.] His [Freud's] reply: "Yes, nature tells a many to marry at 18; and society tells him to marry at 28."

Finally I asked, in general, what analyst he would recommend in America in case I ever wished to undergo analysis. He replied that he would recommend only one man: Brill. (This was in 1920.)

I then departed with a vivid feeling of respect and liking for Freud, even though our short conversation had started at cross purposes. (Allport, 1958, p. 3)

THE EVOLUTION OF A CLASSIC TEXTBOOK

From the latter account, it appears that although Allport flatly rejected Freud's equation of him with the little boy on the tramcar, his rejection of Freudian theory in general did not start as quickly or as emphatically as he implied in other accounts. His continuing ambivalence over the next several years was expressed in his correspondence with a friend and former graduate school classmate, William S. Taylor. In July 1922, two years after his Freud encounter, Allport wrote to Taylor that he would soon be returning to Vienna and Berlin, "and hope that we may correspond rather seriously and fully on some of the matters which puzzle us both, and which we might disentangle in writing. I may be able to give first hand the psycho-analytic views, or I may have an opportunity of securing Freud and Jung's answers to our questions" (Allport, 1922b). As matters turned out, Allport did not meet Freud again and apparently had no significant contact with other European psychoanalysts. Nor were his questions readily disentangled, as his further letters to Taylor indicate. Five months later, for instance, he wrote from Berlin:

The course I have with [Max] Dessoir on "Parapsychologie and Psychoanalyse" is an interesting exposition and destruction of the Freudian formulae. He cannot add much, I believe, to our own criticisms of Freud. Is it not true that some of the fundamental contributions of Freud are as original and significant as the ideas of any one man can ever be in science? Is it not true also that no psychologist who has balance would hesitate to condemn the silly Freudian superstructure? Freud in Vienna is now the old story of a famous man in his own town. He is hooted and hooted. Everyone here laughs at him, and he has no recognition except in a narrow circle of orthodox admirers. Freud would be far better off should he migrate to America. (Allport, 1922c)

After another three months, Allport wrote further from Hamburg: "I have just finished reading Freud's *Vorlesungen* [Introductory Lectures]— miles of them—and remain no more nor less instructed than before taking up the book. He is totally without respect in his own land. Such is the fate of a prophet or a would-be prophet" (Allport, 1923).

Allport did gain a great deal of new information and new perspectives on psychology in Europe, and he occupied himself mainly with issues related to these nonpsychoanalytic approaches during the next decade. But Freud's crucial question to him remained an irritant consciously and perhaps unconsciously, a challenge to his personal and professional identity at several levels. It would be finally addressed—though not addressed finally—during the writing of a pioneering textbook in 1936.

The textbook was *Personality: A Psychological Interpretation,* published in 1937. It was not merely one of the first textbooks in personality psychology; as Maddi and Costa (1972) have observed, "The book had a profound impact on the field, virtually defining for many years what was and was not to be considered important in the study of personality" (p. 139). Allport's official version of how the textbook came to be written deals with rather abstract and intellectual matters:

> My ambition was to give a psychological definition of the field of personality as I saw it. My vision, of course, was influenced by my encounters with social ethics, Anglo-American empiricism and German structural and personalistic theories. I wanted to fashion an experimental science, so far as appropriate, but chiefly I wanted an "image of man" that would allow us to test in full whatever democratic and humane potentialities that he might possess. I did not think of man as innately "good," but I was convinced that by and large American psychology gave man less than his due by depicting him as a bundle of unrelated reaction tendencies. I did not write the book for any particular audience. I wrote it simply because I felt I had to define the new field of the psychology of personality as I saw it. (Allport, 1967, p. 15)

However, in one of his previously unpublished autobiographical statements, Allport offers a much more personally involving account of the book's origins. In so doing, he returns to a familiar topic:

> That book has a strange feature that I have never mentioned to

anyone. I wrote it for no audience. Now, when you're taught to write you're told to have an audience in mind. But, if there was ever a book written because someone had to write it, I think that was it. I didn't think it was a textbook. I didn't think of it as an argumentative treatise. I thought of it as summing up my ideas about human personality. In it, you can see the impact of my encounter with Freud as the origin of my idea that adult motivation is not necessarily a channelling, or conditioning, or overlay of cathected instincts or infantile motivations or fixations.

The result was the concept of functional autonomy. I had no idea at the time that it would be picked up and made an issue of, but it merely seemed to me obvious that motivation was often functionally autonomous of its historical origins in a life. The mainsprings of life get re-wound in the course of development. This was a direct answer to Freud, for Freud had thought that I was suffering from an infantile trauma. I wasn't. If he said I was a brassy young American, he would have been right. But, he didn't. He didn't perceive my contemporary motivation. His error impressed me very much, so that I kept working on the problem of motivation from a point of view of the developing adult. I don't deny that there may be traces of infantilism in all of us or traces of neurosis in all of us. I'm not denying or disparaging at all the Freudian contribution. But, Freud's theory to my mind just is not adequate, because some people *do* grow up *sometimes*, in *some* respects. What interested me was what it meant to grow up and be adult and normal in personality function. That is the focus of my concept of functional autonomy and in general of all the 1937 book, as well as much subsequent writing. (1962, p. 5; Allport's emphases)

That is a very interesting statement, for a number of reasons. First, it reports in greater detail on something we have already heard about elsewhere: how Freud's question had a powerful effect on Allport's subsequent psychological thinking. Second, it emphasizes the magnitude of that effect, by saying that a two-minute exchange with Freud in 1920 led to the writing of a 600-page theoretical-position-paper-*cum*-textbook 16 years later. This is further evidence that Allport had been well primed to react to Freud's question, which hit home in ways that Allport never fully acknowledged.

NOT A LITTLE BOY

Allport's series of denials, toward the end of the passage just quoted, indicates one of the ways in which Freud's question had hit home. " ... Freud had thought that I was suffering from an infantile trauma. *I wasn't.* If he had said I was a brassy young American, he would have been right. But, *he didn't....I don't deny* that there may be traces of infantilism in all or us or traces of neurosis in all of us" (my italics). But that is just what Allport *had* denied about himself, perhaps silently at first but promptly and vigorously, then aloud, over and over again: *I am not that little boy with the dirt phobia.* Keep that sentence in mind—Allport's core response to Freud's interpretation of his behavior—as we examine each element of it.

In my initial analysis of Allport's Freud anecdote, I stressed the denial implicit in the final portion of the core response. "I am *not* someone with a *dirt phobia,*" insisted young Gordon Allport, who had been trained by his parents to be clean in mind and body, and who would later develop a theory of the clean personality in contrast to dirty psychoanalysis. "Who, me, a neurotic dirt-phobe? Never!" was Allport's apparently instant reaction to Freud's unsettling probe. When Allport later felt it necessary to justify presenting what he called "so critical and so brief" an account of psychoanalysis in his *Personality* textbook, he offered a similar denial of its theoretical applicability to nonneurotics: "Psychoanalytic concepts are drawn exclusively from neurotic and pathological material ... and for this reason their applicability to normal personality is in many respects questionable" (1937, p. 181, fn. 27).

But there is more to Allport's reaction, as his 1962 statement on the origins of the *Personality* textbook suggests. He says there, " ... Freud's theory to my mind just is not adequate, because some people *do* grow up *sometimes,* in *some* respects" (p. 5; his emphases). Now back to our core sentence: "I am *not* that *little boy....*"

Regardless of what neurotic symptoms were or were not involved, it was important for Gordon Allport, at age 22 in Sigmund Freud's office, to deny being a little boy. Allport had been the baby in his family, five years younger than the youngest of his three brothers. To a considerable degree, he had remained in the shadow of his brother Floyd, seven years older than he. Floyd Allport graduated from Harvard before Gordon thought seriously of enrolling there. Floyd was a decorated military hero in World War I while Gordon merely served in the Students' Army Training Corps, performing what Gordon himself called "sophomoric" tasks. Floyd was awarded a Ph.D. degree from Harvard on the day that Gordon got his bachelor's degree. At several points in his short autobiography, Gordon refers either to his "generalized inferiority feeling" as a young man (1967, p. 7) or to specific feelings of inferiority toward Floyd (p. 12). In an undated description of his "Personal Experience with Racial and Religious Attitudes," Gordon described himself as having been "a youth of great inferiority feeling...."

I know what it is to be the object of scorn, but for personal and not [group] membership reasons. As I said, this sensitivity gave me a variety of compensatory strivings in myself, and as I overcame my handicaps, I also grew in sympathy with any under-dog" (Allport, n.d.). Early in his academic career he told one correspondent, "I have published several articles of no great importance, and am not to be confused with my more eminent brother, F.H. Allport, of Syracuse University" (Allport, 1928).

Gordon Allport did manage after college graduation to go off on his own for a year, to teach in a small English-speaking school in Constantinople, with nobody around who was likely to make him feel inferior. But at the end of that year he headed back to Harvard, ready to become a graduate student in the psychology department where brother Floyd was already on the faculty—and at this point Freud had the audacity to tell him he was still a little boy! No wonder so much of the 1937 *Personality* textbook and of Gordon Allport's later writing about personality development stress the *discontinuity* between child and man, through the development of the functional autonomy of motives and in many other ways.

ALLPORT AS UNIQUE INDIVIDUAL

Back to our core sentence again: "I am *not that* little boy...." Allport treated as self-evident the fact that he was not the little boy he had seen on the tramcar. Regardless of any possible similarities that Freud might have hypothesized, Gordon W. Allport was *one* person and the little boy was *another* person. Allport's first sentences in his *Personality* textbook are, "As a rule, science regards the individual as a mere bothersome accident. Psychology, too, ordinarily treats him as something to be brushed aside" (1937, p. vii). Allport was not about to permit his own individuality to be brushed aside. Allport ends the book with what is, for a textbook, an unusually stirring paragraph:

> Thus there are many ways to study man psychologically. Yet to study him most fully is to take him as an individual. He is more than a bundle of habits; more than a nexus of abstract dimensions; more too than a representative of his species. He is more than a citizen of the state, and more than a mere incident in the gigantic movements of mankind. He transcends them all. The individual, striving ever for his own integrity, has existed under many forms of social life—forms as varied as the nomadic, feudal, and capitalistic. He struggles on even under oppression, always hoping and plan-

ning for a more perfect democracy where the dignity and growth of each personality will be prized above all else. (pp. 565–566)

This stress on the individual was not altogether uncommon in psychology by the 1930s. Gordon's older brother Floyd had already made it a feature of his own influential approach to social psychology—for instance, by attacking the "fallacy" of the "group mind" early in his 1924 textbook and by arguing instead that the so-called "mental structure" of groups actually consists of "sets of ideals, thoughts, and habits repeated in each individual mind and existing only in those minds" (pp. 8–9). What really distinguished Gordon Allport's position from that of his brother, and from most other psychologists of his day, was Gordon's emphasis on the *uniqueness* of the individual. Early in the final chapter of *Personality*, he states:

> Implicit in the modern point of view is the demand that psychology expand its boundaries, revise its methods, and extend its concepts to accommodate, more hospitably than in the past, the study of the single concrete mental life.
>
> This demand is thoroughly radical. It is directed against the practice in general psychology of drawing the blood and peeling the flesh from human personality, leaving only such a skeleton framework of mind as is acceptable to the sparse canons and methods of nomothetic science. By stripping the person of all his troublesome particularities, general psychology has destroyed his essential nature. The newer point of view reverses the perspective. The person is no longer regarded as a neutral tinted background upon which the all-important design of mind-in-general stands out. Quite the reverse: the uniform design traced by general psychology becomes the ground upon which the integral, three-dimensional, and unique individual emerges as the salient feature. (p. 549)

That is a dramatic declaration of independence from the nomothetic psychoanalysts and behaviorists of Allport's day. Even more, by advocating the study not just of the individual but of the *unique* individual, Allport declared *his* uniqueness in comparison with brother Floyd or with virtually anyone else in psychology at the time. "I am not that little boy," he was saying; "I am nobody but me."

ALLPORT AS AN ADULT

Finally, having dealt with every other element of the core sentence, "I am not *that little boy with the dirt phobia*," we are left with its beginning: "*I am not.*" Erik Erikson, in his psychobiography of Mar-

tin Luther, makes much of Luther's so-called "fit in the choir," when
Luther is said to have shouted out, "It isn't me!" or "I am *not!*" (1958,
p. 23). Declaring what you are not, according to Erikson, is often a way
to establish who you are, what your identity is (p. 36). Gordon Allport,
by his testimony, was not a neurotic, not a little boy, not a generic
personality interchangeable with other personalities; so what was he?
As he suggested in his 1962 "reminiscence" on the origins of the *Personality* textbook ("... some people *do* grow up ..."), he was a grown-
up, a psychologically healthy adult.

And what does that imply? Well, as he said in the book, "There are
as many ways of growing up as there are individuals who grow, and in
each case the end-product is unique. But," he added, "if general criteria
are sought whereby to distinguish a fully developed personality from
one that is still unripe, there are three differentiating characteristics
that seem both universal and indispensable" (1937, p. 213).

Allport did little to demonstrate the universality or indispensability of the three characteristics that he listed. But they are surely characteristics that he felt he himself possessed in full measure, indeed
more than most people—as, on the whole, he did. He identified them as
self-extension, self-objectification, and a unifying philosophy of life
(1937, pp. 213–214). *Self-extension* involves having "a variety of autonomous interests" (p. 213), the incorporation into oneself of the many
things one loves: "Possessions, friends, one's own children, other children, cultural interests, abstract ideas, politics, hobbies, recreation, and
most conspicuously of all, one's *work*" (p. 217, his emphasis). One is
reminded here of the busy Allport, who even as an undergraduate devoted himself enthusiastically to volunteer work with boys' clubs, social
service agencies, the Humane Society, and so forth, while joyfully discovering the new intellectual world of Harvard, Cambridge, and Boston—a far cry from the Freud anecdote's narrowly focused dirt-phobic
boy and his well-starched mother.

Self-objectification includes the development of self-insight and of
that highly correlated quality, a sense of humor. The latter involves,
according to Allport, "the ability to laugh at the things one loves (including of course oneself and all that pertains to oneself), and still to
love them" (p. 223). We might wonder about Allport's degree of self-
insight, as he resolutely insisted that that little boy had no relevance to
himself. But Allport certainly did display a sense of humor about the
matter, and he was *very* self-aware regarding the only level of personality he thought important for normal adults—the conscious level.

Finally among Allport's criteria for a fully developed personality is
a *unifying philosophy of life*, one that represents to a person "his place

in the scheme of things" (p. 214). Allport acknowledged that "there are many ... unifying philosophies," but, he insisted, "Religion is the search for a value underlying *all* things, and as such is the most comprehensive of all the possible philosophies of life" (p. 226; his emphasis). Here the very religious Gordon Allport could feel superior even to his older brother Floyd, who had publicly given up the idea of a "transcendental, monistic god" (Allport, 1933, p. 458). On this point Gordon could also feel superior to Sigmund Freud. He observed that in the recently published *New Introductory Lectures*, "Freud declares himself 'perfectly certain' that this particular class of 'illusions' [i.e., religion] springs from infantilism of the mind" (Allport, 1937, p. 227). Allport thought he knew better; and in knowing better, he recognized himself as the true adult among this company. While discussing his criteria for personal maturity, Allport listed the major limitations of other approaches to the psychology of personality, and here he made one simple complaint about psychoanalysis: *"Freudian psychology* never regards an adult as truly adult" (1937, p. 216; his emphasis). Like every personality theorist before and after him, Allport clearly knew of at least one adult who was truly adult: the theorist himself.

CONCLUSION

I realize that in focusing on the personal sources of his 1937 personality textbook, I am selling Gordon Allport short. I wish he were still around to rally the forces of idiographic psychology; we need someone of his vigor and eloquence. I have been greatly impressed by the wise and pithy editorial correspondence I have seen from his many years as editor of the *Journal of Abnormal and Social Psychology*. If Allport's editorial suggestions had been headed more carefully by Abraham Maslow, for example, the third-force humanistic psychology movement might have proceeded on more solid ground. I have seen much evidence of Allport's private kindness to individuals as different from him and from each other as Jenny Masterson and Harry Murray.

I agree with Allport's statement, in the *Personality* text, that "In biographies ... an inevitable exaggeration of consistency occurs. 'Irrelevant' activities and traits are discarded, and the act of discarding makes for over-simplification .... The writer wishes to extract the 'essence' or meaning of the life. In so doing remarkable unity emerges, more than was ever present in the animate person" (p. 352, fn. 8). Surely there was much more to Gordon Allport than the clean little boy of his Freud encounter. But Allport himself kept telling that story, telling it more often than any other story about himself, and tying it directly to his life's work.

A year after Allport's personality textbook was published, another milestone in personality psychology appeared: Henry Murray's *Explorations in Personality* (1938). Murray dedicated his book in part "To Sigmund Freud, whose genius contributed the most fruitful working hypotheses . . . and to Carl G. Jung, whose writings were a hive of great suggestiveness." Allport had properly dedicated the *Personality* text to his mother, whose virtues and teachings did indeed leave their strong mark upon the book. But he might well have added to his dedication these words: "And to Sigmund Freud, whose question stung me to make this belated (but thoroughly adult) reply."

ACKNOWLEDGMENTS: Extracts from the unpublished papers of Gordon W. Allport are quoted by permission of Robert B. Allport, the Harvard University Archives, the Archives of the History of American Psychology, and the Library of Congress. The excerpt from an unpublished letter by Henry A. Murray is quoted by permission of Nina Murray and the Harvard University Archives. Individuals who provided information during the preparation of this chapter include Robert B. Allport, James W. Anderson, George Atwood, K. R. Eissler, Anthony Greenwald, Henry A. Murray, Dan Ogilvie, Thomas Pettigrew, M. Brewster Smith, Philip J. Stone, and Eugene Taylor. Their helpfulness of course does not make them in any way responsible for my interpretations or conclusions.

REFERENCES

Allport, F. H. (1924). *Social psychology.* Boston: Houghton Mifflin.

Allport, F. H. (1933). *Institutional behavior.* Chapel Hill: University of North Carolina Press.

Allport, G. W. (1922a). *An experimental study of the traits of personality.* Unpublished doctoral dissertation, Harvard University, Cambridge, MA.

Allport, G. W. (1922b). Letter to W. S. Taylor, 25 July. William S. Taylor Papers, Archives of the History of American Psychology, University of Akron, Akron, OH.

Allport, G. W. (1922c). Letter to W. S. Taylor, 18 December. William S. Taylor Papers, Archives of the History of American Psychology, University of Akron, Akron, OH.

Allport, G. W. (1923). Letter to W. S. Taylor, 21 March. William S. Taylor Papers, Archives of the History of American Psychology, University of Akron, Akron, OH.

Allport, G. W. (1928). Letter to W. E. Leonard, 5 April. Gordon W. Allport Papers, Harvard University Archives, Cambridge, MA.

Allport, G. W. (1929). The study of personality by the intuitive method: An experiment in teaching from *The Locomotive God. Journal of Abnormal and Social Psychology, 24,* 14–27.

Allport, G. W. (1937). *Personality: A psychological interpretation.* New York: Holt.

Allport, G. W. (1942). *The use of personal documents in psychological science.* New York: Social Science Research Council, Bulletin 49.

Allport, G. W. (1953). The trend in motivational theory. *American Journal of Orthopsychiatry, 25,* 107–119.

Allport, G. W. (1958). G. W. Allport recalls a visit to Sigmund Freud. Unpublished manuscript, Sigmund Freud Archives, Library of Congress, Washington, DC, October 29.

Allport, G. W. (1962). My encounters with personality theory. Unpublished manuscript, recorded and edited by W.G.T. Douglas, Boston University School of Theology, October 29.

Allport, G. W. (1965). *Letters from Jenny.* New York: Harcourt.

Allport, G. W. (1967). Autobiography. In E. G. Boring & G. Lindzey (Eds.), *A history of psychology in autobiography* (Vol. 5, pp. 1–25). Boston: Appleton.

Allport, G. W. (n.d.). Personal experience with racial and religious attitudes. Unpublished manuscript, Gordon W. Allport Papers, Harvard University Archives, Cambridge, MA.

Elms, A.C. (1972). Allport, Freud, and the clean little boy. *Psychoanalytic Review, 59,* 627–632.

Erikson, E. H. (1958). *Young man Luther.* New York: Norton.

Erikson, E. H. (1969). *Gandhi's truth.* New York: Norton.

Evans, R. I. (1970). *Gordon Allport: The man and his ideas.* New York: Dutton.

Faber, M. D. (1970). Allport's visit with Freud. *Psychoanalytic Review, 57,* 60–64.

Maddi, S. R., & Costa, P. T. (1972). *Humanism in personology: Allport, Maslow, Murray.* Chicago: Aldine.

Morey, L. C. (1987). Observations on the meeting between Allport and Freud. *Psychoanalytic Review, 74,* 135–139.

Murray, H. A. (1938). *Explorations in personality.* New York: Oxford.

Murray, H. A. (1972). Letter to Ada L. Allport, 22 September. Gordon W. Allport Papers, Harvard University Archives, Cambridge, MA.

Ogilvie, D. M. (1984). Personality and paradox: Gordon Allport's final contribution. *Personality Forum, 2,* 12–14.

CHAPTER FOUR

Allport and Murray on Allport's *Personality*
A Confrontation in 1946–1947*

M. BREWSTER SMITH

In the winter of 1946–1947, graduate students in the Department of Social Relations at Harvard, then in its second year, heard Gordon Allport, Henry Murray, and Kurt Lewin each talk about his distinctive approach to personality in the presence of the others and comment about the others' theories. New graduate students were then required to participate in two proseminars: one on methods chaired by Jerome S. Bruner, the other on concepts led by Talcott Parsons. Most of the advanced students turned out for the occasions (December 15, 1946, and January 6, 1947) when these three originators of personality psychology held forth. I was a privileged participant and took full telegraphic notes. I remember sharing the common feeling that we were participating in a joust of Olympians. When I returned to my notes a quarter century later, they still evoked for me the excitement of the occasion. I select here the interchange between Allport and Murray on Allport's theory. What follows is a paraphrase rather than a verbatim recording. I try, however, to err on the side of fidelity rather than felicity of expression. I let each protagonist speak in the first person.

* This chapter is adapted from Smith (1971) with permission.

M. BREWSTER SMITH • Board of Studies in Psychology, University of California, Santa Cruz, California 95064.

Fifty Years of Personality Psychology, edited by Kenneth H. Craik *et al.* Plenum Press, New York, 1993.

ALLPORT ON ALLPORT

I will reply here to the critics of my book, *Personality: A Psychological Interpretation*, and attempt to meet their criticisms insofar as possible. There have been three main criticisms: First, with respect to culture, the book disregards the cultural matrix of personality; second, in regard to its emphasis on uniqueness; and third in regard to its motivational theory.   reply to critics

THE NEGLECT OF CULTURE

In the new Department of Social Relations, the neglect of culture is an unpardonable sin. But the sin was deliberate in this book, and I would commit it again. The book's preface indicates its intended scope, which is concerned with the structural problem, with what personality is rather than how it got that way. In my thinking there is a sharp distinction between personality and social psychology. One must think of personality as a biophysical or biopsychical structure. It may be modified by the field, but it *is* something. Social psychology is everything else. It doesn't make sense to define personality in terms of its social implications. This leaves it with nothing substantial.

I was reacting against Kimball Young's (1930) social psychology and also against the anthropological relativists who said that personality is merely the subjective side of culture—roles and statuses. My position here was supported by the German life history studies (Allport et al., 1941), which showed that personality was not disrupted proportionally to the disruption in culture. I was also reacting against Cooley and G. H. Mead, against James's exaggerated statement about the plurality of social selves, and against Lewin's emphasis on the influence of the momentary field. Murray and Lewin have treated the environment better than I in their concepts of press and field. But I was trying to do something quite different. I may, of course, have exaggerated things in the other direction.

In response to my critics, I readily admit that culture largely determines the formation of the growing personality. It also determines much or most of the variability of personality, and its effects. (The great man theory is wrong). The social factor has everything to do with the evaluation of personality.

UNIQUENESS

The criticism here has come from the statistically minded and from Murray. I am unrepentent. There have been three objections. First, personality becomes inaccessible to science if we are required to regard it as unique. Second, uniqueness is merely quantitative, not qualitative. We can encompass "uniqueness" by finer measures of more variables that jointly produce a fine enough psychography. Third, even though everything concrete is unique, that has not prevented the development of the nomothetic physical sciences.

The first of these issues is one of semantics. Following Windelband, I distinguish two aspects of knowledge: the idiographic and the nomothetic. Most intellectual work requires both of these aspects. In my book, this is visible in the chapter on understanding personality, where inference is contrasted with intuition (attending to, concentrating on the unique object). The two points of view also apply to the treatment of traits as common versus unique and in the chapter on methods. The issue concerning uniqueness is settled in terms of predictive power, which is greater when idiographic knowledge is employed. The evidence is not fully conclusive, but suggests that direct acquaintance works better than general knowledge. But Sarbin (1943) objects.

In regard to the second objection, it is simply an impracticable procedure to approach uniqueness via a million variables, since you would still have to reckon with all interrelationships. One might as well stay on the molar level.

As to the third objection, I am unimpressed by reference to nomothetic physics, since we are dealing not with stones but with personality. Uniqueness is *not* the primary characteristic of stones. My argument with Cyril Burt in the *British Journal of Educational Psychology* summarizes this (Allport, 1946). Burt seeks his key qualities from factor analysis. My key qualities would be personal, not universal; not derived from a hash of all different kinds of personalities. The results of factor analysis are limited by the tests that are put in and by the fact that a hash of the personalities of all participants cannot represent the ego structure of any single one of them.

ISSUES OF MOTIVATIONAL THEORY

In this area I am more vulnerable. Three criticisms have been made of my position: That it does not provide genetic continuity; that it is superficial, lacking in depth, antipsychoanalytic; and that it fails to supply the basis for patterning or cohesion among motives and ought, strictly speaking, to result in a kind of entropy. All of these criticisms have some validity, and I am willing to arbitrate.

First, in regard to geneticism. Bertocci (1940) says that I am an emergent evolutionist, in regard to the emergence of personality and selfhood. Along with McDougall and Murray, Bertocci would like a steady, rechanneled source of motivation. In contrast, I feel (Allport, 1940) that we genuinely learn our motives. The genetic continuity is a matter of overlapping shingles. In the army, illiterates were trained to read. There were powerful motives supporting their learning to read in the army: they had to, shame, homesickness. Once they leave the army, these motives are gone. Will the ex-soldiers lose their skill? No. Why do they continue to read? Is it because of new motives or of old motives to which the reading skill is attached? This makes little difference, since some transformation is necessary.

Next as to the criticism of lack of depth. Remember the times in which my book was written—the excesses of Freudianism prior to Horney, French, Rogers, and Alexander. I follow Adolph Meyer (Lief, 1948) in holding that the mechanisms of abnormality differ from those of normality. In normality, balancing mechanisms predominate; this homeostasis is missing in abnormality. The balancing factors include integration, benign inhibition and repression, ability to adjust to novelty, sthenic emotions of hope and love, insight, and a philosophy of life compatible with reality. In abnormality, we find the dissociative, the unwholesomely repressive, the compulsions and obsessions, the morbid fantasies. Freud was interested in the unbalancing mechanisms and saw them everywhere. He developed a paradigm of personality out of these. In modern psychoanalysis, a more dynamic ego has been admitted. I overreacted to Freud's statement that the ego is not dynamic, the metaphor of the riderless horse. This is very false, but it is not the view of post-Freudians. So the ground is prepared for agreement. I admit I underestimated the remnants of juvenility and unbalancing elements in all of us.

As to the third criticism, my treatment of functional autonomy—mechanisms becoming motives—in Chapter 7 gives the impression of a lot of separate motives going off in different directions without any cohesion. This was my greatest blunder in the 1937 volume. The problem here is somewhat the same as that involved in Lewin's concept of differentiation, which also leads to entropy. But he gets out of the difficulty by his concept of central regions. I tried to handle the problem in an eclectic way in my chapter on the unity of personality. The only new idea in the chapter was that of congruence. I drew from Goethe the idea of unity through striving, through one's major goals. I was afraid of two things—German rhapsodic verbalism and the very sterile American self-psychology represented by Mary Calkins. Soon after my book, Sherif and Cantril (1947) wrote extensively on the ego as did Lewin (1935) and Koffka (1935). I felt the need for empirical study of the ego, and summarized the literature in my 1943 paper on ego psychology (Allport, 1943). This made a persuasive case for the need for a concept of the ego. The studies demonstrating the experimental effects of ego involvement provide an operational definition of the ego, as what makes the difference in these results. This operationally defined ego repairs my concept of functional autonomy.

A motive may be autonomous of its origin, but never of the ego. Mechanisms will not turn into motives unless they serve the life-style of the person. Striving is a descriptive concept; ego structure is the underlying one.

MURRAY ON ALLPORT

Allport is concerned with the ego system; with what is conscious, voluntary, and rational or self-consistent and coherent; what is observable in everyday life or overt and public. He is also concerned with social issues. His concern with a few of the aspects of the ego system is good, but not enough.

The child begins with many energies, needs, and emotions not integrated into the ego system. Unlike Allport, I see personality as beginning before integration is attained. In this period, there is expressive action as differentiated from goal-directed action. This results from the overflow of internal energies on the motor side and from sensory pleasures on the sensory side. This is all id activity, Freud's pleasure principle broadened to include things that Freud was not concerned with. The child is doing this within the sphere of the mother. He gets rewards of admiration, love, and compassion.

From the beginning, barriers are put up against some behaviors. The internalized cultural regulations deriving from the environment are among the most important constituents of personality. Time, place, mode, and object rules run athwart the pleasure principle. Most of the person's needs get satisfied, but within this pattern, not spontaneously.

When a conscious goal-directed system has developed, the ego comes in. The child has begun to think how to arrive at a certain goal. He has to learn, has to make an effort. This is distinct from the early expressive state when he is just blowing off steam. Early the child gets his rewards from his mother without effort. Soon, he has to work to get rewards. He has to learn good from bad. Consciousness and the ego system emerge from barriers and frustration.

Allport presents an ego psychology. I want to include the id—the

child, the involuntary, the unconscious. All of us have a vast Sargasso
Sea of an id: temperament and mood, emotions (we cannot control these—
only the objects and images), needs, and images that have been associated with needs, that is, fantasies. Whenever we engage in undirected
thinking, there is id activity. If love were an ego process, it would be
planned and rational. But it is not. It is usually a compromise between
id and ego. The good as well as the bad emerges from the id. The id
goes along under the ego all the time. I am interested in superordinate
dynamic systems straddling the ego and id.

ALLPORT IN REJOINDER

Our respective approaches to personality can be put in capsule
thus: For Murray, personality is the life history. The most important
question that he wants to know about a person is, what are his fantasies? For Lewin, the person is the life space. The most important
question for him is, what is the situation? For me, personality is the
individual's intentions. The most important question is, what are his
intentions and values?

I have always dealt with two differences with Murray: (1) His
excessive geneticism. I think that the first three years of life don't
matter very much. The child is flexible. (2) His need theory, which is
too McDougallian, too arbitrary. I don't claim to know about native
energies, but feel sure that they are recast as life goes on. A third
major difference I have with Murray concerns the ego concept.

Back in the 1880s, John Dewey used the concept of soul, not theo-
logically but to represent the functions of unity, coherence, and purpos-
iveness. When the soul went out of fashion, it took with it the cognate
concepts and problems—the self. Freudianism brought back the ego as
a related concept—an integrative organizer—but lost its purposive-
ness, seeing the id as the source of all energies.

I have distinguished eight meanings of the ego concept, of which
Murray adopts one. I embrace all eight (See Allport, 1943).

1. The ego as knower. This is rare in psychology, except for Bren-
   tano and the phenomenologists. William James denied the necessity of pure ego in this sense.
2. The ego as object known (e.g., studies of the location of one's
   self, the concept of depersonalization).
3. The ego as primordial selfishness (for example, Sterner,
   LeDantec). Metaphysical egoism has been mainly European.

4. The ego as dominator or status seeker. Ego involvement often means that status or pride is at stake.
5. The ego as passive organizer, in Freud, or as conscious organizer, in Murray.
6. The ego as fighter for ends, the center of purpose.
7. The ego as a segregated system of personality. Here I would classify Koffka and Lewin, except insofar as they say that the ego always tends upward, which involves senses 4 or 6.
8. The ego as subjectified cultural norms, as exemplified in Sherif and Cantril.

When there is ego involvement, experiments show that general traits of personality are obtained. Without ego involvement, there is specificity.

Peter Bertocci pulls out senses 1 and 6, the knowing and wanting ego, which is phenomenologically separate as the self. The other senses represent central aspects of personality which the self evaluates.

The ego need not be conscious. Ego involvement is not coextensive with consciousness or with voluntarism.

COMMENTARY

The themes that Allport and Murray developed in this confrontation are ones that each of them presented more systematically elsewhere. Yet I think there is value in noting what they chose to highlight in each other's presence for an audience of graduate students. Allport and Murray were competing for the favor of *their* graduate students.

Their stylistic differences, the emotional flavor of which eludes my notes, find a record in them: Allport's magisterial marshaling of argument from on high as compared with Murray's less orderly plunge into the midst of the teeming phenomena of personality. What my notes do not convey, but I remember, are Murray's playfully provocative taunting of Allport with id-like phenomena, and Allport's high, pink forehead scalp turning progressively deeper shades of red in response. Indeed, their former student of much earlier times, Saul Rosenzweig (1970), had it right when he matched Murray, Allport, and Boring (the historian of experimental psychology) with the id, the ego, and the superego in Freudian psychoanalysis: the fit is uncanny.

Understandably, from a graduate student's standpoint, Murray got the better of the match. Of the sparring partners, Murray was redolent with charisma that Allport somehow lacked. As a graduate student just before and just after World War II and then as a young faculty member, I was more acutely aware of Allport's limitations and less appreciative of his extraordinary strengths than I came to be in later retrospect (Smith, 1972, 1990). The vignette stands out in my memory of an early morning in December 1948, when on my hurried way to teach, having just greeted my newborn first son at the Boston Lying-in Hospital, I encountered Gordon on the steps of Emerson hall. As he took the customary cigar from my outstretched hand, Gordon beamed his reserved smile and said, "Very nice, Brewster. Every psychologist should have a child and a dog." At the moment I could have throttled him! Thereafter, I understood his doctrine of the "functional autonomy of motives" as his ingeniously designed charter to let him leave untidy animals and children to the behaviorists and psychoanalysts.

But in spite of the undoubted fact that Murray made him uncomfortable and represented a view of personality that was distinctly uncongenial to him, Allport defended Murray with complete magnanimity when it counted most. Only since Triplett's (1983) dissertation have we known about the intense struggles behind closed doors concerning Murray's tenure at Harvard, a closely fought academic battle in which Allport was Murray's indispensable supporter.

REFERENCES

Allport, G. W. (1940). Motivation in personality: Reply to Mr. Bertocci. *Psychological Review, 47*, 533–554.

Allport, G. W. (1943). The ego in contemporary psychology. *Psychological Review, 50*, 451–478.

Allport, G. W. (1946). Geneticism vs. ego-structure in theories of personality. *British Journal of Educational Psychology, 16*, 57–68.

Allport, G. W., Bruner, J. S., & Jandorf, E. M. (1941). Personality under social catastrophe: Ninety life-histories of the Nazi revolution. *Character and Personality, 10*, 1–22.

Bertocci, P. A. (1940). A critique of G. W. Allport's theory of motivation. *Psychological Review, 47*, 501–532.

Koffka, K. (1935). *Principles of Gestalt psychology.* New York: Harcourt, Brace.

Lewin, K. (1935). *A dynamic theory of personality.* New York: McGraw-Hill.

Lief, A. (Ed.) (1948). *The commonsense psychiatry of Dr. Adolph Meyer.* New York: McGraw-Hill.

Rosenzweig, S. (1970). Boring and the *Zeitgeist: Eruditione gesta beavit. Journal of Psychology, 75*, 59–71.

Sarbin, T. R. (1943). A contribution to the study of actuarial and individual methods of prediction. *American Journal of Sociology, 48*, 593–602.

Sherif, M., & Cantril, H. (1947). *The psychology of ego-involvements.* New York: Wiley.

Smith, M. B. (1971). Allport, Murray, and Lewin on personality theory: Notes on a confrontation. *Journal of the History of the Behavioral Sciences, 7*, 353–362.

Smith, M. B. (1972). Toward humanizing social psychology. In T. S. Krawiec (Ed.), *The psychologists* (pp. 212–239). New York: Oxford.

Smith, M. B. (1990). Personology launched. Retrospective review of H. A. Murray, *Explorations in Personality, Contemporary Psychology, 35,* 537–539.

Triplett, R. G. (1983). *Henry A. Murray and the Harvard Psychological Clinic, 1926–1938: A struggle to expand the disciplinary boundaries of psychology.* Unpublished doctoral dissertation, University of New Hampshire.

Young, K. (1930). *Social psychology.* New York: Crofts.

PART THREE

CURRENT STATE OF PERSONALITY PSYCHOLOGY AND ITS TEXTS

CHAPTER FIVE

Pattern and Organization
Current Trends and Prospects for the Future*

LAWRENCE A. PERVIN

In reading over the 1937 personality texts of Allport and Stagner in preparation for a colloquium series in honor of them, I was struck with a passage from the 1980 *Annual Review* chapter by Jackson and Paunonen: "We share with Block the view that these earlier authors frequently expressed central issues in personality theory more cogently than do the writings of some contemporary authors who seem to have rediscovered the same issues" (p. 505). Reference was being made to Allport, Lewin, Murphy, and Murray, but Stagner could have been included as well.†

Although clearly one reads into these writings some of what one believes today, I am struck with the many common points of emphasis in the writings of Allport and Stagner: traits and the underlying consistency of personality, the dynamics of personality functioning, the importance of affect, concern with the development of personality, and the importance of culture and an appreciation for cultural differences.

---

*This chapter is adapted from an address given at the Institute of Personality and Social Research, University of California at Berkeley, Spring 1987.

† It was particularly interesting for me to go back and read Allport, something I have been prone to do over the years, since he was a professor of mine in 1957. At the time I failed to appreciate his enormous wisdom.

LAWRENCE A. PERVIN • Department of Psychology, Rutgers University, New Brunswick, New Jersey 08903.

Fifty Years of Personality Psychology, edited by Kenneth H. Craik *et al.* Plenum Press, New York, 1993.

I would like to focus on the shared emphasis that I found most striking and that forms the theme of this chapter: the organization of personality. Allport was very concerned with the individuality of personality. Sometimes he attempted to focus on the uniqueness of the individual through an emphasis on the uniqueness of the *units* of personality (e.g., unique traits) while at other times he emphasized the uniqueness of the *organization* of personality. Particularly in terms of the latter, it is clear that Allport was concerned with synthesis, organization, patterning, and the "unity of personality." And, while Stagner emphasized the importance of analysis (traits), over time he increasingly became concerned with personality as a dynamic system.

So, taking the concern of Allport and Stagner with the organization of personality as a point of departure, I would like to consider three issues: (1) the nature of the units and structure of personality, (2) the organization of affects, and (3) the organization of the self.

THE UNITS OF PERSONALITY
AND THEIR ORGANIZATION

Concern with the organization of personality confronts us first with the question of the units of personality (Allport, 1958). What is it that is organized? Here I would like to consider how both Allport and Stagner struggled with the conceptual status of traits as the fundamental organizational units of personality and then go on to consider the concept of goals as a unit that they arrived at and which I believe continues to have merit today.

CONCEPTS OF TRAIT AND MOTIVE IN ALLPORT AND STAGNER

Although both Allport and Stagner are considered to be trait theorists, their discussion of the trait concept is of considerable interest. Not only did Allport not view traits as suggesting that the individual behaved the same way in all situations, a point I and others have made previously (Pervin, 1985; Zuroff, 1986), but he suggested that traits expressed a motivational significance. I believe that this reflected an ambivalence and conceptual confusion on Allport's part, one that he never completely resolved. On one hand, he rejected narrow motivational concepts such as instinct and drive because they failed to provide for the individuality of the organism, whereas on the other hand, he remained concerned with the dynamics of behavior—that which activated and directed the organism. In a sense, traditional motivational concepts were seen as too limited to be expressive of the individual, that is, expressive of the overall organization of functioning that resulted in an expressive style for the individual. At the same time, trait concepts were insufficiently dynamic. Thus, he asked whether traits were self-active, and after first suggesting that strictly speaking they were not, he went on to suggest that "in another sense traits do initiate behavior" (Allport, 1937, p. 321). His conclusion was that although not all motives were traits and not all traits were motives, there was some overlap between the two: "Some traits thus seem to have motivational (directional) significance and some mere instrumental significance" (1937, p. 323). Whereas some traits referred to the expressive–stylistic aspect of personality, other traits referred to the motivational component of personality, what Allport called its "telic significance." And it was the traits with motivational significance that played a particularly significant role in the unity of personality.*

Allport also related the distinction between expressive traits and motivational traits to the phenotype–genotype issue. He pointed out that the same behavior in different people could have different roots and that seemingly different behaviors in the same person could have the same root. Whereas stylistic, expressive traits were more phenotypic, motivational traits were more genotypic (Allport, 1937, pp. 324, 358). And while personality psychologists needed to be concerned with both, the latter were "the very springs of conduct" (p. 326). Furthermore, Allport suggested that personality psychologists needed to be concerned with interdependent substructures, some of which would be integrated and others of which would be in conflict. As he expressed it in a 1939 address at Berkeley, "the organism is, after all, but a living system of interdependent motives" (p. 108).

It is here that we may draw an interesting comparison with the views of Stagner, who suggested that although traits were the units of personality, they remained descriptive of behavior rather than explanatory of behavior. And what of explanations? These involved inner drives or impulses: "We cannot then understand personality without understanding motivation" (Stagner, 1937, p. 12). This view is stated even more explicitly in the second edition: "Too many psychologists write as if a trait were an effective cause of behavior. This is quite incorrect and misleading. . . . The trait, then, should be considered descriptive, but not explanatory. The causes of human behavior insofar as we can identify them are the motives which impel us to act and the

---

*Buss (1989) similarly includes both temperament and motive concepts under the trait rubric.

environment which shapes our actions" (Stagner, 1948, p. 144).* And, in the third edition, published in 1961, Stagner went on to view personality as a goal system, a view that he related to Allport's earlier emphasis on goals. An interesting aspect of this apparent shift to a more dynamic, explanatory view is that Stagner suggested that the goal concept was "hardly different from our earlier usage of trait" and that "the concept of trait should be reevaluated as having dynamic implications" (1948, p. 358). Further, he noted that "Allport, after having earlier accepted the separation, seems to have shifted and accepted the notion of identity of trait and motive" (p. 359). Perhaps this is why McClelland was led to suggest that "it appears that Allport has stretched the term *trait* a little too far. He is now using it to account for inconsistencies in behavior, new responses which seem primarily determined by the person's wishes or goals rather than by his past adjustment in similar situations" (1951, p. 214).

In sum, both Allport and Stagner were concerned with the units of personality and with the organization of these units. Both began with a trait concept and struggled with the relation between traits and motives, descriptions and explanations, phenotypes and genotypes. Both came to emphasize the importance of goals, or what Allport (1955) called propriate strivings, for the organization and unity of personality. Both appreciated the complexity of behavior from a systems perspective in terms of the varied roots that the same behavior can have (equifinality), the varied paths that the same motive can follow (equipotentiality), the multidetermination of most behavior, and the potential for conflict as well as coherence or integration in system functioning.

THE GOAL CONCEPT

I would like next to consider goals, both as units of personality and as a basis for understanding the dynamic, organized aspects of personality functioning. In particular, I want to call attention to two aspects of system functioning, multidetermination and conflict, since they have been of interest to me as a clinician and researcher. That most behavior is multidetermined or—as psychoanalysts would have it, over-determined—would appear to be self-evident. Yet, my sense is that it is relatively neglected in our thinking and research. My own work on the goal concept made clear the extent to which people view their own behavior in important situations as involving multiple goals. Rarely do

---

* Wiggins (1973) similarly describes traits as descriptive rather than explanatory.

we do something for one reason alone. Consider, for example, the confessions of a lawyer who seeks to answer the question of why he has fought so hard for the interests of the guilty. In this *Newsweek* article, the author suggests such motives as the following: emotional identification with the underdog, performing well during a trial, a need for power and admiration, winning, beating witnesses, voyeurism, and exhibitionism. He concludes that "in trying to understand myself and my work, I am led ineluctably to the murky and subjective realm of what I brought with me when I first stepped into a courtroom. It was clearly not just the belief that every criminal defendant has a right to counsel" (Wishman, 1981, p. 25). Or, consider the more recent article in the *New York Times* that suggested that women who choose to become surrogate mothers have such diverse and multiple motivations as money, feeling confirmed as a woman, doing something special, altruism, gratitude for the life given them after they were adopted, and guilt over a previous abortion (Goleman, 1987, p. C1). Indeed, this article suggests many of the principles of system functioning that are suggested in the works of Allport and Stagner and that seem particularly key to me: equipotentiality, or the potential for similar motives to lead to quite different (even contrasting) behaviors; equifinality, or the potential for the same behavior to express different motives; and multidetermination, or the principle that behavior expresses the interaction among multiple motives.

Similarly self-evident would appear to be the importance of *conflict* in our lives, here referring to conflict internal to the system, though clearly conflict is a major issue in close interpersonal relations (Peterson, 1989) as well as in the international relations level of system functioning. Lewin (1935) gave considerable attention to the issue of conflict, as did Dollard and Miller (1950) in their extrapolations from psychoanalytic theory to stimulus–response theory, but the concept has ceased to play a major role in most current personality theory and research.

In my earlier research on goals (Pervin, 1984), I examined the implications of goal conflicts for how situations are experienced. Each of ten subjects rated the relevance of 11 conflicts to 20 situations, the conflicts being standard for the group but the situations being idiographic for the subject. The list of conflicts had been drawn from those suggested by a small group of subjects and included items such as "Relax, enjoy versus Do what 'should' do." and "Assert self versus Gain acceptance, approval." Generally, situations that the subjects associated with negative affect were also found to be associated with high conflict.

I have just begun to pursue further this line of research, again having subjects provide situations representative of their daily lives, and have extended the list of goal conflicts to include some suggested by the work of Karen Horney, as well as others suggested by the work of Timothy Leary on interpersonal relations. Some of the issues being investigated are: critical features of situations of goal conflict, the determinants of how conflicts are handled, and sex differences in the nature of goal conflicts and patterns of handling conflict.

While the data are still being analyzed, some of the preliminary findings may be of interest. Of course, it is no surprise to find enormous individual differences in the amount of overall conflict experienced, in the conflicts reported to be most central, and in the reported pattern of handling various conflicts. Overall, there is a tendency for the amount of conflict reported to be associated with separate self-report measures of anxiety, depression, and the tendency to blame oneself for negative events, though not with a measure of defensiveness. These results appear to fit with those reported by Emmons (1989), suggesting a relation between life satisfaction and a "personal strivings system" free of conflict, as well as a relation between conflicts over emotional expression and problems of psychological and physical well-being.

Most of the sex differences considered so far have been small, but a few patterns appear to be emerging. First, males report a higher overall level of conflict than do females. Second, whereas males appear to experience more conflict over intimacy, females appear to experience more conflict in relation to issues of expression of anger and dominance–submission. Finally, whereas males report a greater tendency to handle conflict through doing what feels best or acting impulsively, females report a greater tendency to handle conflict through compromise and avoidance.

A final aspect of the goals concept worthy of consideration is its place in social cognition; that is, the extent to which we anticipate and account for behavior in terms of assumptions we make about the motives or goals of others and ourselves (Pervin, 1989; Read, 1987; Read et al., 1989). This is a point emphasized by Heider (1958) but often neglected in the attribution literature. In a relevant study, Adrian Furnham and I (Pervin & Furnham, 1987) had subjects rate the probability of each of 16 behaviors in 16 situations, with the 16 situations representing all combinations of four situation categories and four goals. The resulting ratings indicated that personal goals influenced behavioral expectations far more than did situational types, with the exception of behaviors associated with affect and the face (e.g., crying).

This tendency for emotions to be perceived to be highly situationally determined is a common finding in the literature.

Furthermore, in an apparent reversal of the "fundamental attribution error," subjects expected their own behavior to vary *less* than the behavior of others! In other words, they expected their own behavior to be more stable than they expected the behavior of others, whereas the "fundamental attribution error" suggests that people see the behavior of others as stable and traitlike and "more accurately" perceive their own behavior as relatively situation-specific. One possibility suggested for this apparent discrepancy with the attribution literature is that goals rather than traits were considered. Another possibility is that expectations rather than postevent attributions were considered. The latter suggests the possibility that people really expect themselves to be far more stable than social psychologists have suggested, at least more stable than they expect others to be. When they do find themselves behaving "inconsistently," they are even more prone to attribute their own behavior in the situation to the situation than they are to attribute the behavior of others. In other words, people may be more trait theorists, or at least motivation theorists, for themselves as well as others than social psychologists have recognized. It may also be of interest to note here the findings of Asch and Zukier (1984) that suggest that people perceive themselves and others as psychological units—units that have patterning and order, units that are complex, and units that have the potential for conflict.

Consideration of the question of social cognition may bring us back to the question of traits versus motives as units of personality. Furnham and I intended to conduct a study comparing trait-based expectations of behavior with goal-based expectations. We never did get around to conducting this study, but my sense is that traits and goals represent two different ways of organizing information about people and social action. Traits have heuristic value in enabling us to package together a great deal of information, to smooth out irregularities, and form relatively global impressions of people that provide for generalized expectancies. Motives have heuristic value in enabling us to make more specific predictions based on an assessment of particular aspects of the individual's personality and situational factors. Overall, one would expect there to be a relationship between traits and motives in the same person, as Allport and Stagner suggested. And, as Asch and Zukier (1984) noted, motives may help us to reconcile apparent discrepancies between traits and specific behaviors. However, traits and motives are distinct concepts, each with its own heuristic value and limitations.

If this is the case in social cognition, then it may suggest a parallel view for us as personality psychologists; that is, as Murray (1938) and McClelland (1951) suggested, we treat traits and motives as distinct concepts, with some overlapping relationships but with differing functional utilities—the former (traits) involving broad consistencies in behavior and expressive of regularities and the latter (motives) involving the interplay between the regular and unusual in the person, or what I have more broadly described as the stasis and flow of behavior (Pervin, 1984). Recent research indicates that it is possible to map trait and goal concepts onto one another, suggesting that study of relationships between the two units may yet be possible (Costa & McCrae, 1988; Read et al., 1989).

I would like to conclude this section by emphasizing the difficulty of devising a system for representing the organization of personality, in particular the organization of goal systems. Ordinarily we think of organization in terms of hierarchical structures and, where assessment is involved, in terms of score profiles. However, it seems to me that the organization of personality is a much more complex matter, involving a more complex relationship among the parts than a hierarchical analysis or profile of scores provides for. What is needed is a system of representation that captures both the dynamics of action and the degree of integration or conflict among the parts. Allport (1937, pp. 246, 358) was critical of the factorial conception of personality as a system of independent elements and, as noted, argued instead for a view of interdependent substructures. Development of a scheme for representing the complexity of organization of personality would go a long way toward providing for appreciating the individuality that Allport so cherished, without resorting to the investigation of unique units for each person. To my mind, George Kelly (1955) came closest to the systems view being emphasized, suggesting that the person's construct system had both structure and fluidity to it.

AFFECT

I would like now to turn briefly to the question of the organization of personality in relation to two additional areas: affect and the self. It is my sense that for some time the importance of affect for personality functioning was a neglected area, with the exception of such individual affects as anxiety and such psychologists as Tomkins (1962). In part, this was because of the emphasis on overt behavior during the 1940s and 1950s, followed by the emphasis on cognition in the period since then. The situation has changed of late, to the extent that affect is a major concern of "cognitive–behavior therapists." However, much remains to be done in the area of the organization of affects within the person.

My own interest in the area of affect was spurred by a number of factors: a long collegial relationship with Silvan Tomkins, dating back to 1962; ongoing practice as a psychodynamically oriented clinician; research on free-response descriptions that primarily elicited affect descriptors of situations; and a study of consistency of response across situations that suggested that similar situations might not elicit similar behaviors if they differed in a characteristic that elicited strong affect (Champagne & Pervin, 1987).

I will describe some of the results of my research on affect and personality, particularly as they relate to the issue of organization and pattern, but let me note that this proved to be the most difficult and frustrating piece of research in which I have engaged. I believe that there is gold there, but the mining is difficult, involving the hazards of digging deep and following false leads.

In any case, the research basically involved subjects rating the relevance of an extended series of affects to situations and people they had identified as being relevant to them. In addition, in one phase of the research, subjects rated a list of prototypic situations and prototypic situation features for various affects to see if subjects could agree about the nature of the situations and defining characteristics of situations critical for each affect. This research followed that suggested by Buss and Craik (1983) in their work on traits. Finally, subjects indicated the second-most likely affect they would experience in each prototypic situation. This procedure was used to consider further relationships among affects and individual differences in the organization of affects in prototypic as well as idiosyncratic situations. A feature of this research, which has tended to be typical of the research I have conducted over the years, is a mix of standard and free-response data, of nomothetics and idiographics, of an interest in general principles established through the study of patterns in individuals.

Generally, similar affect factors were found for individuals, with three positive affect factors (Happy, Attraction–Love, Friendship) and four negative affect factors (Anger Out, Anger In–Blows to Self-esteem, Distress, Envy–Jealousy) being typical. In other words, generally individuals appear to organize affects in reasonably similar ways, at least at the highest level of organization. This was true regardless of whether subjects were rating affects in relation to situations, people, or other affects. At the same time, there were considerable individual differences in the relative importance of individual affects as well as in the relations or correlations between specific affects. In relation to the former, two individuals might have the same mean value for an affect across the situations, but for one subject this might indicate an affect of considerable import while for another it might indicate an affect of minimal import. For example, two individuals had similar overall mean ratings for the affect jealousy. In one subject this meant that it was the least important of all 50 affects rated while for another subject it meant that it was of average importance.

In relation to the latter—the relations among affects—while virtually all subjects reported a high correlation between friendship and trust, there was considerable variability in the extent to which love and trust were seen as related to one another. Similarly, while subjects generally agreed on the prototypicality of situations and situation characteristics, there were considerable individual differences in the next most likely affect to be experienced in a prototypic situation, with this measure of association found to be related for the individual to that determined by an analysis of other affect association data. In other words, even in situations that are so powerful as to elicit virtually the same predominant affect in most individuals, the further affective elaboration will vary considerably from individual to individual.

The data from this research clearly indicate that most situations are experienced in terms of combinations of affects, including at times positive and negative affects. I am reminded here of a patient who recently told me of the range of emotions he experienced while caring for his terminally ill father: love, hate, guilt, sadness, and anxiety. Further, while one can find evidence of an overall, general organization of affects, there exists considerable individual variation in the patterning of relative importance of affects and relationships among affects. These data fit with the results of research I have conducted on the relation between affect and addiction (Pervin, 1988), where different patterns of affect are associated with different drugs and drug versus nondrug states, and with the research of Lewis and Michalson (1982) on the organization of affects in children.

In concluding this section, I would like to note that with the study of a very restricted range of affects, one may miss some affects that, while infrequently experienced, may be of considerable import. Even where an affect is rarely experienced by a particular subject, it may play a key role in the person's functioning, as is so often observed by clinicians. For example, I have recently become quite impressed with the importance of the affect of shame in the organization of personalities of some individuals, regardless of the frequency with which it is experienced. Indeed, much of a person's life may be organized around the feeling of shame, involving how the person interacts with others and feels about the self.

In sum, the importance of the organization of affects in personality functioning is easily lost in studies where but a few major affects are investigated and only nomothetic data analyses are used.

THE ORGANIZATION OF THE SELF

Finally, I would like to consider the question of the organization of the self. Although I have not conducted research in this area for some time, I would like to consider it because it concerned both Allport and Stagner and because it raises profound questions concerning the issue of organization.

In writing the first edition of *Current Controversies and Issues in Personality* (1978), I debated whether to include a chapter on the self. As I noted, interest in the self had waxed and waned, and I was not sure where it was headed. Indeed, in 1955, Allport found it necessary to address the question "Is the concept of the self necessary," concluding, of course, as did Stagner (1948), that the concept of the self was necessary for capturing the organization of personality. Since that time, research on the self has grown enormously so that it now plays a significant role in the areas of personality and social cognition. Yet, it seems to me that little of this research concerns the question of organization or how the person is able to organize variability in behavior over time and across situations into a coherent representation of the self.

We find considerable evidence that people behave differently at different times in their lives, behave differently in different situations, and play different roles or present themselves differently in different situations. As Schlenker (1985) notes in a recent edited book on the self, there is both the inner self, concerned with personal experience, and the outer self, concerned with self-presentation. There is, then, the question of the organization of the inner self, the outer self, and the integration of the two. Scheibe (1985), presenting a historical review in the same book, notes the following frequently quoted passage from James (1890, p. 294):

> Properly speaking, a man has as many social selves as there are individuals who recognize him and carry an image of him in their head. But as the individuals who carry the images fall naturally into classes, we may practically say that he has as many different social selves as there are distinct groups of persons about whose opinion he cares.

However, Scheibe goes on to criticize those who quote this passage with a bias toward division, fragmentation, and pluralism rather than with a more complete view of the self as an inward and active agent. Interestingly, he neglects to mention the work of Allport who, it seems to me, did as much as anyone over the years to keep the concept of the self in the forefront of our attention.

We are aware of the fragmented nature of the self that can often be experienced, reaching extreme proportions in the cases of schizoid personalities and multiple personalities. How, then, do we account for such pathological developments as well as for the ability of most of us to retain some degree of cohesion and integration within inner and outer, between inner and outer, between earlier and later? How is it that we look, feel, and seem very different as adults than as children, and yet retain a sense of continuity? I know that there is important evidence of such continuity (Block, 1971), but I think that even these data leave considerable room for consideration of this question. And how is it that we can feel and look so different in social situations and yet here, too, retain a sense of self, as if one was looking at a holographic image from different angles?

Again we come to fundamental questions of pattern and organization, questions of integration and conflict, questions that were of fundamental concern to Allport and Stagner, and that all too rarely are the focus of concern in today's literature. Perhaps an exception to this, and an indication of things to come, is the interest expressed by a number of authors in the 1985 Schlenker volume in the work of Prescott Lecky on self-consistency. Perhaps another is the recent effort by Cantor and Kihlstrom to consider the self system as a family of selves—a fuzzy set:

> The meaning of the self is given in the family of selves. The unity of self comes from the many overlapping resemblances among the different selves.... You are *yourself* because of this network of overlapping features which are characteristic of the family of selves. And, you are many things in many places with different people.... The self-concept, therefore, must represent both the variety and the unity within each person's family of selves.... As such, the cognitive definition of self can be varied, encompassing more aspects of self than would a representation of a core self, yet still serving as a unified mental structure. (1987, p. 124)

CURRENT STATUS AND PROSPECTS FOR THE FUTURE

In a 1939 APA address given by Allport in Berkeley, he reviewed 50 years of progress in psychology. How do we stand now in the field of personality as we review 50 years of progress since the publication of

Allport's and Stagner's texts? Alternatively, a *Handbook of Personality: Theory and Research* (Borgatta & Lambert, 1968) was published over 20 years ago; how far have we come since then? Having just finished editing a handbook of personality (Pervin, 1990), I find it an opportune time to consider this question as well as the field's prospects for the future. I believe that a review of the current literature presents a relatively optimistic picture of the field, though one that must be tempered by an awareness of periods of past optimism followed by disappointment, specifically in the later 1950s and early 1960s. What most impresses me about the field today is the increased emphasis on the complexity of personality and increased diversity of concepts and research methods utilized. For example, I am encouraged by the greater attention being given to the question of motivation and relations among cognition, affect, and behavior, as well as the use of experience sampling, field study, and case study methods in addition to the traditional use of questionnaires and experimental laboratory methods (Craik, 1986). In addition, my sense is that the division between personality and other parts of psychology, in particular social psychology, has become blurred. Although some see this as a threat and feel that the turf of personality must be safeguarded against intrusion by outsiders, I believe that this is a healthy development since it encourages us to broaden our horizons and make use of conceptual and methodological advances in other areas. I also believe that Allport and Stagner would have been sympathetic to this view. In fact, Allport argued for a psychology of personality, which focuses on the human person without destroying the traditional structure of general psychology, and against a personalist psychology, which seeks to focus on the individual and demolish the entire edifice of general psychology (Allport, 1937, p. 550). As I have noted, both also emphasized the importance of culture and an awareness of cultural differences, an emphasis that I believe is returning to the field.

Historically there have been many issues that have been of continuing concern to personality psychologists. I have attempted to outline these in my 1990 Handbook chapter, which reviews the history of modern personality theory and research, but here I would like to focus on three issues that I see as particularly problematic at this time. Not surprisingly, we will once more see connections to the work of Allport and Stagner. The first issue concerns the interplay between stability and change, what I have called the stasis and flow of behavior. Historically we have become bogged down in the person–situation controversy in a way that I think has been unproductive. The issue is not whether persons or situations are more important, but rather how we can conceptualize the dynamic interplay between the person and the environment over time and across situations; that is, the ways in which people bring coherence to their functioning while remaining adaptive to changing external circumstances. As Mischel (1990) has noted, his influential 1968 book was an effort to call attention to exactly this question, for the most part neglected by trait and psychoanalytic approaches, rather than an attack on the field of personality or the existence of individual differences.

The second issue concerns the kinds of laws and predictions that may be possible for us as personality psychologists. Perhaps the most succinct way to express this is to state the possibility that human behavior is so multiply determined and influenced by highly idiosyncratic meaning structures that general laws and specific predictions may be unrealizable goals. Frequently of late I have come across the suggestion that ultimately psychology will be composed of three segments: neuroscience or neurobiology, artificial intelligence or cognitive science, and some version of folk psychology or hermeneutics. One already sees splits along these lines in many major departments of psychology, the first two often being seen as part of the "hard sciences" and the latter as part of the "soft sciences." Although I do not share this view, it is raised, in one form or another, by some very respectable thinkers who are not necessarily hostile to "soft psychology" generally or personality in particular. One of the most provocative thinkers along these lines is the anthropologist Richard Shweder (1989, 1990), who, in defining the field of cultural psychology and the semiotic person, argues against the view of people as the same wherever you go and instead for a view of people as intentional beings who live in a world that is domain-specific, cross-culturally diverse, and historically variable.

Finally, there is the issue of the organization of personality. Here I fear that little progress has been made. Whether because of the difficulty of the problem, forces in the field that operate against such exploration, or the lack of methodological tools appropriate for such investigation, we find little consideration of pattern and organization in personality functioning. In this sense I am in agreement with Carlson (1984), though I wish to distinguish this issue from consideration of the issues of idiographic versus nomothetic and laboratory versus naturalistic research. In his 1937 text, Allport observed that "the truth of the matter is that the total organization of personality is still a new and poorly formulated problem in psychology. It is a many-sided issue whose solution yet lies in the future" (p. 365). Fifty years later, the problem is hardly new, though the rest of what Allport had to say would still apply: it is poorly formulated, it is many-sided, and the solution lies in the future.

REFERENCES

Allport, G. W. (1937). *Personality: A psychological interpretation*. New York: Holt, Rinehart, & Winston.

Allport, G. W. (1939). Review of fifty years of personality. Paper delivered at the meetings of the American Psychological Association, Berkeley, California.

Allport, G. W. (1955). *Becoming: Basic considerations for a psychology of personality*. New Haven: Yale University Press.

Allport, G. W. (1958). What units shall we employ? In G. Lindzey (Ed.), *Assessment of human motives* (pp. 239–260). New York: Holt, Rinehart and Winston.

Asch, S. E., & Zukier, H. (1984). Thinking about persons. *Journal of Personality and Social Psychology, 46*, 1230–1240.

Block, J. (1971). *Lives through time*. Berkeley, CA: Bancroft.

Borgatta, E. F., & Lambert, W. W. (Eds.) (1968). *Handbook of personality theory and research*. Chicago: Rand McNally.

Buss, A. H. (1989). Personality as traits. *American Psychologist, 44*, 1378–1388.

Buss, D. M., & Craik, K. H. (1983). The act frequency approach to personality. *Psychological Review, 90*, 105–126.

Cantor, N., & Kihlstrom, J. F. (1987). *Personality and social intelligence*. Englewood Cliffs, NJ: Prentice-Hall.

Carlson, R. (1984). What's social about social psychology? Where's the person in personality research? *Journal of Personality and Social Psychology, 47*, 1304–1309.

Champagne, B., & Pervin, L. A. (1987). The relation of perceived situation similarity to perceived behavior similarity: Implications for social learning theory. *European Journal of Personality, 1*, 79–91.

Costa, P. T., Jr., & McCrae, R. R. (1988). From catalog to classification: Murray's needs and the five-factor model. *Journal of Personality and Social Psychology, 55*, 258–265.

Craik, K. H. (1986). Personality research methods: An historical perspective. *Journal of Personality, 54*, 18–51.

Dollard, J., & Miller, N.E. (1950). *Personality and psychotherapy*. New York: McGraw-Hill.

Emmons, R. A. (1989). The personal striving approach to personality. In L. A. Pervin (Ed.), *Goal concepts in personality and social psychology* (pp. 87–126). Hillsdale, NJ: Erlbaum.

Goleman, D. (1987). Motivations of surrogate mothers. *New York Times*, January 20, C1.

Heider, F. (1958). *The psychology of interpersonal relations*. New York: Wiley.

Jackson, D. N., & Paunonen, S. V. (1980). Personality structure and assessment. *Annual Review of Psychology, 31*, 503–551.

James, W. (1890). *Principles of psychology*. New York: Holt.

Kelly, G. A. (1955). *The psychology of personal constructs*. New York: Norton.

Lazarus, R. S. (1990). Theory-based stress management. *Psychological Inquiry, 1*, 3–13.

Lewin, K. (1935). *A dynamic theory of personality*. New York: McGraw-Hill.

Lewis, M., & Michalson, L. (1982). *Children's emotions and moods: Developmental theory and measurement*. New York: Plenum.

McClelland, D. C. (1951). *Personality*. New York: Sloane.

Mischel, W. (1990). Personality dispositions revised and revisited: A view after three decades. In L. A. Pervin (Ed.), *Handbook of personality: Theory and research (pp. 111–134)*. New York: Guilford.

Murray, H. A. (1938). *Explorations in personality*. New York: Oxford University Press.

Pervin, L. A. (1978). *Current controversies and issues in personality*. New York: Wiley.

Pervin, L. A. (1984). The stasis and flow of behavior: Toward a theory of goals. In M. M. Page (Ed.), *Personality: Current theory and research* (pp. 1–53). Lincoln: University of Nebraska Press.

Pervin, L. A. (1985). Personality. *Annual Review of Psychology, 36*, 83–114.

Pervin, L. A. (1988). Affect and addiction. *Addictive Behaviors, 13*, 83–86.

Pervin, L. A. (Ed.) (1989). *Goal concepts in personality and social psychology*. Hillsdale, NJ: Erlbaum.

Pervin, L. A. (Ed.) (1990). *Handbook of personality: Theory and research*. New York: Guilford.

Pervin, L. A., & Furnham, A. (1987). Goal-based and situation-based expectations of behavior. *European Journal of Personality, 1*, 37–44.

Peterson, D. R. (1989). Interpersonal goal conflict. In L. A. Pervin (Ed.), *Goal concepts in personality and social psychology* (pp. 327–362). Hillsdale, NJ: Erlbaum.

Read, S. J. (1987). Constructing causal scenarios: A knowledge structure approach to causal reasoning. *Journal of Personality and Social Psychology, 52*, 288–302.

Read, S. J., Jones, D. K., & Miller, L. C. (1989). Traits as goal-based categories: The importance of goals in the coherence of dispositional categories. Paper delivered at the meetings of the Society of Experimental Social Psychology, Santa Monica, CA.

Scheibe, K. (1985). Historical perspectives on the presented self. In B. R. Schlenker (Ed.), *The self and social life* (pp. 33–58). New York: McGraw-Hill.

Schlenker, B. R. (1985). Preface. In B. R. Schlenker (Ed.), *The self and social life*. New York: McGraw-Hill.

Shweder, R. A. (1989). Cultural psychology: What is it? In J. W. Stigler, R. A. Shweder, & H. Herdt (Eds.), *Cultural psychology: The Chicago symposia on culture and human development* (pp. 1–43). New York: Cambridge University Press.

Shweder, R. A. (1990). The semiotic person of cultural psychology. In L. A. Pervin (Ed.), *Handbook of personality: Theory and research* (pp. 399–416). New York: Guilford.

Stagner, R. (1937). *Psychology of personality*. New York: McGraw-Hill.

Stagner, R. (1948). *Psychology of personality* (2nd ed.). New York: McGraw-Hill.

Tomkins, S. S. (1962). *Affects, imagery, and consciousness*. New York: Springer.

Wiggins, J. S. (1973). In defense of traits. Unpublished paper. University of British Columbia, Vancouver, BC.

Wishman, S. (1981). *Newsweek*, November 9, p. 25.

Zuroff, D. C. (1986). Was Gordon Allport a trait theorist? *Journal of Personality and Social Psychology, 51*, 993–1000.

CHAPTER SIX

The Continuing Relevance of Personality Theory

SALVATORE R. MADDI

In academic circles, the past 20 years have shown a decline in the influence of personality theorizing. For the first part of that period, the person–situation debate fulminated, with the social psychologists and behaviorists joining with some in the personality field to argue that situation rather than person variables account for behavior. Although there were counterarguments raised, some psychologists came to wonder whether personality exists at all, and even those who did not go this far were likely to conclude that the personality area is a mess. Finally, cooler heads prevailed, and an interactional accord was reached in which behavior was regarded as a joint function of situational and person variables, with the emphasis of empirical study being on the interaction of the two.

The interactional accord did not, however, bring back into the academic fold the elaborate form of personality theorizing aiming at comprehensive understanding that characterized earlier times. To the present, personality research has focused on single dependent variables rather than broader swatches of behavior and circumscribed or middle-level theorizing rather than more elaborate conceptualizations. In clinical practice, the comprehensive personality theories still hold sway, though that is a major reason why clinicians are regarded by academi-

SALVATORE R. MADDI • School of Social Ecology, University of California, Irvine, California 92717.

Fifty Years of Personality Psychology, edited by Kenneth H. Craik *et al.* Plenum Press, New York, 1993.

cians as scientifically inadequate. Gone are the research efforts of an earlier time that aimed at subjecting comprehensive personality theories to empirical evaluation. The closest we are to this earlier emphasis now is with the act and prototype theories and research, but these approaches cover only a small portion of the previous agenda of personality study.

Along with this shift away from comprehensive personality theorizing has come a decrease in influence for psychologists who consider themselves to be in the personality area. In the 1970s, personality research became harder to publish and professional organizations hitherto emphasizing personality became progressively more defined by social psychology. Even academic jobs in personality became hard to get, as this area appeared more and more irrelevant. As the 1980s ended, there were signs that this trend might be decelerating or even reversing, as long as the person pursuing personality study combined it with other more central emphases, such as developmental, cognitive, or social psychologies, and eschewed those comprehensive personality theories that appear so antiquated.

At the risk of also appearing antiquated, I wish to argue for the continuing relevance of comprehensive personality theorizing. Indeed, I find it increasingly more important, as academic psychology ever more clearly shows the telltale shortcomings of its 20-year disavowal of efforts at comprehensive understanding of human behavior.

PSYCHOLOGY: THE FRAGMENTED DISCIPLINE

There are many signs that psychology is currently an extremely fragmented discipline. To explicate this contention in what follows, I will find it useful to give some examples, though my aim is not to lay blame. Indeed, blame laying is a sign of fragmentation, and there has been too much of this in our discipline. My stance is that the excessive fragmentation is hurting us and that comprehensive approaches to personality constitute one kind of antidote.

THE PREVALENCE OF WARRING FACTIONS

In recent times, psychology has shown a pronounced tendency toward what Gordon Allport (1955) called "simple and sovereign theorizing." By this, he meant an approach to theorizing that singled out one (or at most a very few) variable or assumption as essential, as all that is needed for understanding. Also part of this approach is a penchant for extolling the virtues of one's own variable at the expense of the variables being extolled by others.

Allport clearly believed simple and sovereign theorizing to be too limited and belligerent, in short, fragmenting to foster the scientific development of a field. It is a kind of misuse of criticality that is unfortunately very much alive in psychology. Indeed, most of the person–situation debate already mentioned hinged on simple and sovereign theorizing. Social psychologists and behaviorists (e.g., Bem, 1972; Mischel, 1968) pounced on some evidence that personality measures show only modest correlations with behavioral indices to argue that it is situational pressures that are really important. Pushed on to the defensive, some personality psychologists responded by insisting that person variables control the lion's share of behavior (e.g., Alker, 1972; Epstein, 1984). The ensuing fight over whether the situationists or the personalists would triumph proceeded merrily despite the existence of findings indicating that the interaction between situation and person variables accounted for the largest portion of behavior variance (e.g., Bowers, 1973). It took years before cooler heads could prevail and the interactional accord was formulated (Bowers, 1973; Ekehammer, 1974). And even now, some psychologists would prefer to keep fighting (e.g., Fiske, 1974).

Nor was this the first time the person–situation debate flared up. Early this century, William McDougall (the Harvard instinct theorist) and John B. Watson (the founder of behaviorism) engaged in long, heated debate over whether instincts or situations were the real cause of behavior. Some feel that one or the other protagonist triumphed, but the debate appears to have been rather inconclusive. Before too long, it was Carl R. Rogers and B. F. Skinner who engaged in another prolonged debate concerning whether person-centered counseling freed persons to follow their own inherent potentialities or merely shaped their behavior in directions favored by their counselors. Despite its focus on what the psychotherapist is really doing, this is clearly a form of the person–situation debate. So inconclusive was the confrontation between these two psychologists that the debate was continued by their students. If there was any upshot of all this effort, it suggested that if the unconditional positive regard person-centered counselors think they are extending to their clients is really a shaping process, its end result is to increase the likelihood of unusual or idiosyncratic responses that could be described as freedom.

Whenever the person–situation debate bursts forth, it ends inconclusively. The reason for this is that it is a false debate in the first place. It takes just a bit of thought to realize that behavior could never be exclusively a function of either person or situation variables. Indeed, behavior is a complex amalgam of both sources of influence and, hence, all that is viable is an interactional accord. Early in the history of American psychology, William James formulated this position as "the transitoriness of instinct." By that he meant that if there are instincts, they are only pure the first time they are expressed. After that, we are confronted with a compound of the instinct and what has been learned in its previous expressions, or what might these days be called an interactional variable.

Had James been heeded, there might not have been person–situation debates in the ensuing years. For that matter, the inconclusiveness of the earlier forms of the debate might have precluded our most recent version of it. Far from giving up criticality of mind, we might have used that capability on issues that can be resolved. That unresolvable issues can generate so much excitement and effort suggests just how deeply entrenched in our discipline is "simple and sovereign theorizing." We have a tendency to want to win wars even more than to deepen understanding of behavior.

Indeed, there is a debate accelerating right now that bears resemblance to the person–situation debates of the past. It involves the behavioral geneticists and the social developmentalists. The attempt to demonstrate that behavior is largely or totally explained by genetic factors is gaining considerable impetus. The empirical argument hinges on the greater similarity in behavior of genetically related children reared apart than of genetically unrelated children reared together. In the hands of some investigators, such observations lead to the conclusion that rearing is unimportant by comparison with genetics. The rejoinder, articulated well by Lois Hoffman (personal communication) is that behavioral similarity is not a good gauge of socialization if family units treat different children differently, as they undoubtedly do. It is common in families for one child to be treated as the leader and another as the scapegoat, for female children to be treated differently from male children, and for birth order to involve different parental behaviors. Thus, it is self-serving for the behavioral geneticists to choose behavioral similarity as a measure of socialization effects. And so the debate goes, inconclusively, generating more competition than clarity, as William James warned us.

Nor is the tendency toward warring factions limited to specifically articulated debates. More general than a debate is the continuing antagonism between academic psychologists and practitioners. Many academicians see themselves as the only true scientists, because they theorize, do research, and teach. Accordingly, they consider the practitioners, whether they be clinical or industrial in their efforts, as somewhere between hacks and hucksters. On their part, many practitioners see themselves as the only really adult psychologists, because they deal with real problems of real people. Accordingly, they consider the academicians to be irrelevant, romantic, trivial, and weak. It is quite rare for a psychologist to believe that academic and practical functions are two sides of the same scientific coin. Each needs the other, the academic to remain grounded in relevancy and the practitioner to resist mindlessness as a reaction to everyday pressures. Needless to say, there are competent and incompetent psychologists in both academics and practice, but this proves nothing about science or relevancy.

Indeed, within the academy there exists the same war over who and what in psychology is the more scientific. The biologically and cognitively oriented psychologists generally regard themselves as scientific insiders, with the others being somewhere between tender-minded and softheaded. In contrast, the social, personality, and developmental psychologists see themselves as truly understanding what is important in the discipline, with the others being somewhere between sterile and silly.

Let me not belabor the point. Virtually wherever one turns in our discipline there are warring factions, and this is a sign of our fractionation.

The Prevalence of Middle-Level Theorizing

For some time now, academic psychology has been dominated by middle-level theorizing. This approach avoids elaborate assumptive systems concerning matters far removed from immediate observation and makes no pretense of comprehensiveness concerning human behavior (Conant, 1947; Merton, 1957, 1968). A definite outcome of commitment to middle-level theorizing is that many discrete hypotheses regarding the same or similar phenomena are likely to exist concurrently in an area. This is because each investigator may well start with just one assumption (e.g., Durkheim's famous hypothesis that suicide rate is a function of the normlessness of a society), applying it in one or more concrete contexts by procedural elaborations that seem dictated merely by methodological concerns or common sense. One positive feature of having many discrete hypotheses is that a lively empirical competition ensues.

But the danger inherent in middle-level theorizing might be called a vanity of small differences or the entrenchment of several hypotheses, the differences between which would appear small and unimportant if only a broader purview were taken. A concerted attempt to theorize comprehensively might collapse the hypotheses together, on the grounds of their being special cases of each other or differing expressions of the same underlying process. But the distrust of comprehensive theorizing precludes such an attempt.

There are too many contemporary research areas in danger of such a vanity of small differences to be included here. One that may suffice as an example is intrinsic motivation. The basic phenomenon studied is the paradoxical decrease in performance of a preferred activity that takes place when an external reward is introduced. Many investigators have proposed explanations of this phenomenon. Deci (1971) suggested a cognitive evaluation hypothesis emphasizing that if a reinforcer is perceived as controlling behavior from an external source, then intrinsic motivation for performing is reduced. Kruglanski (1975) proposed endogenous versus exogenous attribution, similarly focusing on the reasons for instead of the causes of behavior. Then there is the over-justification hypothesis of Lepper and Greene (1975), stressing how behavior originally justified by intrinsic motivation becomes over-justified with the addition of extrinsic reinforcement. Reiss and Sushinsky (1975) offered a competing response hypothesis, suggesting that subjects will be less interested in playful activities to the extent that extrinsic rewards elicit responses that interfere with play responses. There is even a delay of gratification hypothesis (Ross et al., 1976) that focuses on the inhibiting effects of delay between promise and receipt of reward.

The empirical studies done in furtherance of these various hypotheses are intriguing and sophisticated. Each hypothesis has its own kind of empirical support. But, as DeCharms and Muir (1978) conclude in their review, the great bustle of activity in this field has led to little consensus or accumulated sense of understanding, and the problem may be the insufficient theoretical elaboration of the many proposed explanations. The hypotheses remain rich in implicit assumptions. I suspect that at the underlying level of implicit assumptions, there is considerable overlap if not identity among these hypotheses. But our commitment to middle level theorizing precludes exploration of hypothesis overlap and contributes to the fragmentation of psychology.

OVERSPECIALIZATION

So specialized have the subfields of psychology become that there is little or no sense of common cause or even communication across them. Odd though it may be, there is virtually nothing tying together the subfields of cognition, personality, learning, development, social psychology, biopsychology, industrial–organizational psychology, and clinical psychology. There are separate journals with separate readerships, simultaneous sessions in different hotels at annual conventions, misunderstandings and antagonisms in the conduct of academic departmental affairs. In some universities, biologically oriented psychologists belong to different divisions or schools than do socially oriented and clinically oriented psychologists. In other universities there are several departments that include psychologists. Introductory psychology courses and textbooks have become increasingly more fragmented and unwieldy. Indeed, at some universities the traditional introductory psychology course has given way to several alternative courses, each emphasizing some but not all aspects of the field. So fragmented is our field that it has become a Tower of Babel in which many no longer feel that there is any underlying discipline.

Perhaps this fragmentation is one reason why psychology is not a central feature of university organization. Although it is a popular undergraduate major, psychology appears rather peripheral to academic structure and definition. Nor on an individual basis do many psychologists tend to play central intellectual roles among their academic colleagues from other disciplines. Although some psychologists are now beginning to fill administrative roles at universities, this activity does not seem to extend to influencing their colleagues in scholarly ways. This may well be because psychologists have become so specialized that they lack any overall format and agenda that can be persuasive to scholars in other areas.

Certainly, the overspecialization renders it difficult for academic psychologists to address such major problems of a psychosocial nature as poverty, injustice, criminality, physical and mental illness, character development, homelessness, and the like. The research problems that fill our journals tend to be narrower and more esoteric. And there is the alarming tendency to retreat even further from content than that and define our science in terms of methodological prowess. Even in reviewing each others' manuscripts for publication, we are more likely to critique the methods than the content and conclusions. An aspect of this is the tendency to avoid topics for study that appear too complex to be researched easily. It is as if a retreat to methodology is the only thing holding our fragmented field together.

PERSONALITY THEORIZING AS ONE ANTIDOTE

One way to overcome the fragmentation in our field is for psychologists to spend time and imagination considering entire persons in their social milieu. This will help to blend together the various bits and pieces of knowledge currently existing in unintegrated form. Henry Murray (1938) dubbed this holistic study of humans, *personology*, and personality theorizing is its conceptual aspect.

TASKS AND COMPONENTS OF PERSONALITY THEORIZING

In order to appreciate the integrating effect on psychology that personality theorizing could have, it would be well to consider what are the tasks in and components of personality theorizing. Elsewhere (Maddi, 1968/1988) I have contended that personality theories need to include core, peripheral, and developmental statements.

In the core statement, theorists make assumptions about what binds all human beings together, what they all share. Typically, these assumptions refer to unlearned, inborn aspects of motivation, temperament, and potentialities. Implicitly or explicitly, the core statement concerns the overall purpose of human life. For some personality theories, the core statement is heavily biological. Freud (1925), for example, assumed that the mental preoccupation with sexual and aggressive instincts mirror the organismic facts of metabolism. Other personality theories are less concerned with biology, such as Allport's (1955) core assumption that humans all try to achieve *propriate* (self-expression and self-determination) *functioning*. Although the aim of the core statement is to identify how we are all alike, some personality theories record that, within this, inborn individual differences exist. For example, Rogers (1959) assumes that although we are all striving to actualize our inherent potentialities, we are radically differentiated by these potentialities.

The peripheral statement in a personality theory conceptualizes the various life-styles that characterize the thoughts, feelings, and actions of adults (Maddi, 1968/1988). The life styles are typically composed of types (e.g., the Freudian oral, anal, phallic, and genital character types) consisting of related traits, motives, or defenses (e.g., dependency, dominance, gregariousness, need for achievement, reaction formation). The types, traits, and defenses proposed in a peripheral statement refer to motivational and expressive characteristics that are learned, rather than inborn. The peripheral statement is the way in which the theorist explains individual differences in behavior. Although past critiques (e.g., Bem, 1972; Mischel, 1968) have insisted that peripheral theorizing does not give sufficient weight to situational determinants of behavior, personality theories (e.g., Allport, 1937; McClelland, 1951; Murray, 1938) have often defined peripheral characteristics as having joint situational and personal instigation. In any event, the current interactional accord (Ekehammer, 1974; Endler & Magnussen, 1976) indicates the importance of including both sources of behavior in peripheral theorizing.

In its developmental statement, a personality theory conceptualizes how expressions of the core we all share lead to the individual differences in life-style constituting the periphery (Maddi, 1968/1988). Involved here is a consideration of how learning takes place. Typically, personality theories consider child–parent interactions to be formative in the development of life-style. Some personality theories also consider individual–society interactions as important as well. The latter theories tend to assume that personality development continues throughout life, whereas the former consider life-style to be the product of learning in the childhood years.

A touchstone to personality theorizing is a sense that there are behavioral phenomena that can be explained that way (Maddi, 1968/1988). Without this, there would be little reason to theorize at all. An implication of the interest in explaining certain phenomena is the development or adoption of a data language that will specify the units of analysis that will frame the relevant dependent variables. It is true that the agenda of personology is so broad—to understand all the regularities that lend pattern to human behavior—that it has been difficult to be very concrete about a data language. Nonetheless, some theorists, notably Murray (1938), have attempted to start on this problem. Others (e.g., McClelland, 1981) have implied a data language in their dedication to explaining specific behaviors and their covariation.

Added to the components of a personality theory just outlined is an evaluative concern for explanatorily differentiating ideal from common and from psychopathological behaviors that is so frequent among theorists as to be virtually universal (Maddi, 1968/1988). The life-style conceptualized as ideal is considered virtually invulnerable to stressors and maximally expressive of the core (or universal human purpose). In contrast, the other, more common life-styles are considered to permit less full expression of core characteristics and this defines their vulnerability to stressors. The conceptualized breakdown of common life-styles in the face of stressors is the typical way in which personality theories explain psychopathological states. The evaluation of life-styles as ideal or nonideal carries with it a related evaluation of the developmental patterns that lead to them as ideal or nonideal. All of this constitutes a springboard to a conceptualization of psychotherapy, as that which can help persons overcome breakdowns by substituting for the nonideal developmental pattern they experienced previously, a facsimile of the ideal developmental pattern.

INTEGRATING POTENTIAL OF PERSONALITY THEORIZING

Even in this brief outline of the tasks in and components of personality theorizing, it is easy to discern a formidable integrating potential. Properly done, personality theorizing needs input from such areas as learning, cognition, physiological, social, measurement, developmental, and abnormal psychology. Through its integrative format and goals, personality theorizing might also make contributions back to these areas. This contribution to other areas might well be enhanced by the expression of personality theorizing in relevant personality research. With a few exceptions here and there, however, this bright hope has not been realized, and fragmentation and divisiveness reigns in psychology.

One reason why the integrative potential of personality theorizing has not been realized is the result of the very fragmentation and divisiveness itself. When other psychologists shun personality theorizing as unscientific, personologists too often respond by withdrawal into their own scholarly agenda, essentially giving up on their colleagues as trivializers. In the academic world, these personologists often find common cause with more receptive scholars in other fields. The advantage in this is some sense of intellectual community for personologists. The disadvantage is that there is no curb on fragmentation and divisiveness in psychology. My advice to personologists is to use the sense of worth they get from their own work and its acceptance by scholars in other disciplines to continue the struggle to have an integrative effect on their fellow psychologists in other areas. After all, personologists did bother to enter psychology rather than some other discipline. This implies or even defines their commitment to that field, and could help them to overcome any bitterness they might feel at being rejected as unscientific.

Another reason why personality theorizing has not reached its integrative potential in psychology is more internal to personology. Even within personology, there is a kind of fragmentation and divisiveness that takes place. Although each personality theory may well express the breadth and depth that integrates information from other areas of psychology, personologists tend to become committed to one of these theories to the exclusion of the others. Thus, personologists are Freudians, or Adlerians, or Jungians, or Rogerians, or existentialists and have little time or inclination to encounter or be influenced by other approaches. Indeed, this internal fragmentation is often augmented by rivalry, as one's own approach comes to feel more and more familiar and comfortable.

The antidote to this fragmentation within personology is comparative analysis (Maddi, 1968/1988). The first step in a comparative analysis of personality theorizing is to steep oneself in the various theories that exist, trying to understand what the theorists were trying to accomplish in understanding behavior. There are, of course, many existing theories of personality, even if one restricts oneself to just those known to psychologists.

The second step of comparative analysis involves classifying the theories into the smallest number of models that appear to do justice to the aims and approaches of the theories. Here, it is not enough to consider just parts of the theories, as has been done in the common classification of cognitive, trait, behavioristic, and dynamic theories. For example, too much is left out when one classifies Allport as a trait theorist (as he was at least as much cognitive and behavioristic) or Freud as a dynamic theorist (as he heavily emphasized cognition and trait considerations as well). These common classifications get imposed on personality theorying primarily because they reflect the preoccupations of other fields of psychology. But to persist in this is to miss the integrative potential of personality theorizing by reducing it to what will minimally interfere with other areas of psychology. A more instructive classification of personality theories will simultaneously take into account their core, developmental, and peripheral statements. This is admittedly hard to do, and we will probably go through several classificatory efforts before one feels acceptable to most personologists.

My own efforts at this second step of comparative analysis have led to three models, each with two variants. I have called them *conflict* (psychosocial and intrapsychic) *fulfillment* (actualization and perfection), and *consistency* (cognitive dissonance and activation) models (Maddi, 1968/1988). A theory fits into the conflict category if it postulates at the core level two great forces, present at birth, unchangeable, and in opposition to each other; at the peripheral level a life-style that is considered ideal because it is a compromise between the opposing great forces, whereas the nonideal life-styles fail to achieve a compromise; and a developmental statement that defines the ideal interaction between youngsters and parents as a razor's edge, not too permissive and not too punishing. Such theories express the psychosocial variant if one great force is presumed to arise in the individual while the other arises in groups or societies and the intrapsychic variant if both great forces are considered to be present in the individual without any necessary consideration of groups or societies. The prototype of the psychosocial conflict model is Freud's (1933) theory and of the intrapsychic conflict model is Jung's (1933).

In contrast, a theory expresses the fulfillment model if it postulates at the core level only one great force that, because inherent, is unchangeable; at the peripheral level a life-style that is considered ideal in that it expresses the great force more fully than the other, nonideal life-styles; and a developmental statement that emphasizes as ideal interactions between youngster and parents that facilitate expressions of the great force. In this model, psychosocial conflict is recognized as a possible occurrence. But when it occurs, society is regarded as having failed the individual. Such conflicts are considered resolvable and indicate the need for social reform. A theory expresses the actualization variant if the great force involves ever greater expressions of presumed inherent potentialities and the perfection variant if it involves striving to reach behavior patterns regarded as ideal though not programmed in potentialities as such. The prototype of the actualization fulfillment model is Rogers's (1959) theory and of the perfection fulfillment model is existential psychology (Maddi, 1970; May, 1958).

Finally, the third, or consistency, model involves at the core level a negative feedback principle in which there is discomfort with and efforts to decrease discrepancies between some personal norm and actual occurrences; and at the peripheral and developmental levels the retention of behaviors that have proven successful in reducing such discrepancies. In the cognitive dissonance variant, the norm is an expectation or prediction, whereas in the activation variant the norm is a customary level of tension or arousal. Prototypic of the cognitive dissonance variant is the theory of Kelly (1955) and of the activation variant is that of Maddi (1968/1988).

Thus, the end result of the second step of comparative analysis is to highlight the smallest number of categories or models that characterize the existing personality theories. Then the third step is to pinpoint the issues that arise from the disagreements between these categories or models (Maddi, 1968/1988). These issues can be primarily at the core, peripheral, or developmental levels. For example, a largely core issue is whether all, some, or no behavior is defensive. A seminal issue that arises at the developmental level is whether or not there is radical change in behavior after the childhood years are past. Issues at the peripheral level tend to involve differences in the content of lifestyles that are to be regarded as ideal.

The formulation of issues leads readily into the fourth step of comparative analysis, which is to resolve the issues. In an empirical field like psychology, resolution will be sought through research. To be truly relevant, the research should employ a design that permits the favoring of one or the other side of the issue, depending on what results are obtained. Such comparative analytic research is most productive when the design to be employed has been carefully planned so that obtained results can convincingly favor theories on one side of the issue while damaging those on the other. Through a concerted effort at such research, the issues separating models could well be resolved. Once it is clear which model is the most promising, psychologists could either endorse the personality theory or theories well expressing this model or build a new theory that explicitly capitalizes on what has been learned in the comparative analytic research.

Whether or not you find the particular models I have proposed convincing (they are certainly not the only ones it is possible to abstract from existing personality theories), I hope you will appreciate the enormous integrative potential in the comparative analytic approach. At every step of this approach (and especially in the posing of issues and their resolution), individual personologists would be well advised to consult with their colleagues who hold differing theoretical perspectives. There would be, through this task-oriented communication, pressure on all personologists to be clearer and more definite about their theoretical views and the research implications in them. Engaging in comparative analysis would go a long way toward obviating fragmentation within personology. It would also facilitate the integrative effect of personology on other areas of psychology in that many personologists would have to use more explicitly and comprehensively information available from these other areas in order to be specific enough to engage in the collegial aspects of comparative analysis just outlined.

THE EMPIRICAL SPIRIT

If personologists adopted comparative analysis as their method of choice, the personality field would be defined more by the issues needing resolution than by one or another of the existing theoretical approaches. For this kind of commitment one needs an empirical spirit, a willingness to change one's beliefs if convincing research compels that.

This does not mean, however, that a personologist would have to or should lose his or her belief in one personality theory as probably better than the others. Loss of all belief pending the outcome of some future comparative analysis comes perilously close to lack of commitment or alienation. Personologists need to struggle simultaneously to find or develop the personality theory that seems convincing to them and be willing to subject that theory to the empirical rigors of comparative analytic test. Without the former commitment, the hard work of theory refinement and development will languish. Without the latter commitment, the pressures toward fragmentation will stifle progress toward true understanding of human behavior.

TEACHING PERSONALITY

At present, it is most common for psychology curricula to include one advanced undergraduate course on personality and for there to be one or more courses on aspects of this subject matter at the graduate level. Typically, these days, the undergraduate course either emphasizes personality research rather than theory or considers a major theory or theories as examples of what is available. The same pattern appears at the graduate level, though one is more likely to find there the research emphasis rather than the theoretical emphasis.

Although the research emphasis in personality teaching expresses the scientific tradition and aspiration of psychology, it has a serious drawback in terms of the position I have taken in this chapter. Scrutiny of the research appearing in even the most prestigious personality journals illuminates this drawback by showing that rarely do the papers articulate, let alone derive their concerns from, anything approaching comprehensive theories of personality. As personality research is done these days, it involves, at most, middle-level theorizing (Merton, 1957, 1968) in which hypotheses to be tested or questions to be answered are derived from either common sense or other studies similarly conceived.

Because there is little comprehensive theorizing standing behind personality research, courses emphasizing it are not particularly useful in overcoming fragmentation. At most, the research studies cluster in areas of human behavior, such as creativity or aggressiveness, and the course based on them goes from one such area to another. Nowhere is the student encouraged to put the areas together into an overall sense of human behavior. Nowhere is the student stimulated to consider core, peripheral, and developmental concerns in an integrated fashion. This approach to personality teaching recapitulates the fragmentary approach currently seen in the teaching of other areas of our field, notably introductory, social, and biological psychology. Thus, to teach personality by restricting coverage to research studies alone is to fail to alert new generations of budding psychologists to the value of integrative effort. We will be passing on to them a fragmented, divisive field as if that were some sort of ideal.

By contrast, courses covering major personality theories at least encourage the student to consider core, peripheral, and developmental assumptions in overall attempts to understand human behavior. But such courses come with dangers of their own. The major pitfall of courses taught from one theoretical perspective to the exclusion of others is what I have elsewhere (Maddi, 1968/1988) called *partisan zealotry*. In his or her zealous championing of one personality theory, the teacher may insulate the student (especially if this is the only personality course in the curriculum) from the possibility of picking and choosing among various available alternatives. This pitfall is minimized if the teacher goes out of his or her way to alert students to alternative views though they are not emphasized in the course. It is especially useful if there are also courses championing some of these alternative personality theories in the curriculum.

That leaves the type of course that surveys personality theories rather than restricting itself to a favored one. Done well, such a course can certainly alert the student to the comprehensive, integrating function of personality theorizing. The major pitfall of this approach inheres in its survey format and might be called *benevolent eclecticism* (Maddi, 1968/1988) or an uncritical reiteration of the same old theories in the same old ways. Too often, students get through such courses by memorizing madly immediately before the examinations and promptly forgetting everything as soon as the evaluation is over.

It will by now come as no surprise to you that I advocate a comparative analytic approach in personality teaching (Maddi, 1968/1988). With such an approach, the student experiences the comprehensive, integrative format of personality theorizing, learns the content of the major existing theories, experiences an intellectual framework within which to classify and evaluate theories, ponders some of the issues characterizing the personality field, and sees examples of how research can hope to resolve those issues. Should students taking such a course actually become psychologists, they are more likely to approach their field with integrative standards and goals, and value in themselves and others an empirical spirit that transcends but does not replace their personal convictions. Especially because it is hard for those psychologists who have long conducted their careers in more fragmentary and divisive fashion to change that, it is important to educate the succeeding generations of psychologists differently. And comparative analysis is a useful teaching tool in this effort.

A FINAL WORD

Although I started with an analysis of personality theorizing, I have ended with an encouragement to teach the existing personality theories. To some, these theories, though perhaps having a kind of grandeur, are a bit old-fashioned and outmoded. Indeed, Jerome Singer even characterized textbooks surveying these theories as a kind of sojourn through the graveyard. To be sure, his critique was largely about the uncritical nature of such surveys. But he was also objecting in part to emphasizing these old theories.

To my mind there is no reason to either cherish or reject the comprehensive personality theories merely because they exist or may have been formulated some time ago. If they are the subject matter of a comparative analysis, we will see soon enough where they fit into models for understanding human behavior and how their model fares in research-based issue resolution. Then there will be a reason to retain, change, or reject existing personality theories that is based in intellectual concerns rather than fashion. After all, if the concrete personality theories that exist today had not been formulated already, there is every reason to believe that personologists would invent them soon. There is a small number of models for understanding human behavior and a finite number of examples of these models that human imagination can construct.

REFERENCES

Alker, H. A. (1972). Is personality situationally specific or intrapsychically consistent? *Journal of Personality, 40,* 4–16.

Allport, G. W. (1937). *Personality: A psychological interpretation.* New York: Holt.

Allport, G. W. (1955). *Becoming: Basic considerations for a psychology of personality.* New Haven: Yale University Press.

Bem, D. J. (1972). Constructing cross-situational consistencies in behavior: Some thoughts on Alker's critique of Mischel. *Journal of Personality, 40,* 17–26.

Bowers, K. S. (19730. Situationism in psychology: An analysis and a critique. *Psychological Review, 80,* 307–336.

Conant, J. B. (1947). *On understanding science.* New Haven: Yale University Press.

Deci, E. L. (1971). The effects of externally mediated rewards on intrinsic motivation. *Journal of Personality and Social Psychology, 18,* 105–115.

DeCharms, R. C., & Muir, M. S. (1978). Motivation: Social approaches. In M. R. Rosenzweig & W. Porter (Eds.), *Annual review of psychology* (pp. 000–000). Palo Alto, CA: Annual Reviews.

Ekehammer, B. (1974). Interactionism in personality from a historical perspective. *Psychological Bulletin, 81,* 1026–1048.

Endler, N. S., & Magnussen, D. (1976). Toward an interactional psychology of personality. *Psychological Bulletin, 83,* 956–974.

Epstein, S. (1984). The stability of behavior across time and situations. In R. A. Zucker, J. Aronoff, & R. I. Rabin (Eds.), *Personality and the prediction of behavior.* New York: Academic Press.

Fiske, D. W. (1974). The limits for the conventional science of personality. *Journal of Personality, 42,* 1–11.

Freud, S. (1925). Instincts and their vicissitudes. In S. Freud, *Collected papers* (Vol. 4). London: Institute for Psychoanalysis and Hogarth Press.

Freud, S. (1933). *New introductory lectures in psychoanalysis* (W.J.H. Sprott, trans.). New York: Norton.

Jung, C. G. (1933). *Modern man in search of a soul.* New York: Harcourt, Brace & World.

Kelly, G. A. (1955). *The psychology of personal constructs* (Vol. I). New York: Norton.

Kruglanski, A. W. (1975). The endogenous–exogenous partition in attribution theory. *Psychological Review, 82,* 387–406.

Lepper, M. R., & Greene, D. (1975). Turning play into work: Effects of adult surveillance and extrinsic rewards on children's intrinsic motivation. *Journal of Personality and Social Psychology, 31,* 116–125.

Maddi, S. R. (1970). The search for meaning. In M. Page (Ed.), *Nebraska symposium on motivation* (pp. 000–000). Lincoln: University of Nebraska Press.

Maddi, S. R. (1988). *Personality theories: A comparative analysis* (5th ed.). Homewood, IL: Dorsey. (Original publication 1968).

May, R. (1958). Contributions of existential psychotherapy. In R. May, E. Angel, & H. F. Ellenberger (Eds.), *Existence: A new dimension in psychiatry and psychology* (pp. 000–000). New York: Basic Books.

McClelland, D. C. (1951). *Personality.* New York: Dryden.

McClelland, D. C. (1981). Is personality consistent? In A. I. Rabin, J. Aronoff, A. M. Barclay, & R. A. Zucker (Eds.), *Further explorations in personality* (pp. 87–113). New York: Wiley.

Merton, R.K. (1957). The role-set: Problems in sociological theory. *The British Journal of Sociology, 8,* 106–120.

Merton, R. K. (1968). *Social theory and social structure.* New York: Free Press.

Mischel, W. (1968). *Personality and assessment.* New York: Wiley.

Mischel, W. (1973). Toward a cognitive social learning reconceptualization of personality. *Psychological Review, 80,* 252–283.

Murray, H. A. (1938). *Explorations in personality: A clinical and experimental study of fifty men of college age.* New York: Oxford University Press.

Reiss, S., & Sushinsky, L. W. (1975). Overjustification, competing responses, and the acquisition of intrinsic interest. *Journal of Personality and Social Psychology, 31,* 116–125.

Rogers, C. R. (1959). A theory of therapy, personality, and interpersonal relationships, as developed in the client-centered framework. In S. Koch (Ed.), *Psychology: A study of a science* (Vol. 3, pp. 000–000). New York: McGraw-Hill.

Ross, M., Karniol, R., & Rothstein, M. (1976). Reward contingency and intrinsic motivation in children: A test of the delay of gratification hypothesis. *Journal of Personality and Social Psychology, 33,* 442–447.

CHAPTER SEVEN

It's Time to Put Theories of Personality in Their Place, or, Allport and Stagner Got It Right, Why Can't We?

GERALD A. MENDELSOHN

Among the various subfields of psychology, Personality is just about unique in its continued dedication to the teaching of courses and thus to the writing of textbooks devoted to "theory." Where else, save perhaps in the closely allied field of Abnormal Psychology, can one find comparable courses and texts? Surely not in Cognitive or Biological Psychology, for example, and only with difficulty in Social Psychology. The contrast between the fates of Hilgard's (1948) classic *Theories of Learning* and Hall and Lindzey's (1957) comparably classic *Theories of Personality* is telling in this regard. The former, whose last edition was written a decade ago, can scarcely be considered representative of the current generation of textbooks in learning while the latter, in its most recent incarnation (Hall *et al.*, 1985) (and with two additional authors), remains a leading textbook in the field. In what follows, I will be less concerned with the question of why this state of affairs exists than with the question of whether it is a desirable state of affairs. It should come as no surprise after so tendentious an opening that I intend to

GERALD A. MENDELSOHN • Institute of Personality and Social Research, University of California at Berkeley, Berkeley, California 94720.

Fifty Years of Personality Psychology, edited by Kenneth H. Craik *et al.* Plenum Press, New York, 1993.

argue that the continued emphasis on theories of personality is not desirable, that it is both anachronistic and a misleading representation of what, in fact, personality psychologists think about and do.

THE DISTINCTION BETWEEN THEORIZING ABOUT PERSONALITY AND THEORIES OF PERSONALITY

Before I develop the argument whose conclusion I have just stated, two clarifications are in order. First, a distinction between "Theories of Personality" and theorizing about personality needs to be made. By the latter I mean the kind of conceptual analysis that both precedes and follows empirical work. Such theorizing is essential and, if one accepts the proposition that there are no facts apart from theories, inevitable. We have, in fact, been passing through a particularly vigorous period of such theoretical activity, most obviously (but not only) in the debate about the meaning and status of "traits" and situations. In the course of that debate, any number of basic assumptions about personality, including the legitimacy of the concept of personality itself, came under intense scrutiny. If, as I believe, the debate is now largely resolved, that is because of the understandings that it engendered or revived; understandings about, for example, the meaning of traits and "consistency," the compositing of observations and the interaction between persons and situations. Thanks to this kind of conceptualizing, personality is now a healthier field than it has been for years. And when we add in such current developments as the revived interest in long-term motivational sequences and in the self, public and private, the elaboration of the concepts of social intelligence and ego development, the increase in taxonomic activity, the study of the dynamics of stress and coping, and the attempt to comprehend the significance of evolutionary biology for human behavior, it becomes apparent that personality theory is by no means languishing in neglect.

In contrast, I mean the term "Theories of Personality" to apply to those ambitious, broadly encompassing and universalistic statements that claim to identify the basic elements and processes underlying individual psychological activity. These theories are generally identified with a particular person (e.g., Freud, Kelly, Rogers) and by a label written in capital letters (e.g., Analytic Psychology, Personal Construct Theory, Social Learning Theory). More often than not, they originate in clinical observation or armchair reflection and are closely tied to psychotherapeutic considerations. To be sure, there have been many efforts to "validate" several of these theories, or rather, particular elements of these theories, by empirical procedures, but it is essentially to the speculations, insights, and persuasiveness of the individual theorists that they owe their existence. Theories of Personality are, in sum, at an altogether higher level of abstraction and at a far greater remove from empirical research than what I previously described as "theorizing about personality."

Judging from the 15 textbooks (all with publication dates of 1984 or later) that I have before me as I write, there is good agreement about the theorists to whom students should be introduced. The list of the top 20 runs as follows: Adler, Allport, Bandura, Cattell, Dollard (and Miller), Erikson, Eysenck, Freud, Fromm, Horney, Jung, Kelly, Maslow, Mischel, Murray, Rogers, Rotter, Skinner, and Sullivan. Though they form the core group, not all of them appear in every text; Maddi (1989), in his distinguished comparative analysis of personality theories, for example, excludes Sullivan and Horney "because their thinking no longer seems to have great direct impact on the personality field" (p. 14). A number of theorists appear with less frequency than the top 20 but often enough to warrant mention: Guilford, Hartmann, Kohut, Lewin, May, McClelland, Rank, Sheldon, and White. Finally, cameo appearances are made by Angyal, Berne, Binswanger, Boss, Ellis, A. Freud, Goldstein, Maddi, and Perls. A few other names might justifiably be added to the list, but this is, I believe, a reasonably inclusive roster of the writers who define the canon of Theories of Personality as it can be inferred from contemporary textbooks.*

THE GENRES OF TEXTBOOKS IN PERSONALITY

The second clarification has to do with the content of textbooks in Personality. I cannot claim to have done a systematic survey of publisher's lists, but it seems clear that the prototypic textbook is organized to a considerable degree around the presentation of Theories of Personality. There are, of course, exceptions; in fact three genres of textbooks can be distinguished. First, there are those that are explicitly designed to provide coverage of the positions of the theorists deemed most significant by the author(s). Hall and Lindzey is the *locus classicus* of this genre—after the obligatory introductory material, a dozen or so chapters devoted to a theorist or to a group of related theorists,

---

* There are some mysteries about who is included and who is not in textbooks of personality. For example, in what meaningful sense can Skinner be considered a personality theorist and why has Gardner Murphy so completely disappeared from view?

followed by some comparative or summarizing comments. Other formats can be found in which theorists who presumably share a general
orientation are grouped into families that may be variously labeled
strategies, approaches, perspectives, and so forth. Indeed, this seems
to be the predominant trend recently. The cast of characters is the
same, however, and the essential substance of the volume remains the
exposition of their views. I say the "essential substance" because it is
usual to include as well material on some or all of the following: relevant assessment techniques and therapeutic approaches, examples of
pertinent research, critical evaluations, and intertheorist comparisons.
The selection of this additional material is, of course, a function of the
particular theorists chosen for inclusion in the text; it does not result
from an effort to provide representative or systematic coverage of the
issues of concern to contemporary personality psychologists.

The second genre of textbook is organized around topics and issues
in personality rather than Theories of Personality. Stagner's *Psychology of Personality* (1974) provides a good example of the genre. In it
one finds chapters on methods, development, units of analysis (e.g.,
traits, styles), dynamics, and determinants (e.g., biological and socioeco-
nomic factors). Many of the familiar theorists make an appearance, but
briefly and only inasmuch as they have relevance to the topical organization of the book. Examples of this genre vary in the balance they
strike among conceptual analysis, methodological concerns, and presen-
tations of specific areas of empirical research, but they all seek to provide an introduction to and overview of the subject matter of the field
of personality. It may perhaps be unnecessary to point out that the
"subject matter of the field of personality" is by no means coextensive
with the subject matter addressed in the work of the canonical Theorists of Personality.

Finally, there is a third genre of textbooks that is a hybrid of the
two just discussed. Textbooks of this kind are organized into two major
sections, the first devoted to the expositions of the standard Theories
of Personality and the second to reviews of specific areas of empirical
investigation. The areas chosen for inclusion naturally vary from text
to text; some typical choices are aggression, sex roles and gender identity, stress and coping, self-concepts and so on, though in some cases
the topics are broader (e.g., personality development). Inclusiveness is
the hybrid's advantage—there is something for everybody—but the inclusiveness inevitably leads to less depth and detailing than one finds
in the best examples of the other two genres. A more serious limitation
of the hybrids is that the two major sections are rarely integrated in
more than a superficial way. That, too, is inevitable given the casual

relationship that exists in actuality between Theories of Personality and research in personality. I shall elaborate on this point shortly.

It is perhaps ironic that even though the first two significant textbooks in personality, the textbooks that inspired this volume, were of the second genre, the example of the founders has been followed fitfully at best. A number of empirically oriented texts have appeared over the years, it is true, but they have not often run to multiple editions and exemplars are not common today. Rather, the diet offered to undergraduates has been and continues to be based on Theories of Personality, however varied the preparation and the side dishes.

What conclusions can our students, and indirectly our colleagues, be expected to draw from this way of presenting the field of personality? First, that the work of personality psychologists is inspired by and organized around the content of the Theories of Personality; second, that these theories have adequate validity and utility; and finally, that they represent the current state of thinking in the field. If this were not so, why would we in our primary vehicle of self-presentation, the textbook, give pride of place to this content as opposed to some other? But, in fact, none of these conclusions is correct, for Theories of Personality are at the periphery, not at the core, of the contemporary field of personality as it is practiced by professionals and, I believe, for good reason.

THE CRITIQUE OF THEORIES OF PERSONALITY

Now that I have made the necessary clarifications and staked out a position, it is time to defend that position with more than sniping comments. My brief will be in three parts. I will argue first that Theories of Personality are not really theories in any acceptable scientific sense; second, that they are anachronistic; and finally, that they have little to do with the research actually done by personality psychologists.

QUESTIONABLE SCIENTIFIC STANDING OF THE THEORIES

Although it would be most difficult to obtain agreement on precisely what qualities a scientific theory should have, the following statement taken from Hall and Lindzey (1985) seems appropriate for present purposes and reasonably consensual: "We have defined personality theory as a set of assumptions about human behavior, together with the empirical definitions required, first, to move from the abstract statement of the theory to the empirical observations and, second, to test and/or support the theory" (p. 17). Do the Theories of Personality that appear in textbooks conform to this definition? It would be hard to argue that they do. They are rarely systematic in their statement of basic assumptions or concepts and the relationships among them. Key concepts are ill-defined and central issues of methodology and measurement are not addressed. Alternative hypotheses are numerous but unexamined, ad hoc and post hoc interpretations abound, and many, perhaps most, of the propositions of these theories are neither confirmable nor disconfirmable, that is, they are not capable of generating precise predictions. Furthermore, the empirical and observational sources of these theories are questionable on several grounds. Generally, they have been based on small, special, and historically limited samples. Introspection and armchair reflection have more often been their sources than data of a less subjective character. When some sort of evidence is adduced, it is frequently contaminated by the means of its collection (e.g., clinical interactions) and it is frequently impossible to distinguish between the data and the interpretation of the data. This makes replication and intersubjective agreement well-nigh impossible. Thus, the systematic collection and analysis of evidence has had little to do with the origin, modification, acceptance, or fall from grace of the Theories of Personality. Finally, I have never understood why Personality should place such heavy emphasis on theories originating in the study of atypical groups. The study of pathology frequently provides illuminating information, but it seems to me more sensible to regard pathology as a deviation from general patterns than to make inferences about general patterns on the basis of the exceptional. As Maddi (1989) points out, "A theory of psychotherapy is one thing; a theory of personality is another" (p. 617).

The set of objections I have just rattled off obviously apply to some Theories of Personality more than to others, but none is immune to criticism on several of these grounds. Does that mean that I regard them as worthless? Not at all, for they often raise issues of substantial psychological importance and sometimes provide insights about them. The classical Theorists of Personality, however, can scarcely be considered the only thinkers to have struggled with issues of psychological importance or to have provided insights about them. So, too, did the Greek dramatists and philosophers, the medieval scholastics, the Protestant reformers, the Elizabethan playwrights, the Encyclopedists, and the Russian novelists, to note only a few groups of Western writers. The question then becomes what, if anything, have the Theorists of Personality identified as issues or as conceptions of those issues or as approaches to the study of those issues that distinguishes them from the many, many others who have observed and written about human behavior? What is special about their work? Why in our teaching of personality should we pay particular attention to them as sources of ideas in preference to artists, philosophers, and theologians?

The answers to those questions ought to have something to do with psychology as a scientific endeavor. If the Theorists of Personality have particular significance for psychologists who seek to be empirical scientists, it ought to be the case that they present their ideas in a form that facilitates a scientific understanding of personality. But that is precisely what, I have argued, they fail to do. I am not alone in that judgment; the authors of textbooks by and large raise the same criticisms as I have in their evaluations of the theories they present. Hall and Lindzey (1985) for example, explicitly pose the question of whether the personality theories they examine in their book conform to their definition of a theory. Their answer: "Hardly" (p. 17).

What we have, then, are theories in name only. Levy (1970), after coming to the same basic conclusion, suggests the term "conceptions" as more appropriate. Perhaps the term "viewpoints" would do equally well; but whatever term is chosen, the comment by historian Peter Brown (1967) about religious systems seems no less applicable to Theories of Personality: "The quality of a religious system depends less on the specific doctrine, than on the choice of problems that it regards as important, the areas of human experience to which it directs attention" (p. 393). That is a function of genuine importance—there is no reason to doubt that the field would be the poorer had the canonical theorists (among others) not transmitted their understandings and speculations to us. There remains, however, a fundamental difference between "concepts" of personality and "theories" of personality; to ignore that difference is not a service to our students or our field.

QUESTIONABLE CONTEMPORARY RELEVANCE OF THE THEORIES

The second part of my brief concerns the contemporary relevance of the theories of personality. It is a striking fact that of the 38 theorists cited earlier as forming the canon, 16 were born in the nineteenth century and another 19 were born between 1900 and the end of World War I. That leaves only three, Bandura (1925), Mischel (1930), and Maddi (1933) whose careers began after World War II. It is also striking that the theorists who populate the textbooks of 1990 are largely the same as those who populated the textbooks of 1960. Is it surprising in these circumstances that many of our colleagues regard the field of personality as stagnant?

Of course, it does not necessarily follow that because the Theories of Personality are getting on in years, they should be put out to pasture. My father used to say, "Because it's new doesn't mean it's good." To that observation a corollary can be added, "Because it's old doesn't mean it's bad." One could argue, that is, that the Theories of Personality have proven so durable because they are good theories. Given their widely acknowledged deficiencies, however, that seems an unpromising argument. And there are other grounds as well for doubting that the merit these theories may once have possessed has remained undiminished over the years. The time is long past when one could consider theories, scientific or otherwise, as being isolated from the intellectual, social, and cultural milieu of the time of their development. They are embedded in history. This is particularly true of theories such as those in the social sciences that are essentially speculative constructions innocent of systematic empirical grounding. Thus, the bulk of the Theories of Personality reflect the concerns of bygone times. A brief anecdote may illustrate the point. During a discussion with a graduate student in music, I made the obvious point that in his choice and handling of dramatic themes, Wagner was Jungian. "No," the student corrected me, "Jung was Wagnerian." He was, of course, correct; for budding European intellectuals of Jung's generation, Wagner was a force whose influence was felt well beyond the sphere of music (Barzun, 1938, p. 115). Consider, too, Freud's now-rejected theorizing about the psychology of women or how the category of sexual perversion has bit by bit been emptied of content in the post-1960s era.

Now I realize that intellectual issues that have their origins in an earlier period may still have considerable contemporary relevance; we have not ceased to be concerned about unconscious processes, the self, identity, and the like. What has changed, however, is the cultural, intellectual, and scientific context in which we conceptualize and investigate those issues. Moreover, new issues and paradigms, as well as new data and methods that could not have been taken into account or even imagined by the canonical theorists have come to prominence since their work was done. One can conceive a psychoanalysis shaped by a computer model rather than a hydraulic model, but the fact is that the death of Freud and the birth of computers were roughly contemporaneous. History, and with it science, marches on; it is the fate of theories to be discarded, modified, and replaced. There is no good reason to believe that theories of personality have qualities that make them any more enduring than theories in other fields.

Lest I be misunderstood, I should make it clear that I am not counseling ignorance of the past. Thinking about personality did not begin in 1980 or 1960 or at the turn of the century; to understand where we are now, it is essential to understand where we came from. Thus, an awareness of Theories of Personality should be a part of the training of personality psychologists at all levels. Indeed, in my own teaching of personality I devote considerable time to psychoanalytic thinking not only because the shape of the field has been so influenced by Freud's work but also because he was so astute in identifying the problems that any comprehensive approach to personality must address. But if it is an error to be ignorant of the past, it is no less an error to present the past as if it were the present. To do so is to encourage the identification of the field of personality with the spirit and spirits of yesteryear and to ignore or crowd out the vigorous theorizing and research about personality that, as I noted earlier, is very much a part of the contemporary scene. In sum, the more a textbook focuses on Theories of Personality, the more it conveys a distorted and deadening view of the field.

QUESTIONABLE HEURISTIC VALUE OF THE THEORIES

Despite all that I have said so far, there is another criterion for evaluating theories that must be considered before concluding that the canonical Theories of Personality are of historical interest only. This criterion can be summed up as follows: "The bottom line in the evaluation of personality theories is their heuristic value. However vague and poorly developed a theory, if it can be shown to generate significant research, the chances are that it has something important to say about human behavior" (Hall & et al., 1985, pp. 19–20). While the second sentence is perhaps arguable, the first embodies a view that appears in one form or another in most textbooks. The implication of this view seems clear enough: Theories of personality should play a major role in the ongoing research activities of personality psychologists. Whether or not they do is an empirical question, one that can be investigated by examining representative samples of recent articles in the major journals of the field.

To be reasonably up to date and efficient in this research, I have selected for study the most recent complete volumes of two major journals in the field, the *Journal of Personality* (Volume 57, 1989) and the Personality Processes and Individual Differences section of the *Journal of Personality and Social Psychology* (also Volume 57, July–December 1989). The two combined produced a sample of 81 articles in which there is a total of 3799 references. First, I will report the good news for partisans of Theories of Personality. Seventy percent of the articles include at least one reference to one or more of the canonical theorists; moreover, 26 of the 38 and 19 of the "top 20" theorists are cited at least once. But as it says in a good book, "Data giveth and data taketh away." A closer look at the evidence, it turns out, provides a less encouraging picture. Of the 3799 references, only 208 are to a publication authored or coauthored by one of the 38 canonical theorists. Five theorists, Allport, Bandura, Cattell, Eysenck, and Mischel account for 60% of all those references; that is, the remaining 33 theorists combined are cited a mere 84 times (2.2% of the references) and only 11 of them appear more than twice. It is important to add that the great majority of the 208 references are to theorists still living in 1989—1% of the references are to those no longer with us. It should be noted, too, that cognitive social learning and psychometric–structuralist perspectives are the only two that are represented in these journals with any frequency at all. The similar findings of Mendelsohn in 1983 and Levy in 1970 indicate that the neglect of Theories of Personality by researchers is not of recent origin.

If we move beyond counting to ⌐qualitative analysis⌐ it becomes apparent that very few of these references are more than phrases or one-liners, a sort of courteous gesture to our forebears. Here are some typical examples: "A third view is that establishing a sex-typed identity is a major adaptive milestone of childhood and adolescence (Erikson, 1950; Kohlberg, 1966; Mussen, 1969)"; "This tradition [psychobiography] may be said to have been launched by Freud's (1910/1964) classic treatment of Leonardo da Vinci (Elms, 1988), even though its major proponent within personality psychology may have been Gordon Allport (1961), the champion of the idiographic perspective (see also Erikson, 1959, 1969)"; and "Many longitudinal studies have been case studies of adults offering detailed descriptions of individuals but little evidence of generality of results beyond the individual studied (e.g., Allport, 1965; White, 1966)." (These quotations are from Alpert-Gillis & Connell, 1989, p. 98; Simonton, 1989, p. 696; and Moskowitz & Schwartzman, 1989, p. 724, respectively; it should be noted in passing that they include a bit more than 3% of the 208 references to the Theorists of Personality.) Clearly, it is correct and appropriate to make such citations, but they are scarcely an integral or even necessary part of the text; that is, nothing essential, conceptual, or empirical would have been lost had the great majority of the 208 citations been omitted. To put it differently, in very few of the studies examined was a hypothesis derived from or inspired by a Theory of Personality tested, and in no case was the validation or invalidation of one of the Theories or even a part of one of the Theories at issue. That they have a generalized distal influence on research is true to varying degrees, but it is obvious that the proximal influences on research are theoretical positions of more recent vintage and the contemporary empirical literature. At this point I can do no better than to quote Levy (1970): " . . . one interpretation, which seems inescapable, is that these theories of personality are not performing the integrative and heuristic function we expect of a theory" (pp. 84–85).

WHAT IS TO BE DONE?

Now I do not wish to argue that what is, is necessarily the way things ought to be. One cannot dismiss out of hand the possibility that the manifest neglect of Theories of Personality by contemporary researchers has more to do with their ignorance, indifference, laziness, lack of historical sense, and low horizons than with the inadequacies of the classical theories. But that seems to me incorrect on several grounds. First, it is implausible that researchers would not be drawn to theories that are useful, ones that could serve integrative and heuristic functions. Why would they willfully ignore so valuable a resource if it existed? Second, as I argued earlier, the speculative, imprecise, and anachronistic character of the canonical theories do, in fact, render them inadequate for contemporary scientific purposes. It is important to note in this respect that the theorists whose positions are most nearly free of those limitations, for example, Allport, Bandura, Cattell, Eysenck, and Mischel, have a far from trivial influence on current research. Finally, I believe that it is a misreading of the contemporary literature to regard it as devoid of theoretical inspiration or significance. What is true is that, with the exceptions just noted, the theories that figure in the literature are other than those that appear in textbooks. It would be difficult, however, for many, I fear most, of our students to appreciate the fact or even to understand that personality is an evolving field, not one mired in the contemplation of the great figures of its past.

And yet a problem remains. If it is true, as I would have appeared to argue, that the field is in a healthy and productive state, why is there a widespread feeling (one I share) that much of the empirical literature is empty and trivial. Might it not be that by turning away from the theorizing of the canonical theorists or by concentrating on middle-level theories (cf. Maddi, 1984), we have condemned ourselves to the collection of "itty-bitty" facts, to use Allport's (1961) telling phrase? I do not think so. Recent theoretical work based on, say, evolutionary biology or conceptions of ego development may be lacking in the literary allure of psychoanalysis, but it is scarcely lacking in breadth or potential integrative power. And there are any number of other recent theoretical positions of which the same can be said. In sum, the fitful intellectual sustenance to be gained from reading the journals in personality cannot reasonably be attributed to any impoverishment of theoretical possibilities resulting from the neglect of the classical tradition.

Having argued that the tediousness of much current research is not due to the neglect of the classical theorists, I should, at least for the sake of completeness, offer some alternative hypotheses. To be brief, my candidates are the following: (1) the rigidity and rituals of what the field regards as appropriate methodology; (2) the pressures to produce articles at a high and steady rate, a factor that encourages the study of immediate outcomes with procedures that yield a maximum of data with a minimum of effort; (3) laziness; (4) the uneven distribution of research talent; (5) the tendency of many investigators to think like psychologists instead of like functioning social beings when they engage in research; (6) the oversimplification of complex processes and phenomena in order to make them amenable to investigation by the methods that are available and acceptable to the profession; and (7) the sheer difficulty of doing good research on human beings and here I refer to both intellectual and ethical problems. Some might suggest an eighth factor: the failure of researchers to place their empirical work within a firm theoretical context; but I have never been able to detect a correlation between how significant or interesting a study is and the strength of its tie to some explicit theory.

By now the point should be clear: It's time to kick the habit, to break our addiction as teachers to theories of personality. The phrase "as teachers" is, of course, crucial, for what we do as researchers and as theorizers has but a passing resemblance to what we habitually teach, at least to undergraduates. But if we abandon the course in Theories of Personality,* what should we be doing as teachers? The answer to that question is easy—we should be telling students about what we actually do and how and why we do it. To quote myself, "I am convinced that as teachers and writers of textbooks, we can best convey what makes the study of personality consequential and exciting by introducing students to the scientific activity that engages us as professionals" (1983, p. 437). Ironically, that is what Allport and Stagner, in their very different

---

* The typical contemporary textbook in personality could be reserved for its proper setting in courses explicitly devoted to the history of ideas in personality. As it stands now, such courses would be indistinguishable from much of what is presently being taught in the field; but if we were to break the addiction, they could serve an important function.

ways, did some 50 years ago. We could do no better than to take their approach as a model now. In the end, all that I am advocating comes down to this: "Preach what you practice."

REFERENCES

Allport, G. W. (1961). *Pattern and growth in personality*. New York: Holt, Rinehart and Winston.

Alpert-Gillis, L. J., & Connell, J. P. (1989). Gender and sex-role influence on children's self-esteem. *Journal of Personality, 57*, 97–114.

Barzun, J. (1958). *Darwin, Marx, Wagner: Critique of a heritage*. New York: Doubleday.

Brown, P. (1967). *Augustine of Hippo*. Berkeley: University of California Press.

Hall, C. S., & Lindzey, G. (1957). *Theories of personality*. New York: Wiley.

Hall, C. S., Lindzey, G., Loehlin, J. C., & Manosevitz, M. (1985). *Introduction to theories of personality*. New York: Wiley.

Hilgard, J. (1948). *Theories of learning*. New York: Prentice-Hall.

Levy, L. H. (1970). *Conceptions of personality*. New York: Random House.

Maddi, S. R. (1984). Personology for the 1980s. In J. Aronoff, R.A. Zucker, & A. I. Rabin (Eds.), *Personality and the prediction of behavior* (pp. 7–41). Orlando, FL: Academic Press.

Maddi, S. R. (1989). *Personality theories: A comparative analysis* (5th ed.). Chicago: Dorsey Press.

Mendelsohn , G. A. (1983). What should we tell students about theories of personality? *Contemporary Psychology, 28*, 435–437.

Moskowitz, D. S., & Schwartzman, A. E. (1989). Painting group portraits: Studying life outcomes for aggressive and withdrawn children. *Journal of Personality, 57*, 723—746.

Simonton, D. K. (1989). Shakespeare's sonnets: A case of and for single-case histori ometry. *Journal of Personality, 57*, 695–721.

Stagner, R. (1974). *Psychology of personality* (4th ed.). New York: McGraw-Hill.

PART FOUR

PRESENT-DAY PERSPECTIVES ON BASIC ISSUES

CHAPTER EIGHT

Science and the Single Case

IRVING E. ALEXANDER

I must express my gratitude for being asked to participate in this anniversary celebration. The task assigned, a review of "science and the single case," or the continuing saga of the study of the individual, allowed me to reexperience the pleasure I derived in reading Allport's volume (1937) as a graduate student more than 40 years ago. While my present concern is centered in the first and last chapters, I was drawn to rereading the others as well. My impression was that despite the passage of the years, it could still be read with profit by graduate students today. With regard to the scientific study of the individual, the arguments remain timely and persuasive but certainly need retelling in light of our history over the past half-century.

Allport immediately sets the tone of his ideological position by referring to individuality as the supreme characteristic of human nature. He then contrasts this obvious bit of knowledge possessed by the ordinary person to the attitude exemplified in the sciences devoted to the study of life processes that he characterizes as one where "the very existence of the individual [is] somewhat of an embarrassment and [they] are disturbed by his intrusion into their domains" (1937, p. 3).

At the beginning of his last chapter, entitled "The Person in Psy-

Presented in the APA Symposium, "Fifty Years of Personality Psychology," August 28, 1987, New York, New York.

IRVING E. ALEXANDER • Department of Psychology, Duke University, Durham, North Carolina 27706.

Fifty Years of Personality Psychology, edited by Kenneth H. Craik *et al.* Plenum Press, New York, 1993.

chology," he attributes to the modern point of view (undoubtedly his own) the demand that "psychology expand its boundaries, revise its methods, and extend its concepts to accommodate, more hospitably than in the past, the study of the single concrete mental life" (1937, p. 549). In support of this position, he refers, in a footnote, to the definitions of psychology by Wundt, James, and Titchener, all stressing individuality, although he points out the discrepancy between their aims and their ultimate accounts of mental life. Ironically, this turned out to be largely true of Allport's work as well.

Allport's focus on the individual grew out of an antielementaristic stance. He did not want to study part processes but rather how things common to human kind were ultimately put together in any individual. In this sense, he was influenced by various theoretical positions arising in late nineteenth century and early twentieth century Germany, especially the "Verstehende Psychologie" of Dilthey and later Spranger (emphasizing value or meaning) and also the "personalism" of Wilhelm Stern. The dynamic holism of Gestalt psychology also captured his interest although its relationship to the individual was not clearly drawn until the work of Lewin. Finally, we cannot leave the issue of influence without mentioning psychoanalysis, which had its origin in neighboring Austria. Allport was intimately aware of the tenets of psychoanalytic theory and recognized its potentiality for studying the dynamic patterns of individual psychological existence. However, in this first chapter, he enumerates his antipathy toward the search in psychoanalysis for universal causes, its slavish acceptance of Freud's doctrine, its isolation from general psychology, its "one-sided" interest in the problems of psychopathology, and its overemphasis on the sexual motive and on the power of the unconscious. These unacceptable features kept Allport in an ambivalent posture toward Freudian theory. He certainly could not embrace the psychoanalytic position, especially as it related to the direct impact of early experience on later personality development, nor could he deny the importance of information resulting from the study of "unconscious" mechanisms. His solution, in part, was the doctrine of functional autonomy of motives, which reduced the all-embracing power of the original conditions surrounding drive acquisition. Without question, Allport imparted a clear and persuasive message that stressed the importance of the study of the individual to the growth of the understanding of human nature.

The growing strength of a personalistic position in American psychology by the end of the 1930s was obvious. In addition to Allport's clarion voice, a strong statement for the lawfulness of the individual had been made earlier in a brilliant essay by Kurt Lewin in 1930 entitled, "The Conflict between Aristotelian and Galilean Modes of Thought in Contemporary Psychology." In the very same period, the pioneering work of the group led by Henry A. Murray at the Harvard Psychological Clinic was in progress and culminated in their classic report, *Explorations in Personality*, published in 1938, the year after the publication of Allport's book. One powerful chapter in Murray's book contains the extensive descriptions of the results of investigation by multiple techniques, of a single human being, "Case History: Case of Earnst."

When one adds to these milestones the strong interest generated by the appearance of new techniques, the Rorschach (Rorschach, 1921) and the Thematic Apperception Test (Morgan & Murray, 1935), which had the promise of delineating dynamic individual profiles utilizing important personality dimensions, the day of the study of the individual appeared close at hand. Yet, here we are a half-century after Allport's treatise on personality appeared, not all that much farther along the path. Although there have been occasional voices continuing to remind us of this lamentable fact, the general climate in psychology as a discipline has been noticeably unresponsive over the years to the Allportian message until rather recently. I should like to reflect on why this might have been the case.

STUDY OF THE INDIVIDUAL: INHIBITING FORCES

The messages of Allport, Murray, and Lewin regarding the scientific legitimacy, utility, and interest in studying the individual were even more unusual since they were embedded in the social climate of the 1930s, a period whose disastrous economic impact placed particular emphasis on the common fate. Few escaped the ravages of the depression. Certainly at that time the plight of the individual so clearly delineated, nurtured, and protected in our society by the founding fathers was masked by the plight of the many. This particular attitude extended into the following decade fueled by the cooperative, group demands necessary to sustaining a critical, national war effort.

The immediate ramifications of World War II on the study of personality were powerful. Two major needs were quickly specified, both contained under the general umbrella of selection. One was concerned with the identification of the particularly fit (the selection of officers, pilots, special technicians, intelligence agents, etc.), which had formerly been the province of industrial psychologists—the matching of the worker to the job. The other focused on the identification of the particularly unfit, those unsuited psychologically to withstand the demands of a life in the military, a major concern of psychopathologists. The efforts that followed, extensions of the practices that already existed in psychometrics, personality assessment, and psychopathology, were directed away from any emphasis on the understanding of any individual *qua* individual and turned toward the specific question of whether any individual was a member or potential member of any particular designated class. Does he possess the critical attributes necessary to succeed as an airplane pilot? Can he stand the rigors of submarine duty? The ultimate outcome of such study, especially under the press of time, is likely to be the search for clues or signs (usually atomistic and unconnected, sometimes not easily explainable on logical grounds) that will improve a selection ratio. False positives are easily identifiable, false negatives especially in a buyer's market are easily forgotten. In any case, the study of the individual as a dynamic, functioning whole, is lost for presumably the good, utilitarian reasons of efficiency and cost. This was, in my estimation, one of the major impacts of those war years on the study of personality.

In the ensuing years, the study of personality was engulfed and largely dwarfed by the dramatic rise of the field of clinical psychology. One would have thought that its rapid growth as a special discipline might have held out the possibility of a rebirth of interest in the study of the individual. For a variety of reasons, however, this was not to be the case. Part of the difficulty can be traced to conflicting ideologies in the development of a discipline. Those conflicts were multiple. They existed in university departments, between clinical psychologists and their colleagues in more traditional areas of study. In other settings, they were interdisciplinary; power struggles occurred between clinical psychologists and the psychiatrists who administered the hospitals, clinics, and treatment programs in which practical skills were learned. Furthermore, there was strife among clinical psychologists themselves, who were variously split on the importance of training for research or practice in this newly emerging, burgeoning specialty.

Clinical psychology as a unique field was fostered by an anticipated national need: a returning population of young veterans who had been exposed for long periods of time to the stresses of combat and of military life. The need to train a whole new profession to deal with these acute and anticipated long-range problems became a governmental concern. Funds were appropriated and dispensed through the National Institute of Mental Health and the Veterans Administration to create or expand professions dealing with the problems of mental health and illness. One consequence of this effort was that personality as a field of study increased in prominence. Yet the barriers to individual study remained formidable. The training issues from a philosophical and practical standpoint were resolved early. Without professional schools designed to train clinical psychologists, as there were in medicine and social work, a training base had to be selected. Since those who had assumed leadership in this newly emerging field were trained in graduate departments of psychology, the locus of the training was assured. New graduate programs, handsomely supported by government subsidies, were introduced into somewhat reluctant but appropriately entrepreneurial traditional departments of psychology where research was conceived as an entirely nomothetic enterprise, largely experimentally based. The training model adopted for clinical psychology was that of the scientist–practitioner with nomothetic research as the accepted standard for clinical students and faculty alike. The critical messages emanating from the two major landlords with which clinical psychology had come to live—clinical psychiatry and academic psychology—were powerful enough to discourage any serious attempt to study the individual. Clinical psychiatry emphasized the assessment task in the service of medical-type diagnosis that led to nomothetic distinctions and fostered both therapeutic interventions and practical research based on this model. Academic psychology continued to regard the individual in a manner that Allport detested: as a source of "error variance," a constant disturbance in the search for general laws. Career incentives for idiographic research were minimal. For young faculty, idiographic interest seemed a likely road to academic oblivion since research funding for such studies was meager and publication outlets were limited; for graduate students it was an unlikely path to acceptable dissertation projects. These constraints were firmly established in the decade or two following World War II and have tended to restrict the growth of personological investigations ever since.

STUDY OF THE INDIVIDUAL: SUSTAINING FORCES

Given such constraints, one would have expected the ultimate disappearance of the study of the individual except when that could be accomplished by the method of nomothetic comparison. Although this pattern of investigation became dominant, fortunately it did not turn out to be the exclusive model and I should like to briefly trace what seemed to be some of the countervailing forces.

The largest of these remains the unabated curiosity that humans have about other people and about themselves. This interest is reflected both nomothetically and idiographically. Certainly we wish to know about people in general, about women and men, Russians and Chinese, the young and the old, the troubled and the untroubled. But we also want to know what single others who stir strong affects in us are like and how we can come to know with any reasonable degree of certainty how to detect what we wish to know about them. Probability statements about personality characteristics derived from comparative group data are not likely to satisfy that curiosity, since the primary or raw data of experience with individual people are too compelling and complex to be explained in that way.

On another level, though, despite the powerful impact of the spirit of the times in the psychology of the 1950s and 1960s, there remained a few voices who either emphasized the importance of the study of the individual or presented theoretical or methodological schemas that suggested frameworks for such study. Prominent exemplars were Robert White (*Lives in Progress*, 1952/1966/1975), Harry Murray ("American Icarus," 1955), Harold McCurdy (*The Personal World*, 1961), George Kelly (*The Psychology of Personal Constructs*, 1955), Allport (*Letters from Jenny*, 1965), Charles Dailey (*The Assessment of Lives*, 1971), M. B. Shapiro ("The Single Case in Clinical Psychological Research" 1966). Methodological paths were opened by Kelly's Rep Test (1955), Jack Block's development of Stephenson's Q technique (1961), and Julian Rotter's development of incomplete sentences methodology (Rotter & Rafferty, 1950). Many of these writers would probably not have described themselves as thoroughgoing personologists; nevertheless, their contributions helped to keep that tradition alive during a very difficult period.

The scene began to change in the 1970s heralded in part by Carlson's (1971) trenchant analysis of the role of the person in personality research. Within the period of a few years, there appeared a succession of papers introducing new analytical techniques or new applications of analytical techniques for the study of the individual. Rosenberg and Jones (1972) used factor analysis to interpret Theordore Drieser's work. Simonton (1975) introduced time-series analysis. In the ten years from 1967 to 1977, a number of volumes appeared devoted to design and analysis of studies employing the single case (Chassan, 1967/1979; Davidson & Costello, 1969; Hersen & Barlow, 1976; Kratochwil, 1978; Neufeld, 1977). The climate in psychology was becoming more receptive toward idiographic analysis. By 1979, Tomkins had already introduced some of the basic ideas of "script theory," a stance ideally suited for examining the psychological life of an individual, which Tomkins (1987, 1991, 1992) has continued to develop.

At roughly the same time, two psychological volumes appeared—one in psychology (Stolorow & Atwood, 1979) and one in philosophy (Scharfstein, 1980)—that examined the life work relationship of significant contributors to those disciplines. These works were reflective of the fact that psychobiographical analysis, long a scholarly outlet for those in the psychoanalytic tradition, was enjoying a more general rebirth largely stimulated by Erikson's work on Martin Luther (1958) and on Mahatma Gandhi (1969).

The past decade produced a continuation of this vein of interest in the study of the individual. Lamiell's (1981) cogent methodological criticisms of a group comparative approach to knowledge about any particular member of that group served a function similar to that served by Carlson's (1971) paper. He again reminded us that our interest in information about particular people could not be satisfied by the methods of data analyses we were employing. At this point one might wonder why the message about individuality and its importance has to be reintroduced periodically in the history of personality study. Perhaps the problem is similar to all others in which the cogency of the issue is clearly identified but no simple remedy is apparent. Under such conditions we tend to put the problem on the back burner, returning to study that which is customary, feasible, and economical, despite our implicit knowledge that the problems concerning the study of the individual remain largely unsolved.

The study of narratives, or life histories, certainly received positive impetus from the appearance of Runyan's (1982) important volume *Life Histories and Psychobiography*. In it he performed a great service by reviewing both the distant and more recent efforts in these areas. The book has rapidly become the standard introduction to the field. Its contents include not only discussions and critiques of cogent methodological issues, but also clear examples of sound use of data in psychobiographical analysis.

Within a few short years, the *Journal of Personality* (March 1988) devoted a special issue to studies employing life narrative material as basic data for general personality questions or for specific psychobiographical inquiry. The papers sufficiently varied in subject matter illustrated clearly the continuing and expanding interest in such research among personality psychologists. That psychobiography and individual life narrative study were not simply a scattered enterprise was further attested to by the formation in the mid-1980s of the Society for Personology, whose members meet annually to discuss research developments in this field.

THE CURRENT SITUATION

The year 1990 produced two books that further illustrate the increased receptivity for this kind of work in the study of personality. One, Dan McAdams's *The Person,* is cast in a textbook format but constitutes a rather wide departure from traditional personality texts. Although it reviews both theory and research in what has become the province of standard tomes in this area, its focus and major emphasis is on the understanding of the person and not simply of people per se. In this regard, he has devoted a sizable portion of the book, without neglecting traditional coverage, to both theory and research in the personological mode. The book is dedicated to both Allport and Murray. It is superbly written, filled with state-of-the-art literature, and should have a most positive influence on young people beginning the study of personality. The second, *Personology: Method and Content in Personality Assessment and Psychobiography,* by Alexander (1990), will by its title, if nothing else, legitimize the Allport and Murray heritage. It offers methodological guides to the analysis of personal data, reviews what may be critical in preparing young scholars for personological inquiry, and seeks further insights into the interplay between the life as lived and the work accomplished in the histories of Freud, Jung, and Sullivan.

While I have reported briefly on what I see as a revival of serious scholarly work in the personological tradition, I have focused almost exclusively on work emanating from the general area of personality. One cannot overlook the fact that the study of individual lives and their products exists in a variety of fields, both in psychology and in neighboring disciplines. The literature of child development and aging both reflect recent interest in linguistic analysis of individual subjects. Psychohistorical inquiry appears to be flourishing as evidenced by new journals devoted to this kind of inquiry. Certainly political analysts both in the popular press and biographical essays appear to be paying increasing attention to the effect of personality factors in the performance of political leaders. While the increase in scholarly activity is a positive sign, it also serves to point up the multiplicity of problems both theoretical and methodological that must be solved before such study will stand on firm, consensual grounds. Many of these issues are treated at length by Runyan (1982) and McAdams (1990). What role personality psychologists and personologists particularly will play in the development of this field of study will be critical to its essential success. Historians, political scientists, other social scientists, and even literary biographers are not likely to generate either the conceptual or methodological advances necessary to establish this line of inquiry on solid footing. They are more likely to borrow from psychology that which seems available and usable. The extreme emphasis on Freudian or Ericksonian interpretive schemas in psychobiographical work would lend testimony to this conjecture.

These remarks about the role of psychology in the future of personological study leads me to think about more structural and systemic matters. How does one obtain relevant training to do personological work? The answer turns out to be neither clear nor simple. There are no graduate or even postgraduate programs with designations that would lead one unequivocally to competency in the pursuit of personological goals. Interestingly enough, this has always been true in psychology even as far back as the golden days of the Harvard Psychological Clinic in which many of the leading personologists—White, Tomkins, Sanford, Rosenzweig, and MacKinnon—were trained. The usual training path for people with personological interests has been either through clinical psychology or psychoanalytic training programs. The closest institutional setting that could foster such a goal in the recent past was at the University of California, Berkeley, which through its Institute for Personality Assessment Research maintained a strong graduate program in personality.

The developments of recent years would seem to point toward the need for cross-disciplinary cooperation in the preparation of personological specialists. Whether there will be such interdisciplinary programs in the future is a question whose answer does not invite a great deal of optimism on my part. Programs in American education in order to be launched at the present time require rapid, face value, bottom-line payoffs, or else must be entirely self-supporting. The study of single human beings is complex, time consuming, and not always certain to include obvious, immediate benefits. If my analysis is correct, it is very likely that as in the past personologists will develop slowly and in their own unique ways.

REFERENCES

Alexander, I. E. (1990). *Personology: Method and content in personality assessment and psychobiology.* Durham, NC: Duke University Press.

Allport, G. W. (1937). *Personality: A psychological interpretation.* New York: Holt.

Allport, G. W. (1942). *The use of personal documents in psychological science.* New York: Social Science Research Council.

Allport, G. W. (1965). *Letters from Jenny.* New York: Harcourt, Brace and World.

Block, J. (1961). *The Q-sort method in personality assessment and psychiatric research.* Springfield, IL: Thomas.

Carlson, R. (1971). Where is the person in personality research? *Psychological Bulletin, 75,* 203–219.

Chassan, J. B. (1979). *Research design in clinical psychology and psychiatry* (2nd ed.). New York: Irvington. (Original work published 1967)

Dailey, C. A. (1971). *The assessment of lives.* San Francisco: Jossey-Bass.

Davidson, P. O., & Costello, C. G. (1969). *N=1: Experimental studies of single cases.* New York: Van Nostrand-Reinhold.

Erickson, E. H. (1958). *Young man Luther.* New York: Norton.

Erickson, E. H. (1969). *Gandhi's truth.* New York: Norton.

Hersen, M., & Barlow, D. H. (1976). *Single case experimental designs.* New York: Pergamon Press.

Kelly, G. A. (1955). *The psychology of personal constructs.* New York: Norton.

Kratochwil, T. R. (Ed.) (1978). *Single subject research.* New York: Academic Press.

Lamiell, J. T. (1981). Toward an idiothetic psychology of personality. *American Psychologist, 36,* 276–289.

Lewin, K. (1930). The conflict between Aristotelian and Galileian modes of thought in contemporary psychology. *Journal of General Psychology, 5,* 141–177.

McAdams, D. P. (1990). *The person: An introduction to personality psychology.* San Diego: Harcourt Brace Jovanovich.

McAdams, D. P., & Ochberg, R. L. (Eds.). (1988). *Psychobiography and life narratives.* Special issue of the *Journal of Personality, 56,* 1–326.

McCurdy, H. C. (1961). *The personal world.* New York: Harcourt, Brace and World.

Morgan, C. D., & Murray, H. A. (1935). A method for investigating fantasies: The Thematic Apperception Test. *Archives of Neurology and Psychiatry, 34,* 209–306.

Murray, H. A. (1955). American Icarus. In A. Burton & R. E. Harris (Eds.), *Clinical studies in personality* (Chapter XVIII). New York: Harper & Brothers.

Murray, H. A. (1938). *Explorations in personality.* New York: Oxford University Press.

Neufeld, R. W. (1977). *Clinical quantitative methods.* New York: Grune and Stratton.

Rorschach, H. (1921). *Psychodiagnostik.* Bern: Bircher.

Rosenberg, S., & Jones, R. (1972). A method for investigating and representing a person's implicit theory of personality: Theodore Dreiser's view of people. *Journal of Personality and Social Psychology, 22,* 372–386.

Rotter, J. B., & Rafferty, J. E. (1950). *Manual: The Rotter incomplete sentences blank.* New York: Psychological Corporation.

Runyan, W. McK. (1982). *Life histories and psychobiography.* New York: Oxford University Press.

Scharfstein, B. (1980). *The philosophers: Their lives and the nature of their thought.* New York: Oxford University Press.

Shapiro, M. B. (1966). The single case in clinical psychological research. *Journal of General Psychology, 74,* 3–23.

Simonton, D. K. (1975). Sociocultural context of individual creativity: A trans-historical time-series analysis. *Journal of Personality and Social Psychology, 32,* 1119–1133.

Stolorow, R. D., & Atwood, G. E. (1979). *Faces in a cloud: Subjectivity in personality theory.* New York: Aronson.

Tomkins, S. S. (1979). Script theory: Differential magnification of affects. In H. E. Howe & R. A. Dienstbier (Eds.), *Nebraska Symposium on Motivation* (Vol. 26, pp. 00–00). Lincoln: University of Nebraska Press.

Tomkins, S. S. (1987). Script theory. In J. Aronoff, A. I. Rabin, & R. A. Zucker (Eds.), *The emergence of personality* (pp. 147–216). New York: Springer.

Tomkins, S. S. (1991). Affect, imagery, consciousness: The negative affects—anger and fear (Vol. 3). New York: Springer.

Tomkins, S. S. (1992). Affect, imagery, consciousness: Cognition—duplication and transformation of information (Vol. 4). New York: Springer.

White, R. W. (1975). *Lives in progress.* New York: Holt, Rinehart and Winston. (Original work published 1952; subsequent publication 1966)

CHAPTER NINE

Describing Lives
Gordon Allport and the "Science" of Personality

BERTRAM J. COHLER

No one has approached the task of describing lives with greater humility than Gordon Allport, whose contributions have been so important in shaping contemporary psychological inquiry. At the time of his death, in 1967, he was a preeminent figure in the human sciences; his work encompassed social psychology and social ethics as well as personality inquiry. He largely fashioned the concept of social attitudes, and his conjectures about the ways these determine our actions have led to numerous studies of attitude–behavior relations. His integrative work, *The Nature of Prejudice* (1954b), illustrated how multiple perspectives could be brought usefully to bear on a social problem. His historical survey [in the *Handbook of Social Psychology* (1954a) and reprinted in the two editions that followed] has edified numerous psychologists and sociologists and promises to retain its status as a basic source well into the twenty-first century.

Allport identified the central issues regarding both methods of study and substantive areas of inquiry in social psychology. However, he is best known for his contributions to the study of the person. Reviewing the history of personality psychology, Craik (1986) suggests that Allport's 1937 text, along with Stagner's (which appeared in the same year), had much to do with advancing the study of personality from a

BERTRAM J. COHLER • Committee on Human Development, University of Chicago, Chicago, Illinois 60637.

Fifty Years of Personality Psychology, edited by Kenneth H. Craik *et al.* Plenum Press, New York, 1993.

"preidentity" phase to the status of a recognized subdiscipline within psychology. Allport understood the conceptual challenges confronting students of personality; and he skillfully formulated many of the problems that personality research has addressed in the past half-century. Owing partly to Allport's clear and provocative presentation of the central issues, we are now beginning to make a bit of headway on some of them, as documented by several accounts in this volume. To appreciate Allport's vision as a personality theorist, one can compare his early construal of an issue (cross-situational consistency, for example) with today's state-of-the-art achievements on that issue (see Chapter 17, this volume, for a discussion of current theory and research on consistency). On most issues, Allport poses the problem in a way that invites research; and on many issues, there has been research progress.

Allport was an action psychologist. Concerned that psychology should make enduring contributions toward understanding social life and relieving social conflict, he sought to understand the means by which conflict could be reduced within the community and nation and in resolution of international tensions. He was also concerned with the integration of American and European psychology, forging new initiatives for study among psychologists of many nations. His continuing interest in Continental philosophy and psychology led to dialogues with clinicians; he fostered an alliance between existential phenomenology and psychology by taking seriously the works of Binswanger, Victor Frankl, and others. This "third force" [as Allport, following Maslow (1954), described existential psychology] was seen as an alternative to behaviorism and reductionistic psychoanalysis, the two systems of psychology that dominated Western psychology in the decade following World War II. Allport possessed a good knowledge of philosophy. His use of phenomenology may have initially limited his impact in the area of personality. From the vantage point of 1990, though, it is obvious that the phenomenological perspective has exerted significant long-term influences on personality psychology with regard to method as well as content.

Notable features of Allport's career included a continuing commitment to the empirical study of personality processes and a readiness to explore various philosophical approaches. His writings rank among the most comprehensive accounts of the complex relationship between person and social context, including the extent to which understanding of both self and others might be influenced by situational variables. In view of Holt's (1962/1978) critique to the effect that Allport was not a systems theorist, it is interesting to note that much of Allport's discussion of the interplay between person and social context anticipates a systems view. Indeed, in the 1961 revision of Allport's textbook, his main criticism of Stagner's approach is that it places too much emphasis on homeostasis. Allport maintained that Stagner, like many other psychologists at that time, was overly concerned with motivation as a tension-reduction phenomenon and too unwilling to acknowledge the teleological aspects of personality:

> Most current theories of personality take full account of two of the requirements of an open system. They allow interchange of matter and energy, and they recognize the tendency of organisms to maintain an orderly arrangement of elements in a steady state. Thus they emphasize stability rather than growth, permanence rather than change, "uncertainty reduction" (information theory) and "coding" (cognitive theory) rather than creativity. In short, they emphasize *being* rather than *becoming*. Hence, most personality theorists are biologistic in the sense that they ascribe to personality only the two features of an open system that are clearly present in all living organisms. (Allport, 1960, p. 44)

Allport also suggested that Stagner's concept of trait was not operationally defensible, being based on too few indicators (Allport, 1961, p. 337). For this reason, Stagner's position (as presented in his 1951 *Psychological Review* article on homeostasis, for example) seemed likely to overestimate the amount of cross-situational consistency to be expected in a person's actions.

ALLPORT'S APPROACH TO THE STUDY OF THE PERSON

As one of Allport's students and graduate assistants, I had a good opportunity to observe Allport as a teacher and a scholar; I was particularly struck with the dignity and respect he accorded to others. His quotation from Spinoza, leading off *Pattern and Growth in Personality* (1961), is noteworthy: "I have made a ceaseless effort not to ridicule, not to bewail, nor to scorn human actions, but to understand them" (p. vii).

Allport and I did not always agree on the scope and methods of personality inquiry. Allport could not understand my fascination with psychoanalytic approaches to the study of lives; he viewed psychoanalysis as an unnecessarily reductive and restrictive approach. In retrospect, I can appreciate Allport's discomfort with psychoanalytic accounts of personality structure and development.

Allport recognized that portrayal of particular lives and studies of aggregates provided complementary approaches. However, he appeared to mistrust the very person-centered approach that he championed [a paradox noted also by Holt (1962/1978)]. During the course of my doctoral studies, a group of us became interested in the detailed tracking of particular lives over time and were spending much time examining interview and semistructured test data. When we met with Allport to discuss the issues involved in integrating interview and test results, he cautioned us that "idiography was no country for young men." I regarded this as more than a statement of political realities; it conveyed some of Allport's ambivalence regarding the approach that he had so long championed. On the other hand, discussing my fledgling efforts to create what ultimately became the first automated Minnesota Multiphasic Personality Inventory (MMPI) procedure, Allport cautioned me that we know far more about tests than we do about persons.

I should also add that there was some tension between Allport and the personnel of Harvard's Psychological Clinic, including Henry Murray and Robert W. White. A certain amount of rivalry or conflict was to be expected, with so many major figures in contemporary psychology working as colleagues on the same campus. But both Murray and White approached the study of lives from the clinical tradition, applying insights obtained from records of disordered lives in the construction of a theory of "normal" personality development. Allport was concerned directly and mainly with the "normal" personality; his approach relied on philosophical concepts (drawn largely from existentialism) and relevant findings from social and developmental psychology. Even so, Allport was distressed when informed that the *Journal of Abnormal and Social Psychology*, for which he had served as editor, was to become two separate journals; thus he may have believed that both "normal" and "abnormal" psychology could contribute importantly to the understanding of personality.

Allport offered some pointed criticisms of the personality tradition that Murray and his associates had pioneered. In the first place, Allport disagreed with Murray's distinction between traits and dispositions able to evoke action (so-called motives). While some dispositions may appear more central or pervasive in a person's life (so-called cardinal dispositions), Allport maintained that, although dispositions may vary in intensity, all dispositions were able to evoke action. In the second place, Allport disagreed with Murray's psychodynamic model of personality development. Allport particularly mistrusted the epigenetic approach to understanding lives, in which explanations of adult outcomes were inevitably and all too readily linked to presumed childhood origins based on a naive concept of critical period. To some extent,

Allport's notion of functional autonomy can be regarded as a protest against and a kind of replacement for epigenetic explanation.

From his very earliest writing, Allport was concerned with the coherence and integrity of self. He also recognized the constraints imposed on personality study by the fact that one person's attribution of meaning to a particular action need not correspond to another's, and he saw that multiple perspectives would be needed for exploring people's constructions of the world.

With the person—rather than behavior—as the focus of investigation, Allport addressed basic questions of method: What techniques are most appropriate for studying people's lives? Can we obtain a record of a subject's actions, life events, and experiences that simultaneously does justice to the coherence and integrity of the self? What sources of information are most useful for individuals? Which sources are best for aggregates?

The particular "documents of life" a psychologist opts to use will necessarily color his conclusions; and regardless of the documents one selects, problems will be posed by the relationship between subject and observer and the ever-present necessity of interpretation (Crapanzano, 1980; Freeman, 1985; Ricoeur, 1971a, 1971b, 1980, 1981). In these respects, the study of personality differs fundamentally from the natural sciences:

> ... the crisis of social science concerns the nature of investigation itself. The conception of the human sciences as somehow necessarily destined to follow the path of the modern investigation of nature is at the root of this crisis. (Rabinow & Sullivan, 1979, p. 4)

The Interpretive Perspective

Charles Taylor (1985) traces the history of the modern interpretive perspective from the nineteenth-century German philosopher Dilthey through Windelband and Spranger, noting that its present resurgence is due largely to the work of Ricoeur (1971a, 1971b) and Habermas (1971). A major intellectual impetus for this tradition has been the work of the same European scholars who formulated the concept of human sciences to refer to those social sciences that focus on issues of meaning and intent and whom Allport studied early in his career. Upon receiving his doctoral degree in 1922, Allport was awarded a Sheldon traveling fellowship and spent the next two years in Germany and England, where he worked with Stern and studied the writings of Dilthey, Windelband, and Spranger. One product of this effort was the Allport–Vernon (1931) *A Study of Values*.

In "The Study of Personality by the Intuitive Method" (Allport, 1929), a little known but important paper, Allport discussed the contributions of German psychologists pioneering the *Geisteswissenschaften* with their emphasis on *verstehen* methods. He advocated an interpretive methodology:

> The rigid methods employed in the current psychological analysis of personality are prescribed in deliberate imitation of the natural sciences. Whatever the gains may have been, this subservience has resulted in the conviction on the part of many that such methods are insufficient, and that there is a need, especially in dealing with personality, of what Jaspers has called a "psychological psychology." (p. 17)

Reviewing the contributions of Croce, Bergson, Spranger, and others, Allport called for renewed study of personality as both an art and a science. I interpret Allport's use of the word "art" to refer to empathic (*verstehen*) understanding, and the word "science" to refer to disciplined scholarly inquiry focusing on meaning [in which "the image of the man is never lost; it is merely brought into focus" (P. 21)]. Thus Allport anticipated the "interpretive turn" of social science in the second half of the twentieth century (Rabinow & Sullivan, 1979), presenting a persuasive argument against the possibility of a value-free, fully objective psychology of personality.

THE INTERPRETIVE TURN AND THE NOMOTHETIC–IDIOGRAPHIC DEBATE

The Continental phenomenologists and psychologists whose writings seem to have influenced Allport's views on the necessity of interpretation in the social sciences probably provided some of the inspiration for his focus on the study of the person as well. The nomothesis–idiography distinction so important in Allport's work had been elucidated in Windelband's 1904 monograph on history and natural science. History was an interpretive discipline based on more or less singular events, whereas natural science could be nomothetic and deal with aggregated cases.

There has been a continuing controversy in psychology about the relative merits of nomothetic versus idiographic approaches. Holt (1978), for example, suggested that there is a lawfulness to people's lives; in broad outline, the course of each person's life is guided by this aggregate lawfulness. Therefore, the psychologist should in principle be able correctly to infer from the individual to the aggregate, and vice versa. In spite of its logical defensibility, however, Holt's treatment of the problem held little interest for Allport: It did not fully address the rich distinction laid out by Windelband.

Allport (1962) advocated a "morphogenic" perspective, which presumed (1) a unique organization or structure of personality within each person, and (2) no uniqueness of elements (i.e., traits) of which the structure was composed. He was more concerned with advancing the morphogenic point of view than with predicting particular actions, demonstrating behavioral regularity, or highlighting the idiography–nomothesis polarity as initially portrayed by Windelband.

PERSONAL DOCUMENTS

There is now much debate regarding use of personal documents in the study of persons. The issues in dispute include the representativeness of particular life history documents for a particular life, how best to define units in analyzing documents, and the extent to which one may generalize from particular lives to larger groups (Rosenwald, 1988; Runyan, 1982, 1988; Stewart *et al.*, 1988; Weintraub, 1975). Allport was aware of these issues but not centrally interested in them. Rather, he sought to adduce support for his morphogenic view: He hoped to demonstrate that the structure of each person's life, though describable in terms of the same elements assessed via the same methods as anyone else's, was in some important respect unique.

Many of those who have recently discussed the idiography–nomothesis problem in psychology arrive at a position similar to Allport's. Bem (1983), for example, says

> I believe a successful interactional theory . . . is not likely to be idiographic, but it will be morphogenic or person centered. That is, it will not invoke a unique set of variables for characterizing each person . . . but it *will* be concerned with the unique salience and configuration of a common set of variables within the person rather than with the relative standing of persons across those variables. (p. 573)

New methodologies developed for the study of individual lives are also compatible with the morphogenic perspective. Hogan's (1978, 1980, 1981) treatment of career sequences, Chiriboga's (1978) life chart, and Runyan's (1982) portrayal of stage–state analysis are particularly good examples. Although persons share conceptual timetables of optimal development and evaluate their own progress in terms of these (Roth, 1963), the manner in which they negotiate their individual careers shows marked variation as a function of cohort, social status, ethnicity, and other social factors. Little's (1983) concept of personal projects and his method of quantifying one's progress toward completion of such projects are also consistent with the morphogenic approach and can be extended into a life course perspective.

The array of "idiographic" methods that have been explored over the years is reviewed by Runyan (1983). Although they all have potential utility as morphogenic measures, Allport was most comfortable with content analysis of written documents; he liked the fact that these data provided contexts and configurations in which individual traits could be discerned. Although such traits do not permit comparisons across persons ("common" traits fulfill this role), idiographic study is valuable because it enables us to contemplate the structure and coherence of a particular personality (i.e., to define someone's "personal disposition"). If the available documents span an appreciable length of time, this method may also reveal at least some threads of the fabric of continuity that Allport expected to find in a person's life.

In a well-known content analysis, 172 letters written by "Jenny," the mother of Allport's college roommate, were read by clinical judges, who ascribed traits to her on the basis of common sense. "Many of the selected trait names were obviously synonymous, and nearly all fell readily into eight clusters" (Allport, 1966, p. 7). Years later, the same letters were content coded by other judges; factor analysis of their contents yielded seven factors, six of which corresponded to one of the clusters obtained from the original group of clinicians. Allport concludes that although " . . . there is no possibility in this case of obtaining external validation for the diagnosis reached . . . We can say that the direct commonsense perception of Jenny's nature is validated by quantification, coding, and factoring" (1966, pp. 8, 9). In other words, although it is clear what these letters signify about Jenny's nature, they constitute only one source of data. Allport tacitly acknowledges that some significant convergence among different kinds of evidence would provide a more persuasive account of her personal dispositions.

Similarity between the conclusions arising from these two "readings" of Jenny's letters is presented as a tour de force of idiographic analysis. Its results could be useful for nomothetic investigations, too, in that the traits dependably ascribed to Jenny might turn out to be applicable to the description of others as well. Whereas idiographic analysis permits identification of individual traits (which may or may not be useful in describing someone else), nomothetic studies demand that common traits (those which apply to just about everyone) be assessed. The objective of nomothetic work—comparisons among subjects—is meaningful only for common traits.

ALLPORT'S CONSTRUAL OF PERSONALITY STRUCTURE

Allport opposed the mechanistic "drive" theories of his time and those developmental theories that postulated strong links between early childhood experiences and one's adult personality. His psychology is a reaction against behavioristic interpretations (e.g., Miller & Dollard, 1941), which regarded personality as sets of habits or behavior tendencies specific to the particular situations in which they were learned, as well as against those psychoanalytic theories of development that presume powerful and long-lasting motivational consequences of the child's mastering of developmental tasks.

The formulation devised by Allport designates *traits* as the units in terms of which personality is to be described and the *proprium* to account for the individual's sense of selfhood.

TRAITS

Allport based his concept of trait on work by the German type theorist William Stern, whose 1921 textbook on differential psychology Allport had read during his postdoctoral studies in Europe (Evans, 1970) (it is also noteworthy that Allport's books contain numerous references to Stern). Allport's definition changed only slightly over the years and always carried an appeal to physiology: A trait is "a neural disposition of complex order, [which] may be expected to show motivational, inhibitory, and selective effects on specific courses of conduct" (1937, p. 319) and "a neuropsychic structure having the capacity to render many stimuli functionally equivalent, and to initiate and guide equivalent (meaningfully consistent) forms of adaptive and expressive behavior" (1961, p. 347).

In the 1961 edition of his textbook, Allport attempted to specify wherein traits differed from other forms of response readiness or determining tendencies of personality, such as habits (which are less general than traits) and attitudes (which have an object of reference and a value component, pro or con, whereas traits lack both). There are common traits, distributed in an approximately normal manner within a culture, and personal (or individual) traits, which are unique in their organization and interrelationships within the person. Personal traits vary in content from one individual to another and vary in salience within the individual; there are cardinal traits (roughly equivalent to Murray's unity thema), central traits, and secondary traits. Allport is less concerned with issues of intention or motivation than with detailed description; what is important about personal dispositions is their organization within the individual rather than whether they are instrumental or motivational. Indeed, the definition of personal disposition (Allport, 1961, p. 373) is virtually identical with the definition of trait (p. 347), except for a parenthetical addition of the phrase "peculiar to the individual." Morphogenic study, the mapping of personal dispositions in terms of their salience and interconnectedness, is a means of achieving comparatively full knowledge of another person.

Interconnectedness is clearly of prime importance. If the theory cannot specify how the elements go together, it ends by portraying the person as little more than a bundle of traits, some highly salient, some less salient. A theory of personality ought to account for one's feeling of identity or at least attempt to explain how it is that most people achieve and maintain a sense of coherence or integrity of experience.

REALIZATION OF PERSONAL INTEGRITY: THE PROPRIUM

The past two decades have seen an appreciable shift toward subjectivism in personality psychology. This trend has led to a resurgence of interest in the self (including self-esteem) and in phenomenological approaches to personality. The focus is now on subjective organization of experience; there has been a dramatic turning away from the behavioral tradition. Concern with overt actions and their consequences has been replaced, to a large extent, by concern with the ways persons construct meaning in their lives. A partial list of illustrative topics includes the origins and functions of plans and intentions (Ainlay, 1986); autobiographical memory (Rubin, 1986) and its incessant revision (Greenwald, 1980); the social construction of narratives (Elder *et al.*, 1984); wishes, goals, strivings, and projects (Emmons, 1989; Little, 1983); maintenance of self-congruity in the face of inconsistent or dissonant information (Sirgy, 1986); and the ways in which we formulate the meanings of our actions (Wegner & Vallacher, 1987).

Within psychoanalysis, concern has shifted from study of experience-distant concepts derived by analogy from experimental psychology (such as ego functions or processes) to the experience–near realm, focusing on determinants of sense of coherence and capacity for solace. Theorists as diverse as W. D. Winnicott (1965), George Klein (1976), and Heinz Kohut (1971, 1977) have sought to describe dynamics of the process by which one maintains a sense of personal integrity. Within child psychology, works by Kagan (1980, 1981) and Kegan (1982) present constructive–developmental perspectives highlighting the emergence of selfhood.

Lasch (1979) views this emerging focus on subjective experience as a sign of the increased narcissism of our time (reflected in the past decade by proliferation of popular magazines such as *Self*, as well as in other media). However, it is more likely that popular culture, influenced perhaps by psychological research and/or consumer research, has come to appreciate the importance of understanding the means by which the individual realizes personal integration and maintains positive morale. Indeed, the study of the origins and vicissitudes of self–regard (topics considered under the heading of "proprium" in Allport's work) is among the central concerns of the contemporary psychology of personality. Much of this current interest in the self was anticipated by Allport in the two editions of his text.

Allport was much influenced by William James. In the 1937 edition of his personality text, Allport used the concepts and terminology (e.g., "consciousness of self") of James's classic *The Principles of Psychology* (1890/1918, Vol. 1., p. 336) and viewed the self—as James did—as a unity of consciousness representing personal identity, continuous though continually changing. In distinguishing between bodily and social self and in dealing with self-preservation and sense of integrity, Allport also echoes James's earlier formulation of the same concepts.

The 1961 edition of Allport's text presents a different account of the self, one that elaborates James's definition of the self as a "fighter for ends." Here, Allport introduces a new concept, the proprium, which includes the self as both knower and object of knowledge. Propriate striving [which subsumes "directedness" and "intentionality," but is at the same time a dynamic unifying phenomenon, "the cement holding a life together," (p. 126)] dictates our patterns of self-involvement as opposed to mere task involvement. Our sense of self arises from the proprium; propriate strivings are important determinants of "attention, judgment, memory, motivation, aspiration level, productivity, and the operation of personality traits" (p. 128), as well as of our reactions to personally relevant consequences of our acts.

Other propriate states, such as self-esteem and self-image, influence the expression of strivings and the ways we respond to events that befall us. Certain patterns of propriate states, says Allport, are recognizable as pangs of conscience, feelings of inferiority, or a sense of obligation (1961, pp. 134–138).

During the past three decades, efforts by psychologists of various persuasions have brought personal integrity (and closely related topics, such as self-esteem) to a prominent position in the study of personality. The psychoanalysts Kohut (1977, 1984) and Klein (1976), the survey researcher Morris Rosenberg (1979), the cognitive–experiential theorist Epstein (1980, 1981), the social-learning theorist Bandura (1982), and the social psychologists Gergen and Gergen (1983) and Antonovsky (1979, 1987) are just a few of the many writers whose descriptions of the self are highly compatible with Allport's 1961 statement. The writings of Klein and Kohut are perhaps the clearest examples. Klein postulates the existence of an active self that functions as an integrator or synthesizer of one's experiences; when it is operating effectively, the person has a sense of continuity, coherence, and integrity—experience is rendered "self-syntonic." Perceived coherence is by no means a luxury, though. Kohut has documented the impact on lives of the failure to maintain it: People who lack a coherent narrative of the course of their lives report feelings of depletion and low morale. They sometimes resort to disavowal or disowning of their actions in order to maintain a consistent self-narrative, but this is a psychologically risky expedient because it often leads to a sense of fragmentation.

I do not wish to imply that all the self theorists took their cue from Allport's concept of the proprium. They may well have come by their ideas independently or gotten them from others (in 1951, for example, both Carl Rogers and Jean Piaget published books specifying the importance of congruity between percepts and self-structures or schemata). Though Allport was a penetrating thinker and writer, like other scholars he was also both product and agent of the *Zeitgeist*. His works need to be understood in historical perspective as well as on their own merits. I want to suggest that Allport was one of the creators of the *Zeitgeist* of academic psychology in the second half of the twentieth century; as such, it is likely that he influenced some of the self theorists who were his contemporaries and some of those who followed.

CONCLUSIONS

Allport's primary contribution to the study of the person may be less a matter of theoretical notions, methodological prescriptions, or empirical work than of his uncanny ability to comprehend the major issues in the field. As early as his first papers, Allport was aware of the fundamental problems confronting those who wished to study persons, such as the problem of distinguishing between text and interpretation, the advantages and drawbacks of individual difference formulations in the study of personality structure, the fact that traits as well as environments were ever-changing, and the challenges of accounting for continuity and change in lives over time. In his 1937 textbook, Allport was already protesting the view that childhood experiences inevitably shaped one's destiny; he maintained instead that one's own definition of the meaning of self was a powerful factor in determining long-term outcomes.

Concepts such as functional autonomy and propriate strivings were created to account for phenomena of growth and development, change and stability over time and the creative capacities that sometimes enabled individuals to overcome adversity. Allport was able to foresee shifts within both behaviorism and psychoanalysis away from emphasis on the person's reactive tendencies and toward emphasis on the processes by which morale is maintained and the sense of personal congruence is enhanced. And he was able to make some telling contributions of his own, which made it more certain that these shifts in the dominant paradigms of the mid-twentieth century would actually come about.

REFERENCES

Ainlay, S. C. (1986). The encounter with phenomenology. In J. D. Hunter & S. C. Ainlay (Eds.), *Making sense of modern times: Peter L. Berger and the vision of interpretive sociology* (pp. 31–56). New York: Routledge & Kegan Paul.

Allport, G. W. (1929). The study of personality by the intuitive method: An experiment in teaching from *The Locomotive God*. *Journal of Abnormal and Social Psychology, 24*, 14–27.

Allport, G. W. (1937). *Personality: A psychological interpretation.* New York: Holt, Rinehart and Winston.

Allport, G. W. (1954a). The historical background of modern social psychology. In G. Lindzey (Ed.), *Handbook of social psychology* (1st ed., Vol. 1, p. 3–56). Reading, MA: Addison-Wesley.

Allport, G. W. (1954b). *The nature of prejudice.* Cambridge, MA: Addison-Wesley.

Allport, G. W. (1960). *Personality and the social encounter.* Boston: Beacon Press.

Allport, G. W. (1961). *Pattern and growth in personality.* New York: Holt, Rinehart and Winston.

Allport, G. W. (1962). The general and unique in psychological science. *Journal of Personality, 30*, 405–422.]

Allport, G. W. (1965). *Letters from Jenny.* New York: Harcourt, Brace and World.

Allport, G. W. (1966). Traits revisited. *American Psychologist, 21*,1–10.

Allport, G. W. (1968). *The person in psychology: Selected essays.* Boston: Beacon Press.

Allport, G. W., & Vernon, P. E. (1931). *A study of values.* Boston: Houghton Mifflin.

Antonovsky, A. (1979). *Health, stress, and coping.* San Francisco: Jossey-Bass.

Antonovsky, A. (1987). *Unraveling the mystery of health: How people manage stress and stay well.* San Francisco: Jossey-Bass.

Bandura, A. (1982). The psychology of chance encounter and life paths. *American Psychologist, 37*, 747–755.

Bem, D. (1983). Constructing a theory of the triple typology: Some (second) thoughts on nomothetic and idiographic approaches to personality. *Journal of Personality, 51*, 566–577.

Chiriboga, D. (1978). Evaluated time: A life-course perspective. *Journal of Gerontology, 33*, 388–393.

Craik, K. (1986). Personality research methods: An historical perspective. *Journal of Personality, 54,* 18–51.

Crapanzano, V. (1980). *Tuhami: Portrait of a Moroccan.* Chicago: University of Chicago Press.

Elder, Jr., G., Liker, J., & Cross, C. (1984). Parent–child behavior in the great depression: Life-course and intergenerational influences. In P. Baltes & O. G. Brim, Jr. (Eds.), *Life-span development and behavior* (Vol. 6, pp. 111–158). New York: Academic Press.]

Emmons, R. A. (1989). The personal striving approach to personality. In L. A. Pervin (Ed.), *Goal concepts in personality and social psychology* (pp. 87–126). Hillsdale, NJ: Erlbaum.

Epstein, S. (1980). The stability of behavior. II. Implications for psychological research. *American Psychologist, 35,* 790–806.

Epstein, S. (1981). The unity principle versus the reality and pleasure principles, *or* the tale of the scorpion and the frog. In M. Lynch, A. Norem-Hebeisen, & K. J. Gergen (Eds.), *Self-concept: Advances in theory and research* (pp. 27–37). Cambridge, MA: Ballinger/Harper & Row.

Evans, R. (1970). *Gordon Allport: The man and his ideas.* New York: Norton.

Freeman, M. (1985). Paul Ricoeur on interpretation. *Human Development, 28,* 295–312.

Gergen, K. 91982). *Toward Transformation of Social Knowledge.* New York: Academic Press.

Gergen, K., & Gergen, M. (1983). Narratives of the self. In T. Sarbin & K. Scheibe (Eds.), *Studies in Social Identity* (pp. 245–273). New York: Praeger.

Greenwald, A. G. (1980). The totalitarian ego: Fabrication and revision of personal history. *American Psychologist, 35,* 603–618.

Habermas, J. (1971). *Knowledge and human interests.* Boston: Beacon Press. (Original work published 1968)

Hogan, D. (1978). The variable order of events in the life course. *American Sociological Review, 43,* 573–586.

Hogan, D. (1980). The transition to adulthood as a career contingency. *American Sociological Review, 45,* 261–276.

Hogan, D. (1981). *Transitions and social change: The early lives of American men.* New York: Academic Press.

Holt, R. R. (1978). Individuality and generalization in the psychology of personality: A theoretical rationale for personality assessment and research. In R. R. Holt (Ed.), *Methods in clinical psychology: Projective assessment* (Vol. 1, pp. 5–29). New York: Plenum Press. (Original work published 1962)

James, W. (1918). *The principles of psychology.* New York: Holt. (Two volumes; original work published 1890)

Kagan, J. (1980). Perspective on continuity. In O. G. Brim, Jr. & J. Kagan (Eds.), *Constancy and change in human development.* Cambridge, MA: Harvard University Press.

Kagan, J. (1981). *The second year: The emergence of self-awareness.* Cambridge, MA: Harvard University Press.

Kegan, R. (1982). *The evolving self: Problem and process in human development.* Cambridge, MA: Harvard University Press.

Klein, G. (1976). *Psychoanalytic theory: An exploration of essentials.* New York: International Universities Press.

Kohut, H. (1971). *The analysis of the self: A systematic approach to the psychoanalytic treatment of narcissistic personality disorders* (Monograph 1 of the Psychoanalytic Study of the Child Series). New York: International Universities Press.

Kohut, H. (1973). The psychoanalyst in the community of scholars. *The Annual for Psychoanalysis, 3*, 341–370.

Kohut, H. (1977). *The restoration of the self.* New York: International Universities Press.

Kohut, H. (1984). How Does Psychoanalysis Cure? (Eds. A. Goldberg & P. Stepansky) Chicago: University of Chicago Press.

Lasch, C. (1979). *The culture of narcissism: American life in an age of diminishing expectations.* New York: Norton.

Little, B. (1983). Personal projects: A rationale and method for investigation. *Environment and Behavior, 15*, 273–309.

Maslow, A. (1954). *Motivation and personality.* New York: Harper & Row.

Miller, N., & Dollard, J. (1941). *Social learning and imitation.* New Haven: Yale University Press.

Piaget, J. (1951). *The psychology of intelligence.* London: Routledge & Kegan Paul.

Rabinow, P., & Sullivan, W. (1979). The interpretive turn: Emergence of an approach. In P. Rabinow & W. Sullivan (Eds.), *Interpretive social science: A reader* (pp. 1–24). Berkeley: University of California Press.

Ricoeur, P. (1971a). The model of the text: Meaningful action considered as text. *Social Research, 38*, 529–562.

Ricoeur, P. (1971b/1991). What is a text? Explanation and understanding. In K. Blamey & J. B. Thompson (Eds. and Trans.), *From text to action: Essays in hermeneutics* (Vol. II, pp. 105–124). Evanston, IL: Northwestern University Press.

Rogers, C. R. (1951). *Client-centered therapy; its current practice, implications, and theory.* Boston: Houghton Mifflin.

Rosenberg, M. (1979). *Conceiving the self.* New York: Basic Books.

Rosenwald, G. (1988). A theory of multiple-case research. In D. McAdams & R. Ochberg (Eds.), *Psychobiography and life narratives* (pp. 239–264). Durham, NC: Duke University Press.

Roth, J. (1963). *Timetables.* Indianapolis: Bobbs-Merrill.

Rubin, D. (Ed.) (1986). *Autobiographical memory.* New York: Cambridge University Press.

Runyan, W. M. (1982). *Life histories and psychobiography.* New York: Oxford University Press.

Runyan, W. M. (1983). Idiographic goals and methods in the study of lives. *Journal of Personality, 51*, 413–437.

Runyan, W. M. (1988). A historical and conceptual background to psychohistory. In W. M. Runyan (Ed.), *Psychology and historical interpretation* (pp. 3–60). New York: Oxford University Press.

Sirgy, M. J. (1986). *Self-congruity: Toward a theory of personality and cybernetics.* New York: Praeger.

Stagner, R. (1937). *Psychology of personology.* New York: McGraw-Hill.

Stagner, R. (1951). Homeostasis as a unifying concept in personality theory. *Psychological Review, 58*, 5–17.

Stern, W. (1921). *Die differentielle psychologie.* Leipzig: Barth.

Stewart, A., Franz, C., & Layton, L. (1988). The changing self: Using personal documents to study lives. In D. McAdams & R. Ochberg (Eds.), *Psychobiography and life narratives* (pp. 41–74). Durham, NC: Duke University Press.

Taylor, C. (1985). Interpretation and the sciences of man. In C. Taylor (Ed.), *Philosophy and the human sciences: Philosophical papers* (Vol. 2, pp. 15–57). Cambridge: Cambridge University Press.

Wegner, D., & Vallacher, R. (1987). The trouble with action. *Social Cognition, 5,* 179–190.

Weintraub, K. J. (1975). Autobiography and historical circumstances. *Critical Inquiry, 1,* 821–848.

Windelband, W. (1904). *Geschicte und Naturwissenschaft.* Strassburg: Heitz.

Winnicott, D. W. (1965). Ego distortion in terms of the "true" and "false" self. In D. W. Winnicott (Ed.), *The maturational processes and the facilitating environment* (pp. 140–152). New York: International Universities Press.

CHAPTER TEN

Gordon Allport and "Letters from Jenny"

DAVID G. WINTER

As editor of the *Journal of Abnormal and Social Psychology* in 1946, Gordon W. Allport published "Letters from Jenny" (Anonymous, 1946). These letters were in fact selections and abridgements from a series of 301 letters written during the years 1926–1937 from "Jenny" (at the beginning of the correspondence, a 58-year-old widow) to "Glenn" (the college roommate of her son "Ross") and his wife "Isabel." Eighteen years later, Allport republished the letters as a book, adding a retrospective discussion by Isabel and interpretations of Jenny according to existential, depth psychological, and structural–dynamic theory (Allport, 1965). The published letters are about one third of the total correspondence.

In Allport's words, "these letters tell the tragic story of a mother–son relationship, and trace the course of a life beset by outward frustration and defeat" (Anonymous, 1946, p. 318). During the early years of the correspondence, Jenny's extreme possessiveness of her son erupted in periodic suspicions, recriminations, and hatred of any women in his life. Ross's unexpected death in 1929 (from complications of a mastoid infection and operation) was a turning point. Thereafter, according to Isabel's later account, "Jenny's hostility and suspicion turn into full-fledged paranoia, [while] the more benign qualities seem to diminish" (Allport, 1965, p. 156).

DAVID G. WINTER • Department of Psychology, University of Michigan, Ann Arbor, Michigan 48109.

Fifty Years of Personality Psychology, edited by Kenneth H. Craik *et al.* Plenum Press, New York, 1993.

To Allport, these letters were both personally fascinating and professionally useful as a teaching device:

> Speaking for myself I may say that I have found the Letters the most effective case material I have ever encountered for provoking fruitful class discussions of theories of personality. . . . I know of no other case material so rich and exciting and challenging for those who like to explore the mysteries of human nature, whether they be students of psychology or devotees of literature or simply observers of life. (1965, pp. vi, x)

Two of Allport's students carried out content analysis studies of the letters (Baldwin, 1941, 1942; Paige, 1964, 1966). In many personality textbooks (e.g., Hall & Lindzey, 1970, pp. 288–290; Peterson, 1988, p. 292; Phares, 1988, pp. 50, 256–257, 278; Ryckman, 1989, pp. 226–230, Scroggs, 1985, pp. 147–153), the letters are cited as the major (if not the only) example of Allport's concern for studying individual persons through the use of personal documents (Allport, 1942) and "idiographic" (later "morphogenic") methods (Allport, 1962).

GORDON ALLPORT AND "GLENN"

In publishing the letters, Allport identified Glenn and Isabel as "a married couple living and teaching in an eastern college town" (Editor's Introduction to Anonymous, 1946, p. 318). The obvious similarity to Allport's own life (academic positions at Dartmouth and then Harvard), as well as the phonetic similarity of "Glenn" and "Isabel" to "Gordon" and "Ada" (the first name of Allport's wife), naturally led many readers to wonder whether the letters were actually written to the Allports, but he repeatedly denied this. As an editor, he was vague about how he acquired the letters, noting only that Glenn and Isabel "made them available for editing, for analysis, and for publication" (1965, p. vi).

In fact, Gordon Allport and his wife Ada *were* "Glenn" and "Isabel," and "Jenny" actually was the mother of Allport's college roommate. This can be demonstrated in several ways. First, there is photographic evidence. According to the *Freshman Red Book* of the Harvard class of 1919 (Harvard Class of 1919, 1915), Gordon Allport lived in Gore Hall D-41 (now part of Winthrop House) in 1915–1916. The photograph of "Ross" published as the frontispiece in Allport (1965) is the same as the photograph of the only other occupant of that room. Accoding to Harvard University records, "Ross" and Gordon Allport also roomed together in Perkins Hall 30 during 1916–1917, after which Ross joined the United States Ambulance Service in World War I.

Second, the dates of moves of Glenn and Isabel and the birth of their first child match the actual details of the Allports' life. Moreover, all of the facts about "Ross" mentioned in the letters are consistent with the biographical details of Allport's roommate, as printed in the class of 1919 reports published by the Harvard Alumni Office: private preparatory school in Chicago, military service during 1917–1919, and various merchandising positions in New York up to his death.

In publishing the letters, Allport wrote that he disguised the names of all places (except New York and Chicago) and persons when he published the letters (1965, p. vi). For example, Ross is said to have attended Princeton, and Jenny's family of origin was said to be located in Montreal. In fact, however, Allport neglected to alter a few minor details, and these "slips" first suggested to me the real identities of the correspondents. (1) On August 27, 1926, Jenny wrote ironically that "This has been a wonderful week—Pres[iden]t Eliot gone—Valentino gone...." Charles W. Eliot, president of Harvard University from 1869 to 1909, died on August 22 (Rudolf Valentino, the movie star, died the next day), but surely this event would be of greater interest to the mother of a Harvard graduate than to the mother of a Princeton graduate. (2) On a Sunday in November 1929, Jenny wrote:

> Last night when coming home . . . my eye fell on the evening paper "Princeton 10—Yale 6." . . . How lovely for our beloved College to win again. Only 1 year ago yesterday Ross drove me to New Haven to the game. (Allport, 1965, p. 72)

In fact, 10–6 was the score of the Harvard–Yale game in 1929, and it was the Harvard–Yale game (not the Princeton–Yale game) that had been played in New Haven the previous year.

Ross's obituary in the Harvard Class of 1919 fourth report (issued in 1936) was signed by "G. W. A." (obviously Gordon Allport). It includes the following remembrance, which is both consistent with and yet quite different from the Ross of the letters:

> His classmates will remember [Ross] for his distinguished appearance and bearing, for his Irish love of argument, and for his persuasive speech. He took unfailing delight in the gentle pleasures of social and intellectual comradeship. Always prepared to challenge uncritical opinions held merely on the strength of tradition, he exerted a maturing influence on his associates such as might be expected from an instructor but scarcely from a fellow student. Although vigorous in argument, he never harbored grudges nor placed undue emphasis upon mere differences in opinion. He had many friends. (Harvard class of 1919, 1936, p. 189)

What a delicate task writing this obituary must have been for Gordon Allport! The occasion called for praising Ross; yet Allport was also regularly corresponding with Jenny, who kept pouring out her own ambivalent feelings and bitterness about Ross. In fact, Jenny read and edited what he wrote. (A draft of this obituary, with annotations in Jenny's handwriting, is preserved in the Allport papers in the Harvard University Archives.) The obituary concludes with a simple sentence that gives scarcely a hint of the Jenny and Ross saga of the *Letters:* "He is survived by his mother who resides in New York."

UNDERSTANDING THE CASE OF JENNY

While these details may make a diverting detective exercise, is it important to know that the Glenn and Isabel of *Letters from Jenny* were really Gordon and Ada Allport? Is it ethical to disclose these facts? Since Jenny, Ross, and all their relatives, as well as Gordon and Ada Allport, are long since dead, I do not believe that publishing this information violates any rights of privacy or other ethical standards.* In fact, I believe that establishing the identity of Glenn adds to our understanding of Jenny. Knowing that the letters were actually written to Gordon Allport enhances the value of his editorial comments on the case. Thus when he writes that "one might label [Jenny] as hysterical, overprotective, aggressive, asocial, extrapunitive, an isolate, paranoid, having a character disorder [and] extraordinarily expressive" (1965, p. viii), or when he suggests that Jenny might have had an "anal character" (p. 181), a "personally confused sex-identity" (p. 183), or "repressed *guilt*" (p. 184), we may be sure that his comments are based on his personal acquaintance of 22 years (1915–1937) as well as on his editorial study of the letters. Allport's quotations from various student analyses of Jenny (e.g., Allport, 1965, pp. 173, 174, 212, 220) can now be read as having the imprimatur of his own personal experience.

Yet as published, *Letters from Jenny* gives only a one-sided view of Jenny, Ross, and their relationships to Glenn and Isabel. Allport's editorial role necessarily gave him control of everything we know about Jenny. For example, we know nothing whatever of Glenn and Isabel's replies to her letters and how these replies might have affected what she wrote. In his introduction, Allport claimed that "what they wrote

---

* I have retained the pseudonyms "Jenny" and "Ross" because I do not see any reason to use their real names (although they are given in available records). I have used "Glenn" and "Gordon Allport" interchangeably.

to Jenny does not alter the relationship, nor does it affect the flow of the narrative" (1965, p. viii); but without examining both sides of the correspondence, we cannot evaluate such a claim.* Even Jenny's side is incomplete. For "purposes of publication," we are told, "the Letters have been abridged to approximately one-third their original length." Baldwin (1941, p. 19) states that originally there were 301 letters, of which 100 were used in his analysis; but the published book contains at least portions of over 150 letters. We know little about the selection process beyond Allport's vague statement that he "made a special effort to preserve the original proportion of subject matter" (1965, p. vi).† Since the unpublished parts of the correspondence are not in Allport's papers in the Harvard University Archives, we must assume that they were destroyed. Perhaps scattered references to "Jenny" will be found among Allport's other correspondence, teaching notes, or other personal papers that would shed more light on his feelings about the relationship.

Whatever Allport's reasons for editing, commenting on, and publishing the letters, we must realize that he was not a detached editorial observer, but rather a participant in a demanding and difficult relationship. Most readers, for example, find Jenny a difficult and double-binding correspondent, who demanded time and effort while playing on emotions and guilt. Christmas 1926 was an example. On December 15, 1926, she wrote, "Ask dear Isabel *not* to send any Christmas gift this year,

---

* Interestingly enough, Allport discussed these issues in his classic work on the use of personal documents in psychology:

> The use of letters in research ... is complicated by the necessity of considering the personality of the recipient as well as that of the sender, the relationship existing between the two, and the topics of thought that comprise the exchange of letters. (1942, p. 108)

† Baldwin gives the most detailed description of how this selection was made:

> The material eliminated was the personal information which would identify the characters, and most of the incidental chatter common in letters. This included thanks for gifts, answers to questions asked by the correspondents, and similar material. The remaining material in the letters included narratives of past and present experiences, comments on Jenny's attitude toward these experiences, and remarks about the people she met. A fair sample of this material was included in the selection. The selected set of letters was designed to give the same impression of Jenny as the original. (1942, pp. 165–166)

There is some confusion about the exact materials used by Baldwin (1941, 1942). According to Allport (1942, p. 46), Baldwin used the complete text of Jenny's letters, from the beginning through November 2, 1927, a period represented by only 35 whole or partial letters in *Letters from Jenny*. As noted above, Baldwin stated that he used 100 out of 301 letters.

but to send a note so I may receive it about Christmas time, in New York, and so not feel so desperately alone" (Allport, 1965, p. 24). Glenn and Isabel wisely ignored this request, and so on January 5 Jenny wrote, "Your Christmas letter and Christmas box were wonderful. One could never be quite forsaken or alone when one receives such things on Christmas Eve" (p. 26). Seven years later, she thanked Glenn and Isabel for a "splendid" St. Patrick's Day box, but then launched into two paragraphs of criticism: she didn't relish drinking "lukewarm thick tomato juice," the sardines should have been in individual tins, and the cheese was too soft (pp. 116–117).

Through the correspondence, she compelled attention to (if not acceptance of) her repeated vituperations against Ross, with whom Glenn and Isabel also corresponded (to judge from the two letters from Ross excerpted in Allport, 1965, pp. 64, 66). She begged their attention to her financial affairs and dispensed unsolicited and contradictory advice on how to live their own lives and how to raise their child. For Allport, then, publishing the letters and using them as teaching material may have satisfied motives arising out of this complex relationship.

"JENNY" AND ALLPORT'S THEORETICAL IDEAS

All theories are influenced by the theorist's personality and life experience. What part did Allport's experiences with Jenny and Ross play in his own theories? Without a complete study of Allport's life and times, it is impossible to evaluate how much Jenny and Ross were actual influences on his thinking versus how much they were merely effective illustrations of themes and ideas drawn from Allport's own beliefs, temperament, and external influences. Still, a close reading of the letters in conjunction with Allport's theoretical writings suggests some important connections or resonances—if not causal connections—between his experiences with Ross and Jenny on the one hand and some of his major contributions to personality theory on the other.

CONFLICT AND MEDIATION

For example, Allport has long been recognized as a major theorist of prejudice and conflict (see Allport, 1954). From Isabel's recollections, though, we get a vivid description of his practical efforts to mediate an awkward and potentially explosive situation:

> Glenn attended Ross's funeral and cremation, and spent an uncomfortable afternoon trying to keep peace between Jenny and the

fiancee. . . . On the way to the crematory Glenn sat between Jenny and the "chip" [Jenny's word for her son's wife] in the limousine. While the latter was decently silent Jenny kept sending barbed verbal darts across Glenn to her. (1965, p. 153)

Allport's discretion and sense of tact, familiar to those who (like the author) had the privilege of studying or working with him, come through in Isabel's recollection of the time Jenny inquired about moving to their town:

Our friendship would [have been] strained by an endless series of misunderstood actions, flare-ups of temper; and she would have no other target for her hostility than Glenn and myself. We knew that Jenny needed us, but with such a paranoid personality we knew also that our only hope (and hers) was to maintain a civilized but sympathetic distance. . . . So Glenn wrote a kind but frank reply, saying that our plans were uncertain, that my health was not too robust, and in general implying a firm No. We were far from certain how this "rejection" would be received. To our surprise and relief she accepted it without rancor, in fact even with sympathetic understanding (1965, pp. 153–154).

THE IDIOGRAPHIC APPROACH

One of Allport's major contributions to personality theory was the idiographic–nomothetic distinction—studying the unique structure of individuals versus studying general dimensions common to many people—and his related interest in developing idiographic (or morphogenic) methods to capture the uniqueness of the individual personality (Allport, 1962). No doubt the challenge of understanding Jenny—an extraordinary, intractable, and complex person—resonated with this theoretical emphasis on the individual case. Further, perhaps, the difficulty of understanding Jenny probably reinforced his doubts about the possibilities of reducing personality to a short list of universal dimensions (as he perceived Henry Murray, his contemporary at Harvard, to be attempting; see Murray, 1938). Allport's own words illustrate this connection:

Psychologists are on safe ground so long as they talk in abstractions about personality-in-general. Their real test comes when they attempt to explain (or guide or therapeutically treat) a single concrete life. In reflecting on the case of Jenny I find myself wishing that I could take refuge in vague generalizations, but invariably she pins me down with the unspoken challenge, "And what do you make of *me*?" And so, aware as I am of my audacity, I make bold to present this edition of the Letters. (1965, p. x)

Even at the end of his life, Allport wrote about Jenny in his own autobiography: "Here surely is a unique life, calling for psychological analysis and interpretation" (Allport, 1968a, p. 403).

Regardless of how much Jenny influenced Allport's idiographic concerns, his description and analyses of Jenny (1965, Chapters 5–9)—seven or eight major themes, each expressed in adjectives or phrases chosen both to capture the unique individual characteristics of the person and also to reveal whatever latent unities exist beneath superficially divergent behaviors—stands as a model of the Allportian method of personality assessment. His descriptive methods might be compared to art history (tracing the stylistic development of the individual) rather than chemistry (analyzing complex substance into a few basic elements). Allport actually developed such a comparison in a 1938 lecture that was published in a collection of papers on personality (Allport, 1960) while Murray explicitly used the chemistry analogy to describe his own approach (Murray, 1938, pp. 142–143).

THERAPEUTIC SKEPTICISM

Knowing his true role in the Jenny case, we can see in Allport's editorial discussion of the role of Glenn and Isabel a sense of personal powerlessness about the possibility of intervention:

> What Glenn and Isabel wrote to Jenny did not alter the relationship appreciably. Jenny wanted a pair of sympathetic listeners. Having found them she proceeded to pour out the story of her hopes, jealousies, striving and defeat. For eleven years Glenn and Isabel listened willingly but made no effective attempt to alter the life-drama being enacted before them. Indeed, they were powerless to do so. (Anonymous, 1946, p. 316)

While Allport may have *felt* powerless to alter Jenny's life, he did write letters recommending that she be admitted to a church-supported home, some 18 months after Ross's death.*

Allport's feelings of powerlessness to intervene in Jenny's life stand in sharp contrast to his committed activism in many other situations. Yet this powerlessness does echo his professional doubts about the possibility of deep-seated transformations of character through therapy. (Allport's own theory of personality, for example, has few explicit therapeutic implications.) In the introduction to the published letters, Allport asked of Jenny, "Could proper guidance or therapy at an appropriate

---

* Letters from Allport to D. B. Aldrich, April 26, 1931, Allport papers in the Harvard University Archives.

time have helped alter the rigid course of her conduct" (1965, p. viii)? In the end, he was pessimistic: "Glenn and Isabel made a good 'third ear' as does any helpful psychotherapist. But Jenny was incapable of advancing in insight because of the tenacity of her temperament and the set of her world-view" (1965, p. 218).

NORMAL AND ABNORMAL

Judging by his introduction to the book edition of the letters, Allport saw Jenny and Ross locked in the classic drama of Jocasta and Oedipus. Having asked "why [the letters] should be so stimulating and pedagogically effective," Allport then supplied his own answer:

> Every male reader is himself a son. . . . Therefore the bitter dilemma of Ross and his mother often seems to echo the reader's own personal (but usually milder) problem. Like a Greek tragedy the Letters have a universal appeal. (1965, p. vi)

Yet if Allport believed that Ross and Jenny enacted the universal Greek tragedy of Oedipus, in his writings on personality he usually took pains to delimit the universality of the complex to which Freud gave that name. In discussing interpretative autobiographical essays written by students in his courses, for example, he argued that Freudian theory had only limited usefulness (limited, as the following quotation suggests, to circumstances that were almost an exact replica of Jenny and Ross):

> Their Freudian interpretations seemed to fit well if and when the family situation in early life was disturbed. When the father was absent or ineffectual [Ross's father died before he was born], when the mother was notably aggressive, when there was deliberate sex stimulation within the family—in such cases, it seems that the Oedipal formula provides a good fit, together with all its theoretical accoutrements of identification, superego conflict, defense mechanisms, castration threats, and all the rest.
>
> When, on the other hand, the family life is reasonably normal and secure, a Freudian conceptualization seems forced and artificial. If we say, by way of rough estimate, that 60 per cent of the students try a Freudian conceptualization of their own cases, about 10 per cent turn out to be wholly convincing and theoretically appropriate. (1968b, p. 181)

This sharp discontinuity between normal and abnormal is another familiar feature of Allport's personality theory. His views on the role of unconscious defense mechanisms, the importance of early experience, and the usefulness of projective techniques all follow from this fundamental distinction. Two examples illustrate the point:

> I am fully aware of my heterodoxy in suggesting that there is, in a restricted sense, a discontinuity between normal and abnormal motivation, and that we need a theory that will recognize this fact.... There is still a world of difference, if not between normal and abnormal people, then between the healthy and unhealthy mechanisms involved in the development of motivation. (1953, p. 105)

> The issue, as we have said, is of the highest importance for personality theory. If we regard all the acquisitions of an adult (his altruism, his ideals, his mature tastes, and his "ought" conscience) as "secondary," or, as Freud has said, as "transparent sublimations" of id processes, we have an animalistic view of the nature of normal adult personality.... The point at issue, we repeat, is the relative importance of unconscious and conscious functions in forming and maintaining personality. (1961, pp. 148–149)

Elms (1972) described Allport's view of human nature as "the clean personality ... reject[ing] psychological data on such unsavory creatures as rats, children, and neurotics as being largely irrelevant to the understanding of the mature personality" (pp. 630–631). Actually, Allport did not deny the existence of unconscious wishes that distort reality and defeat rational striving. Rather, he was concerned to circumscribe their role, to limit their application, to "segregate" the normal and the abnormal. This is made clear in his final summing up of Jenny:

> We shall have to admit that in her personality neurotic processes took the upper hand. Narrowness, rigidity, inappropriateness marked her behavior. Compulsively she expressed her anger, having little tolerance for frustration. Almost always she dwelt on the past, rigidly and regressively.... If character neurosis is "inflexible self-centeredness" ... then Jenny stands diagnosed.... Toward the end of her life ... from the neurosis an actual psychosis seems to be developing. (1965, p. 221)

FUNCTIONAL AUTONOMY

At the theoretical level, Allport tried to reinforce the distinction between infantile–sexual–pathological and adult–ego–normal with the concept of "functional autonomy" of motives—that the motives that actually influence our everyday behavior are not (or are not any longer) derived from original "primitive" or "primary" drives. Functional autonomy is thus a mechanism by which adult personality processes can be segregated from their infantile roots. More formally, Allport described functional autonomy as an "acquired system of motivation in which the tensions involved are not of the same kind as the antecedent tensions from which the acquired system developed" (1961, p. 229). For Allport, functional autonomy was "an essential element to a sound theory of personality" (Evans, 1971, p. 29); yet for all his discussion over the years, it remains one of his most elusive and controversial concepts (see the discussion in Evans, 1971, pp. 29–39).

By Allport's own analysis quoted above, Jenny was not "functionally autonomous" in the usual sense of the term, for she did not show the mature, sound, "normal" behavior ordinarily connoted by that concept. Nevertheless, in his original paper on functional autonomy (published in the year that Jenny died), Allport illustrated the concept with a hypothetical example of a mother and child that bears a striking resemblance to Jenny and Ross:

> Many young mothers bear their children unwillingly, dismayed at the thought of the drudgery of the future. At first they may be indifferent to, or even hate, their offspring. . . . The only motives that hold such a mother to child-tending may be a *fear of what her critical neighbors will say* . . . a habit of doing any job well, or perhaps a *dim hope that the child will provide security for her in her old age.* . . . In later years not one of these original motives may operate. *The child may become incompetent, criminal, a disgrace to her, and far from serving as a staff for her declining years, he may continue to drain her resources and vitality. . . . She certainly feels no pride in such a child; yet she sticks to him.* (1937, p. 81, emphases added)

Allport used this example, so vividly reminiscent of Jenny, to illustrate functional autonomy, in that the mother's persistence is explained not by an "original" motive of maternality but rather by repeated child-tending behavior that in later years acts as an acquired motive. Yet while the behavior has become functionally autonomous, it is not necessarily adaptive, healthy, mature, or wise.

JENNY AND ROSS IN GORDON ALLPORT'S LIFE

What role did the relationships with Jenny and Ross play in Allport's own experience? Here again, without a complete biography it is difficult to distinguish influence from illustration, or causation from resonance. Still, a few themes can be identified as guides to further exploration.

JENNY AS MOTHER

As quoted above, Allport's introduction to the book edition of the letters suggests that he saw Jenny and Ross in universal terms as mother and son. In some respects, she was also a symbolic "mother" to Allport. For example, a St. Patrick's Day card sent by Jenny in his first year at college (preserved in a scrapbook of his college years) has the following inscription, along with a drawing decoration of four shamrocks*:

> St. Patrick's Day
> in the Morning, 1916
>
> To My Dear Mr. Allport,
>   With warmest St. Patrick's Day greeting from the very Irish Mother of his hyphenated room-mate.
>
> [J. G. Masterson]

Jenny clearly assumed a maternal relation to Glenn and Isabel. She usually addressed letters to "My dearest Boy" or "My dearest Boy and Girl." The published letters begin with Jenny entrusting Glenn with the final duties of a son (arranging her funeral and winding up her affairs), having transferred these duties from Ross because she could no longer "ever again believe one word that left his lips—to ever trust him, or rely on him, to have the smallest faith in him" (Allport, 1965, p. 14). Over the years, she freely offered "maternal" advice to Glenn and Isabel on topics such as hair styles, raising children, and traveling.

Did Jenny resemble Allport's own mother? His autobiography contains only one sentence about her: "My mother had been a school teacher and brought to her sons an eager sense of philosophical questing and the importance of searching for ultimate religious answers" (Allport, 1968a, p. 379). Does this sound like Jenny? Yes and no; they both seem to have had a philosophical bent and a "tenacious temperament," but Jenny's worldview was self-defeating (see Allport's final analysis of Jenny quoted above).

In an analysis of Allport's famous story of his 1920 encounter with Freud, Elms (1972) characterized Allport's father as concerned with "hard work and tight money," two themes with which Allport himself characterized Jenny's letters (1965, pp. 193–194, 201–202). If hard work and money concerns also applied to his own mother, then there are some further points of similarity between the two "mothers."

Allport's privately printed and circulated memoir of his own mother, entitled *The Quest of Nellie Wise Allport* (Allport, 1944), suggests that

---

* Reprinted by permission of the Harvard University Archives.

Nellie (his mother) and Jenny were both similar and different. Like Jenny, Nellie had a strong philosophical interest (but one that kept evolving rather than getting mired in the same self-defeating grooves), a strong sense of autonomy, and great sensitivity to beauty. Early religious training fostered in both women a sense of "unworthiness." In later years, however, Nellie's religious views, broadened with the study of anthroposophy, evolved into a sense of gratitude and serenity, whereas Jenny remained an embittered skeptic, tormented by self-hatred. Perhaps as a result, Nellie was generous and therefore generative, never putting "obstacles in the paths of others" (Allport, 1944, p. 27), while Jenny's *Letters* are the story of obstacles between mother and son.

Ross as Double

If Jenny was a "mother" to them both, then Ross and Gordon Allport were brothers—even closer, perhaps "doubles" (Rank, 1922/1971). Both were born in the Middle West less than a month apart (Ross on October 16, 1897, Allport on November 11). Both went east to Harvard. Both were admitted to college late [as Allport put it, "squeezing through the entrance tests given in Cambridge in early September;" (1968a, p. 380)]. They were roommates for two years. In an early letter, Jenny fondly recalled their first encounter in words that emphasize the brother–double theme:

> Such a lot of things have happened since you, Glenn dear, and Ross stood in the college office waiting to write on your exam. Tall, thin, pale boys, the world and life all before you—anxious, tense—a long time ago. If anyone had said then the day would come when you, Glenn dear, the pale, slim boy, would be the only protection of the other boy's mother, you would have been considerably surprised. (Allport, 1965, p. 20)

World War I

At the end of their sophomore year in the spring of 1917, however, their paths diverged. The United States entered World War I. Ross enlisted in the ambulance corps and went off to France. Returning in 1919, he finished college but was never able to settle down and establish himself. From 1920 until his death in 1929, Ross held and lost jobs with at least four different companies and even served in the Marines for a short time. As he wrote to Glenn shortly before his death, "I am worried about my job which seems shaky, and my life which seems futile" (Allport, 1965, p. 66). As a result of the war, he had become, as

Allport put it, a member of the "lost generation ... distorted, badly adjusted to old scenes and old ambitions" (Allport, 1965, p. 5).

For Gordon Allport, in contrast, "World War I dislocated my program only slightly" (1968a, p. 381). He stayed in college and graduated with his class in 1919. A year teaching English in Istanbul gave "freedom and novelty and [a] sense of achievement" (p. 383). There followed a fellowship for graduate study at Harvard, a traveling fellowship for two years in Germany (where he studied with Wertheimer, Köhler, Spranger, Stern, and Werner) and England. With the offer of an instructorship at Harvard and an invitation to develop a course in the new field of the "psychology of personality," he was clearly launched on a successful and distinguished career.

"Bad Son" and "Good Son"

The same divergence was reflected in their changing relationship to Jenny: Ross became the "bad" son, while Gordon Allport took his place as the "good" son. Two quotations from Jenny's letters make the point:

> What you say is sure to be the wise, and best, thing. You are such a good friend to me that I trust you implicitly—your good judgment, and your kindness. (May 3, 1927; Allport, 1965, p. 39)

> Ah! Glenn, my dear, Ross is not a good son, nor is he a decent fellow. (May 31, 1929; Allport, 1965, p. 65)

In his mother's view, Ross was "sex mad," consorting with a "chip ... of the flapper type"* (May 31, 1929; Allport, 1965, p. 65); but Gordon Allport was faithfully married to "my dearest girl"—"Of course I know you *must* be a nice girl, or Glenn would not have chosen you" (April 27, 1926; Allport, 1965, p. 16). To Jenny, Ross was a "contemptible cur" (May 31, 1929; Allport, 1965, p. 65), but Glenn and Isabel were "the decentest persons I know" (March 17, 1926; Allport, 1965, p. 16).

---

* Baldwin, writing with at least the implicit imprimatur of Gordon Allport, gives the most vivid description of Ross (and Jenny's view of Ross) during this time:

> Ross and his [first] wife were divorced, but Jenny bitterly resented Ross's interest in other women. She found numerous defects in the character of each likely candidate for Ross's affection. A number of girls entered the scene, each to be succeeded by the next in line. Vivien, the last and most prominent, was not disliked at first but her interest in Ross made her thoroughly hated. (1942, p. 165; see also 1941, pp. 22–25)

Return of the Double

In Rank's classic analysis, the double is the "detached personification of instincts and desires which were once felt to be unacceptable, but which can be satisfied without responsibility in this indirect way" (1922/1971, p. 76). Can we find any traces of this "double" relationship with Ross in Allport's writings? For all of their similarities of background and early college experience, Gordon Allport and Ross diverged sharply in temperament, life outcome, and of course relationship to Jenny. Drawing on Rank's analysis, we might speculate that Gordon Allport, raised on "hard work and tight money," would have envied Ross's easygoing, fun-loving manner (B. J. Cohler, personal communication, December 23, 1987). Allport's sharp distinction between normal and neurotic functioning, often laced (as we have seen) with "hypothetical" examples and images suggestive of Jenny and Ross, would then seem to reinforce the difference between his own life and that of Ross. Of course, his theoretical distaste for the infantile, the sexual, and the neurotic was certainly consistent with many other features of his background and temperament, as Elms (1972) suggests (see also Chapter 3, this volume).

Was Ross also feared as well as envied, and the double relationship denied as well as affirmed? Rank suggested that "in the same phenomena of defense the threat also recurs. . . . [the double] reappears in superstition as the messenger of death" (1922/1971, p. 86). Freud maintained that in our unconscious we are all perverse, infantile, and potentially neurotic. If that is true, then how different would Glenn really be from "sex-mad" Ross, bound to his mother in a helpless and hopeless struggle? What would be the protection from Ross's fate? On what grounds would survival be deserved? For Allport, perhaps, a theory of personality that emphasized the discontinuity between normal and abnormal helped to answer these questions.*

SUMMARY

This chapter has established Gordon Allport's true role in the *Letters from Jenny*. I have gone beyond this established fact to speculate

---

* These speculations suggest that Allport's view of Freud would have become more negative after the beginning of the Jenny correspondence (1926) and especially after the death of Ross (1929). Such a prediction could be explored through a close reading of Allport's psychological writings and papers, notes, and professional correspondence between 1921 (when he actually met Freud) and 1937, when he published *Personality: A Psychological Interpretation.*

about how Allport's role affects our interpretation of the Jenny case and to suggest ways in which aspects of the case may relate to Allport's life and personality theory. Of course, these speculations need to be checked against the facts that will emerge from further biographical research on Gordon Allport. In a time when personality psychology has begun to focus on the personalities of its founders, this chapter is a small contribution to that task.

ACKNOWLEDGMENTS: I am grateful to Abigail Stewart, Alan Elms, Bertram Cohler, Jeffrey Paige, Robert Hogan, and several anonymous reviewers for reading the manuscript for this chapter and giving suggestions. Naturally, they bear no responsibility for any of my conclusions.

REFERENCES

Allport, G. W. (1937). The functional autonomy of motives. *American Journal of Psychology, 50*, 141–156.

Allport, G. W. (1942). *The use of personal documents in psychological science*. New York: Social Science Research Council, Bulletin 49.

Allport, G. W. (1944). *The quest of Nellie Wise Allport* (revised). Privately printed. (Available in the Allport papers, Harvard University Archives.)

Allport, G. W. (1953). The trend in motivational theory. *American Journal of Orthopsychiatry, 25*, 107–119.

Allport, G. W. (1954). *The nature of prejudice*. Reading, MA: Addison–Wesley.

Allport, G. W. (1960). Personality: A problem for science or for art? In G. W. Allport, *Personality and social encounter* (pp. 3–15). Boston: Beacon Press.

Allport, G. W. (1961). *Pattern and growth in personality*. New York: Holt, Rinehart & Winston.

Allport, G. W. (1962). The general and the unique in psychological science. *Journal of Personality, 30*, 405–422.

Allport, G. W. (1965). *Letters from Jenny*. New York: Harcourt, Brace.

Allport, G. W. (1968a). An autobiography. In G. W. Allport, *The person in psychology* (pp. 376–409). Boston: Beacon Press.

Allport, G. W. (1968b). Crises in normal personality development. In G. W. Allport, *The person in psychology* (pp. 171–183). Boston: Beacon Press.

Anonymous. (1946). Letters from Jenny. *Journal of Abnormal and Social Psychology, 41*, 315–350, 449–480.

Baldwin, A. L. (1941). *A statistical method for investigating the structure of personality*. Unpublished doctoral dissertation, Harvard University.

Baldwin, A. L. (1942). Personal structure analysis: A statistical method for investigating the single personality. *Journal of Abnormal and Social Psychology, 37*, 163–183.

Elms, A. L. (1972). Allport, Freud, and the clean little boy. *Psychoanalytic Review, 59*, 627–632.

Evans, R. (1971). *Gordon Allport: The man and his ideas*. New York: Dutton.

Hall, C. S., & Lindzey, G. (1970). *Theories of personality* (2nd ed.). New York: Wiley.

Harvard Class of 1919. (1915). *Freshman red book.* Cambridge, MA: Harvard University.

Harvard Class of 1919. (1936). *Harvard Class of 1919 fourth report.* Cambridge, MA: Harvard University Alumni Office.

Murray, H. A. (1938). *Explorations in personality:* New York: Oxford University Press.

Paige, J. M. (1964). *Automated content analysis of "Letters from Jenny."* Unpublished honors thesis, Harvard University.

Paige, J. M. (1966). Letters from Jenny: An approach to the clinical analysis of personality structure by computer. In P. J. Stone (Ed.), *The General Inquirer: A computer approach to content analysis* (pp. 431–451). Cambridge, MA: MIT Press.

Peterson, C. (1988). *Personality.* San Diego: Harcourt, Brace.

Phares, E. J. (1988). *Introduction to personality* (2nd ed.). Glenview, IL: Scott, Foresman.

Rank, O. (1971). *The double.* Durham: University of North Carolina Press. (Originally published 1922)

Ryckman, R. M. (1989). *Theories of personality* (4th ed.). Monterey, CA: Brooks/Cole.

Scroggs, J. R. (1985). *Key ideas in personality theory.* St. Paul, MN: West.

CHAPTER ELEVEN

Allport's Personal Documents
Then and Now

LAWRENCE S. WRIGHTSMAN

It was my pleasure to spend a rather extensive amount of time with Gordon Allport during the spring semester of 1966, when he was a visiting fellow at the East–West Center in Honolulu and I was a faculty member at the University of Hawaii. He was a gentle and gracious man who was willing to share his past experiences and to facilitate the development of younger colleagues. I remember fondly that he volunteered to fill out an attitude scale I had recently constructed (the Philosophies of Human Nature Scale), and he even scored his own scale responses. Twenty-five years later, I still deeply value my association with him.

The very first words in the Preface to Allport's *Personality* were: "As a rule, science regards the individual as a mere bothersome accident" (1937, p. vii). Allport's science, of course, was just the opposite. It placed the individual at the very focus of investigation.

OVERVIEW

My goal in this chapter is to compare the status of personal documents 50 years ago and now. Allport's (1942) monograph, *The Use of Personal Documents in Psychological Science*, published five years after his *Personality* text, served as a beacon for those interested in the use

LAWRENCE S. WRIGHTSMAN • Department of Psychology, University of Kansas, Lawrence, Kansas 66045.

Fifty Years of Personality Psychology, edited by Kenneth H. Craik *et al.* Plenum Press, New York, 1993.

of autobiographies, memoirs, diaries, collections of letters, and similar materials as raw material for the analysis and interpretation of personality and behavior.

Within a decade of Allport's monograph, there had been a fertile development of the personal documents approach. Charlotte Buehler (1935), Else Frenkel-Brunswik (Frenkel, 1936; Frenkel-Brunswik, 1939), John Dollard (1935), Henry A. Murray (1938), Jerome Bruner (Allport et al., 1941), Alfred Baldwin (1940, 1942), and other prominent psychologists used diaries, life histories, and other autobiographical material to understand responses to catastrophe, mechanisms of self-deception, and changes over the life cycle, among other matters. After World War II, interest dwindled. There are exceptions, of course; Robert White's (1975) continuing interest in the growth of personality; the intensive case analyses of a small number of adult males by M. Brewster Smith, Bruner, and White (1956) done in an attempt to understand how opinions are developed and maintained; and the analysis of Theodore Drieser's writings by Seymour Rosenberg and Russell Jones (1972) in order to understand Dreiser's implicit personality theory.

Several years ago (Wrightsman, 1981), I argued that the "state of the art" regarding the use of personal documents in psychology had not—until shortly before the 1980s—advanced beyond that summarized in Allport's 1942 monograph. Happily, I can report my impression that the "rebirth" in the use of these materials that was beginning to emerge in the late 1970s has continued and increased.

In looking retrospectively at 50 years of the use of personal documents, I will attempt to compare the purposes, the theoretical perspectives, and the methods then and now. As space permits, I will provide some recent and current examples; I regret that I will not have the space to mention a greater number of the excellent contemporary examples.

In reviewing Allport's perspective, I have primarily relied on three of his writings: his *Personality* text, the previously mentioned SSRC monograph, and his book, *Letters from Jenny* (1965). (In actuality, he had little to say about such materials in the book that has generated this volume; "personal documents" is not in the index, and there is only a brief section on "personal records.")

THE PURPOSES OF PERSONAL DOCUMENTS IN PSYCHOLOGICAL RESEARCH

Allport saw personal documents as materials that can tell us "what goes on in people's minds" (1942, p. vii). He defined the personal document as "... any self-revealing record that intentionally or unintentionally yields information regarding the structure, dynamics, and functioning of the author's mental life" (1942, p. xii). He limited the term to first-person documents; this restriction has continued. Allport was well aware of the problems in the representativeness of the single case and the problems in the validity of subjective records (1944, p. xi). But, he wrote, "... the psychologist ... must ask even of the deceptive and trivial documents why they were written and, further, why they are dull or deceptive" (1942, p. xiii).

Allport observed that the ways of using personal documents varied considerably. Chapter 3 of his SSRC monograph lists and annotates 21 different purposes for use of personal documents. Table 1 reprints these, using Allport's labels and providing his definitions and some examples of his and some of mine. Allport would acknowledge that some of these purposes overlap with each other.

Looking at these purposes through the filter of the 50 intervening years, we can note several salient characteristics of this categorization:

1. It is a surprising hodgepodge of purposes, in the sense that some of these reflect anticipated benefits to the author of the document, while most deal with the value of personal documents for the social scientist or the psychotherapist.

2. Some of the uses are now routine ones, such as analyzing collections of letters in order to understand the personality of the letter writer or asking a psychiatric patient to write a brief autobiography. In contrast, other purposes identified by Allport have seemingly been ignored; for example, Number 19, as a source for generating questionnaire items, has not often been utilized (Richard Christie's Machiavellianism scale being an exception).

3. Some of these purposes lead to creative ideas, based on unusual types of personal documents. Number 18 suggests that exchanges of letters could be used to study the nature of friendship or marriage. Allport, in 1942, saw this resource as almost overlooked by social psychologists.

Extending this idea, a specific type of personal document—an advertisement in a lonely hearts column of a newspaper—has recently been used by social psychologists to study self-presentation and social needs. In one study, Harrison and Saeed (1977) content analyzed more than 800 such advertisements, focusing on differences in the ads placed by women and men. Women were more likely to describe themselves in terms of physical attractiveness and men were more likely to specify this as a want. Men more often mentioned financial security as an attribute of theirs; women were more likely to seek it. Deaux and Hanna

TABLE 1. Allport's List of Purposes for
Psychologists' Use of Personal Documents[a]

1. *Phenomenological investigations*
   DEFINITION: "interest in complex phenomenal states" (p. 37). [Allport's famous
   quotation (p. 37): "If we want to know how people feel: what they experience
   and what they remember, what their emotions and motives are like, and the
   reasons for acting as they do—why not ask them?"]
   EXAMPLE: Galton's accounts of the imagery of his correspondents.
2. *The study of religious experience*
   EXAMPLE: Several investigators (Hoffding, Clark, etc.) have analyzed diaries and
   autobiographies from the point of view of religious experience.
3. *Study of the psychological effects of unemployment*
   EXAMPLE: Zawadski and Lazarsfeld (1935) analyzed autobiographies of unemployed
   writers in Poland, leading to a grouping into four types.
4. *Mental life of adolescents*
   RATIONALE: G. Stanley Hall and others have argued that personal documents are
   the *best* means of studying adolescence because the "experiences peculiar to
   adolescence are inaccessible to adults whose later encounters with love and life
   have the effects of recasting to tally the nascent and turbulent groping of
   adolescents in their struggle to come to terms with physical reality and social
   responsibility" (Allport, 1942, p. 39).
   EXAMPLE: Norman Kiell, in 1964, collected a set of autobiographical materials
   prepared by adolescents in an effort to demonstrate that the internal and
   external agitations of the adolescent are present in every part of the world and
   hence only partly determined by culture.
5. *Didactic uses*
   RATIONALE: It has been claimed that practice in writing self-reports increases
   insight, powers of observation, and self-control in adolescents.
6. *Practical use of experience records*
   RATIONALE: Social progress may result from the analysis of vivid stories about one's
   personal experiences.
   EXAMPLE: Clifford Beers's *A Mind That Found Itself* (1928).
7. *Autoanalysis*
   PURPOSE: Autobiographical outpourings that aim at catharsis may be useful as
   teaching devices or as an aid in evolving a theory of personality.
   EXAMPLE: W. E. Leonard's *Locomotive God* (1927).
8. *Historical diagnoses*
   PURPOSE: To shed light on the personalities of writers, artists, and other gifted
   people.
   EXAMPLE: Bragman's studies of Rossetti (1936); Squires's study of Dostoevsky
   (1937).
9. *Supplement to psychiatric examination*
   PURPOSES: Besides providing new leads for diagnosis, there may be a therapeutic
   value, "initiating and helping to guide the course of treatment" (p. 44).
10. *The subject's verification and validation*
    PURPOSE: A "rebuttal" by a subject to another's analysis of him or her.
    EXAMPLE: John Dewey (1904) responded to his expositors and critics in a series
    entitled *The Library of Living Philosophy*.

11. *Mental effects of special physical conditions*
    PURPOSE: Autobiographical materials may help "to keep the influence of physical factors in perspective" (p. 45).
12. *Light on creative processes and the nature of genius*
    PURPOSE: To study creativity.
    EXAMPLE: Willa Cather's (1927) account of her conception and writing of *Death Comes for the Archbishop.*
13. *The psychologizing of the social sciences*
    PURPOSE: The application of "psychohistory" and "psychobiography" to historical or cultural phenomena. (These terms were generated later than Allport's 1942 monograph.)
14. *The psychologizing of literature*
    PURPOSE: The probing of motivation by literary critics and biographers.
    EXAMPLE: Robert Sears's (1979) comparison of Mark Twain's letters and his novels, to identify periods of depression in his life.
15. *Illustration*
    PURPOSE: "Perhaps the commonest use of documents is to provide illustrative material for authors who wish to exemplify some generalization already in mind" (p. 48).
16. *Induction*
    PURPOSE: To derive general principles from raw material or particulars.
    EXAMPLE: Charlotte Buehler's *Lebenspsychologie,* based on 200 life histories.
17. *Occupational and other types*
    PURPOSE: The derivation of types, or clustering cases according to similarities.
    EXAMPLE: Donley and Winter's (1970) scoring of U.S. presidential inaugural addresses in order to classify them on strength of achievement, affiliative, and power motives.
18. *Interpersonal relations*
    PURPOSE: "The possibility of using exchanges of letters between two persons as a means of studying the dyadic relations of friendship, of marriage, of the parent–child bond seems almost overlooked by social psychologists" (p. 50).
19. *First step in the construction of tests and questionnaires*
    PURPOSE: To provide insights for generating items in standardized tests and questionnaires.
20. *Reinforcement and supplementation*
    PURPOSE: "Often the personal document merely falls into place as one of several methods in a battery. It serves no other purpose than adding credibility to the total picture developed through interviews, tests, ratings, institutional reports, or other methods" (p. 51)
    EXAMPLE: Thomas and Znaniecki's study of Polish peasants (1918).
21. *Methodological objectives*
    PURPOSE: Social scientists may use personal documents "simply in order to find out how they may be used to the best advantage" (p. 51). There is an allusion here to theory development; focus is not so much on the individual or on general laws of behavior, as it is on "the *process* by which the significance of behavior becomes known and evaluated" (p. 51).
    EXAMPLE: Allport's derivation of an empirical–intuitive theory of understanding from the reactions of students in reading Leonard's *Locomotive God.*

---

[a]From Allport (1942, Chapter 3). All quoted material is from this source.

(1984), using a similar set of documents, followed up by analyzing the content of lonely hearts advertisements placed by homosexual and heterosexual men and women. Deaux and Hanna concluded that both the advertiser's gender and his or her sexual preference were related to both self-identified attributes and needs in a companion.

4. Another observation, based on Allport's list of purposes, is the surprising—at least to me—lack of emphasis on theory testing in Table 1. In contrast, I would expect that contemporary psychologists, if asked about the value of personal documents, would list as the premiere value their clarification of theory.

For example, Swede and Tetlock (1986) note that controversy surrounds many aspects of the construct of implicit personality theory. How many basic dimensions underlie an individual's trait perceptions? Is it appropriate to seek a dimensional representation of implicit theories of personality? Not only is there disagreement over the answers to these questions, but also theories and models that provide a good fit with regard to group data may not be supported by data from separate individuals (Kim & Rosenberg, 1980). Swede and Tetlock (1986) point to the idiographic analyses of individual respondents as a way of producing inductive generalizations on this topic.

5. Finally, I detect a shift in a direction hinted at with regard to the accuracy of personal documents. As I have indicated, Allport was primarily concerned with reliability and deception (whether conscious or unconscious). But he also asked why—why deceptive? The shift has been even more toward the *process* involved; for example, what were the determinants of the process of writing the personal document or narrating an event? Also, what are the perceptual and interpretive processes of the social scientist who analyzes and interprets the documents (*Items*, 1981)? Allport was concerned that oversimplification and arbitrary conceptualizations could limit the value of personal documents. Now, however, there is

> an acceptance . . . that these filtering processes are an inherent and meaningful part of any communication about the world. A scientist or humanist should not seek to eliminate the filters but rather be conscious of them and account for them as a part of the research or creative process. (*Items*, 1981, p. 21)

THEORETICAL PERSPECTIVES— ALLPORT'S AND THE PRESENT

A second contrast between Allport's work and the present deals with theoretical perspectives. Allport himself, in *Letters from Jenny* (1965), carried out one of the most visible and extensive analyses of personal documents. Between the ages of 58 and 70, Jenny Gove Masterson wrote more than 300 letters to two young friends, a married couple who were living in a nearby Eastern college town. Her friendship with the young man extended back to the time—a decade before—when he had been a college roommate of Jenny's son, Ross. The exchange of letters began in March 1926 and continued without interruption—an average of a letter exchanged about every two weeks—for 11½ years, until Jenny's death in October 1937.

Allport, after reprinting excerpts from most of the letters, analyzed Jenny's personality from three theoretical perspectives: existential (or phenomenological), depth (or psychoanalytic), and structural–dynamic. Allport carried out his interpretations in the early 1960s before psychology had felt the impact of dialectic thinking.

We now have other and, I believe, more appropriate models for interpreting sets of letters (Wrightsman, 1988). Different theories of personality seem congenial with different types of personal documents. Autobiographies and memoirs are retrospective, and often there are significant acts of filtering, reframing, and justifying within them; their analyses seem most congenial with deterministic theories such as psychoanalysis or social-learning theory. In contrast, diaries and collections of letters are more relevant to a dialectic theory, because they represent an ongoing, but constantly changing, production of raw material.

My reading of Jenny Masterson's letters leads me to conclude that what is missing from Allport's analyses is a focus on the dynamic, constantly changing relationship between Jenny and her son, Ross, who was clearly the most important person or object in her worldview. Jenny's feelings shift from trust and love to distrust and revulsion and back again. We could employ various ways of labeling the dialectic that is operating within Jenny: a tug between trust and distrust of Ross; pulls between insistence on her financial independence and her reliance and dependence on Ross and others; vacillations between realistic planning and helpless despair. Thus can contemporary theory enrich the interpretations of personal documents.

METHODOLOGIES—ALLPORT'S VERSUS THE PRESENT

Obviously the greatest difference between the status of personal documents in Allport's time and now is not with regard to purposes, theory testing, or theoretical perspective—it is in regard to methodology. The growth of sophisticated statistical analyses and high-speed computers has led to a massive shift toward more fine-grained analyses carried out on the data generated from personal documents. Table 2

TABLE 2. Contemporary Types of Studies Using Personal Documents

1. Rosenberg and Jones (1972): The implicit personality theory of Theodore Dreiser

In a study whose methodology has served as a guide for subsequent work, Seymour Rosenberg and Russell Jones applied content analysis and factor analysis to determine the implicit personality theory of one person: Theodore Dreiser, the author of *Sister Carrie* and *An American Tragedy*. Dreiser was chosen because his book, *A Gallery of Women*, published in 1929, contained detailed character descriptions. The book consists of 15 different stories, each a portrayal of a different woman known by Dreiser. Thus, each person is described in 20 to 50 continuous pages, and a variety of people are so described. By listing each character mentioned in any of these stories and each trait ascribed to him or her, Rosenberg and Jones identified 241 characters and 6761 descriptive units from the book.

Statistical analysis sought to determine what traits clustered together. (It is trite but true to observe that these analyses could not have been completed when Allport's 1942 monograph was published.) Results indicated that traits associated with women were quite different from those associated with men. Furthermore, the dimension of conformity versus nonconformity emerged as an important construct in Dreiser's descriptions of people, but conformity was not associated only with the female sex, as the usual stereotype would have predicted.

The detailed, quantitative analysis of literary and other written materials has been used in some of Rosenberg's more recent work and served as a model for Swede and Tetlock's (1986) recent analysis of Henry Kissinger's implicit personality theory.

2. DeWaele and Harre (1979): Assisted autobiography as a psychological method

In a very useful, original, and detailed book chapter, DeWaele and Harre described procedures for the creation of an "assisted autobiography," which is "really a continuous process of negotiated autobiographical reconstruction" (1979, p. 193). Then they provide a means for analysis of the contents of the autobiography. The chapter includes a 15-page appendix that serves as a checklist of various aspects of the content of the life story. Although the chapter is not relevant to advances in statistical analysis, it provides a "fresh look" at methodology in the broad sense and reflects a humanistic perspective that assumes that research is a negotiated cooperative interaction between the investigator and the research subject.

3. Tetlock (1981): A comparison of preelection and postelection statements by twentieth-century U.S. presidents.

Philip Tetlock coded public statements and addresses by presidents from McKinley through Carter for integrative complexity. Statements made prior to election were compared with statements made in the first month, the second year, and the third year in office. In addition to repeated-measures analyses of variance, Tetlock used (more conservative) quasi-F-ratios to evaluate the data, by considering some effects (time period and paragraph sampling unit) as random, not fixed, effects. Results indicated that except for Herbert Hoover, presidential policy statements became more complex after assuming office.

Similarly, Suedfeld and Rank (1976) demonstrated that the long-term success of revolutionary leaders was related to the cognitive complexity of their public statements. Equally important is the content analysis of speeches and interviews of Soviet Politburo members, to aid in understanding their personal characteristics, done by Margaret Hermann (1980). She has also applied this content analysis to President Reagan's public statements.

4. Berman (1985): Analysis of the diary of an older person

Harry J. Berman of Sangamon State University, Springfield, Illinois, is developing a methodology for examining the diaries and journals of older people, in order to understand how they deal with the events of late adulthood. The analysis is driven by concepts from psychoanalytic theory and Daniel Levinson's stage theory of adult development (1978). This is a useful approach in the sense that the experiences of older people are distinct from those of younger ages.

5. Stewart and Healy (1985): The study of adaptation to stress and life change

The explosion of interest in adult psychological development that we have witnessed in the last decade has given renewed interest to the study of autobiographies. Daniel Levinson and his colleagues (1977) elicited autobiographies from their subjects as part of their investigation of stages in men's development. Abigail Stewart and Joseph Healy have analyzed autobiographies in identifying reactions to stressful events and adaptation to life changes.

---

lists a brief sampling of representative procedures in contemporary research. It is probably irresponsible to try to pick only a few examples, and even more so, considering that I have tried here to consider "methodology" in the broadest sense—not just data collection and analysis procedures—but the relationship of researcher to subject, the imbeddedness of method in theory, and the use of a variety of materials beyond the classic letters, diaries, and autobiographies.

CONCLUSION

What would Allport say if he were suddenly revived and confronted with the breadth of use of personal documents in contemporary psychology and other social sciences? He would be gracious, of course, although I imagine he would feel regret that there was such a long latency before his 1942 monograph had much impact. He would welcome the increase in number and variety of studies in the last decade. He would find it gratifying that in 1986, the Social Science Research Council, which sponsored his 1942 monograph, announced its plans to appoint a Committee on Personal Testimony (Crapanzano et al., 1986). And he would applaud the fact that the American Council of Learned Societies was co-sponsoring this new committee, because in his time the barriers between the social sciences and the humanities were less formidable than they became in the 1960s and 1970s. [There are indications that more interdisciplinary cooperation is occurring now, according to Crapanzano et al., (1986).] I think he would be amazed and a little disturbed by the profusion of statistical methods—and especially the cost in carrying them out. (He once told me that every piece of research he had completed was unfunded, with the exception of the information transmission research he did for the government during World War II.) He might be surprised that some fundamental problems, such as how to generalize knowledge from a single case, have still not been systematically examined. I believe he would urge us, in his gentle way, not to forget the whole person as we apply our new and sophisticated analyses to the investigation of personal documents.

REFERENCES

Allport, G. W. (1937). *Personality: A psychological interpretation*. New York: Holt, Rinehart and Winston.

Allport, G. W. (1942). *The use of personal documents in psychological science*. New York: Social Science Research Council.

Allport, G. W. (Ed.) (1965). *Letters from Jenny*. New York: Harcourt Brace, and World.

Allport, G. W., Bruner, J. S., & Jandorf, E. M. (1941). Personality under social catastrophe: An analysis of German refugee life histories. *Character and Personality, 10,* 1–22.

Baldwin, A. L. (1940). The statistical analysis of the structure of a single personality. *Psychological Bulletin, 37,* 518–519.

Baldwin, A. L. (1942). Personal structure analysis: A statistical method for investigating the single personality. *Journal of Abnormal and Social Psychology, 37,* 163–183.

Beers, C. W. (1928). *A mind that found itself* (5th ed.) New York: Doubleday.

Berman, H. J. (1985, March). On the brink: Elizabeth Vining's "Being Seventy." Unpublished paper presented at conference on "Humanistic Perspectives on the Aging Enterprise in America," Center for the Study of Aging, University of Missouri, Kansas City.

Bragman, L. J. (1936). The case of Dante Gabriel Rosetti. *American Journal of Psychiatry, 92,* 1111–1122.

Buehler, C. (1935). The curve of life as studied in biographies. *Journal of Applied Psychology, 19,* 405–409.

Cather, W. (1927). A letter from Willa Cather: A short account of how I happened to write *Death comes for the Archbishop. Commonweal, 7,* 713–714.

Crapanzano, V., Ergas, Y., & Modell, J. (1986, June). Personal testimony: Narratives of the self in the social sciences and the humanities. *Items, 40*(2), 25–30.

Deaux, K., & Hanna, R. (1984). Courtship in the personal column: The influence of gender and sexual orientation. *Sex Roles, 11,* 363–375.

Dewey, J. (1904). *The library of living philosophy:* University of Chicago Press.

DeWaele, J.-P., & Harre, R. (1979). Autobiography as a psychological method. In G. P. Ginsburg (Ed.), *Emerging strategies in social psychological research* (pp. 177–224). New York: Wiley.

Dollard, J. (1935). *Criteria for a life history*. New Haven, CT: Yale University Press.

Donley, R. W., & Winter, D. G. (1970). Measuring the motives of public figures at a distance: An exploratory study of American presidents. *Behavioral Science, 15,* 227–236.

Frenkel, E. (1936). Studies in biographical psychology. *Character and Personality, 5*, 1–35.

Frenkel-Brunswik, E. (1939). Mechanisms of self-deception. *Journal of Social Psychology, 10*, 409–420.

Harrison, A. A., & Saeed, L. (1977). Let's make a deal: An analysis of revelations and stipulations in lonely hearts advertisements. *Journal of Personality and Social Psychology, 35*, 257–264.

Hermann, M. G. (1980). Assessing the personalities of Soviet Politburo members. *Personality and Social Psychology, 6*, 332–352.

Items (1981, June). The uses of personal testimony. *35*(1/2), 20–21.

Kiell, N. (1964). *The universal experience of adolescence.* New York: International Universities Press.

Kim, M. P., & Rosenberg, S. (1980). Comparison of two structural models of implicit personality theory. *Journal of Personality and Social Psychology, 38*, 375–389.

Leonard, W. E. (1927). *The locomotive god.* New York: Century.

Murray, H. A. (1938). *Explorations in personality.* New York: Oxford University Press.

Rosenberg, S., & Jones, R. A. (1972). A method for investigating and representing a person's implicit theory of personality: Theodore Drieser's view of people. *Journal of Personality and Social Psychology, 22*, 372–386.

Sears, R. R. (1979, June). Mark Twain's separation anxiety. *Psychology Today*, pp. 100–104.

Smith, M. B., Bruner, J. S., & White, R. W. (1956). *Opinions and personality.* New York: Wiley.

Squires, P. C. (1937). Fyodor Dostoevsky: A psychopathological sketch. *Psychoanalytic Review, 24*, 365–385.

Suedfeld, P., & Rank, A. D. (1976). Revolutionary leaders: Long-term success as a function of cognitive complexity. *Journal of Personality and Social Psychology, 34*, 169–178.

Swede, S. W., & Tetlock, P. E. (1986). Henry Kissinger's implicit theory of personality: A quantitative case study. *Journal of Personality, 54*, 617–646.

Stewart, A. J., & Healy, J. M. (1985). Personality and adaptation to change. In R. Hogan & W. Jones (Eds.). *Perspectives on personality: Theory, measurement, and interpersonal dynamics* (pp. 117–144). Greenwich, CT: JAI Press.

Tetlock, P. E. (1981). Pre- to post-election shifts in presidential rhetoric: Impression management or cognitive adjustment? *Journal of Personality and Social Psychology, 41*, 207–212.

Thomas, W. I., & Znaniecki, F. (1918). The Polish peasant in Europe and America. Boston: Gorham Press.

White, R. W. (1975). *Lives in progress: A study of the natural growth of personality* (3rd ed.). New York: Holt, Rinehart and Winston.

Wrightsman, L. S. (1981). Personal documents as data in conceptualizing adult personality development. *Personality and Social Psychology Bulletin, 7*, 367–385.

Wrightsman, L. S. (1988). *Personality development in adulthood.* Newbury Park, CA: Sage.

Zawadski, B., & Lazarsfeld, P. (1935). The psychological consequences of unemployment. *Journal of Social Psychology, 6*, 224–251.

CHAPTER TWELVE

Conceptions of Self and Identity

A Modern Retrospective on Allport's View

ROY F. BAUMEISTER

My particular task for this volume is to comment on the status of work on self and identity in relation to what Allport had to say. I take as my point of departure Allport's (1943) paper entitled "The Ego in Contemporary Psychology," for it serves as a clearer and more thorough statement of his views on the self than does the 1937 text that was the occasion for our symposium.

ALLPORT'S VIEWS IN RETROSPECT

In reading Allport's wise and insightful comments about the self from nearly half a century ago, one is struck by how many of his comments are still useful and germane. This is not to say, however, that nothing has been learned in the past half-century. I wish to comment on six of Allport's points about the self.

First, he predicted an increase in the psychological study of the self. Writing in 1943, when the psychology of self was just getting started, he said "we may safely predict that ego-psychology will flourish increasingly" (p. 476). There is little doubt but that his prediction has been confirmed. The decade of the 1940s saw the psychoanalytic movement take new notice of the ego, resulting in an expanded appre-

ROY F. BAUMEISTER • Department of Psychology, Case Western Reserve University, Cleveland, Ohio 44106.

Fifty Years of Personality Psychology, edited by Kenneth H. Craik *et al.* Plenum Press, New York, 1993.

ciation of its importance and capabilities. Each decade since has added its views and its data, as not only psychology but indeed all the social sciences and humanities became fascinated with the nature of selfhood and identity.

Second, it is remarkable to note that Allport was willing to attempt a comprehensive summary of self, listing if not integrating all major aspects of it that psychology had found. A similar comprehensive inventory is desperately needed today. Our theories and findings about self have expanded all out of control, and few attempt to provide an overview or even to fit their data into a comprehensive theory of the self. For a great scholar like Allport to attempt such an overview in the 1940s was intellectually audacious; for anyone to attempt it today, without years of work, is almost absurd. Yet in a sense it fails to do justice to Allport's memory for us not to try. Later in this chapter, I shall attempt to provide at least an outline of what such a comprehensive theory of self would require today.

Third, one notes that Allport sometimes confused self and personality. This confusion persists today; it is hard to draw the line. Most of us would say that the self is not the same thing as the totality of personality; perhaps the self should be considered part of personality. All personality traits do not belong in the self. One's score on extraversion, for example, is not a measure of self. The reason for the confusion between self and personality has to do with the self-concept, which does potentially include all one's traits—or at least one's beliefs about one's traits. A recent work defined the self as "a person's mental representation of his or her own personality" (Kihlstrom et al., 1988, p. 146). While this definition leaves out interpersonal aspects, social identity, the decision-making aspect of self, and perhaps a few others, it does effectively call attention to the relation between self-concept and personality. Self includes one's ideas about one's personality.

Fourth, Allport had fairly little to say about identity. Erik Erikson had not yet coined the term *identity crisis*. Writing in 1943, in the middle of World War II, Allport did not see the Americans as obsessed with their identity crises, with finding themselves, and so forth. Since then, this has become an area of major focus. Identity, as a socially constructed definition of self, has been an increasingly important feature of self research over the past several decades. In Allport's day, the self was understood primarily in terms of the psychodynamic ego, but later generations of scholars have come to appreciate the need to augment the notion of ego with an understanding of cultural factors, interpersonal processes, and so forth.

Fifth, Allport emphasized the unity of self. The self is indeed experienced as a unity. Allport spoke of the self as a unifying principle in personality.

Modern research has lost sight of this aspect of the self to some degree, and today's researchers might well benefit from being reminded of Allport's discussion of this principle. Researchers today speak of various aspects of self-concept, of the dimensionality of self-esteem, of individual self-schemas for each trait, and other matters, as if these are fairly independent. The focus is on the parts and aspects of the self. Too little attention is paid to the unifying aspect of the self as a whole.

An important example concerns the notion of potentialities. Heidegger's existential concept of potentiality was recently revived by Markus and Nurius (1986) to show that people have different conceptions of future possibilities for themselves. Calling these "possible selves," however, has misled some readers to think that it refers to a multiplicity of selves, concealing the vitally important fact that it is in every case the same self that is at issue. A person can imagine him- or herself in various catastrophic fashions—as someday being a criminal, or a drug addict, or not getting tenure—but this is quite different from imagining someone else in those circumstances. The emotional power and force of possible selves derives from the fact that it is *oneself* who is imagined thus. In other words, it is not really a matter of different or multiple "possible selves," but rather one's same self with different attributes, different definitions, or different circumstances.

Probably a major reason for the modern loss of the sense of the unity of self is the declining interest in morality, both socially and in psychological theory. In moral action, the self participates as a unity; the whole individual is implicated in moral action. The declining interest in moral issues removes this unifying force from prevailing conceptions of selfhood. In its place, the new view of humanity regards the individual as a bundle of situational responses, with minimal continuity.

Sixth, Allport noted that the most important motivation associated with the self is the desire to maximize self-esteem; that is, to avoid loss of esteem and if possible to increase it. The motivational importance of self-esteem is as strong and widespread in today's psychology as it was back then. The only difference is that today we cite different references (and, to be sure, we have accumulated a great deal more evidence), but it is the same effect.

Today, however, we would have to augment this motivation with at least one other major motivation of the self, namely control (also known as choice or personal freedom). Abundant evidence has associated the self with control. The self seeks to gain, maintain, and exercise control. This general principle has been shown in many contexts, ranging from the importance of choice in cognitive dissonance (e.g., Linder *et al.*, 1967; on the self, see Baumeister & Tice, 1984), to reactance theory (Brehm, 1966; also Baer *et al.*, 1980), to systematic efforts to distort feedback so as to preserve views of self as having control (Greenwald, 1980; Taylor & Brown, 1988). Moreover, both objective and subjective control are sought. That is, even when the self cannot really be in control, it wants to think it is. Hence Langer's (1975) work on the illusion of control or Alloy and Abramson's (1979) evidence that non-depressed people overestimate their degree of control.

ALLPORT'S INTEGRATIVE PROJECT

In 1943, Allport was willing to sketch an overview of what was known about the ego. It is worth asking what such an outline would look like if someone were to attempt it today.

I would suggest three major headings as necessary to cover what is now known about the self: the natural self, the conceptual self, and the action self. I am not proposing a new theory of self here; rather, I am trying to say what categories would be needed to integrate and make sense of all the knowledge that has been accumulated about the self. At best, this is (as I suggested earlier) an outline of what a comprehensive theory of self might look like.

THE NATURAL SELF

The natural self includes the two inevitably or innately given aspects of selfhood. First, there is the physical body. Nowadays in psychology we do not pay all that much attention to the body as an aspect of self, except perhaps in developmental psychology. Developmentalists recognize the importance of the bodily self because their attention is repeatedly forced back to the ineluctable fact that self-knowledge begins with awareness of one's own body. It is also important to keep in mind that outside the modern, industrialized world, self has always been equated very much with body. The psychological self, as a network of inner experience and identity definition, is far from universal. But bodies exist all over the world. Bodies are culturally universal. Self starts with body.

The other aspect of the natural self is that little window of consciousness that is sometimes called the "knower." Like the body, the knower is cross-culturally universal. Every conscious individual has one. It is the owner of sensations and experiences, the subjective aspect of consciousness. Everyone (in the world) is tied to his or her perspective on the world, the little point from which everything else is seen. This aspect, too, has received less emphasis in modern psychology than in the past.

The knower and the body are the basic aspects of self in that they are universal. They comprise the natural starting point of the self, given by our very nature, so it seems fair to call them together the natural self. Psychology has shown little interest in these aspects of selfhood in recent years. The natural self exists, is real, and is undeniably a fundamental part of self, but for some reason it does not attract a great deal of attention from researchers these days.

THE CONCEPTUAL SELF

Let us turn now to the conceptual self. This is the self as a construct, as something made out of meaning rather than given directly by biology and phenomenology (in contrast to the natural self). Modern psychology has shown considerable interest in the conceptual self. Again, one must distinguish two (overlapping) subcategories: identity and self-concept.

Self-concept refers to the person's mental representations of the self as well as self's attributes. It includes one's beliefs about one's body, one's personality, and perhaps one's material possessions as well. The evaluative dimension of self-concept is quite important: self-esteem. Most self-concept research ends up being self-esteem research. People have global conceptions of themselves as having a certain degree of value and they also have evaluations of their various specific attributes. Now, psychology has seen self-esteem research go back and forth in its preference for focusing on global self-esteem or on attribute-specific self-esteem. Probably both are real and important. But there is no denying that the good–bad dimension is a core aspect of self-concept (Greenwald *et al.*, 1988).

Identity refers to a composite *definition* of self, constructed out of several partial definitions that include social roles, personal values, identifications, and so forth. In my 1986 book on identity (Baumeister, 1986), I suggested that identity has the following functional aspects. There is an interpersonal aspect of identity, which includes social roles as well as reputation, as is evident in the "public self" of self-presentation research (e.g., Baumeister, 1982; Schlenker, 1980). Identity, after all, enables you to live in the world of people, so it has a strong interpersonal aspect.

Identity also includes a potentiality aspect. That is, identity is not a purely static conception or definition of self in the immediate present, but rather is known as going somewhere. Identity is goal directed. Having an identity includes having some idea of what you are here for, of what you wish to achieve or become.

And lastly, identity includes a structure of values and priorities. Historically this may be somewhat new as an aspect of individual identity. In the past, values were not personal values; rather, values were part of the common culture, held by consensus and regarded by everyone as objective facts. Now, however, people are confronted with a welter of possible, conflicting values, and they construct their own personal set out of them. Identity crisis begins with a reevaluation of one's basic values. The reasonably finished set of values is fundamental for the self's further work, including forming a concept of one's potentiality and, more generally, making decisions throughout life. It would be wrong to say that identity makes the choices—because making choices is a function of our third category, namely the action self—but identity furnishes a basis for making stable, coherent, consistent choices.

The study of identity crises is probably one of the biggest developments in the area of self that has occurred since Allport wrote his early works. First there were Erik Erikson's (1950, 1968) ideas based on clinical impressions. These immediately captured the collective imagination, and the term "identity crisis" was heard throughout our culture. Then in the 1960s, James Marcia (e.g., 1966, 1967) pioneered a way of studying identity crises empirically, and since then a small flood of articles has examined the correlates of identity crisis. When I set out to work on the book on identity, I wanted to give an account of the process of identity crisis, but I could not find anything in the literature that spelled it out. Research had focused on correlates of identity crisis, but not on processes. So, with Dianne Tice and Jeremy Shapiro, I undertook to construct a process model. We tried to read everything we could get our hands on and integrate these into one overarching account of the process of identity crisis (Baumeister et al., 1985).

But we failed. We concluded that the task was inherently impossible, because there is not one basic process but rather two. These are worth considering, because they indicate how identity can fail and how people seek to repair it. A person can have an identity crisis when his or her identity is not working right; that is, when the identity is inadequate for dealing with the behavioral issues and decisions that confront the person. Although we like to imagine identity crises as somehow bubbling up from inside, they seem instead to occur in response to various life and environmental demands that reveal the inadequacy of one's identity.

We labeled the two types of identity crisis *identity deficit* and *identity conflict*. Identity deficit crises mean having not enough identity: There is not enough in one's identity to make the choices that need to be made. The identity deficit has been shown to be much more common with males than with females, and it seems to be most common in adolescence and then again at mid-life. It is a matter of not knowing what one wants to be, not having personal commitments and beliefs, lacking a long-term life plan, and so forth. The person shows mood swings, experiments with lots of new possible identifications and ideas, ruminates over grand issues, reflects a great deal on his or her own actions and their possible meanings, and so forth. Erik Erikson's work helped us to see this period of vacillation and personal turmoil as a form of personal experimentation. The individual tries on new ideas, traits, loyalties, and futures just as a shopper might try on new clothes to see what fits and what elicits a favorable reaction from others.

The other is identity conflict, which means too much identity. That is, faced with some choices or demands, the different parts of identity make conflicting demands on the person or they prescribe contradictory, incompatible courses of action. For example, the opportunities and demands of one's chosen career may conflict with obligations to family and children. Likewise, the immigrant wants to retain allegiance to the old culture but also embrace the new one. Identity conflicts can occur at any point in life; unlike identity deficits, they seem to have no particular developmental link. There is no experimentation or search for new identifications, no trying out of new patterns. Rather, there is only the anguished struggle for a path of compromise and often the guilt-filled repudiation of one of the conflicting elements.

THE ACTION SELF

Lastly, let us turn to the action self. The two subheads here refer to the agent, who makes the choices and decisions, and the motivational aspect of self. The self is both an actor and a wanter.

The agent is the active element of self. It is what decides, initiates, chooses. This is a familiar and vitally important aspect of self. This was perhaps the core of Freud's original concept of the *ego*, and it is no less valid and important today.

The motivational aspect includes what the self desires. Actually, the term "motivation" tends to connote something impersonal, perhaps unconscious, perhaps situationally induced, and so when referring to the self it may be more appropriate to use the term "desire." The self's main desires are the desire to maximize self-esteem and the desire to maximize control. Deprived of esteem, people are unhappy. They are depressed, humiliated, sad, angry, even mentally ill, and they often find themselves unable to perform effectively at many tasks or unable to cope with setbacks. Likewise, deprived of control, people are unhappy. They experience stress, they get ulcers and other illnesses, they may suffer from learned helplessness, they show reactance, and again they may find themselves unable to perform effectively or to cope. Research shows that people who have both high self-esteem and high feelings of control and efficacy are an unusually happy group, far out of proportion to the objective circumstances in their lives (Argyle, 1987; Campbell, 1981).

Esteem and control are not the only motivations associated with self. Swann (1987) has shown that people often seek confirmation of their views about themselves. The self desires stability and perhaps some form of immortality, whether through lasting fame or through the living legacy of one's offspring.

CONCLUSION

I think that these three main parts of the self are sufficient to cover what is currently known and thought about the self. Some of these notions were already old hat in Allport's day, whereas others had scarcely been studied then but have received all of their attention in the recent decades. Still, that is where we are now in the psychology of self.

I wish to conclude with one further impression. When I set out to write my first book on identity, my starting point was the modern dilemma of identity. Finding oneself, self-actualization, knowing oneself, and all the other clichés that suggest that problems of identity are rampant in modern life. The attempt to furnish an account of identity today in Western culture led me into a project that kept me fascinated for several years and taught me a great deal.

Yet, when I finished that book, I felt that I had not really solved my original problem, which was understanding this core dilemma of modern life. I had indeed given an account of the dilemma of identity, but I also concluded that much of what we call identity problems is not really a matter of identity. Rather, it is a matter of the meaning of life. Finding oneself, and all the rest, is often not a quest for identity per se, but rather a search for a meaningful life. The underlying malaise is not a lack of self-knowledge but a lack of purpose and meaning in how one interprets one's own existence. The natural sequel to my study of identity is therefore a study of life's meaning, and I have spent several years on that project (Baumeister, 1991).

This confusion of identity issues and meaning-of-life issues is apparent in psychology as well as in the popular culture, and it is not easy to untangle them. The cause of this confusion is not mere conceptual sloppiness. Rather, in my research on the meaning of life, I have come to see that the confusion is almost deliberate. Modern Western culture has left us with some severe, distinctive shortcomings and problems in creating a meaningful life. We have come to hope and think that individual identity contains the solutions to these problems. We want the self to be an answer to our problems of life's meaning. As a result, we are coming to place more and more emphasis on the self as a fundamental source of meaning, purpose, and value. The self is used to fill the value gap, or the existential vacuum, or whatever you want to call it. As the culture has turned away from the religious and moral certainties of the past, we have tried to get the individual self to take over many of their guiding functions. Today, the highest goals in life for many people involve knowing oneself, cultivating one's potential, fulfilling oneself, and so forth; these replace the older ideas of serving God and country and fulfilling socially based moral obligations. The self now has to serve as a basic value, and that is something it was not originally cut out for.

The fascination with self that pervades our culture—and our academic psychology—is more than an idle curiosity about what is inside the individual. The quest for self is so urgent, so important, because the self is taking over many of the basic functions of providing us with a meaning for life.

As I argued in my book on identity, the major trend in our history has been to place more and more demands on the individual self. Asking the self to provide us with enough purpose and value to make life meaningful is only our latest, and perhaps our most unfair demand. But it is one we make in deadly earnest.

REFERENCES

Alloy, L. B., & Abramson, L. Y. (1979). Judgment of contingency in depressed and non-depressed students: Sadder but wiser? *Journal of Experimental Psychology: General, 108,* 441–485.

Allport, G. W. (1937). *Personality: A psychological interpretation.* New York: Holt.

Allport, G. W. (1943). The ego in contemporary psychology. *Psychological Review, 50,* 451–478.

Argyle, M. (1987). *The psychology of happiness.* London: Methuen.

Baer, R., Hinkle, S., Smith, K., & Fenton, M. (1980). Reactance as a function of actual versus projected autonomy. *Journal of Personality and Social Psychology, 38*, 416–422.

Baumeister, R. F. (1982). A self-presentational view of social phenomena. *Psychological Bulletin, 91*, 3–26.

Baumeister, R. F. (1986). *Identity: Cultural change and the struggle for self.* New York: Oxford University Press.

Baumeister, R. F. (1991). *Meanings of life.* New York: Guilford Press.

Baumeister, R. F., & Tice, D. M. (1984). Role of self-presentation and choice in cognitive dissonance under forced compliance: Necessary or sufficient causes? *Journal of Personality and Social Psychology, 46*, 5–13.

Baumeister, R. F., Shapiro, J. J., & Tice, D. M. (1985). Two kinds of identity crisis. *Journal of Personality, 53*, 407–424.

Brehm, J. W. (1966). *A theory of psychological reactance.* New York: Academic Press.

Campbell, A. (1981). *The sense of well-being in America.* New York: McGraw-Hill.

Erikson, E. H. (1950). *Childhood and society.* New York: Norton.

Erikson, E. H. (1968). *Identity: Youth and crisis.* New York: Norton.

Greenwald, A. G. (1980). The totalitarian ego: Fabrication and revision of personal history. *American Psychologist, 35*, 603–613.

Greenwald, A. G., Bellezza, F. S., & Banaji, M. R. (1988). Is self-esteem a central ingredient of the self-concept? *Personality and Social and Psychology Bulletin, 14*, 34–45.

Kihlstrom, J. F., Cantor, N., Albright, J. S., Chew, B. R., Klein, S. B., & Niedenthal, P. M. (1988). Information processing and the study of the self. In L. Berkowitz (Ed.), *Advances in experimental social psychology* (Vol. 21, pp. 145–178). San Diego, CA: Academic Press.

Langer, E. (1975). The illusion of control. *Journal of Personality and Social Psychology, 29*, 253–264.

Linder, D. E., Cooper, J., & Jones, E. E. (1967). Decision freedom as a determinant of the role of incentive magnitude in attitude change. *Journal of Personality and Social Psychology, 6*, 245–254.

Marcia, J. E. (1966). Development and validation of ego-identity status. *Journal of Personality and Social Psychology, 3*, 551–558.

Marcia, J. E. (1967). Ego identity status: Relationship to change in self-esteem, "general maladjustment," and authoritarianism. *Journal of Personality, 35*, 118–133.

Markus, H., & Nurius, P. S. (1986). Possible selves. *American Psychologist, 41*, 954–969.

Schlenker, B. R. (1980). *Impression management.* Monterey, CA: Brooks/Cole.

Swann, W. B. (1987). Identity negotiation: Where two roads meet. *Journal of Personality and Social Psychology, 53*, 1038–1051.

Taylor, S. E., & Brown, J. (1988). Illusion and well-being: Some social psychological contributions to a theory of mental health. *Psychological Bulletin, 103*, 193–210.

CHAPTER THIRTEEN

Current Status of the Motive Concept

ROBERT A. EMMONS

INTRODUCTION

The period from 1968 until the early 1980s was not a prosperous one for personality psychology. There was growing disenchantment with the traditional individual differences paradigm and with the apparent lack of theoretical progress being made in the field. Authors of the *Annual Review* chapters on personality regularly bemoaned the state of the field. Apparently feeling a seven-year itch, the most trenchant critiques appeared at septimal intervals (Adelson, 1969; Rorer & Widiger, 1983; Sechrest, 1976). The major reason for the dissatisfaction was the failure of trait measures to predict specific behaviors and the failure of trait indicators to correlate appreciably with each other. The most popular solution to the behavioral consistency controversy, the person X–situation interaction approach, was misguided from the start. Personologists since the time of Allport argued that situations and persons are not independent of each other, that people seek out and avoid situations on the basis of their psychological propensities. This has now been demonstrated in several empirical studies (Diener *et al.*, 1984; Emmons & Diener, 1986; Emmons *et al.*, 1986; Snyder & Ickes, 1985). Clearly it makes no sense to partition variance to persons and situa-

ROBERT A. EMMONS • Department of Psychology, University of California, Davis, California 95616.

Fifty Years of Personality Psychology, edited by Kenneth H. Craik *et al.* Plenum Press, New York, 1993.

187

tions when those situations are to a great degree a function of the individuals who inhabit them. Furthermore, it has been proposed that stability and consistency in personality may be due in large part to the selection, evocation, and manipulation of environments congruent with the self (Buss, 1987; Emmons & Diener, 1986).

It is my belief that the behavioral consistency controversy was prolonged because of a failure to sufficiently take into account the role of motivation within personological functioning. Emphasis on traits and the goal of predictability led to an absence of interest in motivation and the equally worthy yet perhaps more complex goals of explanation and understanding. This was particularly disturbing as the pioneers in the field (Allport, Murray, Stagner, Lewin, McClelland) all stressed the dynamic striving character of behavior—its movement toward goals, goals that are largely idiosyncratic. Of central interest to both Allport and Stagner was motivation. For Allport, "motivation is the go of personality, and is, therefore, our most central problem" (1937, p. 218). According to Allport, the intentions and motivational dispositions "tell us what sort of future a person is trying to bring about, and this is the most important question we can ask of any mortal" (1937, p. 223). In addition, the unity of the self, according to Allport, is reflected in goal-directed striving. Similarly, Stagner noted that "discussing personality without regard to dynamics (i.e., motivation) is like describing the exterior of an automobile ... ignoring the characteristics of the engine" (1937, p. 257). Both Allport and Stagner firmly believed in the idiographic basis of motivation. Allport championed the notion of personal dispositions, of which there were two types: stylistic and motivational. Stagner offered a cultural interpretation of motivation in which he argued that the motives toward which people strive are culturally determined, but also agreed that "to know completely the motivation of any personality, we must study that person" (1937, p. 306).

Gordon Allport cast a very large shadow. He not only overshadowed Ross Stagner, but also his older brother, Floyd Allport, well-known to social psychologists but less so in personologist circles. The same year that Allport and Stagner were publishing their seminal texts, 1937, Floyd Allport published an article in *Character and Personality* (which of course became the *Journal of Personality* in 1945) entitled "Teleonomic Description in the Study of Personality." In this article, Floyd Allport proposed that personality traits were of limited utility for describing the personality of an individual. While some might dismiss this as a sibling rivalry, Allport was making an important point. An individual's personality might be better described, according to Floyd, in terms of what the person seems to be "trying to do" or the purpose or purposes that a person seems to be trying to carry out. Allport coined the term "teleonomic trend" to describe these behavioral tendencies, which he claimed were more dynamic and discriminating than trait terms. Allport also suggested that these teleonomic trends could be used to understand apparently inconsistent behavior (Pervin, 1983). It appears that our founding fathers were also involved in the consistency controversy, an issue that continued to occupy the time of a good many of us some 50 years later. Allport's concept of teleonomic trend became the topic of many a doctoral dissertation for his students, some of whom went on to achieve considerable prominence. These included Norman Frederiksen, John Valentine, Theodore Vallance, Arnold Tannenbaum, Richard Solomon, Wilbur Gregory, and Charlotte Simon. Unfortunately, the influence of the concept did not spread far from Syracuse University and never really caught on. A possible reason for this may have been the cumbersome method of assessing these trends, which required observers ratings from a large number of peers. Floyd Allport did not believe that what an individual said about his or her motives should be taken at face value. There is reason, however, to believe that the concept was abandoned prematurely. With the current emphasis on goal-directed behavior and idiographic approaches to motivation (Frese & Sabini, 1985; Pervin, 1989), the time seems ripe for its renewal. To this end, I have been developing the concept of a "personal striving" (Emmons, 1986), a modern-day descendant of the teleonomic trend. Personal strivings are idiographically coherent patterns of goal strivings and represent what an individual is typically trying to do. In other words, personal strivings refer to the typical types of goals that a person hopes to accomplish. Each individual can be characterized by a unique set of personal strivings. For example, a person may be "trying to appear attractive to the opposite sex," "trying to be a good listener to his or her friends," and "trying to be better than others." Personal strivings can be thought of as superordinate abstracting qualities that render a cluster of goals functionally equivalent for an individual. A personal striving is a unifying construct; it unites what may be phenotypically different goals or actions around a common quality or theme. Thus, a striving can be achieved in a variety of ways and satisfied through any one of a number of concrete goals.

It has become fashionable to posit hierarchical action control systems (Carver & Scheier, 1981; Hyland, 1988; Vallacher & Wegner, 1987). In such a hierarchy, personal strivings are situated between global, diffuse motives and concrete, specific actions, and, as such, represent a desirable yet unexplored middle ground in the hierarchy of personality functioning. Unlike teleonomic trends, personal strivings are not restricted to the behavioral domain. They may be cognitive, affective, or behavioral in nature. Also, our interest has been in what the person is consciously trying to do. Gordon Allport is known for suggesting that if you want to find out something about a person, ask that person directly. So we did. We also agree with Bernie Weiner's (1986) dictum that the royal road to the unconscious is less valuable than the dirt road to consciousness.

The heuristic value of the personal striving concept has now been demonstrated in a number of studies, including predicting levels of subjective well-being (Emmons, 1986); the influence of conflict and ambivalence on psychological and physical well-being (Emmons & King, 1988); the relationship between self-complexity and affective reactivity (Emmons & King, 1989); and daily life events and well-being (Emmons, 1991). A review of the personal striving literature can be found in Emmons (1989).

OTHER CURRENT APPROACHES

Stated simply, current approaches to motivation fall into one of two types. First is the motive concept as defined by McClelland (1951, 1985) and his students (Atkinson & Birch, 1970; McAdams, 1985, 1988a; Winter & Stewart, 1978). These authors define a motive disposition as a class or cluster of affectively tinged goals, or a recurrent preference for certain experiences. A small number of social motives, namely the "big three" of achievement, affiliation–intimacy, and power, are sufficient to describe and explain behavior and experience. A more recent exemplar of this approach is McAdams's (1985) concept of "imago," defined as "an idealized and personified image of the self" (p. 178). Imagoes are the central elements of a person's identity and are centered around the themes of intimacy and power. Imagoes are broad, superordinate constructs that encompass interpersonal styles, values and beliefs, and personal needs and motives (McAdams, 1988a).

Scoring systems for the major motives based on analysis of stories told in response to pictures similar to those in the Thematic Apperception Test (TAT) are well-established and well-validated. It would appear that psychometric concerns over the use of the TAT have subsided. The literature on social motives continues to grow. Some of the more impressive uses have been in the application of social motives to predicting important life outcomes such as physical health (Jemmott, 1987; McClelland, 1989) and presidential performance (Winter, 1987).

The other major type of motivational unit being adopted by investigators is idiographic in nature. In addition to the personal striving concept discussed earlier, several other goal units have been proposed. Klinger (1977) developed the notion of a "current concern" out of dissatisfaction with the failure of the motive dispositions to predict spontaneous thought content. A current concern is a hypothetical motivational state in between the identification of a goal and either the attainment of the goal or disengagement from it. This hypothetical state guides a person's ongoing thoughts, emotional reactions, and behavior during the time it is active. A similar though independently developed concept is the personal project (Little, 1983, 1989; Palys & Little, 1983). Rooted in Murray's concept of a serial program, personal projects are extended sets of actions intended to achieve a personal goal. Lastly, Cantor (Cantor & Kihlstrom, 1987; Cantor & Langston, 1989) recently developed the concept of life task, defined as "problems that people are currently working on" (Cantor & Kihlstrom, 1987, p. 4). These life tasks, consensual in nature but idiographically defined, organize and give meaning to a person's everyday activities and are especially salient during life transitions, such as marriage or graduation from college. Klinger (1989), Cantor and Zirkel (1990) and Emmons (in press) provide an elaboration of and a critical review of the similarities and differences among these goal units.

Recently, McClelland and his associates (McClelland et al., 1989; Weinberger & McClelland, 1990) have distinguished two forms of motivation. One is an affectively–biologically based system, termed "implicit motives," and the other a cognitively–experientially based system, termed "self-attributed motives." These correspond to the social motive and idiographic goal approaches described earlier. These two systems are believed to develop independently, to operate independently of each other, and to predict different classes of behavior. The degree to which they are independent, however, is disputable. Emmons and McAdams (1991) found significant relations between personal strivings (a form of self-attributed motives) and motive dispositions as assessed by a picture-story exercise (implicit motives). Future research should identify conditions under which implicit and explicit motives converge or fail to.

While the late 1960s and 1970s represented a stagnant period in personality psychology's growth, recently there has been a much needed injection of new directions and fresh perspectives into the field. These range from interest in biological influences on personality (Buss, 1984; Kenrick et al., 1985) to studying the naturally occurring stream of behavior and private experience using innovative methods (Craik, 1986; Singer & Kolligian, 1987) to a resurgence of interest in focusing on persons and lives (McAdams, 1988b). No longer do we feel obligated to cite Walter Mischel in the opening paragraph of our articles nor apologize for the sad state of affairs of the field. A renewal of interest in motivational concepts has played a significant role in this revival. It is appropriate that on this 50th anniversary we are returning to an idiographic analysis of motivation. There has been a clear shift from the nomothetic social motives, which dominated the motivational literature over the past 30 years, toward more molecular, idiographic goal units, which are tied closer to everyday naturally occurring experience. Goals possess many desirable properties. Their hierarchical structure with links to both higher and lower levels, the flexibility and discriminativeness yet coherence that the concept implies and its amenability to individual differences measurement make the goal concept a highly desirable unit of analysis for personality psychology.

RECOMMENDATIONS

We have seen a proliferation of concepts in recent years, and more can be expected. This is a healthy sign, but somewhere down the road it needs to be tempered by attempts to demarcate the boundaries between these concepts. Surely if we asked a subject to provide a separate list of his or her personal projects, current concerns, life tasks, and personal strivings, there will be some overlap. The degree of overlap will partially depend on the instructional set used. Attention needs to be directed toward clarifying three types of relationships both within and between the hierarchical control of action:

1. The horizontal structure. What is the relationship between these motivational units of analysis? To what degree would one's current concerns, say, overlap with one's life tasks? Could the current concerns be derived from the life tasks? Would the life tasks emerge from a clustering analysis of the current concerns? Some, perhaps most, current concerns and personal projects would not achieve status as life tasks or personal strivings, such as the examples mentioned earlier, even though they may serve as compelling temporary guides for thought and action. Attention needs to be directed toward specifying the time frame and category width of these respective concepts.

2. The vertical structure. Can these idiographic units of analysis be related to units at a more abstract level of analysis, such as the nomothetic motives? As an example, we have developed a system for coding personal strivings into the major motive systems, such as achievement, affiliation–intimacy, and power. Similarly, Cantor and Kihlstrom (1987) note that at a general level of description, life task

themes for college students center on issues of intimacy and achievement. It may very well be that at an abstract level of analysis, most personalized goal concerns tap either agency or communion (McAdams, 1985). Although movement to a broader level of analysis violates the idiographic nature of these constructs, it is recognized that for certain purposes a more superordinate level of description is desirable. Substantial literatures have developed around each of the major motive systems (Aronoff & Wilson, 1985; McClelland, 1985), so it is essential to integrate this level of analysis with the more circumscribed idiographic units. The Emmons and McAdams (1991) study mentioned earlier suggests that this is indeed feasible.

3. Interhierarchical relationships. What is the relation of these motivational units to nonmotivational units, such as to personality traits? One can classify acts into traits categories, as in the act-frequency approach (Buss & Craik, 1983); however, acts can also be classified in terms of what the person is trying to do, as in the personal striving approach (Emmons, 1989a,b). These two theoretical systems offer different ways for classifying everyday experience and will add to our knowledge of the relations between trait-based and motive-based accounts of action (Alston, 1970, 1975; Buss & Craik, 1983; Emmons, 1989b).

The complexity of relationships within, between, and across personality and motivational hierarchies is likely to be considerable. But it is a complexity that should be embraced rather than avoided. As we celebrate the 50th anniversary of Allport's, Murray's, and Stagner's pioneering works, let us not be discouraged by the complexity of personality. After all, there is nothing in Allport, Stagner, or Murray that would have led us to believe that the study of personality was going to be easy. And surely there is enough work remaining to be done to keep us busy for at least another 50 years.

REFERENCES

Adelson, J. (1969). Personality. *Annual Review of Psychology, 19*, 217–252.

Allport, F. (1937). Teleonomic description in the study of personality. *Character and Personality, 5*, 202–214.

Allport, G. W. (1937). *Personality: A psychological interpretation.* New York: Holt, Rinehart & Winston.

Alston, W. P. (1970). Toward a logical geography of personality: Traits and deeper lying personality characteristics. In H. D. Kiefer & M. K. Munitz (Eds.), *Mind, science, and history* (pp. 70–105). Albany, NY: SUNY Press.

Alston, W. P. (1975). Traits, consistency, and conceptual alternatives for personality theory. *Journal for the Theory of Social Behavior, 5*, 17–48.

Aronoff, J., & Wilson, J. P. (1985). *Personality in the social process*. Hillsdale, NJ: Erlbaum.

Atkinson, J. W., & Birch, D. (1970). *The dynamics of action*. New York: Wiley.

Buss, D. M. (1984). Evolutionary biology and personality psychology: Toward a conception of human nature and individual differences. *American Psychologist, 39,* 1135–1147.

Buss, D. M. (1987). Selection, evocation, and manipulation. *Journal of Personality and Social Psychology, 53,* 1214–1221.

Buss, D. M., & Craik, K. H. (1983). The act-frequency approach to personality. *Psychological Review, 90,* 105–126.

Cantor, N., & Kihlstrom, J. F. (1987). *Personality and social intelligence*. Englewood Cliffs, NJ: Prentice-Hall.

Cantor, N., & Langston, C. (1989). Ups and downs of life tasks in a life transition. In L. A. Pervin (Ed.), *Goal concepts in personality and social psychology* (pp. 127–167). Hillsdale, NJ: Erlbaum.

Cantor, N., & Zirkel, S. (1990). Personality, cognition, and purposive behavior. In L. A. Pervin (Ed.), *Handbook of personality theory and research* (pp. 135–164). New York: Guilford Press.

Carver, C. S., & Scheier, M. F., (1981). *Attention and self-regulation: A Control theory approach to human behavior*. New York: Springer.

Craik, K. H. (1986). Personality research methods: A historical overview. *Journal of Personality, 54,* 18–51.

Diener, E., Larsen, R. J., & Emmons, R. A. (1984). Person X situation interactions: Choice of situations and congruence models of interactionism. *Journal of Personality and Social Psychology, 47,* 580–592.

Emmons, R. A. (1986). Personal strivings: An approach to personality and subjective well-being. *Journal of Personality and Social Psychology, 51,* 1058–1068.

Emmons, R. A. (1989a). The personal striving approach to personality. In L. A. Pervin (Ed.), *Goal concepts in personality and social psychology* (pp. 87–126). Hillsdale, NJ: Erlbaum.

Emmons, R. A. (1989b). Exploring the relations between motives and traits: The case of narcissism. In D. M. Buss & N. Cantor (Eds.), *Personality psychology: Recent trends and emerging directions* (pp. 32–44). New York: Springer-Verlag.

Emmons, R. A. (1991). Personal strivings, daily life events, and physical and psychological well-being. *Journal of Personality, 59,* 453–472.

Emmons, R. A. (in press). Motives and life goals. In S. Briggs, R. Hogan, & W. Jones (Eds.), *Handbook of personality psychology*. Orlando, FL: Academic Press.

Emmons, R. A., & Diener, E. (1986). Situation selection as a moderator of response consistency and stability. *Journal of Personality and Social Psychology, 51,* 1013–1019.

Emmons, R. A., & King, L. A. (1988). Conflict among personal strivings: Immediate and long-term implications for psychological and physical well-being. *Journal of Personality and Social Psychology, 54,* 1040–1048.

Emmons, R. A., & King, L. A. (1989). Personal striving differentiation and affective reactivity. *Journal of Personality and Social Psychology, 56,* 478–484.

Emmons, R. A., & McAdams, D. P. (1991). Personal strivings and motive dispositions: Exploring the links. *Personality and Social Psychology Bulletin, 17,* 648–654.

Emmons, R. A., Diener, E., & Larsen, R. J. (1986). Choice and avoidance of everyday situations and affect congruence: Two models of reciprocal interactionism. *Journal of Personality and Social Psychology, 51,* 815–826.

Frese, M., & Sabini, J. (1985). *Goal directed behavior: The concept of action in psychology.* Hillsdale, NJ: Erlbaum.

Hyland, M. E. (1988). Motivational control theory: An integrative framework. *Journal of Personality and Social Psychology, 55,* 642–651.

Jemmott, J. B. (1987). Social motives and susceptibility to disease: Stalking individual differences in health risks. *Journal of Personality, 55,* 267–298.

Kenrick, D. T., Montello, D. R., & MacFarlane, S. (1985). Personality: Social learning, social cognition, or sociobiology? In R. Hogan & W. H. Jones (Eds.), *Perspectives in personality* (Vol. 1, pp. 201–234). Greenwich, CT: JAI Press.

Klinger, E. (1977). *Meaning and void: Inner experience and the incentives in people's lives.* Minneapolis: University of Minnesota Press.

Little, B. R. (1983). Personal projects: A rationale and method for investigation. *Environment and Behavior, 15,* 273–309.

Little, B. R. (1989). Personal projects analysis: Trivial pursuits, magnificent obsessions, and the search for coherence. In D. M. Buss & N. Cantor (Eds.), *Personality psychology: Recent trends and emerging directions* (pp. 15–31). New York: Springer-Verlag.

McAdams, D. P. (1985). *Power, intimacy, and the life story: Personological inquires into identity.* Homewood, IL: Dorsey Press.

McAdams, D. P. (1988a). Biography, narrative, and lives: An introduction. *Journal of Personality, 56,* 1–18.

McAdams, D. P. (1988b). Personal needs and personal relationships. In S. Duck (Ed.), *Handbook of research on personal relationships* (pp. 7–22). New York: Wiley.

McClelland, D. C. (1951). *Personality.* New York: Dryden.

McClelland, D. C. (1985). *Human motivation.* Glenview, IL: Scott, Foresman.

McClelland, D. C. (1989). Motivational factors in health and disease. *American Psychologist, 44,* 675–683.

McClelland, D. C., Koestner, R., & Weinberger, J. (1989). How do self-attributed and implicit motives differ? *Psychological Review, 96,* 690–702.

Palys, T. S., & Little, B. R. (1983). Perceived life satisfaction and the organization of personal project systems. *Journal of Personality and Social Psychology, 44,* 1221–1230.

Pervin, L. A. (1983). The stasis and flow of behavior: Toward a theory of goals. In M. M. Page (Ed.), *Nebraska Symposium on Motivation* (pp. 1–53). Lincoln: University of Nebraska Press.

Pervin, L. A. (1989). *Goal concepts in personality and social psychology.* Hillsdale, NJ: Erlbaum.

Rorer, L. G., & Widiger, T. A. (1983). Personality structure and assessment. *Annual Review of Psychology, 34,* 431–463.

Sechrest, L. (1976). Personality. *Annual Review of Psychology, 27,* 1–27.

Singer, J. L., & Kolligan, J. (1987). Personality: Developments in the study of private experience. *Annual Review of Psychology, 38,* 533–574.

Snyder, M., & Ickes, W. (1985). Personality and social behavior. In G. Lindzey & E. Aronson (Eds.), *Handbook of social psychology* (Vol. 3, pp. 881–910). Hillsdale, NJ: Erlbaum.

Stagner, R. (1937). *Psychology of personality.* New York: McGraw-Hill.

Vallacher, R. R., & Wegner, D. M. (1987). What do people think they're doing: Action identification and human behavior. *Psychological Review, 94,* 3–15.

Weinberger, J., & McClelland, D. C. (1990). Cognitive versus traditional motivational models. In R. M. Sorrentino & E. T. Higgins (Eds.), *Handbook of motivation and cognition* (Vol. 2, pp. 562–597). New York: Guilford Press.

Weiner, B. (1986). Attribution, emotion, and action. In R. M. Sorrentino & E. T. Higgins (Eds.), *Handbook of motivation and cognition* (pp. 281–312). New York: Guilford Press.

Winter, D. G. (1987). Leader appeal, leader performance, and the motive profile of leaders and followers: A study of American presidents and elections. *Journal of Personality and Social Psychology, 52,* 196–202.

Winter, D. G., & Stewart, A. J. (1978). The power motive. In H. London & J. E. Exner, Jr. (Eds.), *Dimensions of personality* (pp. 391–448). New York: Wiley.

CHAPTER FOURTEEN

The Ability to Judge Others from Their Expressive Behaviors

BELLA M. DePAULO

Allport (1937) had a very strong opinion about where to look in order to figure out the content and structure of people's personalities: Look at their expressive movements. That is, look not only at what people are doing, but how they are doing it; listen not only to what they are communicating, but also the manner in which they are communicating it. In telling us to take these expressive movements very seriously, Allport was not telling us to disregard what people are doing or trying to do. In fact, he maintains that what people are trying to do is most fundamental in revealing the nature of their traits. But still, he cautioned, we should not ignore the "hows" of behavior. Sometimes the ways that people do things are redundant with the fact that they are doing those things. To embellish Allport's own example a little (1937, pp. 464–465), if a group of people were to walk to Yankee Stadium every time the Yankees had a home game, that behavior would suggest that they were very enthusiastic about Yankee baseball. If, in addition, one were to observe that on the way to the Stadium, they all had bubbly faces and sprightly gaits, and that their tee shirts, hats, watches, and tote bags were all emblazoned with the Yankee insignia, that information would only serve to underscore the information already available from the knowledge that they attend every game. But, Allport

BELLA M. DePAULO • Department of Psychology, University of Virginia, Charlottesville, Virginia 22903.

Fifty Years of Personality Psychology, edited by Kenneth H. Craik *et al.* Plenum Press, New York, 1993.

claimed, expressive movements can do more than simply tell us the same information in a different way. Allport believed that expressive behavior is unconsciously determined and therefore can provide a clue to deep-seated aspects of personality that are not always evident in the content of behavior.

THE CONSISTENCY OF EXPRESSIVE BEHAVIORS

Allport had a very broad view of the kinds of behaviors that might be meaningfully expressive. Some of these are very familiar to contemporary students of nonverbal communication, including cues such as facial expressions, body postures, speech fluency, and vocal intensity. Other expressive cues that interested Allport are somewhat less familiar to us now—cues such as the speed with which we draw things, the size of the check marks that we make when filling out checklists, and the degree to which we overestimate the size of angles. Still other cues are ones that were once of some interest to psychologists, but, with a few exceptions, are no longer taken very seriously. These include styles of handwriting and the pressure applied to one's pen or pencil while writing.

Allport thought that these very diverse expressive behaviors fell into three basic clusters of expansiveness, emphasis, and outward tendency or extraversion. But if he had modern data-analytic techniques at his disposal, his heart would be not in the specific clusters but in the unrotated first factor. He believed that one of the fundamental truths about expressive behaviors was that they all simultaneously expressed the same trait. To cite one of his favorite quotes, "One and the same spirit is manifest in all."

Allport's assumption, then, is clearly one of consistency of expressive movements. He believed that different expressive behaviors were consistent with each other and that any given expressive behavior, for a particular individual, would be consistent across time and across situations. His expectations were not absolute, however. Instead, he cautioned that we should never expect consistency to be perfect. If it were, then we could take any one expressive behavior and learn everything about personality from it. In contrast, Allport's belief was that we need to look at the entire *patterning* of expressive cues and that we should expect to find as much consistency in expressive behavior as there is in the personality itself—not more and not less. Expressive behavior, like personality, includes much that is consistent, but it is also marked by conflict and contradiction.

Despite the words of caution in Allport's conclusions, the thrust of his perspective was very optimistic with regard to the questions of whether we can expect to be able to understand accurately other people's feelings and traits. The promise of this perspective was not lost on subsequent researchers, and there have been attempts to search for consistencies across different kinds of expressive behaviors and for links between personality and expressive behavior.

Though no one is quite ready to tie a ribbon around the results of this research and present it to the ghost of Gordon Allport, I think it is fair to say that some progress has been made. You can see evidence of that progress in the refinement in the kinds of questions that are posed. We no longer ask simply whether there is consistency nor even just how much consistency there might be; we now ask where we should look for this consistency—in what kinds of people, what kinds of situations, and along what sorts of dimensions? And we are all very sensitized to the importance of asking the complementary question of when not to expect any consistency at all.

Allport, in his 1937 book, bemoaned the fact that there was very little research on the relationship between particular traits and particular expressive behaviors, and noted that methodologically, researchers were not at all sure how to go about producing the relevant data. Representative of the immature state of the literature at that time was Adler's suggestion, based on no data, that one way to distinguish optimists from pessimists was to observe them when they are sleeping; pessimists, he said, would "curl themselves into the smallest possible space and . . . draw the covers over their heads" (quoted in Allport, 1937, p. 486). Contemporary researchers would know how to substantiate (or insubstantiate) this particular claim empirically, but have not quite brought themselves to do so. However, researchers have documented other stable expressive differences; for example, we know about the loud voices of extraverts (Scherer, 1979) and the fidgety and withdrawn behavior of the socially anxious (Leary, 1983; Schlenker & Leary, 1982).

THE DELIBERATE REGULATION
OF EXPRESSIVE BEHAVIORS

I think one very important development in the study of expressive behavior that cannot be fully credited to Allport is the literature on the deliberate regulation and control of expressive behaviors (see DePaulo, 1991, 1992; DePaulo et al., 1992). Although Allport was willing to admit—though somewhat grudgingly, I think—that people might try deliberately to disguise their expressive behaviors, he was willing to concede this only for specific behaviors or for short periods of time. When it came to what he referred to as *style*, or the totality and complexity of all expressive behaviors taken together, he did not think that deliberate disguise was even a possibility. In his words, "Style ... develops gradually from within; it cannot for long be simulated or feigned" (1937, p. 493; see also Hogan *et al.*, 1985).

Enter Erving Goffman (1959), and a growing list of followers and semifollowers. From an impression management perspective, many behaviors do not emanate purely and spontaneously from the true personality within; rather, they are the product of deliberate regulation and control. Even behaviors that appear perfectly spontaneous and natural are not necessarily so; instead, they might be the creations of especially smooth and skilled self-presenters. Or, it may be the case that the expressive behaviors in question are being emitted un-self-consciously at the moment, but only because they were carefully constructed at one time in the past, then practiced and practiced and practiced until they became habitual and thus nearly indistinguishable from truly spontaneous expressions (cf. Schlenker, 1980). So the first point about the deliberate regulation of expressive behaviors is that it may well occur quite frequently.

The second point is that deliberate attempts at controlling one's expressive behaviors can ruin expressive consistency. If, for example, upon demolishing a much-loathed opponent at tennis, you allow yourself just a little tiny smile, woe to the researcher who tries to find smug mirth in every other aspect of your expressive behavior, too.

Third, attempts at deliberate regulation can also enhance expressive consistency (Lippa, 1983). If a person wanted to convince you that she was an extravert, she might deliberately try to convey extraversion in every way she could think of. She might try to don an extraverted posture and extraverted gestures, she might speak with an extravert's voice, and put on an extraverted face. So, consistency across different expressive behaviors might be accentuated. Deliberate control can also increase the consistency of the link between traits and expressive behaviors. I think that most people believe that their true personalities, as they construe them, are immediately apparent to others (cf. DePaulo *et al.*, 1987). They seem to feel that there is no need to make an effort to appear to be the way they think they really are, because they will appear that way even if they do not try. However, when it is really important to them that another person should be aware of their virtuous personality traits, they might not take any chances. The person in this situation who believes she is an extravert and really is an extravert will take great pains to make sure that her extraversion is abundantly clear to her partner. This is deliberate regulation, but it is regulation that strengthens the link between personality and expressiveness rather than shattering it.

A further point about deliberate attempts at expressive control is that they are not always successful. Freud (1959, p. 94), of course, delighted in warning us that if we try to keep a secret, betrayal will ooze out of us at every pore. When the data on this issue rolled in, they suggested that some pores are much "oozier" than others. For example, when people are not too aroused or emotional, they tend to be very successful at regulating their facial expressions. Research on deception provides some interesting demonstrations of this. When the stakes for telling a successful lie are not too high, liars are very good at using their faces to fool their targets. In fact, in those situations, their targets might actually have a somewhat better chance of detecting the lie if they cannot see the liar's face at all. However, as the stakes go up, and it becomes more important to the liar to get away with the lie, facial expressions and sometimes other nonverbal cues, too, are likely to "leak" the information that the liar is trying to hide (DePaulo & Kirkendol, 1989; DePaulo et al., 1985).

Deliberate attempts at regulation can fail for other reasons, too. For example, some people are unaware of their expressive behaviors or insensitive to their impact on others; still others realize that such behaviors are impactful, but are inept at controlling them. Further, sometimes the very act of trying to control expressive behaviors backfires, and the person's behavior appears to others to be awkward, unnatural, or overly controlled (DePaulo, et al., 1983).

The final point I want to make about the impression management perspective on expressive behaviors is that it suggests a different way of conceptualizing such behaviors. From this perspective, expressive behaviors are not always unbridled expressions of a true underlying personality. Instead, they might sometimes be better regarded as manifestations of social skills—skills that can perhaps be practiced and trained (Argyle & Kendon, 1967; Friedman, 1979). From this perspective, socially anxious individuals are not necessarily stuck with their stammering, gaze avoidance, and desperate nods and smiles, and even extraverts can learn to calm down and shut up.

I see the impression management perspective as complementary to, rather than competitive with, Allport's ideas about un-self-conscious expressiveness. Certainly there are times, such as when we are caught up in the emotion of the moment, that we are spontaneously and un-self-consciously expressive. Further, even when we do try purposefully to regulate our expressive behaviors, even these attempts may be stamped with the ink of our own personal styles.

ALLPORT'S SIX QUESTIONS ABOUT THE FACE

Allport realized that much remained to be learned about expressive behaviors, especially facial behaviors, and he outlined six questions that he thought could guide the scientific study of the face. The first of these sounds much like a quaint hypothesis from 50 years ago. Allport asked whether "native factors in personality, such as temperament and intelligence, are reflected in the bodily form and structure [such as "the bony configuration of the face"]; whereas acquired traits are represented in muscular sets and changes" (1937, p. 482). The other five questions, though, could almost serve as chapter headings in a contemporary textbook on the face.

The second question Allport posed was about the eyes. Allport wondered whether "the subtleties of glance ... are especially rich in expressive significance?" (1937, p. 482). Fifty years later, we now know much about the flavor of that richness. We know that gaze can express affiliation and liking and dominance and status. We know that it can be used to gain information, to avoid giving away information, and to regulate the flow of conversation. We know that it can grab a target's attention and arouse that person, so that she is primed to figure out why she is being observed. Finally, I think it would please Allport to hear that patterns of gazing have been empirically linked to gender, culture, psychiatric status, and, of course, personality (e.g., Argyle & Cook, 1976; Ellsworth & Langer, 1976; Ellsworth & Ludwig, 1972; Exline, 1972; Fehr & Exline, 1987).

Allport's third question was, "Can patterns of facial expression ... be analyzed into the contraction of separate muscles?" (1937, p. 482). It took researchers about 40 of the 50 years to get to this question in a comprehensive way, but the end results are truly elegant. In Ekman's Facial Action Coding System (Ekman & Friesen, 1976), for example, any facial movement can be described in terms of the separate facial muscles whose triggering produced that movement (see also Izard, 1983). This, of course, is just what Dr. Allport ordered.

Allport's fourth question was about smiling. "Why," he asked, "is the smile so disarming a pattern of expression?" Allport undoubtedly had a charming smile in mind when he posed this question, and we still do not have a complete answer to the question of why such smiles can be so disarmingly charming. But we do know that they are not all so scintillating; they can be perfidious as well as polite and sociable, artful as well as ingenuous, and miserable as well as mirthful (e.g., Brunner, 1979; Bugental *et al.*, 1971; Ekman & Friesen, 1982; Ekman, Friesen, & O'Sullivan, 1988; Kraut & Johnston, 1979). And, true to tradition, research has uncovered stable individual differences in at least some of these uses of the smile (e.g., Hall, 1984).

Judge for yourself whether this fifth question has a contemporary ring to it. Allport asked, "Why so frequently does an affective reaction to liking or disliking a stranger precede (and sometimes preclude) objective judgment?" He goes on to note that sometimes when we have a strong affective reaction to someone we just met, it may be because that person is similar to some other person about whom we feel strongly. Allport goes on to ask, "[If this is so, then] why is the *affective* judgment swifter than the conscious recognition of similarity?"

The sixth question Allport raised takes us back more directly to the issue with which we began—that of the ability to judge others accurately on the basis of their expressive behaviors. In formulating this last question, Allport referred to an impactful study conducted by Landis in 1924. In this study, Landis tried to elicit spontaneous emotional reactions in very involving and realistic ways. For example, one of the tasks that Landis asked his subjects to perform was to slice the head off a live rat. What he found was that when his subjects were chopping off the rat's head, some of them looked disgusted, but others looked rather somber, and still others actually laughed. This study, and others showing similar results, had a devastating impact on future research on nonverbal expressiveness. For all the wrong reasons, theorists jumped to the inappropriate conclusion that we simply could not expect people to be able to make accurate judgments of others based only on their facial expressions. Allport was particularly prescient on this issue; he thought he smelled a rat. "If," he asked, "... patterns of expression differ markedly from individual to individual, how does it happen that we are able to judge other people as well as we do?" Allport was a great believer in intuition, and in this case his intuition told him that people can indeed in many instances make accurate judgments about others on the basis of their facial expressions. The missing link in the Landis study was the one between the situation of chopping off a rat's head and the particular emotion experienced by each individual subject. Different subjects presumably experienced different emotions or sets of emotions and had different self-presentational goals. Years later, researchers would try to manipulate the emotions experienced by subjects, so that on any given trial, they were experiencing one of the basic emotions in a relatively pure form. When researchers such as Izard (1971) and Ekman (1972; Ekman & Friesen, 1986) elicited emotions such as surprise, happiness, sadness, anger, fear, disgust, and (most recently) contempt in this very careful way, they found that the resulting facial expressions could be recognized by persons on every continent and in every little village into which these researchers ventured. This research, of course, was on accuracy of emotion perception, and Allport was even more interested in accuracy of personality perception. But that issue, too, has resurfaced, and with a theoretical and methodological vengeance. At this very moment, three recast papers on accuracy of person perception are already in print in *Psychological Bulletin*: David Funder's (1987), Dave Kenny and Linda Albright's (1987), and Arie Kruglanski's (1989). Accuracy is back—and just in time for this fiftieth anniversary celebration.

REFERENCES

Allport, G. W. (1937). *Personality*. New York: Holt.

Argyle, M., & Cook, M. (1976). *Gaze and mutual gaze*. Cambridge, England: Cambridge University Press.

Argyle, M., & Kendon, A. (1967). The experimental analysis of social performance. In L. Berkowitz (Ed.), *Advances in experimental social psychology* (Vol. 3, pp. 55–98). New York: Academic Press.

Brunner, L. J. (1979). Smiles can be back channels. *Journal of Personality and Social Psychology, 37*, 728–734.

Bugental, D. E., Love, L. R., & Gianetto, R. M. (1971). Perfidious feminine faces. *Journal of Personality and Social Psychology, 17*, 314–318.

DePaulo, B. M. (1992). Nonverbal behavior and self-presentation. *Psychological Bulletin, 111*, 203–243.

DePaulo, B. M. (1991). Nonverbal behavior and self-presentation: A developmental perspective. In R. S. Feldman & B. Rime (Eds.), *Fundamentals of nonverbal behavior* (pp. 351–397). Cambridge: Cambridge University Press.

DePaulo, B. M., Blank, A. L., & Hairfield, J. G. (1992). Expressiveness and expressive control. *Personality and Social Psychology Bulletin, 18*, 276–285.

DePaulo, B. M., Kenny, D. A., Hoover, C. W., Webb, W., & Oliver, P. V. (1987). Accuracy of person perception: Do people know what kinds of impressions they convey? *Journal of Personality and Social Psychology, 52*, 303–315.

DePaulo, B. M., & Kirkendol, S. E. (1989). The motivational impairment effect in the communication of deception. In J. Yuille (Ed.), *Credibility assessment* (pp. 51–70). Belgium: Kluwer Academic Publishers.

DePaulo, B. M., Lanier, K., & Davis, T. (1983). Detecting the deceit of the motivated liar. *Journal of Personality and Social Psychology, 45*, 1096–1103.

DePaulo, B. M., Stone, J. I., & Lassiter, G. D. (1985). Deceiving and detecting deceit. In B. R. Schlenker (Ed.), *The self and social life* (pp. 323–370). New York: McGraw-Hill.

Ekman, P. (1972). Universals and cultural differences in facial expressions of emotion. In

J. K. Cole (Ed.), *Nebraska symposium on motivation, 1971* (Vol. 19, pp. 207–283). Lincoln: University of Nebraska Press.

Ekman, P., & Friesen, W. V. (1976). Measuring facial movement. *Environmental Psychology and Nonverbal Behavior, 1,* 56–75.

Ekman, P., & Friesen, W. V. (1982). Felt, false, and miserable smiles. *Journal of Nonverbal Behavior, 6,* 238–252.

Ekman, P., & Friesen, W. V. (1986). A new pan-cultural facial expression of emotion. *Motivation and Emotion, 10,* 159–168.

Ekman, P., Friesen, W. V., & O'Sullivan, M. (1988). Smiles while lying. *Journal of Personality and Social Psychology, 54,* 414–420.

Ellsworth, P. C., & Langer, E. J. (1976). Staring and approach: An interpretation of the stare as a non-specific activator. *Journal of Personality and Social Psychology, 33,* 117–122.

Ellsworth, P. C., & Ludwig, L. M. (1972). Visual behavior in social interaction. *Journal of Communication, 22,* 375–403.

Exline, R. V. (1972). Visual interaction: The glances of power and preference. In J. K. Cole (Ed.), *Nebraska symposium on motivation, 1971* (Vol. 19, pp. 163-206). Lincoln: University of Nebraska Press.

Fehr, B.J., & Exline, R. V. (1987). Social visual interaction. In A. W. Siegman & S. Feldstein (Eds.), *Nonverbal behavior and communication* (2nd ed., pp. 225–348). Hillsdale, NJ: Erlbaum.

Freud, S. (1959). *Collected papers.* New York: Basic Books.

Friedman, H. (1979). The concept of skill in nonverbal communication: Implications for understanding social interaction. In R. Rosenthal (Ed.), *Skill in nonverbal communication.* Cambridge, MA: Oelgeschlager, Gunn, & Hain.

Funder, D. C. (1987). Errors and mistakes: Evaluating the accuracy of social judgment. *Psychological Bulletin, 101,* 75–90.

Goffman, E. (1959). *The presentation of self in everyday life.* Garden City, NY: Doubleday.

Hall, J. A. (1984). *Nonverbal sex differences.* Baltimore, MD: Johns Hopkins University Press.

Hogan, R., Jones, W. H., & Cheek, J. M. (1985). Socioanalytic theory. In B. R. Schlenker (Ed.), *The self and social life* (pp. 175–198). New York: McGraw-Hill.

Izard, C. E. (1971). *The face of emotion.* New York: Appleton-Century-Crofts.

Izard, C. E. (1983). *The maximally discriminative facial movement scoring system* (rev. ed.). Unpublished manuscript, University of Delaware.

Kenny, D. A., & Albright, L. (1987). Accuracy in interpersonal perception: A social relations analysis. *Psychological Bulletin, 102,* 390–402.

Kraut, R. E., & Johnson, R. E. (1979). Social and emotional messages of smiling: An ethological approach. *Journal of Personality and Social Psychology, 37,* 1539–1553.

Kruglanski, A. W. (1989). The psychology of being "right": The problem of accuracy in social perception and cognition. *Psychological Bulletin, 106,* 395–409.

Landis, C. (1924). Studies of emotional reactions: II. General behavior and facial expression. *Journal of Comparative Psychology, 4,* 447–509.

Leary, M. R. (1983). *Understanding social anxiety.* Beverly Hills, CA: Sage.

Lippa, R. (1983). Expressive behavior. In L. Wheeler & P. Shaver (Eds.), *The review of personality and social psychology* (Vol. 4, pp. 181–205). Beverly Hills, CA: Sage.

Scherer, K. R. (1979). Personality markers in speech. In K. R. Scherer & H. Giles (Eds.),

Social markers in speech (pp. 147–209). Cambridge: Cambridge University Press.

Schlenker, B. R. (1980). *Impression management: The self concept, social identity, and interpersonal relations.* Monterey, CA: Brooks/Cole.

Schlenker, B. R., & Leary, M. R. (1982). Social anxiety and self-presentation: A conceptualization and model. *Psychological Bulletin, 92,* 641–669.

CHAPTER FIFTEEN

Judgments of Personality and Personality Itself

DAVID C. FUNDER

My topic is accuracy in personality judgment and the kind of research we need to do *if* we are interested in it. I emphasize the "if" because, perhaps surprisingly, not everybody is interested in accuracy, not even every psychologist who studies judgments of personality—a point I shall return to below. But one psychologists who surely was interested in how accurate personality judgments might be was Gordon Allport.

ALLPORT ON PERSONALITY JUDGMENT

One of our co-symposiasts has been known to refer occasionally to the good Doctor Allport as "Saint Gordon." It is true that in some circles Allport's classic 1937 volume has attained nearly the status of a sacred text. So let us go directly to this esteemed book, which includes a short chapter on "The Ability to Judge People." Allport began with a brief overview of the topic as he saw it, a half-century ago:

> From the psychologist's point of view some of the most important problems involved in judgments of personality are the following: (1) the nature and reliability of first impressions, (2) the chief factors involved in judging, (3) the value of interviews, (4) the ques-

DAVID C. FUNDER • Department of Psychology, University of California, Riverside, California 92521.

Fifty Years of Personality Psychology, edited by Kenneth H. Craik *et al.* Plenum Press, New York, 1993.

tion whether ability to judge people is general or specific, (5) the qualifications of a good judge, (6) the relative excellence of men and women as judges, (7) the types that are best known to us, and (8) common sources of error in judgment.* (1937, p 499)

Today, with 50 years of hindsight upon the research that followed this statement, one might want to add or subtract a bit from this list, and reorder some of its priorities. At least, I would. But still, five decades after it was set down, Allport's compendium of research issues concerning the accuracy of personality judgment remains a fair list. Indeed, the list inspires me to a couple of observations.

First, Allport thought that the topic of interpersonal judgment belonged to the field of personality psychology. This viewpoint contrasts in an interesting way with the situation today, when the topic seems more often regarded as lying within the bailiwick of social psychology or even more recently cognitive–social psychology.

Second, Allport thought the topic of accuracy belonged to personality psychology for a particular reason, one he probably considered too obvious to mention. Allport assumed that there was something "real" for judgments of personality to describe. Therefore, the study of judgments of personality could not avoid being inextricably entwined with the study of personality itself.

This is emphatically *not* the working assumption of social or cognitive–social psychology nowadays. Indeed, the very idea that there might be something out there to judge is assiduously avoided, even sidestepped, by the vast majority of modern research on personality judgment. Judgments of personality are commonly regarded as little more than interesting social phenomena that have little if anything to do with any reality beyond the realm of social judgment itself. As a result, the study of personality judgment has been all but evicted from what Allport would consider its rightful place within personality psychology.†

RESEARCH ON THE PROCESS OF JUDGMENT

For the most part, modern research on interpersonal judgment takes one of two forms. The first and more dominant form is concerned with the process of judgment. The basic strategy is to propose a model

---

* Ken Craik brought this passage to my attention several years ago. Since then, I have exploited it many times to establish my own *bona fides* as a personality psychologist.

† Indeed, things have gotten so bad that even some personality psychologists seem to think there is something wrong with including the study of interpersonal judgments within the field of personality (e.g., Carlson, 1984).

of the judgmental process and then present subjects with experimental stimuli designed to allow the assessment of the degree to which their judgments of these stimuli follow predictions derived from the model. This strategy is fine so far as it goes and is an excellent way to illuminate the process of judgment. However, in much of this research, the process model is given a normative status, so that when subjects' judgments fail to match the model's prescriptions, the researcher is emboldened to conclude not only that the model poorly describes human judgment, but that human judgment itself is flawed. For instance, Bayesian inference provides a mathematical model of how information concerning prior probabilities should be combined when making predictions concerning future outcomes. Many experiments have asked subjects to make probability judgments on the basis of numerical priors, and found that subjects' models consistently deviate from Bayes' prescriptions. These results were typically taken to reveal "errors" or "fallacies" of judgment (e.g., the "base rate fallacy"; see Nisbett & Ross, 1980, for many more examples).

This is not the place to reprise my critique of the error literature (but please see Funder, 1987). For present purposes, it is sufficient to make the point that research on judgmental error, perhaps ironically, says *nothing* about judgmental accuracy, for the same reason that research on errors in visual judgment, or "optical illusions," should not lead us to conclude that people cannot see. Illusions such as the Ponzo or Muller–Lyer effects reveal mechanisms of visual judgment that are usually adaptive; indeed, they reveal important aspects of how accurate visual perceptions can arise (Gregory, 1971). Only in the artificial and rather surreal environment of the laboratory do they lead to visual mistakes. I believe that much the same is true about many if not all of the errors that have been demonstrated in the domain of social judgment. A parsimonious explanation of why so many exist might be that they are the result of judgmental heuristics that ordinarily produce correct judgments in real life, even though they can lead to incorrect judgments within laboratory environments. I realize that this is a controversial opinion, but what should not be controversial is that error research is simply not informative about the accuracy of judgment, one way or the other.* Even though research on judgmental error can be

---

* Indeed, research on the judgment process, such as error research, was originally and explicitly designed to avoid accuracy issues. The brilliant insight of Asch (1946) was that interesting and important information about the process of judgment could be obtained in experiments in which subjects judged stimuli that were wholly artificial. As Jones (1985) pointed out, "Asch solved the accuracy problem by bypassing it." What Jones

importantly informative about the process of judgment, it does not address accuracy as Allport thought of it.

RESEARCH ON INTERJUDGE AGREEMENT

A bit closer to the mark is a second kind of research on judgments of personality that focuses on the phenomenon of interjudge agreement. After an initial burst of enthusiasm for this topic died down some years ago (Taft, 1955), the study of agreement has enjoyed something of a renaissance more recently (Kenny & La Voie, 1984). Sometimes different judges of the same individual's personality agree with each other or with the individual him- or herself in their judgments, and sometimes they do not (e.g., Funder & Colvin, 1988; Funder & Dobroth, 1987). This fact would seem to have obvious implications for judgmental accuracy.

However, like researchers on judgmental process, researchers on interjudge agreement also often seem to go out of their way to avoid becoming entangled in accuracy issues. They have tried to avoid dealing with accuracy through the use of either of two related strategies. The first was commonly used during the first wave of agreement research, which occurred from about 1930 to about 1960: Many studies were performed in which acquaintances of the judgmental target were asked to describe, not the personality of the target, but how the target would describe his or her own personality. Then the target filled out forms to describe himself or herself. The degree of congruence between these two evaluations could of course be measured directly and was assumed to reflect the acquaintances' degree of social sensitivity or empathy (e.g., Gage & Cronbach, 1955; Taft, 1966).

The more recent wave of agreement research, conducted during the 1980s, has for some reason often utilized almost exactly the opposite approach: Investigators ask the target of judgment to describe, not his or her own personality, but how he or she believes he or she will be described by others. Then acquaintances fill out forms to describe the

---

meant was that by inventing a research paradigm that allowed accuracy issues to be finessed through the use of artificial stimuli, Asch had provided a way to address other important issues concerning the process of judgment. It seems ironic as well as unfortunate that, over the years, researchers seemed to forget all this and began to make the fundamental mistake of interpreting research on process and error as implying that human judgment is flawed. That is *not* what Asch had in mind. (Incidentally, human judgment may well be flawed. But error research is not constituted in such a way as to find out.)

target. The degree of congruence between these two evaluations can again be measured directly and is assumed to reflect the target persons' "ability to know what kinds of impressions they convey" (DePaulo *et al.*, 1987, p. 311).

Both kinds of agreement, as studied in the 1930s and in the 1980s, are surely important in their own right. It is interesting to see how well we can predict what somebody else will say about himself or herself, and it would be useful to know the degree to which our impressions of ourselves are held mutually by the people with whom we deal on a daily basis. However, the study of neither sort of agreement is equivalent to the study of judgmental accuracy. We may call our intelligent acquaintance "dumb" and he may be aware of our misperception. We may be crooked folk who manage to convince everybody else that we are honest and be well aware of our success. The result in both instances would be high interjudge agreement of the two sorts just mentioned, but low accuracy.

Moreover, an exclusive concern with judgments themselves and how well they agree can lead researchers to forget about or even avoid thinking about what might really be out there to be judged. And that will lead them to fail to gather further data that might actually help determine whether or not the judgments are accurate. For instance, if a target and acquaintance disagree about the presence of some personality trait, perhaps we could find a way to measure directly the relevant behavior of the target and settle the issue.* But as long as the researcher is content merely to assess congruence between judgments, for their own sake, the question will not even arise. This kind of research, therefore, also often sidesteps the issue of accuracy as Allport thought of it.

CRITERIA FOR ACCURACY

Of course, there is a good reason why all these researchers work so hard to avoid the accuracy issue; they are not just being perverse. The reason is that in order to study the accuracy judgments, it would seem, you need a criterion. And what criterion can one use to evaluate the accuracy of a judgment of personality?

---

* I do not underestimate the problems in gathering the sort of behavioral data that would allow the accuracy of judgments of personality to be assessed. My point is that unless one takes the accuracy question seriously, by focusing on more than just the relationship between different judgments, one will not even begin the formidable task of formulating and gathering such data.

To many, this question has seemed to raise an insurmountable obstacle. Colleagues have advised me many times, in the most friendly way, to drop my research on accuracy because of precisely this problem. But I maintain that finding a criterion for use in accuracy research is not really all that hard or all that mysterious if one simply remembers the lessons of a classic article you probably read in graduate school, if not as an undergraduate: I refer to an article on "construct validity" by Cronbach and Meehl (1955).

That landmark article, which can be read as a philosophical rebuttal to logical positivism and concrete operationalism, addresses the question of how to evaluate a new personality test. If one had a new test of "sociability," say, against what criterion could you prove it to be valid? The answer, say Cronbach and Meehl, is that there is not one. Or, as I sometimes like to change the emphasis, there is not *one*. Rather, all you can do is correlate your new test with as much other information about your research subjects as you can gather and hope that the pattern of convergent relations among independent data sources will, in the end, support the essential validity of your construct.

The task of assessing the accuracy of a personality judgment is exactly the same. If a bunch of subjects rate each other on "sociability," by what criterion can we assess whether these judgments are actually accurate? The answer you probably can see coming: There is not one; there is not *one*. All you can do is gather all the information about these subjects' behaviors that you can, including, I would hope, some fairly concrete indices of social participation, and assess whether or not the pattern of convergent relations among independent data sources increases or decreases your confidence in the accuracy of the subjects' judgments.

THE ACCURACY PROJECT

I have described elsewhere (e.g., Funder, 1989) a study of my own that tries to study accuracy through this tactic. What we have done to gather self-judgments and peer-judgments of the personalities of about 160 subjects. We have also administered a wide variety of personality and ability inventories to these subjects. Finally, and perhaps most interestingly, we have videotaped the behavior of each of these subjects in three different laboratory situations. (In a further project just beginning, we are also including reports and observations of subjects' behavior in daily life.)

The data we have gathered allow us to assess various kinds of agreement and disagreement between acquaintances' judgements of personality and between acquaintances' judgments and self-judgments (Funder & Colvin, in press). But they also allow us to assess the degree of relationship between judgments of personality and at least some of the actual behaviors of the persons who are judged. Our basic analytic scheme is to examine the accuracy of personality judgment, by this kind of criterion, as a function of four potential moderators: (1) "good judge," the possibility that some persons are more accurate judges of personality than are others; (2) "good target," the possibility that some individuals are easier to judge than others; (3) "good trait," the possibility that some traits are easier to judge or that some behaviors are easier to predict than are others; and (4) "good information," the possibility that the accuracy of judgment is affected by the type and amount of information that is available to the judge.

It may not escape the notice of some readers that this is actually a very old-fashioned kind of research. The basic design, which is to gather a large amount of information about the personality of each subject and then see how different kinds of information interrelate, is a strategy that was used more than 50 years ago by Allport (1977) and also by Murray (1938).

This fact may seem unsurprising to those cynics who believe that research in personality tends to go around in circles. A little more optimistically, a few years ago Jack Block (1968) suggested that at least sometimes personality research might advance "helically," so that each time we go around we have elevated ourselves a bit above where we were before. However you prefer to look at it, I do believe that the field of personality psychology could more forward just now, by moving backward a bit and studying judgments of personality the old-fashioned way: By taking them seriously as possible indicators of something that might, just conceivably, really exist.

ACKNOWLEDGMENT: The author's research is supported by grant MH42427 from the National Institute of Health.

REFERENCES

Allport, G. W. (1937). *Personality: A psychological interpretation.* New York: Holt.

Asch, S. E. (1946). Forming impressions of personality. *Journal of Abnormal and Social Psychology, 41,* 258–290.

Block, J. (1968). Personality measurement: Overview. In D. L. Sills (Ed.), *International Encyclopedia of the Social Sciences* (Vol. 12, pp. 141–179). –New York: Macmillan and Free Press.

Carlson, R. (1984). What's social about social psychology? Where's the person in personality research? *Journal of Personality and Social Psychology, 51*, 1200–1207.

Cronbach, L. J., & Meehl, P. E. (1955). Construct validity in psychological tests. *Psychological Bulletin, 52*, 177–193.

DePaulo, B. M., Kenny, D. A., Hoover, C. W., Webb, W., & Oliver, P. V. (1987). Accuracy of person perception: Do people know what kinds of impressions they convey? *Journal of Personality and Social Psychology, 52*, 303–315.

Funder, D. C. (1987). Errors and mistakes: Evaluating the accuracy of social judgment. *Psychological Bulletin, 101*, 75–90.

Funder, D. C. (1989). Accuracy in personality judgment and the dancing bear. In D. M. Buss & N. Cantor (Eds.), *Personality psychology: Recent trends and emerging directions*. New York: Springer-Verlag.

Funder, D. C., & Colvin, C. R. (1988). Friends and strangers: Acquaintanceship, agreement, and the accuracy of personality judgment. *Journal of Personality and Social Psychology, 55*, 149–158.

Funder, D. C., & Colvin, C. R. (in press). Congruence of self and others' judgments of personality. In S. Briggs, R. Hogan, & W. Jones (Eds.), *Handbook of personality psychology*. Orlando: Academic Press.

Funder, D. C., & Dobroth, K. M. (1987). Differences between traits: Properties associated with interjudge agreement. *Journal of Personality and Social Psychology, 52*, 409–418.

Gage, N. L. & Cronbach, L. J. (1955). Conceptual and methodological problems in interpersonal perception. *Psychological Review, 62*, 411–422.

Gregory, R. L. (1971). Visual illusions. In R. C. Atkinson (Ed.), *Contemporary Psychology* (pp. 167–177). San Francisco: Freeman.

Jones, E. E. (1985). Major developments in social psychology during the past five decades. In G. Lindzey & E. Aronson (Eds.), *The handbook of social psychology* (3rd ed., Vol. 1, pp. 47–107). New York: Random House.

Kenny, D. A., & LaVoie, L. (1984). The social relations model. In L. Berkowitz (Ed.), *Advances in experimental social psychology* (Vol. 18, pp. 141–179). New York: Academic Press.

Murray, H. A. (1938). *Explorations in personality*. New York: Oxford University Press.

Nisbett, R., & Ross, L. (1980). *Human inference: Strategies and shortcomings of social judgment*. New York: Prentice-Hall.

Taft, R. (1955). The ability to judge people. *Psychological Bulletin, 52*, 1–23.

Taft, R. (1966). Accuracy of empathic judgments of acquaintances and strangers. *Psychological Bulletin, 52*, 1–23.

CHAPTER SIXTEEN

Gordon Allport

Father and Critic of the Five-Factor Model

OLIVER P. JOHN AND RICHARD W. ROBINS

Over the past 50 years, Gordon Allport's views of personality, and of personality psychology as a science, have had a guiding and pervasive influence. In this chapter, we examine Allport's role in bringing about one of the most significant empirical advances in the field. Allport and Odbert's (1936) psycholexical study of English language personality descriptors laid the empirical and conceptual groundwork from which the Five-Factor Model (FFM) of personality eventually emerged. One might therefore consider Allport one of the fathers of the FFM. Like many fathers, however, he might not have approved wholeheartedly of his offspring.

The FFM is an empirically derived classification of personality traits, based on the intercorrelations among trait ratings across individuals. At the most general (superordinate) level there are five relatively independent content domains, often labeled Extraversion (energetic, sociable, assertive), Agreeableness (loving, pleasant, trusting), Conscientiousness (reliable, organized, efficient), Neuroticism (anxious, nervous, worrying), and Openness (imaginative, curious, broad interests). The history of the FFM has been reviewed by John, Angleitner, and Ostendorf (1988), and several recent reviews have been devoted to the

OLIVER P. JOHN AND RICHARD W. ROBINS • Department of Psychology, University of California, Berkeley, California 94704.

Fifty Years of Personality Psychology, edited by Kenneth H. Craik *et al.* Plenum Press, New York, 1993.

current empirical and conceptual status of this model (Digman, 1990; Goldberg, 1990; John, 1990; McCrae & Costa, 1990).

To be sure, Allport did not anticipate this particular model, nor would he have considered it a sufficient account of all functions and purposes of personality description. Indeed, the FFM is not based on idiographic methods, nor does it explicate the neuropsychic structures Allport believed to underlie personality. Yet, although Allport was an ardent proponent of idiographic approaches, he was not, as some have portrayed him, an opponent of nomothetic approaches. Allport (e.g., 1962) stated very clearly that psychology should aim to understand both the common and the particular in human behavior; to emphasize one to the exclusion of the other would improperly restrict the scope of psychological science. "The psychology of personality, I have therefore explicitly maintained, should be *both* nomothetic and idiographic... abstract dimensions have their place" (Allport, 1946, pp. 133–134). Allport also recognized the need in the field of personality psychology for "a satisfactory taxonomy of personality and its hierarchical structure" (Allport, 1968, p. 48). It is this need that the FFM addresses.

ALLPORT—FATHER OF THE FIVE-FACTOR MODEL

To construct such a "satisfactory taxonomy," Allport and Odbert (1936) followed Klages's (1926/1932) and Baumgarten's (1933) German research and used the natural language as a starting place. The English dictionary served as their source of personality attributes: "Each single term specifies in some way a form of human behavior; each term is a record of commonsense observation, inexact perhaps, but nevertheless constituting an authentic problem for the science that has taken as its task the purification and codification of commonsense views of human nature." (Allport & Odbert, 1936, p. vi).

ALLPORT AND ODBERT'S "PSYCHOLEXICAL STUDY"

Allport and Odbert (1936) selected personality-relevant terms from the 550,000 terms in *Webster's New International Dictionary*. Terms were included in the final list if they were judged to possess "the capacity... to distinguish the behavior of one human being from that of another" (p. 24); thus, terms referring to common and nondistinctive behavior were eliminated. With the addition of a few common slang terms not (yet) included in *Webster's*, the final list amounted to almost

18,000 terms "designating distinctive forms of personal behavior. At first this seems like a semantic nightmare. Yet, it is obvious that trait-names bear some relation to the underlying structural units of personality, and it is our duty to discover, if we can, what this relation is" (Allport, 1937, pp. 353–354). This task, which Allport and Odbert (1936, p. vi) thought would keep a psychologist "at work for a lifetime," has indeed occupied personality psychologists for more than 50 years.

Allport and Odbert (1936) tried to bring some order to the semantic nightmare they had created. They classified their 18,000 terms, on conceptual grounds, into four categories. Only the first category contained terms designating personal traits ("generalized and personalized determining tendencies—consistent and stable modes of an individual's adjustment to his environment"), such as sociable, aggressive, and introverted (p. 26). The second category included temporary states, moods, and activities, such as rejoicing, abashed, and elated. The third category consisted of highly evaluative social and character judgments of personal conduct and reputation, such as average, worthy, and irritating. Although these terms presuppose some traits within the individual, they do not indicate the specific attributes that give rise to an individual's evaluation by others or by society in general. The last category included physical characteristics, capacities and talents, terms of doubtful relevance to personality, and terms that could not be assigned to any of the other three categories.

Norman (1967) subsequently elaborated Allport and Odbert's initial classification and divided the domain into seven content categories: Stable "biophysical" traits, Temporary states, Activities, Social roles, Social effects, Evaluative terms, Anatomical and physical terms, as well as Ambiguous and Obscure terms not intended for further consideration. Allport and Odbert's and Norman's category systems illustrate that the natural language of personality represented in dictionaries includes many different types of concepts. Individuals can be described by their enduring *traits* (e.g., irascible), by the *internal states* they typically experience (furious), by the *physical states* they endure (trembling), by the *activities* they engage in (screaming), by the *effects* they have on others (frightening), by the *roles* they play (murderer), and by the general *evaluations* of their conduct by society (unacceptable, bad). Moreover, individuals differ in their anatomical and morphological characteristics (short) and in the personal and societal evaluations attached to these appearance characteristics (cute).

REPLICATING ALLPORT AND ODBERT IN GERMAN:
A PROTOTYPE MODEL

Allport and Odbert, as well as Norman, employed mutually exclusive categories in their classifications and Allport and Odbert noted that their "four-fold classification is at best only approximate and to a certain extent arbitrary" (1936, p. 27). In addition, agreement among the judges was not particularly high. An inspection of the classifications quickly shows that the categories overlap and have fuzzy boundaries. This observation led some researchers to conclude that distinctions between classes of personality descriptors are arbitrary and should be abolished (Allen & Potkay, 1981).

However, the "unclear cases" that fall on the boundaries between categories create a problem only if one insists on classical definitions in terms of necessary and sufficient attributes. Chaplin, John, and Goldberg (1988) presented an alternative, prototype conception where each category is defined in terms of its clear cases rather than its boundaries; category membership need not be discrete but can be defined as continuous. Chaplin et al. (1988) applied this prototype conception to three classes of person descriptors, namely traits, states, and activities. They found that although the classification of a few descriptors was difficult, the core of each category was distinct from each of the others and could be differentiated by a set of conceptually derived attributes. For example, prototypical states were seen as temporary, brief, and externally caused; in contrast, prototypical traits were seen as stable, long-lasting, and internally caused and needed to be observed more frequently and across a wider range of situations than states before they were attributed to an individual. These findings closely replicated the classifications made by Allport and Odbert and by Norman and generally confirmed that their initial conceptual definitions of traits and states are widely shared.

Whereas the two previous studies had both examined American English, Angleitner, Ostendorf, and John (1990) carried out a "psycho-lexical study" of the German personality vocabulary. Their study was based on the prototype conception proposed by Chaplin et al. (1988) and improved on the earlier studies of English in several methodological respects. In particular, they used a continuous measure of prototypicality for each descriptor in each category by employing ten independent judges and also scored several types of reliability and validity indexes. The resulting German "personality lexicon" is much more convenient than the unwieldy Allport and Odbert lists because continuous prototypicality values are available for each person descriptor in 13 different content categories. All terms can be listed in the order of their membership in any of the categories, making it particularly easy to select subsets of prototypical traits, states, and so on from the total pool. In general, however, the findings in German were consistent with the American ones and further demonstrated that the conceptual distinctions initially made by Allport and Odbert are rooted in a common understanding of personality.

REDUCING THE SEMANTIC NIGHTMARE: FIVE BROAD DIMENSIONS UNDERLYING TRAIT TERMS

Allport and Odbert's four categories provided some structure but did not eliminate the "semantic nightmare" created by the staggering size and complexity of the four lists, which would give personality psychologists bad dreams even today. A reduction and further organization of the terms were therefore badly needed. Allport, however, felt it was safer to err in the direction of overinclusiveness and argued that a large number of fine-grained distinctions within each behavioral domain was scientifically useful and necessary. For example, he considered the more than 200 words related to politeness "a meager enough vocabulary for the possible shadings and forms of *polite* behavior... 'synonyms' should not be avoided; if anything they should be multiplied, in order to do more justice to the variety and number of those overlapping dispositions" (Allport & Odbert, 1936, p. 34).

It is hard to fathom that Allport truly believed that 200 (!) terms are insufficient for the scientific description of individual differences in politeness. Although we appreciate his interest in the richness of the unique and particular and his concern for detail, we also believe that abstraction is necessary in science. One of the goals of scientific theories is a parsimonious representation of the most important aspects of the subject matter. In fact, despite his advocacy of specificity in the study of personality descriptors, Allport also anticipated the procedures that eventually would lead to the discovery of the FFM:

> Theoretically it would be possible to apply this ingenious method [of factor analysis] to a complete list of trait-names, such as that contained in this monograph. One might determine the amount of overlap in meaning between all the terms as they are commonly understood and employed. The investigator might then declare that such and such trait-names are roughly synonymous and that only one of them needs to be retained *if what is desired is a vocabulary of completely independent terms*. The trait-names would be

grouped, and only a single representative would be saved for each
group. (Allport & Odbert, 1936, pp. 32–33, emphasis in original)

Even in this passage, however, Allport expressed his distrust of generalization and felt compelled to remind his readers that the discovery of
a few broad dimensions is but one goal of personality research.

Inspired by the blueprint contained in the above quote and less
wary of the dangers of generalization, Cattell (1943, 1945a,b) reduced
Allport and Odbert's list of 4500 trait terms to a mere 35 trait variables, using both semantic and empirical clustering procedures (for a
review, see John et al., 1988). If Allport was too wary of abstraction,
Cattell (who eliminated more than 99% of the terms Allport had so
tenaciously defended) could have used some of Allport's fastidiousness.
In Cattell's defense, however, it should be mentioned that the small
number of variables was dictated primarily by the data analytic limitations of his time, which made factor analyses of large variable sets
prohibitively costly and complex. On the basis of several oblique factor
analyses of this small set of variables, Cattell concluded that he had
identified 12 personality factors, which were eventually incorporated in
his Sixteen Personality Factors Questionnaire (Cattell et al., 1970).
Subsequent investigators, however, failed to replicate Cattell's factors
(see Digman & Takemoto-Chock, 1981; John, 1990).

At the same time as Cattell, Eysenck (1947; 1952) and Guilford
(1959; Guilford & Zimmerman, 1956) developed and promoted their own
models of personality structure, which differed from Cattell's and from
each other, both in the number and the nature of the factors. Although
Allport was discouraged by these incompatible factor models, he remained convinced that "scalable dimensions are useful dimensions, and
we hope that work will continue until we reach firmer agreement concerning their number and nature" (Allport, 1958, p. 252).

Twenty years later, Fiske (1978) expressed the view that little had
changed in the interim: "the empirical factors obtained by one investigator are not congruent with those developed by any other researcher . . .
no trend toward consensus on a standard set of conceptual dimensions,
either from a priori theorizing or from empirical analyses, is evident"
(pp. 14–15). Curiously, Fiske reached this conclusion, although he had
been the first (Fiske, 1949) to demonstrate a replicable five-factor solution in a subset of Cattell's variables. Fiske was also aware of Tupes
and Christal's finding that "five relatively strong and recurrent factors
and nothing more of any consequence" (1961, p. 14) could be identified
in both Cattell's own data sets and in newly collected ones. And by
1963, Norman had published his now classic replication of these five

factors, which eventually became known as the "Big Five" (Goldberg, 1981)—a title chosen not to reflect their greatness but to emphasize their extraordinary breadth and level of abstraction.

In fact, then, Fiske's appraisal of the evidence available in 1978 was entirely too negative, though symptomatic of the mood of the field at the time. Mainstream personality psychologists either ignored the five factors or rejected them as linguistic fictions because of their origin in the natural language. With few exceptions (e.g., Goldberg, 1976), that perception endured, perhaps because the field was preoccupied with issues such as the response style debate and the person–situation debate, both of which raised considerable doubt about the feasibility and sensibility of research on personality structure (Block, 1977).

THE EMPIRICAL BASIS OF THE FIVE FACTORS

As Block (1977) anticipated, the controversies of the late 1960s and 1970s did not produce a paradigmatic shift but led to a gradual improvement in the methodological quality and sophistication of the research, especially in the realm of multivariate procedures (e.g., Everett, 1983). The field emerged from this period of self-criticism and doubt with a renewed belief in the fundamental importance and scientific viability of trait concepts.

RESEARCH IN THE LEXICAL TRADITION

In the early 1980s, Goldberg (1980, 1981) and Digman and Takemoto-Chock (1981) demonstrated anew the empirical generalizability of the Big Five factors. Similar five-factor structures were subsequently identified in sets of variables that were much broader and selected more systematically from the dictionary than Cattell's 35 variables (Goldberg, 1990). Moreover, the Big Five dimensions also emerged when the personality descriptions were made by experienced personality and clinical psychologists (John, 1990).

The finding that experts and lay judges do not differ systematically in the factor structures of their personality descriptions may seem surprising at first; one might expect experts' notions of personality to differ from "folk concepts" (Tellegen & Waller, in press). However, it is important to realize that the Big Five factors, although derived from ratings of common language trait terms, are *not* folk concepts defined as "everyday variables that ordinary people use in their daily lives to understand, classify, and predict their own behavior and that of others"

(Gough, 1987, p. 1). Whereas each of the individual trait terms represented in the Big Five structure is a folk concept, the five factors represent a higher level of abstraction. They were derived from intercorrelations among trait ratings and, therefore, may not represent any individual's folk theory. For example, the empirical discovery of the Surgency (or Extraversion) factor implies that attributions of sociability, energy, and dominance tend to covary across individuals, whether or not the individual making these attributions is aware of these population correlations. Nor does the discovery of the Big Five imply that individual "folk" actually use these broad concepts when thinking about and describing themselves or others. The difficulty undergraduates have in remembering the five factors in their personality courses provides testimony against the folk concept status of the Big Five.

RESEARCH IN THE QUESTIONNAIRE TRADITION

While the researchers in the lexical tradition were consolidating the evidence for the Big Five, the need for an integrative framework became more pressing among researchers who prefer to measure personality with questionnaire scales. Joint factor analyses of questionnaires developed by different investigators had shown that two broad dimensions, Extraversion and Neuroticism, appear in one form or another in most personality inventories. Beyond these "Big Two" (Wiggins, 1968), however, the various questionnaire-based models had shown few signs of convergence. For example, Eysenck observed that "Where we have literally hundreds of inventories, incorporating thousands of traits, largely overlapping but also containing specific variance, each empirical finding is strictly speaking only relevant to a specific trait .... This is not the way to build a unified scientific discipline" (1991, p. 786).

Again, the situation began to change in the early 1980s. Costa and McCrae had developed the *NEO Personality Inventory* to measure three broad personality dimensions: *N*euroticism, *E*xtraversion, and *O*penness (see McCrae & Costa, 1990, for a review). In 1983, however, they realized that their NEO system closely resembled three of the Big Five factors, but did not encompass traits in the Agreeableness and Conscientiousness domains. They therefore extended their model with scales measuring Agreeableness and Conscientiousness, and demonstrated that their five questionnaire scales converged with adjective-based measures of the Big Five (McCrae & Costa, 1985).* Subsequent re-

---

* See McCrae and John (1992) for a discussion of differences between the lexically based and the questionnaire-based factor structures.

search showed that these five factors could be recovered in various other personality questionnaires, as well as in self-ratings on Block's (1961) California Adult Q-Set (see McCrae & Costa, 1990).

THE EMERGING CONSENSUS AND
HEURISTIC POTENTIAL OF THE BIG FIVE

The convergence between the lexical and questionnaire approaches led to a dramatic change in the acceptance of the five factors in the field. With regard to their empirical status, the findings accumulated since the early 1980s show that the five factors replicate across different types of subjects, raters, and data sources, in both dictionary-based and personality-questionnaire studies. Indeed, even the more skeptical reviewers were led to conclude that "agreement among these descriptive studies with respect to *what* are the appropriate dimensions is impressive" (Revelle, 1987, p. 437; also Briggs, 1989; McAdams, 1992). There seems to be an emerging consensus that the five-factor taxonomy "captures, at a broad level of abstraction, the commonalities among most of the existing systems of personality description, and provides an integrative descriptive model of personality research" (John, 1990, p. 96).

The availability of a general and replicable classification of personality traits and the emerging consensus it spawned precipitated an explosion of interest in the five dimensions. The heuristic and applied value of this taxonomy is only now being realized. Researchers from diverse areas of psychology have begun to use it as a framework to organize and summarize their findings. For example, Barrick and Mount (1991) reviewed the extensive literature on personality predictors of job performance and found consistent trends in what previously had been viewed as a morass of inconsistent findings: Regardless of the type of job and performance outcome measures, scales related to the conscientiousness factor predicted job performance. Scales related to extraversion predicted performance only in jobs involving social contact, such as sales; the other three factors were not systematically related to job performance.

CONCEPTUAL STATUS OF THE FACTORS:
FROM THE BIG FIVE TO THE FIVE-FACTOR MODEL

The change in the empirical status of the Big Five was accompanied by a shift in its conceptual status. So far, we have discussed the discovery and the evidentiary basis of the five factors. How should this empirical finding be interpreted? Some researchers believe that the Big Five constitute a theory of personality. For example, Hogan and Hogan (1989) referred to the five dimensions as the " 'big five' theory" (p. 274), and Digman and Takemoto-Chock (1981) described them as "an impressive theoretical structure" (p. 164). Such claims are difficult to evaluate because the concept of theory, especially in personality psychology, is so ambiguous (Chapter 7, this volume).

Initially, the five factors were tied to the natural language of trait description and, therefore, were properly interpreted as dimensions of trait description or attribution (John et al., 1988), rather than as dimensions of personality or traits. Strictly speaking, the Big Five structure provides only a taxonomy of trait descriptions. Although these trait descriptions are usually thought to reflect observable regularities in behavior (e.g., Norman & Goldberg, 1966), the lexical tradition makes no explicit assumptions (or claims) about the ontological status of the trait terms or about the causal origin of the regularities to which the trait terms refer. The Big Five structure was derived through purely empirical and purposely atheoretical procedures; theoretical considerations, such as questions about the existence and explanatory status of traits, were deemed unimportant.

However, these questions are of considerable importance to the Five-Factor Model. The FFM represents one interpretation of the Big Five dimensions: Although the FFM adopts the Big Five as its basic structural model, it also includes a number of theoretical assumptions that do not necessarily follow either from the lexical approach or from the empirical discovery of the five factors. The FFM can be viewed as a particular instance of trait theory and makes the following major claims (McCrae & Costa, 1990): Personality can be described in terms of five broad content domains, each of which subsumes several more narrowly defined and correlated subsets or facets; individual differences in these domains are stable over long periods of time, have a genetic basis, and derive in part from as yet unspecified internal (e.g., physiological) mechanisms; individuals can be described both in general terms by their scores on the five dimensions and in more detail by their scores on the larger number of facets. It is now widely assumed that the FFM has the same conceptual status as other questionnaire-based models of personality structure advocated by trait theorists such as Eysenck (e.g., 1986), Guilford (e.g., 1959), Cattell (e.g., Cattell et al., 1970), or Tellegen (e.g., 1985).

In light of these differences, the FFM of personality traits should be distinguished from the Big Five, an empirically derived taxonomy of personality trait descriptors. Specifically, we suggest that the empirically derived factors be referred to as the Big Five, to distinguish them from the FFM, which advances more extensive conceptual claims.

ALLPORT—CRITIC OF THE FIVE-FACTOR MODEL

TRAIT THEORY AND PERSONALITY THEORY

The FFM is a structural model of individual differences and, like most dimensional models of individual differences, provides an account of personality that is primarily descriptive (rather than explanatory), focused on variables (rather than on the individual person), and postulates molar or generalized (rather than molecular) dimensions of personality. Allport, on the other hand, subscribed to a broader definition of personality theory. He agreed with Kluckhohn and Murray (1953), who argued that a theory of personality must address several goals: to describe and to explain the ways in which people are (1) like all other people (i.e., general or nomothetic laws), (2) like some other people (i.e., individual differences), and (3) like no other people (i.e., individual or idiographic laws). In other words, individual differences are only one, albeit important, part of personality. A theory of personality requires more than a descriptive taxonomy of broadly defined dimensions of individual differences.

Throughout his career, Allport emphasized three additional issues a theory of personality should address: (1) the causal "neuropsychic" structures that underlie personality, (2) the idiographic analysis of individual lives, and (3) the richness contained in the nuances that can be expressed by individual personality descriptors. In the remainder of this chapter, we discuss each of these concerns, focusing on their implications for an Allportian evaluation of the FFM.

DESCRIPTION AND EXPLANATION

Whether the Big Five dimensions are believed to reflect summaries of behavior over time or causal mechanisms that exist within the person depends on one's conception of personality traits. In general, we can distinguish two conceptions of traits: (1) the summary (or categorical) view, articulated by Wiggins (1974) and by Buss and Craik (1984), and (2) the causal view espoused, for example, by Allport (1937) and

Cattell (1957).* Adherents of the summary view conceptualize traits as descriptive summaries of an individual's past behavioral conduct and refrain from invoking traits as causal or explanatory concepts. For example, if Gordon has exhibited a certain frequency of fastidious acts in the past, we can appropriately describe Gordon's behavior with the trait label "fastidious."

The causal view holds that traits are causal entities corresponding to as yet unknown neuropsychic structures. According to this view, to assert that Gordon is "fastidious" is to infer an internal generative mechanism that causes Gordon to behave in ways that we can label, in common language terms, as fastidious. These two positions differ with regard to the ontological status they accord the trait concept: The summary view does not regard traits as real entities, whereas the causal view regards traits as entities that exist "in our skins" (Allport, 1968, p. 49).

If one adopts a summary conception of traits, then the five dimensions must be interpreted as descriptive, reflecting the fundamental content domains within which observed regularities in behavior can be described (see Hogan, 1983). For example, Hogan and Hogan (1989) interpreted the five factors as "broad dimensions of interpersonal evaluation" (p. 274), suggesting that the factors represent categories of behavior that people find useful and convenient in describing socioculturally important characteristics of others. This theoretical interpretation of the five factors is consistent with the core assumption of the lexical approach that those individual differences that are most salient and socially relevant in people's lives will eventually become encoded into their language (Allport, 1937; see John et al., 1988).

In contrast, if one adopts a causal conception of traits, the five dimensions must be based on underlying causal mechanisms, which researchers should strive to discover.† This is the position Cattell (1957) and Eysenck (1990) adopted in their own models of personality structure. Researchers in the FFM tradition, however, have not taken such an explicitly causal stance toward the FFM and remain more circumspect: "Most contemporary psychologists would acknowledge that there must be some neurophysiological or hormonal basis for personality, but it is unlikely that we will ever find a single region of the brain that

---

* A third view (Ryle, 1949; see also Wright & Mischel, 1987; Zuroff, 1986) treats traits as dispositions, defined as tendencies to behave in certain ways in certain kinds of situations. Whether or not dispositions are causal concepts remains a matter of debate.

† This causal interpretation does not imply that the five factors are isomorphic with the underlying causal structures or that they constrain the number of these structures.

controls Neuroticism, or a neurotransmitter that accounts for Extraversion, or a gene for Openness" (McCrae & Costa, 1990, p. 25).

Revelle (1987) has criticized the FFM for its "lack of any theoretical explanation for the *how* or *why* of these dimensions" (p. 437). Briggs (1989) has expressed similar reservations about the atheoretical nature of the FFM. McAdams (1992) addresses these concerns in some detail. And Allport, no doubt, would have agreed wholeheartedly with all three of them. We also agree that eventually a taxonomic system should be predicated on causal and dynamic principles. However, the critics overlook the fact that "in any science, the taxonomy precedes causal analysis; we must analyze and classify the entities in our field of study before we can frame meaningful theories concerning their behavior. The astronomer classifies stars, the chemist elements, the zoologist animals, the botanist plants; the student of individual differences must do likewise" (Eysenck, 1991, p. 774).

Although descriptive and classificatory concerns have dominated the work on the FFM, the five dimensions, most notably Extraversion and Neuroticism, have been the target of various physiological and mechanistic explanations (see Rothbart, 1989). Similarly, Block and Block's (1980) notion of Ego Control may shed some light on the mechanisms underlying the Conscientiousness and Extraversion factors. Likewise, Tellegen's (1985) interpretation of Extraversion and Neuroticism as persistent dispositions toward thinking and behaving in ways that foster positive and negative affective experiences promises to connect the FFM with individual differences in affective functioning. Other explanatory accounts may come from areas as diverse as evolutionary biology, psychoanalytic theory, and motivational theories.

Whereas Allport emphasized the need to understand the neuropsychic structures underlying traits, many personality psychologists believe that for most of their research they "need not understand the physiological basis of traits" (McCrae & Costa, 1990, p. 25). Given the limits of our current knowledge (see Eysenck, 1990, for a review), the difference between descriptive and causal approaches may be more academic than consequential. Indeed, "Allport's attempt to use traits as explanatory terms was not especially useful. Allport's theory did little more than describe the observed regularities in behavior. Allport's traits may explain behavior in the sense that they identify the cause of the behavior as an internal property of the organism . . . but this explanation is too vague to be satisfying or heuristically valuable" (Zuroff, 1986, p. 999).

Perhaps more useful at this juncture is the development of conceptual definitions of the factors. Thus far, the factors have been defined extensionally, that is, by listing the most prototypical trait adjectives, Q-sort items, or questionnaire scale for each factor (e.g., McCrae & John, 1992). For example, the first factor of the Big Five can be defined by adjectives such as talkative, assertive, active, energetic, outgoing, outspoken, and so on (John, 1990: Table 3.2). This descriptive stage was a necessary first step toward generally accepted factor definitions, and some disagreements remain about the precise composition of the factors (McCrae & John, 1992).

However, such extensional definitions tell us little about the conceptual basis for the particular constellation of personality traits captured by each factor. What are the features common to the traits of each factor? One way to identify features is through detailed conceptual analyses of the behaviors to which the traits in each domain refer. For example, in an analysis of traits from the Agreeableness domain, John (1986) showed that traits related to altruism (e.g., kind, generous, charitable) refer to behaviors that involve voluntary efforts intended to benefit someone else without expecting reciprocity.

Such conceptual analyses lead to intensional definitions that can provide the basis for a causal understanding of each factor. For example, if we know that traits comprising the Agreeableness domain involve the intention to benefit others, we can examine the motivational, evolutionary, or physiological basis of such behaviors. If the FFM is to be rooted in dynamic and psychological processes, a conceptual analysis can help bridge the gap in our understanding between theoretically and empirically derived models of personality structure.

NOMOTHETIC AND IDIOGRAPHIC

So far we have addressed Allport's concerns about the descriptive and explanatory potential of individual difference dimensions. Although Allport viewed individual differences as central to an understanding of personality, he was also concerned with traits as they exist within the individual, and he therefore emphasized the need for idiographic approaches in personality psychology.

The FFM is often described as a model of personality structure (e.g., Digman, 1990). The term *personality structure*, however, has always had two, rather different meanings: one associated with the nomothetic, the other with the idiographic approach. The model of personality structure specified by the FFM is a spatial representation describing the major dimensions of individual differences based on the intercorrelations among traits across individuals. Such a dimensional

model of personality structure, however, should not be confused with
the structure of personality as it exists *within* a particular individual:

> Factors are simply a summary principle of classification of many
> measures... [they] offer scalable dimensions; that is to say, they
> are common units in respect to which all personalities can be com-
> pared. None of them corresponds to the cleavages that exist in any
> single personality. (Allport, 1958, pp. 251–252)

In other words, nomothetic dimensions do not constitute a model
of personality structure if we mean by structure the particular configuration, patterning, and dynamic organization of the individuals' total set
of characteristics (York & John, 1992). Idiographic analyses are needed
to elucidate the ways in which the five personality factors combine
within particular individuals; although not strictly idiographic, typological analyses represent a person-centered approach that can identify groups or subsets of individuals who have similar configurations of
characteristics and share the same basic personality structure (Block,
1971).

Research on the FFM has yet to examine the ways in which the
five factors combine into a coherent personality within individuals and
whether there exist groups or categories of individuals who have similar configurations of these five characteristics. Allport believed that
each individual possesses a unique constellation of traits, some common, others individual; in his view, the functional relations among these
traits are unique for each individual. Taken as a whole, these relations
form a unified system, a personality, that is implicated in all the behaviors of the individual. Allport considered these unique psychological
structures and dynamics more useful for explaining behavior than the
general laws implicit in a nomothetically derived taxonomy: "Factors
fall far short of our demand for a doctrine of elements that will offer as
close an approximation as possible to the natural cleavages and individ-
ualized structural arrangements of each single life. The search must go
on" (Allport, 1937, p. 248).

Despite this pessimistic appraisal of the utility of factors, idiographic analyses might benefit from employing the five content categories specified by the FFM in some of their analyses. In particular, it
seems entirely feasible (and potentially quite interesting) to apply the
five content domains to idiographic analyses of the personal accounts
contained in life history narratives (McAdams, 1989), the personal constructs generated in Kelly's (1955) REP test and in free self-descrip-
tions (John, 1989), or the personal projects (Little, 1989) and personal
strivings (Emmons, 1989) that individuals use to structure their lives

and work toward their goals. Although the five dimensions have not been used in this way, their origin in the natural language makes them ideally suited for applications in this type of person-centered research.

MOLAR DIMENSIONS AND INDIVIDUAL TRAITS

As we have argued earlier, some of Allport's writings suggest that he appreciated the need to reduce the semantic nightmare he created with his list of 4500 trait terms and derive a more practicable system. More often than not, however, he was extremely skeptical about the prospect of seeing the rich and differentiated personality-descriptive language reduced to a few broad dimensions. Exasperated by the observation that "the number of distinguishable qualities is so great and the number of trait names so few," he worried about "certain statistically-minded psychologists" who "hold that the number of independent variables in human nature is relatively small and determinable, and they accordingly deny that each separate trait-name signifies some distinction so essential that it should not be neglected."* A factorial reduction of the personality vocabulary, Allport continued, is a mixed blessing: "Those who seek 'unique factors' would consider the accomplishment highly significant. Those, on the other hand, who hold a theory of overlapping traits would not" (Allport & Odbert, 1936, pp. 31–32).

The "theory of overlapping traits" has many adherents among contemporary psychologists, and the appeal of Allport's doctrine of specificity is often underestimated. Following Allportian tradition, the five factors have been criticized for being too broad to capture all of the variance in human personality (Briggs, 1989; Mershon & Gorsuch, 1988). For example, Briggs (1989) argued that "our success in reducing the natural trait language to its basic dimensions should not be taken to mean that these dimensions are optimal for description or prediction ... the distinctions among constructs subsumed by any one of these five factors are at least as important conceptually as the distinctions among the five factors themselves" (pp. 251–252). Similarly, Allport once described broad factors as resembling "sausage meat that has failed to pass the pure food and health inspection" (1958, p. 251).

These objections overlook the fact that personality can be conceptualized at different levels of abstraction and breadth. Many trait domains

---

* This Allportian inclination to attend to and value the specific descriptive function that each trait term might perform has also been highlighted by Buss and Craik (1985).

are hierarchically structured (Hampson *et al.*, 1986). The five factors indeed represent a rather broad level in the hierarchy of person descriptors (although not the highest possible level, as John *et al.*, 1991, have shown). The advantage of categories as broad as the five factors is their enormous bandwidth, their disadvantage is their low fidelity: In any hierarchical taxonomy, one loses information as one moves up hierarchical levels.

The hierarchical level an investigator selects depends on the particular descriptive and predictive goals of the research. For example, an idiographic analysis (e.g., a case study) of an individual life may require numerous fine distinctions—perhaps even 200 words for politeness. In contrast, for a nomothetic analysis (e.g., screening job applicants for selection interviews), a few broad dimensions might be sufficient. At this point, the FFM is not well-specified at lower levels of abstraction. The "facet" scales McCrae and Costa (1990) developed to assess the next level below the five factors and Goldberg's (1990) hierarchical analyses of trait adjectives are steps in the right direction. Nevertheless, considerable conceptual and empirical work remains to be done in order to achieve a more explicit and consensual specification of the five factors at lower levels of abstraction.

Although incomplete as a fully hierarchical structure, the FFM is already more than a classification of personality traits. It can also serve as an integral part of construct validation because it provides us, as Briggs (1989) notes, "with a framework for building rating scales and omnibus inventories that will represent the domain of personality terms broadly and systematically . . . (and) allows us to locate the seemingly boundless supply of new constructs and measures within a known configuration" (p. 247). Eventually, a comprehensive hierarchical taxonomy will permit the placement of all personality trait constructs into an overarching nomological network. This taxonomy, when supplemented with general propositions about the relations among personality constructs and between personality constructs and behavior, can facilitate an understanding of the structures of personality that are believed to underlie traits.

Allport recognized the importance of such a hierarchical system: "Ultimately, of course, our hope is to be able to reduce molar units to molecular and, conversely, to compound molecular units into molar" (Allport, 1958, p. 241). The development of a hierarchical taxonomy of personality descriptive constructs should ultimately advance our understanding of the patterned coherence of individual personalities to which Allport devoted his life's work.

OLIVER P. JOHN AND RICHARD W. ROBINS

CONCLUSIONS

pe that these excursions into Allport's diverse and influential
writings have served to illustrate a major theme in his psychology.
Again and again, Allport emphasized that personality research must be
both descriptive *and* explanatory, both nomothetic *and* idiographic,
both molar *and* molecular: "No doors should be closed in the study of
personality" (Allport, 1946, pp. 133–134). At this point in its development, the Five-Factor Model of personality traits can satisfy only the
descriptive, the nomothetic, and the molar goals articulated by Allport.
Many contemporary criticisms of the FFM address long-standing Allportian interests in explanatory, idiographic, and molecular contextual
accounts of personality. Allport thus continues to define the broad agenda
of personality and personological research for the years to come.

ACKNOWLEDGMENTS: The preparation of this chapter was supported, in
part, by National Institute of Mental Health grants MH-49255 and MH-
43948. The second author was supported by a National Science Foundation Graduate Fellowship. The support and resources provided by the
Institute of Personality and Social Research at the University of California, Berkeley, are also gratefully acknowledged. We would like to
thank Kenneth H. Craik, Lewis R. Goldberg, Jeffre M. Jackson, Sarah
E. Hampson, Gerald A. Mendelsohn, Myron Rothbart, Gerard Saucier,
Auke Tellegen, Kristina Whitney, and Raymond N. Wolfe for their comments and suggestions on an earlier draft.

REFERENCES

Allen, B. P., & Potkay, C. R. (1981). On the arbitrary distinction between states and
traits. *Journal of Personality and Social Psychology, 41,* 916–928.
Allport, G. W. (1937). *Personality: A psychological interpretation.* New York: Holt.
Allport, G. W. (1946). Personality psychology as science: A reply. *Psychological Review,
53,* 132–135.
Allport, G. W. (1958). What units shall we employ? In G. Lindzey (Ed.), *Assessment of
human motives* (pp. 238–260). New York: Reinhart.
Allport, G. W. (1962). The general and the unique in psychological science. *Journal of
Personality, 30,* 405–422.
Allport, G. W. (1968). Traits revisited. In *The person in psychology: Selected essays by
Gordon W. Allport* (pp. 43–66). Boston: Beacon Press.
Allport, G. W., & Odbert, H. S. (1936). Trait-names: A psycho-lexical study. *Psychological
Monographs, 47,* (No. 211).
Angleitner, A., Ostendorf, F., & John, O. P. (1990). Towards a taxonomy of personality
descriptors in German: A psycho-lexical study. *European Journal of Personality, 4,*
89–118.

Barrick, M. R., & Mount, M. K. (1991). The Big Five dimensions and job performance: A meta analysis. *Personnel Psychology, 44*, 1–26.

Baumgarten, F. (1933). Die Charaktereigenschaften. [The character traits.] In *Beitraege zur Charakter- und Persoenlichkeitsforschung* (No. 1). Bern: A. Francke.

Block, J. (1961). *The Q-sort method in personality assessment and psychiatric research* (reprinted 1978). Palo Alto, CA: Consulting Psychologists Press.

Block, J. (1971). *Lives through time.* Berkeley, CA: Bancroft Books.

Block, J. (1977). Advancing the science of personality: Paradigmatic shift or advancing the quality of research? In D. Magnusson & N. S. Endler (Eds.), *Psychology at the crossroad: Current issues in interactional psychology* (pp. 37–63). Hillsdale, NJ: Erlbaum.

Block, J. H., & Block, J. (1980). The role of ego-control and ego-resiliency in the organization of behavior. In W. A. Collings (Ed.), *Minnesota symposia on child psychology* (Vol. 13, pp. 39–101). Hillsdale, NJ: Erlbaum.

Briggs, S. R. (1989). The optimal level of measurement for personality constructs. In D. M. Buss & N. Cantor (Eds.), *Personality psychology: Recent trends and emerging directions* (pp. 246–260). New York: Springer-Verlag.

Buss, D. M., & Craik, K. H. (1984). Acts, dispositions, and personality. In B. A. Maher & W. B. Maher (Eds.), *Progress in experimental personality research* (Vol. 13, pp. 241–301). New York: Academic Press.

Buss, D. M., & Craik, K. H. (1985). Why *not* measure that trait? Alternative criteria for identifying important dispositions. *Journal of Personality and Social Psychology, 48*, 934–946.

Cattell, R. B. (1943). The description of personality: Basic traits resolved into clusters. *Journal of Abnormal and Social Psychology, 38*, 476–506.

Cattell, R. B. (1945a). The description of personality: Principles and findings in a factor analysis. *American Journal of Psychology, 58*, 69–90.

Cattell, R. B. (1945b). The principal trait clusters for describing personality. *Psychological Bulletin, 42*, 129–161.

Cattell, R. B. (1957). *Personality and motivation structure and measurement.* Yonkers-on-Hudson, NY: World.

Cattell, R. B., Eber, H. W., & Tatsuoka, M. M. (1970). *Handbook for the Sixteen Personality Factor Questionnaire (16PF).* Champaign, IL: Institute for Personality and Ability Testing.

Chaplin, W. F., John, O. P., & Goldberg, L. R. (1988). Conceptions of states and traits: Dimensional attributes with ideals as prototypes. *Journal of Personality and Social Psychology, 54*, 541–557.

Digman, J. M. (1990). Personality structure: Emergence of the five-factor model. *Annual Review of Psychology, 41*, 417–440.

Digman, J. M., & Takemoto-Chock, N. K. (1981). Factors in the natural language of personality: Re-analysis and recomparison of six major studies. *Multivariate Behavioral Research, 16*, 149–170.

Emmons, R. A. (1989). Exploring relations between motives and traits: The case of narcissism. In D. M. Buss & N. Cantor (Eds.), *Personality psychology: Recent trends and emerging directions* (pp. 32–44). New York: Springer-Verlag.

Everett J. E. (1938). Factor congruence as a criterion for determining the number of factors. *Multivariate Behavioral Research, 18*, 197–218.

Eysenck, H. J. (1947). *Dimensions of personality.* London: Routledge and Kegan Paul.

Eysenck, H. J. (1952). *The scientific study of personality.* London: Routledge and Kegan Paul.

Eysenck, H. J. (1986). Models and paradigms in personality research. In A. Angleitner, A. Furnham, & G. Van Heck (Eds.), *Personality psychology in Europe: Vol. 2. Current trends and controversies* (pp. 213–223). Lisse, The Netherlands: Swets & Zeitlinger.

Eysenck, H. J. (1990). Biological dimensions of personality. In L. A. Pervin (Ed.), *Handbook of personality: Theory and research* (pp. 244–276). New York: Guilford Press.

Eysenck, H. J. (1991). Dimensions of personality: 16, 5, or 3?—Criteria for a taxonomic paradigm. *Personality and Individual Differences, 12,* 773–790.

Fiske, D. W. (1949). Consistency of the factorial structures of personality ratings from different sources. *Journal of Abnormal and Social Psychology, 44,* 329–344.

Fiske, D. W. (1978). *Strategies for research in personality: Observation versus interpretation of behavior.* San Francisco: Jossey-Bass.

Goldberg, L. R. (1976). Language and personality: Toward a taxonomy of trait–descriptive terms. *Istanbul Studies in Experimental Psychology, 12,* 1–23.

Goldberg, L. R. (1980, May). *Some ruminations about the structure of individual differences: Developing a common lexicon for the major characteristics of human personality.* Paper presented at the annual convention of the Western Psychological Association, Honolulu.

Goldberg, L. R. (1981). Language and individual differences: The search for universals in personality lexicons. In L. Wheeler (Ed.), *Review of personality and social psychology* (Vol. 2, pp. 141–165). Beverly Hills, CA: Sage.

Goldberg, L. R. (1990). An alternative "description of personality": The Big-Five factor structure. *Journal of Personality and Social Psychology, 59,* 1216–1229.

Gough, H. G. (1987). *Administrator's Guide to the California Psychological Inventory.* Palo Alto, CA: Consulting Psychologists Press.

Guilford, J. P. (1959). *Personality.* New York: McGraw-Hill.

Guilford, J. P., & Zimmerman, W. S. (1956). Fourteen dimensions of temperament. *Psychological Monographs, 70,* (10, No. 417).

Hampson, S. E., John, O. P., & Goldberg, L. R. (1986). Category breadth and hierarchical structure in personality: Studies of asymmetries in judgments of trait implications. *Journal of Personality and Social Psychology, 51,* 37–54.

Hogan, R. (1983). A socioanalytic theory of personality. In M. M. Page (Ed.), *Nebraska Symposium on Motivation, 1982: Personality—Current theory and research.* Lincoln: University of Nebraska Press.

Hogan, J., & Hogan, R. (1989). How to measure employee reliability. *Journal of Applied Psychology, 74,* 273–279.

John, O. P. (1986). How shall a trait be called?: A feature analysis of altruism. In A. Angleitner, A. Furnham, & G. van Heck (Eds.), *Personality psychology in Europe: Current trends and controversies* (pp. 117–140). Berwyn: Swets North America.

John, O. P. (1989). Toward a taxonomy of personality descriptors. In D. M. Buss & N. Cantor (Eds.), *Personality psychology: Recent trends and emerging directions* (pp. 261–277). New York: Springer-Verlag.

John, O. P. (1990). The "Big Five" factor taxonomy: Dimensions of personality in the natural language and questionnaires. In L. A. Pervin (Ed.), *Handbook of personality theory and research* (pp. 66–100). New York: Guilford Press.

John, O. P., Angleitner, A., & Ostendorf, F. (1988). The lexical approach to personality: A historical review of trait taxonomic research. *European Journal of Personality, 2,* 171–203.

John, O. P., Hampson, S. E., & Goldberg, L. R. (1991). The basic level in personality trait hierarchies: Studies of trait use and accessibility in different contexts. *Journal of Personality and Social Psychology, 60,* 348–361.

Kelly, G. A. (1955). *The psychology of personal constructs* (Vols. 1, 2). New York: Norton.

Klages, L. (1932). *The science of character.* London: George Allen & Unwin. (Original work published 1926)

Kluckhohn, C. M. & Murray, H. A. (1953). *Personality in nature, society, and culture.* New York: Knopf.

Little, B. R. (1989). Personal projects analysis: Trivial pursuits, magnificent obsessions, and the search for coherence. In D. M. Buss and N. Cantor (Eds.), *Personality psychology: Recent trends and emerging directions* (pp. 15–31). New York: Springer-Verlag.

McAdams, D. P. (1989). The development of a narrative identity. In D. M. Buss and N. Cantor (Eds.), *Personality psychology: Recent trends and emerging directions* (pp. 160–174). New York: Springer-Verlag.

McAdams, D. (1992). The Five-Factor Model in personality: A critical appraisal. *Journal of Personality, 60,* 329–361.

McCrae, R. R., & Costa, P. T. (1985). Updating Norman's adequate taxonomy: Intelligence and personality dimensions in natural language and in questionnaires. *Journal of Personality and Social Psychology, 49,* 710–721.

McCrae, R. R., & Costa, P. T. (1990). *Personality in adulthood.* New York: Guilford.

McCrae, R. R., & John, O. P. (1992). An introduction to the Five-Factor Model and its applications. *Journal of Personality, 60,* 175–215.

Mershon, B., & Gorsuch, R. L. (1988). Number of factors in the personality sphere: Does increase in factors increase predictability of real-life criteria? *Journal of Personality and Social Psychology, 55,* 675–680.

Norman, W. T. (1967). *2,800 personality trait descriptors: Normative operating characteristics for a university population.* Ann Arbor: Department of Psychology, University of Michigan.

Norman, W. T., & Goldberg, L. R. (1966). Raters, ratees, and randomness in personality structure. *Journal of Personality and Social Psychology, 4,* 681–691.

Revelle, W. (1987). Personality and motivation: Sources of inefficiency in cognitive performance. *Journal of Research in Personality, 21,* 436–452.

Rothbart, M. K. (1989). Temperament and development. In G. A. Kohnstamm, E. Bates, & M. K. Rothbart (Eds.), *Handbook of temperament in childhood* (pp. 188–247). Chichester, England: Wiley.

Ryle, G. (1949). *The concept of mind.* New York: Barnes & Noble.

Tellegen, A. (1985). Structures of mood and personality and their relevance to assessing anxiety, with an emphasis on self-report. In A. H. Tuma & J. D. Maser (Eds.), *Anxiety and the anxiety disorders* (pp. 681–716). Hillsdale, NJ: Erlbaum.

Tellegen, A., & Waller, N. G. (in press). Exploring personality through test construction: Development of the Multidimensional Personality Questionnaire. In S. R. Briggs & J. M. Cheek (Eds.), *Personality measures: Development and evaluation* (Vol. 1). Greenwich, CN: JAI Press.

Tupes, E. C., & Christal, R. C. (1961). *Recurrent personality factors based on trait ratings* (Tech. Rep. No. ASD-TR-61-97). Lackland Air Force Base, TX: U.S. Air Force.

Wiggins, J. S. (1968). Personality structure. *Annual Review of Psychology, 19,* 293–350.

Wiggins, J. S. (1974). *In defense of traits.* Unpublished manuscript, University of British Columbia, Vancouver, Canada.

Wright, J. C., & Mischel, W. (1987). A conditional analysis of dispositional constructs: The

local predictability of social behavior. *Journal of Personality and Social Psychology,*
53, 1159–1177.

York, K. L., & John, O. P. (1992). The four faces of Eve: A typological analysis of women's personality at midlife. *Journal of Personality and Social Psychology, 63,* 494–
508.

Zuroff, D. C. (1986). Was Gordon Allport a trait theorist? *Journal of Personality and
Social Psychology, 51,* 993–1000.

CHAPTER SEVENTEEN

To Predict Some of the People More of the Time

Individual Traits and the Prediction of Behavior

PETER BORKENAU

Walter Mischel's (1968) book, *Personality and Assessment,* was extremely important for the development of personality theory and research in the last two decades. Mischel pointed to the modest cross-situational consistency of behavior that he interpreted as a sign of situational specificity. Moreover, he pointed to the low validity of personality measures in predicting isolated acts of subjects. What he did not mention, however, was that Gordon Allport (1937) had already opposed similar arguments by Hartshorne and May (1928) some decades earlier. Whereas Mischel (1968) referred to Hartshorne and May's study at length, he did not mention Allport's counterarguments. It was mainly Allport who had imaginatively defended the concept of traits against the objections of those who proposed to analyze individual differences at the lower level of habits instead of traits.

Mischel's (1968) theses were first responded to by some theoretical papers. Bowers (1973), for instance, criticized situationism and suggested interactionism as an alternative, whereas Wachtel (1973) suggested that personality may be more important for the choice of situations than for the responses that are elicited from subjects in experi-

PETER BORKENAU • Department of Psychology, University of Bielefeld, W-4800 Bielefeld 1, Germany.

Fifty Years of Personality Psychology, edited by Kenneth H. Craik *et al.* Plenum Press, New York, 1993.

mental settings. Among the first empirical studies designed with Mischel's critique in mind were Jaccard's (1974) on single-act and multiple-act criteria and Bem and Allen's (1974) on individual differences in cross-situational consistency. Bem and Allen (1974) referred to Allport's work at length. The present chapter explores how their approach worked empirically and the extent to which it embodied Allport's ideas.

ALLPORT'S CRITIQUE OF HARTSHORNE AND MAY

Hartshorne and May (1928) examined the consistency of personality among schoolchildren. In an ambitious investigation of moral character, they arranged situations in which the honesty of subjects could be observed. Of major importance, in the present context, was their finding that the average correlation among their various tests of honesty was .23. Hartshorne and May must somehow have felt the ambiguity of this finding. Usually, they emphasized the specificity of behavior, arguing, for instance, "that honesty or dishonesty is not a unified character trait in children of the ages studied, but a series of specific responses to specific situations" (Hartshorne et al., 1929, p. 243). At other places, however, they admitted some support for a more global concept of honesty as a trait:

> Just as one test is an insufficient and unreliable measure in the case of intelligence, so one test of deception is quite incapable of measuring a subject's tendency to deceive. That is, we cannot predict from what a pupil does on one test what he will do on another. If we use ten tests of classroom deception, however, we can safely predict what a subject will do on the average whenever ten similar situations are presented. (Hartshorne & May, 1928, p. 135)

Thus Hartshorne and May obtained findings in support of the aggregation principle, implying that behavior is situationally specific at the level of single activities but consistent at the dispositional level. This view has more recently been emphasized by Epstein (1979; Epstein & O'Brien, 1985). Other readers of Hartshorne and May, however (e.g., Mischel, 1968), cited their study as unequivocal support for a situationist stance. This conclusion is not unambiguously supported by Hartshorne and May's data, but it is in agreement with their general claim that alleged traits, such as deception, helpfulness, cooperativeness, persistence, and self-control, are "groups of specific habits rather than general traits" (Hartshorne et al., 1930, p. 1).

By contrast, Allport (1937) emphasized that individuals differ not only in the degree to which they show common traits, but also in terms of which traits are even relevant. "Strictly speaking, no two persons ever have precisely the same trait. Though each of two men may be *aggressive* (or *esthetic*), the style and range of the aggression (or estheticism) in each case is noticeably different" (Allport, 1937, p. 297). Allport's definition of personality traits makes allowance for this notion. He defines a trait as a "generalized and focalized neuropsychic system (peculiar to the individual), with the capacity to render many stimuli functionally equivalent, and to initiate and guide consistent (equivalent) forms of adaptive and expressive behavior" (Allport, 1937, p. 295). Thus each individual may have his idiosyncratic equivalence classes of situations and behaviors. Consequently, Allport criticized the use of factor analysis (Allport, 1961, p. 331), a technique that presumes that all dimensions are equally useful for describing each individual and that individual differences are appropriately accounted for by different factor scores on the same set of underlying dimensions (see Eysenck & Eysenck, 1980, for this view). Taking Allport's perspective, the cross-situational consistency coefficients reported by Hartshorne and May are not particularly meaningful. "The low correlations between the tests employed prove only that children are not consistent *in the same way*, not that they are inconsistent with *themselves*" (Allport, 1937, p. 250; italics in the original). By this he meant that a particular behavior may serve various traits, the traits being more stable than cross-situational correlations indicate:

> It may be that child A steals pennies because he has a consistent personal trait of *bravado* based upon his admiration for the gangsters he reads about in the tabloids and sees on the screen; child B steals because he has a persistent *interest in tools and mechanics* that drives him to buy more equipment than he can honestly afford; child C, suffering from a gnawing *feeling of social inferiority*, steals pennies to purchase candy to buy his way into favor with his playmates. Child D does not steal pennies, but he lies about his cheating, not because he has a general trait of dishonesty, but because he has a general trait of *timidity* (fear of consequences); child E lies because he is afraid of hurting the feelings of the teacher whom he adores; child F lies because he is *greedy for praise*. Each of these children behaved as he did toward these tests, not because he had specific habits, but because he had some deep-lying and characteristic trait. All that the Character Education Inquiry discovered was that the particular trait of honesty, as defined in the usual ethical terms and tested in various conventional situations, was not one of which the children possessed constant individual degrees, especially in the face of perhaps a stronger tendency of each child to express some trait other than honesty through the behavior of lying and

stealing. The children did not all have the *same* trait, but they had nevertheless their own traits. (Allport, 1937, p. 251–252; italics in the original)

Thus Allport suggested that it is not situational factors that account for the low cross-situational consistency of particular behaviors. Rather, in this passage he is claiming that persons are consistent with themselves and implying that such consistency is what enables others—acquaintances and psychologists alike—to predict their behaviors from knowledge of their individual dispositions. Cross-situational consistency estimates, however, presume that all subjects do possess exactly the same trait, albeit to different degrees.

Furthermore, Allport points out that there may be qualitatively important mismatches between subjects' actual traits and the trait conjectured by the investigator; these will, of course, tend to reduce the apparent consistency of personality.

The error of probing for consistency in the wrong place (and failing to find it, pronouncing in favor of specificity) has been likened by G. B. Watson to the absurdity of asking whether a person using the public library has a trait causing him to take out only books with red or with blue covers. Of course he hasn't. If only the bindings were studied, no consistency should be expected. But if the *subject-matter* of the chosen books was investigated, well-organized traits of interest would appear. (Allport, 1937, p. 256; italics in the original)

And concerning the problem of misinterpreting individual traits as situational specificity, he stated: "Statistical methods are ordinarily applied only to those variables to which all people may be ordered. If many people do not happen to fit the variable then the illusion of specificity results" (Allport, 1937, p. 256).

BEM AND ALLEN'S ELABORATION OF ALLPORT'S IDEAS

Bem and Allen (1974) acknowledged that previous studies had found cross-situational consistency to be discouragingly low. They realized that this pattern of findings might be due in part to a mismatch—for some subjects at least—between the trait under investigation and the trait actually operating to determine the behavior of interest. Thus, despite the low cross-situational consistency coefficients obtained in psychological research, lay persons believe that individuals are consistent because human intuition operates on idiographic rather than on nomothetic assumptions. Individuals appear as consistent because there is no implicit assumption that all individuals, albeit to a different extent, should have the same traits. Rather, trait words are usually selected from the huge vocabulary of thousands of trait-descriptive terms (Allport & Odbert, 1936) such that they fit the specific equivalence classes of the individual being described. For instance, we distinguish between persons who can be counted on to keep their promises and persons who are habitually punctual. But if a person has one of these traits and not the other, we do not speak of him as inconsistently dependable. We do not first impose a trait term and then modify it by describing the instances that fail to fall into that equivalence class. Rather, we attempt first to organize the person's behaviors into rational sets and label them afterward.

All this is a paraphrase of Allport's ideas, as Bem and Allen readily admitted. However, Bem and Allen also suggested a procedure to overcome the main shortcoming of Allport's idiographic approach; its inability to yield testable hypotheses. This is probably the main reason why Allport's ideas, although documenting an ingenious insight, did not inspire a considerable research program (Allport, 1966). Research psychologists are simply not interested in investigating the personalities of particular ordinary individuals. Rather, they search for general principles. The main contribution of Bem and Allen's (1974) article, therefore, was its conceptualizing and initiation of a research program rooted in Allport's (1937) ideas. The kernel of this program was: "Separate those individuals who are cross-situationally consistent on the trait dimension and throw the others out . . . . we believe that the rewards for this small idiographic commitment can even be paid in the sacred coin of the realm: bigger correlation coefficients" (Bem & Allen, 1974, p. 512).

Bem and Allen (1974) tested their prediction for two personality traits, friendliness and conscientiousness. Subjects completed an 86-item personality inventory, rated themselves on two traits (e.g., "In general, how friendly and outgoing are you?"), and indicated their cross-situational variability for these traits (e.g., "How much do you vary from one situation to another in how friendly and outgoing you are?"). Ratings of friendliness and conscientiousness by parents and peers and several behavior observations served as criteria for cross-situational consistency. Two measures of trait variability were used: (1) the self-rated situational variability and (2) a so-called ipsatized variance index (IVI), which was the ratio of the individual's variance on the multiple-item scale of the trait and the variance of all responses to the 86-item inventory. The effects of self-reported variability were assessed by: (1) correlations among ratings of various judges (self, parents, peers, etc.), (2) correlations among observed behaviors, and (3) correlations between judges' ratings and observed behaviors. It turned out that the response to the "How much do you vary" item for friendliness, but not the corresponding IVI, predicted individual differences in consistency for friendliness. In contrast, the IVI but not the response to the "How much do you vary" item for conscientiousness predicted individual differences in consistency for conscientiousness.

Bem and Allen's (1974) study was intriguing and widely cited. There are more than 500 citations listed in the Social Science Citation Index up to 1991. Most of the citations welcomed this fresh approach to the study of personality. The more critical comments, however, referred to two main problems: the one theoretical and the other one empirical—whether Bem and Allen's study was really idiographic and whether the phenomenon could be replicated. I will discuss these two issues in turn.

WAS BEM AND ALLEN'S STUDY TRULY IDIOGRAPHIC?

The answer to the first question is clearly negative, as already admitted by Bem (1983). According to Allport (1937), "idiographic" refers to the unique organization of traits within individuals, whereas Bem and Allen intended to distinguish between persons to whom a trait is more or less applicable. Though not idiographic in the strict sense, however, Bem and Allen's approach does offer a way of testing one of Allport's ideas.

Allport distinguished between individual traits and common traits: "Common traits are those aspects of personality in respect to which *most* mature people within a given culture can be compared" (Allport, 1937, p. 300, italics added). Common traits cannot provide a full description of a person's dispositions; but they are important because they permit individuals to be compared on common scales. Moreover, Allport emphasized the distinction between persons who can be compared on a common trait and others who cannot. With regard to honesty, for instance, he wrote:

> There are honest people, dishonest people, and atypical people—honest in most respects, but not always capable of resisting temptation.... Honesty is either a general characteristic or a set of specific habits ... depending also upon your method, and upon the particular individual you happen to be studying. (Allport, 1937, p. 255)

Thus it may be that Bem and Allen identified those subjects who were "typical" with regard to the dimensions under study. They had then derived testable hypotheses from one of Gordon Allport's ideas. To state, however, that their study was an instance of the classic moderator variable strategy instead of bearing on the idiographic–nomothetic distinction (Mischel & Peake, 1982, footnote 8) confuses the theoretical side with the methodological side of the issue. The moderator variable strategy is a particular statistical method of data analysis that may be used to investigate an unlimited number of psychological theories and hypotheses (Saunders, 1956; Tellegen *et al.*, 1982).

One avoidable shortcoming of Bem and Allen's study, however, was the choice of their moderator variable. They sought to identify those subjects who were cross-situationally consistent by asking subjects how much they varied from one situation to another in how friendly or conscientious they were. By operationalizing consistency in this manner, Bem and Allen appear to have been using three concepts—trait applicability, cross-situational consistency, and lack of situational variability—interchangeably, thus blurring some important distinctions. A trait may be inapplicable for describing a person, not so much because it does not fit the equivalence class of situations for an individual, but rather because it does not fit the person's equivalence class of behaviors. Bem and Allen provide a good illustration by their example of a student so dedicated to study that he has time for little else and is therefore negligent in most other areas of his life. This student would more appropriately be classified as achievement oriented rather than as conscientious, independent of the situational variability of his achievement-related activities. This is because the equivalence class of behaviors referred to by the term "conscientious" refers not only to achievement-related behavior, but also to behaviors like keeping one's home in order, being meticulous about grooming, and so on. Thus trait applicability and cross-situational consistency are related but different concepts.

It is also necessary to consider cross-situational consistency as separate from situational variability. Magnusson (1976) noted the distinction between absolute consistency and relative consistency. Absolute consistency implies that situations make no difference at all, whereas relative consistency implies that the average behavior of a subject sample may change from one situation to another, with the rank order of subjects presumably remaining the same across situations. For instance, most persons are likely to be more anxious while giving a speech to a large audience than while talking to a friend. The mean anxiety level is therefore different in the two situations. It may well be, however, that the individuals who are more anxious while talking to a friend are the same ones as those who are especially anxious when giving a speech to a large audience. Now, consider that subjects are asked how much their trait varies from one situation to another. It is likely that they consider their absolute consistency, whereas Bem and

Allen intended to assess their relative consistency. I submit that relative consistency is difficult to ask for without long-winded explanations of statistical concepts. This difficulty, however, is easily bypassed by asking subjects the more accurate question of how applicable, relevant, or important a trait is to describe their personality. Trait applicability was asked for by Borkenau and Amelang (1985), trait relevance was asked for by Zuckerman and associates (Zuckerman et al., 1988, 1989) and trait importance was asked for by Cheek (1982). These and other recent studies of the variables that influence self × peer agreement are attempts to replicate and to extend the results of Bem and Allen's (1974) study.

THE REPLICABILITY OF BEM AND ALLEN'S FINDINGS

TRAIT RELEVANCE OR TRAIT EXTREMITY?

Studies of trait variability and trait importance as moderators face the methodological problem that the less-variable subjects, or those for whom the trait is more important, are those who are either extremely low or extremely high on that trait. Variability and importance are therefore confounded with trait extremity (Paunonen, 1988; Rushton et al., 1981; Stones & Burt, 1978). More extreme values on both poles of a dimension, however, imply larger standard deviations and, other things being equal, higher correlations. Higher correlations for the less variable group, or for those subjects for whom a trait is more important, can therefore simply reflect the biased sampling of more extreme cases. This was a major argument advanced by critics of Bem and Allen's study (Chaplin & Goldberg, 1984; Paunonen & Jackson, 1985; Rushton et al., 1981).

Two techniques have been used to overcome this problem. Bem and Allen (1974) conducted separate median splits for subjects at each of the seven points of the trait rating scale. Thus subjects who had a moderate trait rating for friendliness needed a higher self-rated variability than subjects with an extreme rating on the friendliness dimension in order to be assigned to the more variable subgroup. Thus extremity and variability were unconfounded by adjusting the distributions of trait ratings within the more- and the less-variable subgroups. The other approach to the problem is to conduct regression analyses or moderated regression analyses (Borkenau & Amelang, 1985; Tellegen et al., 1982) instead of computing correlations. In contrast to correlations, regression coefficients do not increase with the variance of the variables (Hanushek & Jackson, 1977).

WHO ARE THE TRAIT-CONSISTENT SUBJECTS?

Bem and Allen (1974) reported correlations among trait ratings, correlations among behavior observations, and correlations between trait ratings and behavior observations. Moreover, they compared the intraindividual variances of the friendliness and conscientiousness measures for the variable and unvariable subjects. Thus there is a problem as to whether these measures of actual consistency may all be used interchangeably. Mischel and Peake (1982) claimed that it was the correlations among behavior observations only that indicated cross-situational consistency of behavior. This is appropriate as far as cross-situational consistency is concerned. But what measures are appropriate to identify those persons who are "typical" for a trait according to Allport?

It is likely to be the correlations among ratings by various knowledgeable informants that best indicate the applicability of a trait. Low correlations (or high intraindividual variances) among judges are likely to indicate that the informants formed different impressions of the targets' behavior. Consider once more the totally dedicated student who finds no time to keep his apartment in order. He may be rated by some informants as extremely conscientious and by others as not at all conscientious, depending on which aspect of conscientiousness the judges choose to focus on. Because the target is inconsistently conscientious, judges' ratings of his conscientiousness are unlikely to agree. The same argument applies to the equivalence class of situations. If subjects are more conscientious than others in some situations but less conscientious in other situations, various judges who observe the targets in different settings will probably form different impressions.

By contrast, correlations among behavior observations face the problem that targets must have the trait as operationalized by the researcher in order that high cross-situational consistency coefficients are obtained (Allport, 1937). Therefore, if the correlations among behavior observations are *not* lower for subjects with a low self-rated trait applicability, this may indicate: (1) that subjects are not able to provide valid judgments of whether their equivalence classes are appropriately described by the trait under study; (2) that they regard the trait as undescriptive of their behavior in general, although it is descriptive of the particular behavior being investigated by the experimenter; or (3) that they regard the trait as irrelevant in terms of their everyday life situations, despite the fact that it is descriptive of their behavior in the situations being investigated. Thus there are numerous reasons why correlations among behavior observations may be difficult to predict from ratings of trait applicability. It is therefore not surprising that two of the three published studies using behavior observations (Chaplin & Goldberg, 1984; Mischel & Peake, 1982) failed to replicate Bem and Allen's findings. The one study that produced positive results (Zanna et al., 1980) used attitudes instead of traits.

WAS THE SEARCH FOR MODERATORS SUCCESSFUL?

A meta-analysis of the studies that investigated trait variability, trait applicability, trait importance, or trait relevance as moderators of self–peer agreement has recently been published by Zuckerman et al. (1989). The meta-analysis shows a reliable moderator effect in the expected direction. This reflects the fact that there are studies with higher rater agreement for cross-situationally stable subjects (Bem & Allen, 1974; Kenrick and Stringfield, 1980; Mischel & Peake, 1982) or subjects for whom a trait is applicable (Borkenau & Amelang, 1985), important (Cheek, 1982), or relevant (Zuckerman et al., 1988, 1989), and studies that do not produce this finding (Chaplin & Goldberg, 1984; Paunonen & Jackson, 1985). By contrast, there are no published studies that show reliably higher correlations for inconsistent subjects. Moreover, self-rated applicability of a trait to oneself, self-rated trait importance, and self-rated trait relevance are equally efficient moderators as the self-rated cross-situational variability of behavior. Thus, although trait appropriateness is preferable on theoretical grounds (Amelang & Borkenau, 1986; Zuckerman et al., 1989), there is no evidence that suggests the superiority of this variable as a moderator. How can this finding be explained?

One possibility is that subjects do not distinguish between the variability of a trait and its applicability to oneself, its importance, and its relevance. Correlations among self-ratings of variability, applicability, importance, and relevance rarely surpass .20 (Burke et al., 1984; Paunonen, 1988; Zuckerman et al., 1988, 1989); this finding led Zuckerman and co-workers (1989, p. 283) to conclude that trait relevance and trait consistency are relatively independent of one another. But both are so unreliable that a significant correlation between them is not to be expected. Borkenau (1981) checked the stability of self-rated variability that was measured at six-month intervals and found that these stability coefficients did not differ from zero. In contrast, the average six-month stability of the trait ratings was .30. Borkenau (1981) and Chaplin and Goldberg (1984) found low or zero correlations between self-rated variability for a trait and the ipsatized variance index for the same trait. Thus low correlations among measures of trait variability and related concepts are difficult to interpret. The low reliability of measures of trait variability raises important questions about the wisdom of continuing to study it.

Zuckerman *et al.* (1988, 1989) also compared rating measures and ranking measures of trait relevance, whereby the latter required a ranking of several traits for their variability or relevance. Rating measures confound trait × person interactions with systematic individual differences in trait relevance. They do not only identify the traits that are of particular importance for each person, but also those persons who generally believe that traits are useful to describe their personality. In contrast, ranking measures do not reflect systematic individual differences in trait relevance, as the sum of all ranks is the same for all subjects. Zuckerman *et al.* (1989) found that ranking measures of moderators produced greater effects than rating measures. Moreover, Borkenau and Amelang (1985) found moderator effects when using an adjective generation technique to identify trait-relevant subjects. Thus, if the considerable technical problems are overcome, the moderator variable approach may be useful to somewhat increase the prediction of ratings for some of the people.

CONCLUSIONS

The Bem and Allen approach should be evaluated in two respects: (1) whether it really helped to predict some of the people more of the time and (2) whether it revitalized Allport's ideas. As far as prediction is concerned, it has not been clarified in more than a decade's time whether the phenomenon first reported by Bem and Allen is reliable or not. Some authors (Chaplin & Goldberg, 1984; Paunonen & Jackson, 1985) found that the phenomenon is not replicable, whereas others, including myself, found confirming evidence. Even if there is such a phenomenon, however, it is highly elusive.

And what about the revitalization of Allport's ideas? Unfortunately, Gordon Allport died seven years before Bem and Allen (1974) published their study. It would have been interesting to hear his reactions. I wonder whether he would have applauded this approach. Allport argued against the routine use of statistical methods, and he emphasized that personality is an organized whole. He tried to understand the individuality of the single person. By contrast, Bem and Allen suggested an approach that led to exactly those mass investigations that Allport considered unlikely to prove fruitful in understanding personality. I conjecture that Gordon Allport, if still alive, would be more likely to share Lawrence Pervin's (1985) view on the state of personality research; that is, that one learns more about people from personal contact than from reading the personality literature. Thus, although Bem and Allen's work is one of the major offshoots during the last decades of Allport's theorizing, I think Allport himself would have regarded it as a bastard child.

REFERENCES

Allport, G. W. (1937). *Personality: A psychological interpretation.* New York: Holt.

Allport, G. W. (1961). *Pattern and growth in personality.* New York: Holt.

Allport, G. W. (1966). Traits revisited. *American Psychologist, 21,* 1–10.

Allport, G. W., & Odbert, H.S. (1936). Trait-names: A psycholexical study. *Psychological Monographs, 47* (1, No. 211).

Amelang, M., & Borkenau, P. (1986). The trait concept: Current theoretical considerations, empirical facts, and implications for personality inventory construction. In A. Angleitner & J. S. Wiggins (Eds.), *Personality assessment via questionnaires: Current issues in theory and measurement* (pp. 7–34). Berlin: Springer.

Bem, D. J. (1983). Further déjà vu in the search for cross-situational consistency: A reply to Mischel and Peake. *Psychological Review, 90,* 390–393.

Bem, D. J., & Allen, A. (1974). On predicting some of the people some of the time: The search for cross-situational consistencies in behavior. *Psychological Review, 81,* 506–520.

Borkenau, P. (1981). *Intraindividuelle Variabilität und differentielle Vorhersagbarkeit* [Intraindividual variability and differential prediction]. Unpublished doctoral dissertation, University of Heidelberg, Germany.

Borkenau, P., & Amelang, M. (1985). Individuelle Angemessenheit von Eigenschaftskonstrukten als Moderatorvariable für die Übereinstimmung zwischen Selbst- und Bekanntenratings [Individual appropriateness of traits as a moderator of self-peer agreement]. *Diagnostica, 31,* 105–118.

Bowers, K. S. (1973). Situationism in psychology: An analysis and a critique. *Psychological Review, 80,* 307–336.

Burke, P. A., Kraut, R., & Dworkin, R. H. (1984). Traits, consistency, and self-schemata: What do our methods measure? *Journal of Personality and Social Psychology, 47,* 568–579.

Chaplin, W. F., & Goldberg L. R. (1984). A failure to replicate the Bem and Allen study on individual differences in cross-situational consistency. *Journal of Personality and Social Psychology, 47,* 1074–1090.

Cheek, J. (1982). Aggregation, moderator variables, and the validity of personality tests. *Journal of Personality and Social Psychology, 43,* 1254–1269.

Epstein, S. (1979). The stability of behavior: I. On predicting most of the people much of the time. *Journal of Personality and Social Psychology, 37,* 1097–1126.

Epstein, S., & O'Brien, E. J. (1985). The person–situation debate in historical and current perspective. *Psychological Bulletin, 98,* 513–537.

Eysenck, M. W., & Eysenck, H. J. (1980). Mischel and the concept of personality. *British Journal of Psychology, 71*, 191–204.

Hanushek, E. A., & Jackson, J. E. (1977). *Statistical methods for social scientists.* New York: Academic Press.

Hartshorne, H., & May, M. A. (1928). *Studies in the nature of character: Vol. 1. Studies in deceit.* New York: Macmillan.

Hartshorne, H., May, M. A., & Maller, J. B. (1929). *Studies in the nature of character: Vol. 2. Studies in service and self-control.* New York: Macmillan.

Hartshorne, H., May, M. A., & Shuttleworth, J. B. (1930). *Studies in the nature of character: Vol. 3. Studies in the organization of character.* New York: Macmillan.

Jaccard, J. J. (1974). Predicting social behavior from personality traits. *Journal of Research in Personality, 7*, 358–367.

Kenrick, D. T., & Stringfield, D. O. (1980). Personality traits and the eye of the beholder: Crossing some traditional philosophical boundaries in the search for consistency in all of the people. *Psychological Review, 87*, 88–104.

Magnusson, D. (1976). The person and the situation in an interactional model of behavior. *Scandinavian Journal of Psychology, 17*, 253–271.

Mischel, W. (1968). *Personality and assessment.* New York: Wiley.

Mischel, W., & Peake, P. K. (1982). Beyond déjà vu in the search for cross-situational consistency. *Psychological Review, 89*, 730–755.

Paunonen, S. V. (1988). Trait relevance and the differential predictability of behavior. *Journal of Personality, 56*, 599–619.

Paunonen, S. V., & Jackson, D. N. (1985). Idiographic measurement strategies for personality and prediction: Some unredeemed promissory notes. *Psychological Review, 92*, 486–511.

Pervin, L. A. (1985). Personality: Current controversies, issues, and directions. *Annual Review of Psychology, 36*, 83–114.

Rushton, J. P., Jackson, D. N., & Paunonen, S. V. (1981). Personality: Nomothetic or idiographic? A response to Kenrick and Stringfield. *Psychological Review, 88*, 582–589.

Saunders, D. R. (1956). Moderator variables in prediction. *Educational and Psychological Measurement, 16*, 209–222.

Stones, M. J., & Burt, G. (1978). Quasi-statistical inference in rating behavior. *Journal of Research in Personality, 12*, 381–389.

Tellegen, A., Kamp, J., & Watson, D. (1982). Recognizing individual differences in predictive structure. *Psychological Review, 89*, 95–105.

Wachtel, P. L. (1973). Psychodynamics, behavior therapy, and the implacable experimenter: An inquiry into the consistency of personality. *Journal of Abnormal Psychology 82*, 324–334.

Zanna, M. P., Olson, J. M., & Fazio, R. H. (1980). Attitude–behavior consistency—An individual difference perspective. *Journal of Personality and Social Psychology, 38*, 432–440.

Zuckerman, M., Koestner, R., DeBoy, T., Garcia, T., Maresca, B. C., & Satoris, J. M. (1988). To predict some of the people some of the time: A reexamination of the moderator variable approach in personality theory. *Journal of Personality and Social Psychology, 54*, 1006–1019.

Zuckerman, M., Bernieri, F., Koestner, R., & Rosenthal, R. (1989). To predict some of the people some of the time: In search of moderators. *Journal of Personality and Social Psychology, 57*, 279–293.

CHAPTER EIGHTEEN

The Scientific Credibility of Commonsense Psychology

GARTH J. O. FLETCHER

By the early 1980s, the idea that ordinary human social cognition is rational or scientific in character was under serious attack in personality and social psychology. Personality psychology was in the throes of the debate concerning whether behavior was consistent across situations and, although the jury was still out on the issue, powerful voices and persuasive data suggested that the concept of personality traits was a quaint shibboleth of commonsense psychology. As Nisbett and Ross (1980) put it, "the personality theorists' (and the layperson's) conviction that there are strong cross-situational consistencies in behavior may be seen as merely another instance of theory-driven covariation assessments operating in the face of contrary evidence" (p. 112).

In social cognition circles, a flood of research on errors and biases in social judgment apparently demonstrated that laypeople were subject to an extraordinary range of invidious social judgment biases—laypeople were purported to underestimate the causal role of situational determinants of behavior and overestimate the role of personal determinants (the so-called fundamental attribution error), to be poor statisticians, to be unduly influenced by prior theories while underutilizing data, and much more (for reviews, see Markus & Zajonc, 1985; Nisbett & Ross, 1980; Ross, 1977). As Fiske and Taylor (1984) con-

---

GARTH J. O. FLETCHER • Department of Psychology, University of Canterbury, Christchurch 1, New Zealand.

Fifty Years of Personality Psychology, edited by Kenneth H. Craik *et al.* Plenum Press, New York, 1993.

cluded in their textbook, *Social Cognition:* "Instead of a naive scientist entering the environment in search of the truth, we find the rather unflattering picture of a charlatan trying to make the data come out in a manner most advantageous to his or her already held theories" (p. 88).

This issue and related arguments impact on personality psychology and theory in various ways. First, the degree of rationality inherent in everyday social cognition is an important question in relation to general personality theories. Second, much current personality research and theory is derived from the personality theory embedded in common-sense psychology (see Chapter 19, this volume). Consider, for example, the development of the big five personality structure as articulated by McCrae & Costa (1985): extroversion, neuroticism, conscientiousness, agreeableness, and openness. The factorial analyses that produce these factors are based on ratings of personal dispositions drawn from the English language. Hence, the resultant personality structure is essentially an explication of the general personality theory inherent in our language and in laypeople's personality schemata. To put the matter bluntly, if commonsense psychology goes down the gurgler, then so do large portions of contemporary personality psychology.

Assessments of the rationality or scientific credibility of common-sense social cognition depend on the normative model it is compared with. The first section of this chapter will draw on some contemporary philosophy of science and sketch some central elements in scientific cognition. I shall then use this analysis as a framework to analyze and evaluate recent social psychological and personality research in terms of the rationality of ordinary social cognition and in relation to the scientific credibility of our commonsense psychological theories that undergird everyday social judgment.

A REALIST THEORY OF PSYCHOLOGICAL SCIENCE

The idea of a realist approach to psychology that transcends a narrow empiricism is not new. For example, Allport (1966) recommended that we adopt what he termed "heuristic realism": He writes

> Galloping empiricism ... dashes forth like a headless horseman. It has no rational objective; uses no rational method other than math-ematical; reaches no rational conclusion. It lets the discordant data sing for themselves. By contrast, heuristic realism says ... the area we carve out should be rationally conceived, tested by rational methods, and the findings should be rationally interpreted. (p. 40).

Like Allport, I believe that a variant of scientific realism offers the most appropriate and viable scientific model for psychology. Scientific realism is a wide-ranging theory of science; thus, I will consider only a few central components of this approach that are most relevant to the later discussion*: truth as a scientific aim, the relation between theory and data, and a generative concept of causality.

TRUTH AS A SCIENTIFIC AIM

According to scientific realism, scientific theories routinely postulate unobserved theoretical entities to explain phenomena; for example, cognitive mechanisms and personality constructs in psychology or subatomic particles in physics. The nub of a realist approach is that these deep-structural theories are *intended* to adequately refer to and represent a world, some of which is independent of human cognition. Hence, one of the pivotal aims of science is to construct true theories about that world. However, the drive toward "truth" is conceptualized here as a guiding ideal or idealized horizon (McMullin, 1983), which can be conceived of as a highly valued, though unobtainable, goal of scientific enquiry.

THE RELATION BETWEEN THEORY AND DATA

The hypothetico-deductive model is probably the most commonly accepted normative model in personality and social psychology. According to this model, observational claims are deducted from theories, then tested. A variant of this model proposed by Popper (1959), which still has a considerable following in psychology, posits that such tests can falsify but not verify theories. Yet the hypothetico-deductive model and Popper's falsificationist version have been subject to compelling attacks from philosophers over the last three decades and retains few adherents in contemporary philosophy of science.

Probably the major reason for the demise of hypothetico-deductivism in philosophy of science is simply because it does not fit the way science appears to work. For example, this model implies that scientists should drop theories like hotcakes when faced with disconfirming data. In fact, the numerous analyses carried out by philosophers of science examining historically important episodes of scientific change in the physical sciences show that this is not what happens to all (e.g., see

---

* For philosophical accounts of scientific realism see Bhaskar (1978), Hooker (1987), and McMullin (1984); for more psychologically oriented treatments, see Howard (1985), Manicas and Secord (1983), and Greenwood (1989).

Feyerabend, 1975; Kuhn, 1970). The same point holds good for social psychology and personality research, which is full of controversies in which apparently disconfirming data have failed to convince the proponents of the original theories that their hypotheses or theories were false; examples would include the debate between self-perception theory and cognitive dissonance theory, the role of consensus information in social judgment (see Ross & Fletcher, 1985), and whether trait-related behavior is consistent across situations (see Chapter 17, this volume).

However, what to the orthodox empiricist appears to be a blatant disregard for evidence can instead be construed as perfectly legitimate strategies for dealing with recalcitrant data, including positing methodological deficiencies in the relevant research, reinterpreting the data so as to render them consistent with one's preferred theory, or simply modifying the original theory.

The thrust of my argument can be summed up in the aphorism that *theory is underdetermined by data*. This point implies that there is no algorithm that connects data to theory selection. Instead, theory evaluation within a scientific community is always a judgment call that proceeds in a relatively disheveled fashion involving a complex and subtle interplay between conceptual and empirical concerns.

The loose relation between data and theory perhaps explains why dissent and argument are permanent features of psychology, and indeed all science. However, scientific disciplines, again including psychology, can hardly be described as irredeemably inchoate: controversies are resolved, consensus is often attained, and progress is made.What explains the existence of this consensual aspect of psychology? My short answer is in terms of the rational structure of science, which provides an interlocking set of normative values, rules, and aims that regulate theory appraisal and development. These values include some important epistemic criteria used for theory evaluation, apart from the consistency between theory and data or predictive accuracy (Fletcher & Haig, 1990; Howard, 1985).

Consider, for example, the following epistemic criteria proposed by Fletcher and Haig (1990): *Explanatory depth* involves the postulation of one or more underlying causal mechanisms to account for the surface phenomena. A theory that manages to integrate and explain hitherto disparate items of knowledge possesses the valuable property of *unifying power*. A theory whose content is not marred by logical inconsistencies has *internal coherence* while a theory that is consistent with other entrenched or accepted theoretical knowledge has the virtue of *external coherence*. *Fertility* refers to the ability of a theory to stimulate further fruitful lines of research or generate novel and powerful extensions to our knowledge base. The notion of *simplicity* has proved difficult to formulate; nevertheless, scientists are frequently attracted by theoretical elegance rather than cumbersome complexity. Finally, the successful *application* of a mature theory counts as an important epistemic value in a science concerned to give us useful knowledge.

The first criterion (that of explanatory depth) is especially relevant to scientific realism and embraces a particular theory or concept of causality known as a generative concept. To conclude this section, I turn to a brief examination of this concept.

A Generative Concept of Causality

A generative concept of causality proposes that causal relations between events, or between events and dispositional properties, contain some sort of necessary connection or bond that is embedded in the nature of things. A generative account can usefully be contrasted with an approach, usually identified with David Hume, that construes causality purely in terms of regularity. A regularity theory of causality interprets a causal relation as one in which the events are regularly conjoined in space and time, with the cause preceding the effect. The major problem with this approach is that it becomes difficult to conceptually distinguish between bona fide cause–effect relations and coincidental noncausal relations that may be perfectly regular (e.g., night following day). A generative theory solves this problem.

A generative causal account has at least two other important features from my perspective. First, this approach is consistent with realism's demand for producing deep-level explanatory theories that represent hypothetical generative mechanisms. Second, it happily accommodates current cognitive, social psychological, and personality approaches that postulate cognitive–structural models as being causally implicated in the generation of cognition, affect, or behavior.

It is instructive to evaluate the rationality of the layperson's thinking and also the scientific credibility of the layperson's social psychological–personality theories using our thumbnail sketch of a realist account of scientific cognition as a normative model. I will attempt these tasks next.

EVALUATING THE LAYPERSON'S SOCIAL COGNITION: SCIENTIST OR SIMPLETON?

As noted previously, science, according to a realist account, is centrally concerned with the truth value of its theories. But can the same be said for laypeople in their everyday social cognition? As indicated in the introduction, powerful voices within social psychology have answered no! One challenge to the notion that laypeople are seriously interested in truth emanates from the view that humans are more interested in retaining a flattering and positive self-concept than in truth. Indeed, there is a large body of evidence that suggests normal human cognition is characterized by unrealistically positive views of the self, exaggerated perceptions of personal control, and unrealistic optimism (for reviews, see Greenwald, 1980; Taylor & Brown, 1988).

However, this self-serving picture of human cognition is not necessarily antithetical to the layperson's employment of the more dispassionate scientific values of accuracy and logic in the pursuit of truth. The work of Trope (1979, 1980) and others (Strube et al., 1986) has shown that subjects will, at times, prefer tasks that provide good diagnostic information concerning their own level of ability, even when such tasks have the potential of providing ego-threatening feedback.

In short, both cognitive–rational and motivational models of social cognition are correct; people are both rational and rationalizers—at times concerned with explanation, at times with justification, at other times both, and at still other times with neither. Viewed in this way, the proper question becomes to what extent and under what conditions are lay social judgments determined by self-serving motivational factors.

A second major claim to emanate from mainstream social cognition, and one that apparently lays waste the scientific credibility of ordinary cognition, is that laypeople are simply unwilling to modify or abandon beliefs, hypotheses, or theories in the face of disconfirmatory evidence (Fiske & Taylor, 1984; Nisbett & Ross, 1980). However, the above postulate is derived from research and theorizing that largely embodies adherence to the sort of clear-cut algorithmic connection between theory and data that I previously challenged. To recap, I argued that there was no such clear-cut relation between theory and data, and that it was not uncommon for scientists to retain theories in the face of disconfirmatory evidence. Science is inherently conservative in terms of theory change and for obvious reasons. If we revamped or abandoned our theories strictly and immediately according to the vicissitudes of our data, we would indulge in theory change with unsettling regularity. Moreover, the standard situation in science is to have evidence that both confirms and disconfirms our preferred theory. The layperson's conservatism, on this view, should not necessarily be labeled as unscientific.

Once again, the correct question to ask is to what extent the layperson ignores data that run against extant theories or hypotheses.

In fact, the evidence concerning this issue shows that the layperson's hypotheses or theories *are* usually influenced by data—the claim that subjects' performance is less than optimal is based on the usual finding that subjects underutilize the data, according to some normative model of inference such as Bayes's theorem or to the standard Fisherian analysis using significance tests (for reviews substantiating this point, see Einhorn & Hogarth, 1981; Higgins & Bargh, 1987; Ross & Fletcher, 1985). One can view the glass as half full or half empty and be impressed or dismayed at the layperson's attention to predictive accuracy.

A second pivotal point is that if we dispense with a standard hypothetico-deductive framework and accept the idea that there are several epistemic criteria available for theory evaluation, then this can alter the standard interpretation of the layperson's performance in research tasks. Why? Because psychologists typically do not consider all the epistemic values that their subjects may quite reasonably be considering. Take, for example, the study by Lepper, Ross, and Lau (1986), concerned with belief perseverance, in which two groups of high school subjects performed very well or very poorly at solving novel problems under the guidance of either thoroughly effective or ineffective instructional films. In spite of being made aware at a later time of the impact of the instructional films, subjects continued to draw unwarranted inferences (to use the author's words) concerning their own levels of ability that were based on their original performances.

But consider the plausible possibility that subjects would have tried to explain their initial performance and sought to integrate this new information with their extant knowledge. If we consult our prior list of epistemic values, this implies that subjects were utilizing values of *explanatory depth, unifying power,* and *internal and external coherence.* In turn, this bolstering of the initial ability attributions may have rendered these judgments less susceptible to sudden revision when information was received that, from the experimenter's perspective, apparently decisively invalidated the subjects' original ability attributions. It is all too easy to place subjects in research contexts that produce inaccurate subject inferences, but this does *not* entail that such judgments are necessarily irrational or unwarranted.

Finally, let me briefly consider the overall research literature on errors and biases in social judgment. Several authors have drawn similar conclusions based on literature reviews of this research (Fletcher & Haig, 1990; Klayman & Ha, 1987); namely, under unfavorable conditions that promote a casual, automatic, or data-driven style of information processing, laypeople will typically rely on fallback heuristics or easily used rules of thumb. On one hand, these heuristics are often reliable, adaptive, and effective devices; on the other, they produce characteristic biases or errors under certain conditions (Nisbett & Ross, 1980). However, under more friendly processing conditions, that provide useful cues or promote more in-depth information processing, these default heuristics tend to be corrected or discarded, hence reducing resultant biases and errors. These favorable processing conditions include adequate processing time (Fletcher et al., 1990a), a light memory load (Gilbert et al., 1988), having the problem framed in a familiar context (Griggs & Cox, 1983), having cues that help in strategy choice (Hinz et al., 1988), possessing adequate knowledge or sufficient schema complexity to process the information (Fletcher et al., 1986), and being sufficiently motivated to carry out an in-depth analysis (Tetlock, 1988).

Take as an example the celebrated bias known variously as the correspondence bias or the fundamental attribution error: the tendency to underestimate the causal role of situational determinants of behavior and overestimate the causal role of the internal determinants (Ross, 1977). Recent studies have suggested that under conditions that encourage an in-depth and careful processing of the stimulus materials, compared to a superficial and casual analysis, correspondence bias will decrease (Fletcher et al., 1990; Gilbert et al., 1988; Tetlock, 1985).

Individual differences form another, though not commonly researched, class of conditions that may influence social inference biases. Fletcher and his colleagues have examined the role that the complexity of attributional schemata has in relation to the level of expertise exhibited in social judgment, using a recently developed scale termed the Attributional Complexity Scale (Fletcher et al., 1986). This 28-item scale includes seven attributional subconstructs that vary along a simple–complex dimension, including the level of motivation to explain human behavior, the tendency to indulge in metacognitive attributional thinking, the tendency to infer complex causal explanations that are both internal and external, the tendency to infer causes from the distant past, and so on. Initial results have confirmed that this scale possesses good internal reliability, convergent and discriminant validity, concurrent validity, and predictive validity (Brookings & Brown, 1988; Fletcher et al., 1986; Flett et al., 1989).

Using the Attributional Complexity Scale, Fletcher and his colleagues, and others, have found that subjects who possess complex attributional schemata produce more accurate trait and attitude judgments than do those with simple schemata, but that such an advantage appears to be manifested most strongly under conditions that encourage in-depth information processing that is goal driven (Devine, 1989; Fletcher et al., 1988, 1990, 1992). In a reaction-time study Fletcher et *al.* (1992) also found that attributionally complex subjects displayed a clear-cut tendency to control the amount of processing time according to the difficulty level of the causal problem; in contrast, attributionally simple subjects did not control their processing time at all according to the difficulty level of the causal problem. Truly, some laypeople appear to be better naive (social) scientists than others.

CONCLUSION

To conclude this section, I think it is apparent that to view the layperson as a lazy thinker, uninterested in truth, and replete with biases and shortcomings in his or her social thinking is at best an exaggerated half-truth. However, the extent to which one judges the rationality of social judgment, or even the propriety of labeling a mode of thought as a "bias" or an "error," will be determined, in part, by the normative framework adopted. If the normative framework of science advanced here is accepted, then the layperson's social cognition, under certain conditions, looks remarkably similar to that of our prototypical scientist.

FOLK PERSONALITY–SOCIAL PSYCHOLOGY THEORIES:
TOUCHSTONE OR CROCK?

Introductions to social psychology or personality texts often seek to distance these disciplines from common sense. A commonly adopted strategy to demonstrate the relative paucity of common sense is to contrast commonsense maxims that appear contradictory, such as "birds of a feather flock together" and "opposites attract," and proceed to argue that research is needed to go beyond such crude and unhelpful formulations. In contrast to the standard textbook litany, I will argue that substantial elements of personality and social psychological theorizing are clearly derived from commonsense psychological theory.

Of course, most personality and social psychologists happily admit to their interest in commonsense psychological theory, insofar as that theory is causally implicated in the generation of behavior. The schemata and cognitive processes that people use in making judgments and interacting with others are part and parcel of "naive" commonsense theory; hence, common sense is, in part, the subject matter of personality and social psychology. Moreover, personality and social psychological theories also routinely borrow concepts and principles from common sense in building scientific theories; such theories abound with commonsense concepts such as attitude, intention, trait, need, drive, belief, emotion, goal, and so forth. Of course, these concepts are typically refined and more precisely defined in their new theoretical homes than according to their colloquial usages, but the concepts are usually ensconced in theoretical frameworks that are quintessential "common sense"—what Dennett (1987) calls the "intentional stance." The "intentional stance" involves treating humans as rational systems that have certain goals; we can predict and explain behavior by assuming that humans will attempt to achieve those goals, in virtue of various mental states such as beliefs, aspirations, knowledge, attitudes, and so forth.

Empirical examinations that have been made of the similarity between psychological and commonsense theories support my contention concerning the close links between professional and commonsense psychology (for a review, see Furnham, 1989). For example, substantial overlap has been found between lay conceptions and psychologists' theories concerning the introversion–extroversion personality dimension (Semin & Krahe, 1987), intelligence (Sternberg et al., 1981) delinquency (Furnham & Henderson, 1983), and depression (Rippere, 1977).

Although there may be debate concerning the nature and degree of convergence between the theories of the layperson and those of the personality and social psychologist, there is relatively little dispute over the claims that there is considerable overlap between the two spheres. Fierce debate, however, has waxed over the questions of whether commonsense psychological theory is true and whether it is doomed to be replaced by theories with sterner scientific credentials. The answers to these latter questions are not necessarily related to the scientific status of everyday social cognition. It is possible that ordinary folk rely on muddled or fallacious theories because of their limited access to the powerful experimental and research techniques that are available to the professional research psychologist, rather than because they are other than immaculately rational and suitably curious about human behavior. Nonetheless, conclusions concerning the silliness of commonsense psychological theory are relevant to an overall assessment of everyday cognition.

Over the last decade, there has been considerable debate among philosophers of science concerning the feasibility or status of what is referred to as "folk psychology" (see Fletcher & Haig, 1990). The arguments have resolved around the status of "beliefs" or other cognitive attributions in commonsense psychology. For example, one of the most vigorous attacks on folk psychology theory has been developed by Churchland (1984, 1985) who claims that folk psychology is destined for extinction on the grounds that our commonsense psychological framework is a false and radically misleading conception of the causes of human behavior and the nature of cognitive activity. Common sense, it is argued, will be replaced in due course by a mature neuroscience. Although Churchland produces little empirical evidence for his negative assessment of folk psychology, he does present a variety of arguments that I have not the space here to evaluate. However, his central contention is

> ... that neuroscience is unlikely to find "sentences in the head" or anything else that answers to the structure of individual beliefs and desires. On the strength of this shared assumption, I am willing to infer that folk psychology is false, and that its ontology is chimerical. Beliefs and desires are of a piece with phlogiston, caloric, and the alchemal essences. (Churchland, 1988, p. 508)

One major problem with Churchland's position is that folk psychology is narrowly represented as a cognitive theory. In fact, it seems obvious that common sense also contains a sophisticated and subtle theory of personality and social behavior. This personality theory is typically conceived of by psychologists as consisting of schemata that embrace a large set of personality dispositions that are organized to represent a general personality structure. Factor-analytic studies suggest that such personality schemata can be described in terms of general dimensions such as social desirability and intellectual desirability (e.g., Rosenberg *et al.*, 1968). Certain traits are thus seen as naturally co-occurring; for example, skillful and intelligent, clumsy and naive, humorless and unsociable, and helpful and sincere.

Now a huge number of personality dispositions appear to refer to the behavioral as well as the mental spheres. For example, attributions of warmth, introversion, or aggressiveness imply certain loosely defined classes of behaviors, as well as some sort of mental component such as emotional events (e.g., introverted people feel more uncomfortable in company). In addition, many dispositions contain an interpersonal component; for example, dispositions such as warm, sensitive, abrupt, and so forth assume an interactional context. In short, folk psychology is closer to a personality and social psychological theory rather than simply a theory of mind. Moreover, a considerable amount of research attention has been allocated by personality and social psychologists to the question of whether this theory is accurate or reasonable, and the results suggest that commonsense theory may have considerably more going for it than suggested by Churchland's damning indictment.

Several influential reviews of the literature in the 1960s (e.g.,

Mischel, 1968) suggested that there was relatively low consistency of behavior across situations or between self-rated dispositions and individual behaviors (usually resulting in correlations lower than .3). However, it has become clear from the recent flurry of research and critical argument that when behavior is aggregated, rather than treated as single instances, the resultant consistency correlations are much higher (up to .7) (see Kenrick & Funder, 1988, for a recent review). This level of consistency is all that is required as a basis for folk psychology, given that many commonsense, dispositional concepts are loosely defined in terms of rough families of behaviors (e.g., sociable, assertive, unfriendly).

Another line of attack on the validity of folk personality theory has argued that the pattern of correlations produced when subjects rate other people on a set of personality scales is a product of the semantic relations between the traits rather than the empirical relations between the traits—a thesis known as the semantic distortion hypothesis (see, for example, D'Andrade, 1974; Shweder, 1975). The evidence produced for this claim includes demonstrations that subjects' ratings of the semantic meanings of trait terms produces a factor structure similar to that derived from ratings of real people.

However, against the semantic distortion hypothesis, two recent ingenious studies have shown that when semantic effects are controlled, the pattern of correlations among the trait ratings is affected very little (DeSoto et al., 1985; Weiss & Mendelsohn, 1986). Moreover, several studies have shown that, under certain conditions, there is good agreement between self-personality judgments and judgments of peer raters on particular traits and also reliable interjudge agreement concerning the individual being rated (for a recent review, see Funder, 1987). As Kenrick and Funder (1988) have pointed out, these results cannot be explained in terms of the semantic distortion hypothesis.

DISPOSITIONS AS CAUSAL EXPLANATIONS

It is clear from casual observation and analysis of the everyday attribution of dispositions, and also recent research (Asch & Zukier, 1984; Hastie, 1984), that our commonsense model of dispositions is, in part, a deep-structural model in that many dispositions are perceived as causes for other traits or specific behaviors. This characterization of commonsense personality theory is consistent with the proposition that the concept of causality implicit in everyday cognition is generally closer to a generative rather than a regularity theory of causality. The question of what status to accord dispositional or trait concepts in academic psychology is a considerably more contested issue that I shall now discuss.

The major competing views on dispositions are conveniently captured by Zuroff (1986) in his recent discussion of whether Allport was a trait theorist:

> There are three basic positions on the reality of traits. As is well known, Allport held that traits are real, causal entities that correspond to as yet unknown neurophysiological structures. An opposing view is that traits are purely descriptive; they summarize a person's past behavior, but they have no real existence and are certainly not causal entities (Buss & Craik, 1983; Wiggins, 1974). A third possibility is that traits are dispositional concepts (Ryle, 1949). . . . . the dispositional view of traits . . . is that they describe a tendency to perform a certain class of acts when the individual is placed in a certain class of situations. Dispositions are distinct from summaries because they do not imply anything about the actual occurrence of behavior; in the absence of the eliciting stimuli, even a strong disposition will not be manifest in the stream of behavior. Although there are some philosophers who view dispositions as causal concepts (Armstrong, 1969; Hirschberg, 1978), they are generally not considered to provide causal explanations, and, of course, they are not entities. (p. 996)

One major difficulty, both with personality theory and in the debate surrounding this issue, is the disagreement concerning what "dispositions" and "traits" are taken to include. Some psychologists treat these two concepts (traits and dispositions) as equivalent, some do not. Some theorists think all internal dispositions, such as abilities, needs, beliefs, and attitudes, should be excluded from the study of personality; others include a broad range of personal dispositions including those just listed. Fletcher (1984) and Newman and Uleman (1989) have suggested that some classes of disposition qualify for causal status while others do not. For example, many dispositions seem to refer to patterns of observable behavior and perhaps best fit the descriptive summary approach: for example, talkative, punctual, and untidy. Other dispositions appear to be attributions to the "mind" and to clearly represent potential causes for behavior or mental events: for example, beliefs, abilities, and states of knowledge. Still another enormous class of dispositions appear to fall into both camps containing both a causal, usually mental, component and a set of behaviors that are regularly evinced: for example, tolerant, warm, independent, stubborn, confident, and insecure.

The attempt to build a personality theory operating purely with a summary–descriptive definition of dispositions, such as Buss and Craik's (1983) act frequency approach, cannot handle cases where dispositions are rarely or never manifested. This approach also ignores or postpones the all-important task of building explanatory theories (see Block's [1989] devastating critique of the act frequency approach). This criticism also applies to the remaining approach, that Zuroff (1986) terms the dispositional account of traits. In this view, ascribing a disposition is tantamount to a lawlike statement that states a person is liable to behave in characteristic ways under certain conditions. The major problem with this approach is again that it lacks explanatory power; it merely describes empirical regularities and fails to deal with the underlying cognitive or personological constructs that can cause and hence explain such regularities.

The causal–explanatory approach to at least a subset of dispositions, is, of course, the option favored by realists. For the realist account, to ascribe a disposition is to ascribe a property that enables the person to behave in a particular way under appropriate conditions. Hence, dispositions are causes, and the enabling relation is a causal relation. In consequence, realists, like Allport, assert what Zuroff and others deny; namely, that dispositions can function as genuine causal explanations.

One common objection to interpreting dispositions as causes is that they are simply promissory notes for causal explanations. Zuroff (1986), for example, notes that "An explanatory system that makes use of trait concepts must embed the trait terms in a process theory that redeems the promissory notes if it is to generate new findings and deeper understandings" (pp. 999–1000). We certainly accept the notion that dispositional explanations tend to operate as placeholders for later more insightful and complex causal accounts. However, unlike promissory notes, dispositional explanations in psychology cannot usually be exchanged for fuller explanations on demand. Patience may be rewarded, however. The lesson to be learned from the development of good scientific theories in other fields is that dispositional explanations often require prolonged cultivation for small yield. For example, 25 years passed before the Sutton–Boveri hypothesis of chromosomal gene location provided the first independent test of Mendel's theory of the gene. Indeed, it is my view that recent work that has examined traits or individual differences from a social cognitive perspective is currently cashing in some of these promissory notes (e.g., Fletcher & Fincham, 1991; Higgins & Bargh, 1987; Showers & Cantor, 1985).

CAVEATS AND CONCLUSIONS

One theme running through this chapter has been that common sense may be more subtle and sophisticated than is often appreciated and that much of the research and theorizing (of both philosophers and psychologists) may be vitiated by their often cavalier specification of the content and structure of our folk psychology theory. Being anxious to avoid falling into the same trap, I would stress there are some important and obvious differences between commonsense theory and the corpus of "scientific" psychological theories.

Commonsense psychological theories, to a large extent, consist of tacit knowledge, whereas "scientific" theories are laid out in comparatively explicit detail. In addition, commonsense psychological theories seem to have a wider range of uses and aims than scientific theories and consist of a more amorphous, flexible and sprawling set of concepts and models than most psychological theories.

Finally, I have argued for the scientific credibility of commonsense psychology and have suggested that under certain conditions laypeople are considerably more rational in their social judgments than suggested by mainstream social cognition. This does not mean, however, that personality and social psychologists should exploit commonsense psychology in an unreflexive fashion or that folk psychology *necessarily* represents the correct psychological theory (as, of course, could be said of any theory in science). To treat common sense as a resource for theory building is a fine strategy, but to sanctify it is quite another matter—caveat emptor!

REFERENCES

Allport, G. W. (1966). Traits revisited. *American Psychologist, 21,* 1–10.

Armstrong, D. M. (1969). Dispositions are causes. *Analysis, 30,* 28–36.

Asch, S., & Zukier, H. (1984). Thinking about persons. *Journal of Personality and Social Psychology, 46,* 1230–1240.

Bhaskar, R. (1978). *A realist theory of science* (2nd ed.). Sussex: Harvester Press.

Block, J. (1989). Critique of the act frequency approach to personality. *Journal of Personality and Social Psychology, 56,* 234–245.

Brookings, J. B., & Brown, C. E. (1988, April). *Dimensionality of the attributional complexity scale.* Paper presented at the meeting of the Midwestern Psychological Association.

Buss, D. M., & Craik, K. H. (1983). The act frequency approach to personality. *Psychological Review, 90,* 105–126.

Churchland, P. M. (1984). *Matter and consciousness.* Cambridge, MA: MIT Press.

Churchland, P. M. (1985). Reduction, qualia, and the direct introspection of brain states. *The Journal of Philosophy, 82,* 8–28.

Churchland, P. M. (1988). The ontological status of intentional states: Nailing folk psychology to its perch. *Behavioral and Brain Sciences, 11,* 507–508.

D'Andrade, R. G. (1974). Memory and the assessment of behavior. In H. M. Blalock (Ed.), *Measurement in the social sciences.* Chicago: Aldine-Atherton.

Dennett, D. C. (1987). *The intentional stance.* Cambridge, MA: MIT Press.

Desoto, C. B., Hamilton, M. M., & Taylor, R. B. (1985). Words, people, and implicit personality theory. *Social Cognition, 3,* 369–382.

Devine, P. (1989). Overattribution effect: The role of confidence and attributional complexity. *Social Psychology Quarterly, 52,* 149–158.

Einhorn, H. J., & Hogarth, R. M. (1981). Behavioral decision theory: Processes of judgment and choice. *Annual Review of Psychology, 32,* 53–88.

Feyerabend, P. K. (1975). *Against method.* London: New Left Books.

Fiske, S. T., & Taylor S. E. (1984). *Social cognition.* Reading, MA: Addison-Wesley.

Fletcher, G. J. O. (1984). Psychology and common sense. *American Psychologist, 39,* 203–213.

Fletcher, G. J. O., & Fincham, F. D. (1991). Attribution processes in close relationships. In G. J. O. Fletcher & F. D. Fincham (Eds.), *Cognition in close relationships* (pp. 7–35). Hillsdale, NJ: Erlbaum.

Fletcher, G. J. O., & Haig, B. (1992). *The layperson as "naive scientist": An appropriate model for social psychology?* Unpublished manuscript, University of Canterbury, Christchurch, New Zealand.

Fletcher, G. J. O., Grigg, F., & Bull, V. (1988). The organization and accuracy of personality impressions: Neophytes versus experts in trait attribution. *New Zealand Journal of Psychology, 17,* 68–77.

Fletcher, G. J. O., Reeder, G. D., & Bull, V. (1990). Bias and accuracy in attitude attribution: The role of attributional complexity. *Journal of Experimental Social Psychology, 26,* 275–288.

Fletcher, G. J. O., Rhodes, G., Rosanowski, J., & Lange, C. (1992). Accuracy and speed of causal processing: Experts versus novices in social judgment. *Journal of Experimental Social Psychology, 28,* 320–338.

Flett, G. L., Pliner, P., & Blankstein, K. R. (1989). Depression and components of attributional complexity. *Journal of Personality and Social Psychology, 56,* 757–764.

Funder, D. C. (1987). Errors and mistakes: Evaluating the accuracy of social judgment. *Psychological Bulletin, 101,* 75–90.

Furnham, A. F. (1989). *Lay theories: Everyday understanding of problems in the social sciences.* Oxford: Pergamon Press.

Furnham, A., & Henderson, M. (1983). Lay theories of delinquency. *European Journal of Social Psychology, 13,* 107–120.

Gilbert, D. T., Pelham, B. W., & Krull, D. S. (1988). On cognitive busyness: When person perceivers meet persons perceived. *Journal of Personality and Social Psychology, 54,* 733–741.

Greenwald, A. G. (1980). The totalitarian ego: Fabrication and revision of personal history. *American Psychologist, 35,* 603–618.

Greenwood, J. D. (1989). *Explanation and experiment in social psychological science.* New York: Springer Verlag.

Griggs, R. A., & Cox, J. R. (1983). The elusive thematic-materials effect in Wason's selection task. *Quarterly Journal of Experimental Psychology, 35,* 519–533.

Hastie, R. (1984). Causes and effects of causal attribution. *Journal of Personality and Social Psychology, 46,* 44–56.

Hinz, V. B., Tindale, J. E., Nagao, D. H., Davis, J. H., & Robertson, B. A. (1988). The influence of the accuracy of individuating information on the base rate information in probability judgment. *Journal of Experimental Social Psychology, 24,* 127–145.

Hirschberg, N. (1978). A correct treatment of traits. In H. London (Ed.), *Personality: A new look at meta-theories* (pp. 45–68). New York: Halstead Press.

Hooker, C. A. (1987). *A realistic theory of science.* New York: State University of New York Press.

Howard, G. S. (1985). The role of values in the science of psychology. *American Psychologist, 40,* 255–265.

Kenrick, D. T., & Funder, D. C. (1988). Profiting from controversy: Lessons from the person–situation debate. *American Psychologist, 43,* 23–34.

Klayman, J., & Ha, Y. W. (1987). Confirmation, disconfirmation, and information in hypothesis testing. *Psychological Review, 94,* 211–228.

Kuhn, T. S. (1970). *The structure of scientific revolutions* (2nd rev. ed.). Chicago: University of Chicago Press.

Lepper, M. R., Ross, L., & Lau, R. R. (1986). Persistence in inaccurate beliefs about the self: Perseverance effects in the classroom. *Journal of Personality and Social Psychology, 50,* 482–491.

Manicas, P. T., & Secord, P. F. (1983). Implications for psychology of the new philosophy of science. *American Psychologist, 38,* 399–413.

Markus, H., & Zajonc, R. B. (1985). The cognitive perspective in social psychology. In G. Lindzey & E. Aronson (Eds.), *The handbook of social psychology* (3rd ed., pp. 137–230). New York: Random House.

McCrae, R. R., & Costa, P. T. (1985). Updating Norman's "adequate taxonomy": Intelligence and personality dimensions in natural language and in questionnaires. *Journal of Personality and Social Psychology, 49,* 710–721.

McMullin, E. (1983). Values in science. In P. D. Asquith & T. Nickles (Eds.), *Proceedings of the 1982 Philosophy of Science Association* (Vol. 2, pp. 3–23). East Lansing, MI: Philosophy of Science Association.

McMullin, E. (1984). A case for scientific realism. In J. Leplin (Ed.), *Scientific realism* (pp. 8–40). Los Angeles: University of California Press.

Mischel, W. (1968). *Personality and assessment.* New York: Wiley.

Newman, L. S., & Uleman, J. S. (1989). Spontaneous trait inference. In J. S. Uleman & J. A. Bargh (Eds.), *Unintended thought* (pp. 155–188). New York: Guilford Press.

Nisbett, R. E., & Ross, L. (1980). *Human inference: Strategies and shortcomings of social judgment.* Englewood Cliffs, NJ: Prentice-Hall.

Popper, K. (1959). *The logic of scientific discovery.* London: Hutchinson. (Original work published 1935)

Rippere, V. (1977). Commonsense beliefs about depression and antidepressive behaviour: A study of social consensus. *Behaviour Research and Therapy, 15,* 465–470.

Rosenberg, S. C., Nelson, C., & Vivekananthan, P. S. (1968). A multidimensional approach to the structure of personality impressions. *Journal of Personality and Social Psychology, 16,* 619–626.

Ross, L. (1977). The intuitive psychologist and his shortcomings: Distortions in the attribution process. In L. Berkowitz (Ed.), *Advances in experimental social psychology* (Vol. 10, pp. 173–220). New York: Academic Press.

Ross, M., & Fletcher, G. J. O. (1985). Attribution and social perception. In G. Lindzey & E. Aronson (Eds.), *The handbook of social psychology* (3rd ed., pp. 73–122). New York: Random House.

Ryle, G. (1949). *The concept of mind.* New York: Barnes & Noble.

Semin, G. R., & Krahe, B. (1987). Lay conceptions of personality: Eliciting tiers of a scientific conception of personality. *European Journal of Social Psychology, 17,* 199–209.

Showers, C., & Cantor, N. (1985). Social cognition: A look at motivated strategies. *Annual Review of Psychology, 36,* 275–305.

Shweder, R. A. (1975). How relevant is an individual difference theory of personality? *Journal of Personality, 43,* 455–485.

Sternberg, R. J., Conway, B. E., Ketron, J. L., & Bernstein, M. (1981). People's conception of intelligence. *Journal of Personality and Social Psychology, 41,* 37–55.

Strube, M. J., Lott, C. L., Le-Xuan-Hy, G. M., Oxenberg, J., & Deichmann, A. K. (1986). Self-evaluation of abilities: Accurate self-assessment versus biased self-enhancement. *Journal of Personality and Social Psychology, 51,* 16–25.

Taylor, S. E., & Brown, J. D. (1988). Illusion and well-being: A social psychological perspective on mental health. *Psychological Bulletin, 103,* 193–210.

Tetlock, P. (1985). Accountability: A social check on the fundamental attribution error. *Social Psychology Quarterly, 48,* 227–236.

Trope, Y. (1979). Uncertainty-reducing properties of achievement tasks. *Journal of Personality and Social Psychology, 37,* 227–236.

Trope, Y. (1980). Self-assessment and task performance. *Journal of Personality and Social Psychology, 18,* 201–215.

Weiss, D. S., & Mendelsohn, G. A. (1986). An empirical demonstration of the implausibility of the semantic similarity explanation of how trait ratings are made and what they mean. *Journal of Personality and Social Psychology, 50,* 595–601.

Wiggins, J. S. (1974). *In defense of traits.* Invited address at the Ninth Annual Symposium on Recent Developments in the Use of the MMPI, Los Angeles.

Zuroff, D. C. (1986). Was Gordon Allport a trait theorist? *Journal of Personality and Social Psychology, 51,* 993–1000.

CHAPTER NINETEEN

A Commonsense Approach to Personality Measurement

RAYMOND N. WOLFE

The sun, the moon, the clouds, and the stars provided ancient astrologers with clues to people's characters and destinies. Other oracles relied on other sources of information: The hydromancer read the airs, winds, and waters; the necromancer consulted with the dead; the haruspex interpreted patterns of lightning or the entrails of a sacrificed animal; the alchemist read shapes formed by a thin stream of molten lead poured into a bowl of water. These soothsayers were regarded as unenlightened by their rivals and descendants, who offered more personalized pronouncements based on elements of the client's own physical structure: The chiromancer read the lines on one's palm; the physiognomist, facial features; the phrenologist, skull conformation. More recently, psychologists have sought to discern people's character by interpreting records of their self-expression, such as samples of handwriting, projective test responses, and nonverbal behavior. Today's methods of personality measurement arose from this venerable tradition. Many of them still contain remnants of the occult (the word comes from the Latin *occultus*, past participle of a verb meaning to cover up, to hide) that need to be dispelled.

When personality measurement began to emerge as a subdiscipline of psychology in the 1920s and 1930s, much of it took place in psychiat-

---

RAYMOND N. WOLFE • Department of Psychology, State University of New York, Geneseo, New York 14454-1401.

Fifty Years of Personality Psychology, edited by Kenneth H. Craik *et al.* Plenum Press, New York, 1993.

ric institutions. As Szasz (1968, 1977) and others have pointed out, an adversarial relationship exists between patients and clinicians in such settings; assessment in this context is primarily a ritual adjunct to pejorative labeling.* It therefore behooved the early clinical psychologists to swathe this part of their craft in mystery. They did so by developing instruments that were bewildering to laypersons. Projective tests were well suited to this purpose and soon became a basic tool of the clinical trade.

Objective inventories, some of them consisting of hundreds of statements presented for endorsement, tended to be similarly bewildering. The person taking such tests could not be very sure of what was being measured or how; this was thought to be a desirable state of affairs from the psychologist's standpoint. Confronted by a great many statements diverse in content, and ignorant of how one's endorsements were to be scored, weighted, combined, and mapped onto a personality profile, the test taker would be hard put to dissimulate systematically in responding. Even so, psychologists thought that further safeguards against strategic self-presentation were necessary; procedures intended to detect lying, self-contradiction, and random responding were devised and incorporated into many scales.

Adversarial logic was not confined to the psychiatric hospital and the mental hygiene clinic. Psychologists in university and industrial settings mistrusted their subjects too. Many of the instruments developed for use with college samples were constructed in the same way as clinical tests, with subscales designed to spot deliberate or undeliberate fakery on the part of respondents. Scales that assessed only a single construct contained buffer items to partly conceal the purpose of the test by misleading the test taker about what was presumably being measured. It was taken for granted that an appreciable proportion of subjects either could not or would not give truthful reports about themselves.†

Partly because of its origins in clinical psychology, then, early personality measurement resembled espionage. It was a cat-and-mouse-like endeavor, with the psychologist seeking clever ways to penetrate the subject's supposedly elaborate and shifting psychic defenses. The question always in the background (and often at the focus of attention, as in the extensive work on response styles) was How can students of

---

* Anderson (1981) describes the polity's need for experts who are willing to assume the responsibility of identifying surplus individuals and populations. Szasz (1977, chap. 14) describes the distinction between technical and ceremonial uses of assessment.

† For an interesting discussion of deception in modern psychology, see Scheibe (1978).

personality obtain trustworthy self-reports from their subjects? Sustained attacks on the problem gained little ground. Their outcomes compel two conclusions: There is no solving it, and in seeking to solve it, one is likely to mystify oneself. Szasz (1984) provides a coda: "But should we not rather rejoice that men who seek to deceive others, even with the best of intentions, in the end only deceive themselves? So long as that remains true, there is hope for mankind" (p. 169).

The institutional machinery of science is designed to facilitate self-correction; its workings are evident in a trend toward increasing straightforwardness in personality measurement that seems to have begun in the 1930s. Gordon Allport had a hand in it. His teachings, together with efforts of many other psychologists (e.g., Campbell & Fiske's introduction in 1959 of multitrait–multimethod analysis) and the parapposite development of electronic data processing led to some salutary advances.

Allport urged psychologists to rely on common sense in trying to understand personality (Allport, 1937) and in devising and using assessment procedures (1961, p. 399). He advocated multimethod measurement wherever feasible, but tended also to favor direct over indirect methods (e.g., objective over projective techniques) (Allport, 1953). Finally, he contributed objective measures of his own (Allport & Allport, 1928; Allport & Ross, 1967; Allport et al., 1960).

Objective personality assessment started to emphasize direct measures in the 1960s. Instruments appeared in which every item was face valid. Investigators began to act on the assumption that if you want to find out something about someone, the best way to do it is to ask him, as clearly and directly as possible, and take his answer at face value. From the standpoint of the earlier personality testers, a psychologist would be naive to proceed this way.

But there is much in favor of such a commonsense approach. It is conservative; it does not presume that the psychologist can know more about a person than the person himself can know or will tell. It is parsimonious in that it minimizes the number of inferential steps between the response and the psychologist's inference about where the subject stands on a particular trait dimension. It is demystifying: The psychologist need not masquerade as a wizard; the subject can participate as a reporter about himself (in Jessor's phrase, "an ethnographer of his own life") rather than as a fugitive adversary. And with regard to technical adequacy, tests based on commonsense assumptions compare favorably with tests based on other rationales (Ashton & Goldberg, 1973; Scott & Johnson, 1972).

The steps in developing an instrument via the commonsense approach were specified by Jackson (1970). Outcomes of my own studies convince me that, in certain circumstances, the sequence he prescribes is more efficient than any other. In this chapter, I define the circumstances in which Jackson's method is superior and present embellishments of it, along with some minor qualms.

The would-be test builder is confronted by a long list of challenges, many of which are difficult to meet. To ignore any of them, or to fail to meet any of them, reduces the probability that the measure will be able to hold up under multitrait–multimethod analysis. But with certain subject populations and under certain conditions, the method described here is the best available. The present prescription may be helpful also to users of personality tests; to select wisely from an array of inventories, prospective users need to know the hurdles that test builders ought to have negotiated en route to their final lists of items.

The prescription for commonsense measurement consists of answers to three broad questions:

1. Under what conditions is it most reasonable to assume that subjects will give truthful reports about themselves in responses to personality test items?
2. Given these conditions, how can one devise a suitable set of prospective items?
3. Given such a list of items, what criteria can one apply so as to retain the best and eliminate the poorest?

VERIDICALITY

The assumption that subjects will describe themselves accurately on personality tests is most defensible when there are grounds for believing that subjects are

1. able to read and understand the instructions and content of each item;
2. motivated throughout the test to give honest and accurate responses;
3. free from confusion about what the scale as a whole is intended to measure; and
4. free from confusion about the meaning of each item.

The importance of these conditions can hardly be overemphasized. If the subject is illiterate, not motivated to reply truthfully, or confused about what it is he is being expected to report about himself, his responses are worse than useless in the hands of a psychologist who erroneously believes them to be useful. To the extent that any of the conditions is not fulfilled, it is extremely difficult to know what, if anything, a response signifies.

The literacy condition implies some obvious limits. Objective personality tests are ill-suited for subjects below the age of 10, for subjects whose intelligence is below the normal range, for poorly educated adults—that is, anyone whose reading ability is suspect; their applicability with elderly people is also questionable:

> Currently available personality tests have not proven reliable with older adults. Test items are likely to have been written for and normed on younger and better-educated persons. Older persons may also fatigue more easily, may not like being asked the sorts of questions often included in personality tests, and may be more inhibited and subject to response sets. (Hogan *et al.*, 1985, p. 43)

Further delimiters are implied by the second condition, motivation. Willingness to participate and to give veridical self-reports may be low, for example, among subjects in total and near-total institutions, where inmates and staff are likely to be adversaries. Even in ostensibly ideal institutional settings, such as university research centers or psychology departments, subjects may take a dim view of the assessment enterprise. Their attitudes can be adversely affected by information from sources over which the individual investigator has little control: the mass media, the campus grapevine, the subjects' own educational experiences, the ambiance created by recent and current research events.

It is also likely that the investigator's local reputation can influence a potential subjects' expectancies concerning participation in a particular project. Ordinary ethical conduct is essential. Research promises must be kept. One must be direct and honest with subjects in all phases of a study, from initial recruiting through the final providing of feedback in the form of group results. Confidentiality of results must be maintained during and after a study. Beyond their importance with regard to subjects' rights, these rules are an integral part of the fabric of straightforward assessment.

Another part of the fabric is the test materials themselves. In creating these, the investigator must take pains to assure that they will not mislead the subject either by design or through carelessness. The test builder has to labor over general and specific instructions until they are as simple and unmistakable as can be. Instructions should also include an invitation to the subject to signal the examiner if further clarification of purpose, items, materials, or anything else about the testing situation is desired.

In the body of the questionnaire, all items intended to measure a particular trait should be grouped together* and headed by a designation of the trait name (e.g., "The items on this page are intended to measure how energetic you are" or "Items 8 through 17 pertain to satisfaction with life"). Although earlier psychologists would have recoiled from such clarity and directness (it invites dissimulation by the subject), such headings turn out to be valuable because they serve to reduce misunderstandings on the part of the subject.†

Response format should be as simple and unmistakable as possible. A yes–no or true–false format is ideal; however, the Likert format provides a range that is psychometrically advantageous in the early stages of test construction. So here, a compromise is recommended: Likert format throughout item analysis and up to the point at which the instrument has exhibited a satisfactory array of multitrait–multimethod relationships and then it may be feasible to switch to a simpler format.

Instructions and the items themselves should consist of words that are easy to read, arranged in short, simple, self-referential statements (Amelang and Borkenau [1986, pp. 27–28]) cite several empirical studies showing that items having these features tend to be more valid than items lacking them. The meaning of each item must be as unequivocal as human ingenuity can make it. And this meaning should correspond in an obvious way to the trait-name heading under which the item appears. Where these conditions are fulfilled, it becomes possible to begin to exploit ordinary language and common sense in the measurement of personality.

---

* Interspersal of items measuring various traits has been a common practice in the construction of global inventories. By itself, this does not amount to a serious defect because sets of dependable items tend to yield dependable variables whether they are interspersed or not; such sets of items tend to cohere predictability, more or less regardless of the field of items in which they are embedded. Interspersion is thus to some extent defensible; but because it is a potential source of confusion to the test taker, the commonsense approach forbids it.

† Although "transparency" of items has been regarded as a defect (e.g., Epstein, 1984, p. 312), it is necessary and desirable from a commonsense standpoint. Aiming to enlist the subject as a reporter of his own characteristics and seeking to achieve this end by facilitating accurate self-report, straightforward assessment seeks to maximize clarity and directness without insulting the respondent's intelligence. The work of Knowles (1988) demonstrates that the responses of college students, at least, become more reliable as it becomes clearer to the subject exactly what it is that he's being asked to report about himself; this implies that higher-quality responses are obtained when the trait being measured is known than when it is unspecified or concealed or disguised.

DEVISING ITEMS

PRELIMINARY ASSUMPTIONS

The commonsense approach makes no distinction between traits and behavioral dispositions. It simply presumes that people differ in terms of the traits they possess. It is compatible with most definitions of dispositional constructs, including the causal, act frequency, and conditional views described by Wright and Mischel (1987, p. 1160). It is premised on the beliefs that there are individual differences in the strength of people's dispositions to act in certain ways; that these are measurable and worth measuring; that in circumstances conducive to veridicality an efficient way to do this is to ask appropriate self-referential questions grouped together in scales; and that such scales should be devised by the rational method. Finally, it assumes that a scale must measure one and only one construct [Briggs and Cheek (1986), and Wolfe and Kasmer (1988), illustrate the confusions that can arise when psychologists use scales that measure more than one construct] and that a relatively small number of items will suffice for a given construct.

A personality scale is one way of operationalizing a construct that is embedded in a theory. The theory identifies the construct (along with other constructs); the scale quantifies it. It is therefore necessary to start with a theory or a minitheory that specifies two or more constructs and the supposed relationships between them. This accords the theory its warranted logical priority and at the same time compels the test builder to start thinking in terms of convergent and discriminant validity at the very outset.*

To devise good items within these constraints is an exacting task. Sustained attempts to meet this challenge sometimes produce the (perhaps illusory) impression that one's understanding of the construct and theory at issue has been sharpened by the effort (although, at a later stage, subjects' responses can, and must be permitted to, have a decisive role in this respect) (Jackson, 1970, p. 75). It seems plausible, though, that one may acquire greater awareness of a construct's meaning by trying repeatedly to distinguish between its "core" and its "correlates" [or, in Wright and Mischel's terms, central and peripheral acts, respectively (1987, p. 1163)]. This is one of the aspects of scale con-

---

* These points echo two of the essential principles of scale development laid down by Jackson (1970, p. 63).

struction in which Campbell and Fiske's (1959) ideal—refining theory and measurement at the same time—can be realized.

FROM THE THEORY TO THE ITEM

The more fully a theory specifies its constructs' relationships with behavior and with each other, the easier it becomes to devise items. The construct of religiosity within Jessor and Jessor's (1977) theory of problem behavior, for example, is quite well specified in terms of its behavioral referents and its presumed direction of correlation with other constructs. Given this rich nomological net, one can readily generate prospective religiosity items. The construct of private self-consciousness described by Fenigstein, Scheier, and Buss (1975), for example, is poor by comparison, with regard to both behavioral referents and connections with other constructs. It is consequently difficult to think of items likely to be sensitive to individual differences in private self-consciousness and not something else. Data described by Angleitner, John, and Lohr (1986) show that those dimensions of a construct that are most fully explicated in the theory tend to be most heavily represented among test items (pp. 67–76); this should be true by design alone, but is also probably due in part to ease of generating items.

Angleitner and co-workers identify six categories of item content: characteristic activities; attribution of traits to oneself; wishes, interests, and preferences; biographical facts; attitudes and beliefs; and others' reactions to oneself. These can be thought of as the reportable facets or dimensions of a construct—the ways it may manifest itself tangibly enough for the person to recognize it and therefore be able to give an accurate self-description regarding it. Proportions of item content in the finished scale ought to correspond approximately to the theory's specifications as to how the construct is supposed to manifest itself. Item writers should therefore apportion their efforts accordingly (even though it often turns out that the number of items created in a given content category is a poor predictor of the number ultimately retained). The number of items initially devised will depend on many variables apart from richness of theoretical detail: desired length of the finished scale, number of item writers, their familiarity with the construct and theory, and their steadfastness.*

---

* Item writing can be done as a convivial activity or both solitarily and in groups. Brainstorming sessions can facilitate this phase of the work; when they are part of the process, productivity is doubtless affected by group dynamics as well.

Each item is describable in terms of surface characteristics and meaning characteristics (Angleitner et al., 1986, pp. 80–93). Surface characteristics can be determined objectively: They are length (number of words or letters, number of clauses), complexity (person, voice, tense, mood, negation), and sentence type (grammatical case). Meaning characteristics are not so readily ascertained, but can be rated reliably by trained judges: They are ambiguity, comprehensibility, abstractness, self-reference, and desirability of endorsement.

The prescription for straightforward assessment is clear for all features of the item itself. Shortness is prized. Word count should be held to perhaps 15 at most. Qualifying words and phrases should be held to a minimum. The longer an item is, the more complex it is likely to be; the more complex it is, the more alternative interpretations it permits; the more interpretations it permits, the more interpretations subjects will give it; the more interpretations subjects give it, the less psychometrically useful it becomes.

Simplicity and directness are also prized (Scott & Johnson, 1972). Items should be stated in the first person, the active voice, the present tense (except, of course, for biographical facts), and the indicative mood. Negatives are to be avoided; they are confusing (Holden & Fekken, 1990; Matlin, 1983, p. 142), and, as Fletcher (1984) argues, "For mental dispositions, ... positive instances of behavior should assume a much more potent diagnostic role than negative instances" (p. 210) [the findings of Ahlawat (1985)* and Funder and Dobroth (1987) support Fletcher's position].

Declarative and interrogative sentences seem to be equally suitable, although the respondent's task becomes more difficult when both are included in the same scale (response format has to be compatible with sentence type; complications arise when format varies within a scale). Some rules of thumb for writing simple items: Avoid commas, connectives, negatives, and subjunctives.

Angleitner and co-workers present criteria for evaluation of meaning characteristics, along with results of preliminary analyses of 1051 items. The five meaning characteristics turn out to be weakly related to one another, although some pairs yield significant correlations. Ambiguity, for example, correlates –.22 with comprehensibility and .26 with abstractness. Some surface characteristics are also associated with certain elements of meaning (e.g., item length correlates approximately –.60 with comprehensibility).

* I am indebted to Michelle Picioccio for bringing Ahlawat's excellent research to my attention.

After items are written and edited into presentable form with respect to their surface characteristics, their meaning characteristics should be evaluated independently by judges using Angleitner and coworkers criteria, or some variation thereof. This step can identify statements that need to be altered because they are equivocal or otherwise suspect. Improvements in clarity cost less, of course, if they can be achieved early in the sequence. The wisdom of eliminating prospective items at this stage is questionable, although some deselection here may be justified if a great many items are available. (Where possible, one ought to avoid imposing unnecessarily on subjects.) Because psychometric criteria provide the most defensible grounds for item elimination, however, most decisions to retain or not are best left until a later stage. Itemmetric facts are associated with and in a sense underlie psychometric facts (for documentation, see Angleitner et al., 1986; Holden et al., 1985) but should not be used in lieu of them. A dependable psychometric technology for item selection exists; test builders can and should rely on it.

Still, the importance of itemmetric analysis as a first step can hardly be disputed. Straightforward assessment demands that a test item must not bewilder the subject; careful examination of an item's surface and meaning characteristics provides a good safeguard against such bewilderment.

From Itemmetrics to Psychometrics

When each of the face valid items designed to measure a particular construct has been tailored to the point where its surface and meaning characteristics are satisfactory, the test builder will be eager to administer the first draft of the new scale to subjects. But should the test builder be seeking to devise measures of other constructs as well (a useful strategy not only in the interests of theory development but also because it more or less compels one to focus on discriminant validity right from the outset), it may be more efficient to delay data collection until all prospective items in all the scales have satisfied itemmetric requirements.

A large sample—at least 200—of the subject population the test is intended for must then be recruited and tested under good physical (adequate space, seating, lighting, and ventilation; comfortable temperature; freedom from external distractors, etc.) and psychological (freedom from coercion, from time constraints, from concerns about confidentiality, etc.) conditions.

The distribution of responses to each item is first examined for central tendency and dispersion. Any item that yields either a sharply peaked distribution or an asymmetrical distribution is at once suspect; nevertheless, all items should be retained for further analysis. It is quite likely that items showing little dispersion of response and/or appreciable skewness will fare poorly in other analyses. Items exhibiting either of these features can be suspected of eliciting style-determined rather than content-determined responses (Jackson, 1970, p. 73) and will not correlate highly with total scale score (Angleitner et al., 1986, p. 96).

Estimates of homogeneity are calculated next. These include inter-item and item-total correlations, Kuder-Richardson reliability, and coefficient alpha. To justify the tester's procedure of adding together the subject's responses to different items, it is necessary that these responses exhibit a high level of homogeneity across items: 1.00 is the ideal. Classical measurement theory specifies interchangeability of items as a necessary condition for additivity. In practice, however, it turns out that the content of pairs of items that intercorrelate above .5 is often markedly redundant. Students of personality should therefore be willing to accept sets of items with interitem correlations in the range of .2 to .4, which "would seem to offer an acceptable balance between bandwidth and fidelity" (Briggs & Cheek, 1986, p. 115). Although there is room for debate as to what constitutes an optimal level of correlations among items, it is obvious that negative interitem correlations or very low positive interitem correlations raise major questions about the meaning of a total score that is the sum of responses to such diverse items.

One can increase Kuder-Richardson reliability and the value of coefficient alpha by lengthening the scale with parallel items (i.e. items that merely restate the content of items that already cohere). Some psychologists may have resorted to this expedient in order to be able to report higher reliability values.

Can the desired level of internal consistency be obtained through more legitimate efforts? For a scale to be properly content-saturated (Jackson, 1970), all of its items have to show purity by exhibiting high loadings on the factor the scale is supposed to measure and zero loadings on factors the scale is not supposed to measure; in other words, every item must pass the tests of convergent and discriminant validity. Jackson's (1967) development of the Personality Research Form follows the steps dictated by this rationale. He started with a fairly detailed theory—Murray's (1938) theory of psychogenic needs—and sought to develop a separate scale for each of the 20 needs; these constitute an excellent base from which to establish the necessary discriminant validity. More than 100 candidate items were written for each scale. After sustained efforts at refinement, he arrived at finished scales, most of which exhibited both types of validity.

I would like to think that useful instruments can be devised without undertaking so Herculean a task. However, there is no getting around the fact that several scales need to be developed simultaneously (or, alternatively, that other established scales have to be used along with those being developed) if discriminant validity is to be considered systematically from the beginning.

Test builders with aims more modest than Jackson's can avail themselves of many techniques for sifting prospective items. Beyond interitem correlations and other well-known estimates of internal consistency stands a large array of factor analytic methods, many of which offer the kind of information needed in deciding to retain, eliminate, or alter prospective items. These should be exploited, but it needs to be done thoughtfully. The danger is that in using techniques so efficient, so streamlined, one may forget that it is necessary to touch base from time to time with fresh batches of empirical reality in the form of data from new and different groups of subjects (with $N=200$ or more in each group to assure stability of the correlation matrix).

Having calculated coefficient alpha for a set or subset of more than enough prospective items, for example, one may winnow through the set by recalculating alpha repeatedly, each time with a different suspect item removed. If the value of alpha goes up when a given item is removed, that item is a good candidate for discarding. When all the items thus identified are discarded, coefficient alpha for the remaining items is acceptably high. Another example: One has an abundance of items that could conceivably form a set of clusters compatible with theory. One then goes fishing for this particular structure through successive approximation, conducting one factor analysis after another and eliminating one or more items at each step. After several such analyses, one may arrive at the desired structure. In both of these examples, the investigator capitalizes on idiosyncracies of the data set at hand, thereby decreasing the likelihood of successful cross-validation.

It is, of course, absolutely necessary that stable factor structures be demonstrated sooner or later. This is always a difficult challenge, but it is somewhat easier to meet when test builders are following the commonsense procedure. After two or three careful revisions followed by new data collections, the items and scales start to become known quantities. Their action becomes fairly predictable; the likelihood of unpleasant surprises (e.g., shrinkage on cross-validation, occurrence of unexpected or uninterpretable factor structures) diminishes rapidly.

As Jackson says, "Successive attempts must be made to approach a variety of optimal properties" (1970, p. 65). At the item level, these properties include all the elements of itemmetric adequacy, plus convergence with the other items, discriminant validity with respect to items known to measure other constructs that are theoretically unrelated to the construct at issue (and preferably a large number of such other constructs, the more the better), and freedom from the influence of desirability. Most psychometricians would also insist on adding temporal stability to this already rather daunting list.

FROM THE ITEM TO THE SCALE

The next question is, given a set of items each of which exhibits all of these optimal properties, can they be assembled into a scale that faithfully represents the construct? Jackson (1970) invites attention to content bias as a potential problem: It is quite possible that items intended to measure one or another facet or manifestation of the construct will have been eliminated disproportionately. In such a case, the test builder must backtrack, perhaps to the stage of preparing brand-new items, and work again through the itemmetric–psychometric sequence. At some point, the test builder is loath to retrace these steps one more time and decides to present the scale as "finished" (all this means is that the test builder has chosen—to use Kafka's classic oxymoron—to temporarily abandon the effort to improve it further). The finished scale, then, may misrepresent the construct in some important way or ways. It is in this respect that the psychological adage "The measure *is* the theory" is importantly true (see Rocklin & Revelle, 1981, for an example).

Degree of correspondence between scale and construct is the central question of content validity. The answer to it is usually arrived at through inspection and informed opinion; statistical analysis of responses is less decisive on this matter than on the other elements of a scale's adequacy. With consensus to the effect that the scale does fairly represent the construct, this requirement is met. If consensus is not sought, or is sought but not obtained, either of two scenarios is likely to ensue. In the first, multitrait–multimethod analyses call attention to the disparity and lead to attempts at revising the scale in order to improve the match.

In the second, the measure can threaten to supplant or become the theory. This is particularly likely when the test builder and the theorist are the same person. Given the considerable investment of effort that test construction entails, the psychologist may well be motivated to make a "satisficing" compromise in judging the match between scale and construct, and this conclusion will probably favor the scale at the expense of the theory. In presenting the scale, then, the psychologist may be motivated to play down or ignore altogether the elements of mismatch. Consequences of the second scenario are harmful indeed: Confusion is sown among students; prospective users of the scale are misled. Thus measurement, which ought to be the servant of theory, can come to dictate it even before the data are in.*

SCALE BREADTH VERSUS SCALE LENGTH

Constructs differ in breadth (Hampson *et al.*, 1986) as well as with regard to the richness of the nomological net in which they are embedded. As breadth and/or number of specified relationships within the net increase, so does the difficulty of devising a scale that can adequately represent all facets of the construct without using a very large number of items. The trade-off between length and breadth is the focus of an edifying debate between Burisch (1984a,b, 1985, 1986) and Paunonen and Jackson (Paunonen, 1984; Paunonen & Jackson, 1985).

Burisch argues for shortness. He demonstrated that length is not necessarily associated with validity and makes a convincing case for the cost–benefit advantages of scales consisting of less than ten items. Paunonen and Jackson contend that aggregating across larger numbers of items (say, 16 or 20 per scale) produces a more reliable measure and one that better represents the construct's various facets. A longer scale, they claim, should therefore be capable of predicting a greater variety of criterion behaviors and might fare better in cross-validation. In the end, however, Paunonen and Jackson concede that "As observed by Burisch ... a *judiciously* abbreviated test can for practical purposes be as useful as the full measure in certain instances" (1985, p. 341, italics in original).

Burisch's position does seem radical in that it tends to divorce the instrument from the theory. Psychologists should, he says, present

---

* Later on, as empirical results begin to accumulate, the psychologist may be tempted to let data lead the theory more powerfully than they ought to. This temptation needs to be resisted because, like the method of resolving mismatch in the second scenario, it is conducive to a sterile state of affairs in which methodology takes complete precedence over theory. If this imbalance of power is permitted to prevail, future historians of psychology will find it easy to sum up twentieth-century developments in personality research: "Advances occurred in the area of measurement, as psychologists progressed from reifying traits to reifying trait–method combinations."

subjects with easily understood trait labels or undisguised content-oriented statements rather than with restatements of the theoretical definition of the construct. It is more necessary that subjects give accurate reports about themselves than that the scale represent all facets of a construct. The scale's fidelity to the construct is beside the point if subjects are unable or unwilling to give truthful responses to it:

> That is why it is not wise to keep them busy for too long, have them read lengthy instructions, or require them to strain their brains on word meanings different from everyday usage. This trap avoided, it is also important not to fool ourselves regarding the quality of the resulting data. Given the coarse grain of the language we converse in, we should stop expecting major breakthroughs from polishing verbal instruments. (Burisch, 1984n, pp. 96—97)

Several recent reports address the question: At what point does one begin to encounter diminishing returns with regard to scale length? Along with Burisch's demonstration that the number of items in the Hamburger Depressions-Skala can be drastically reduced, there have been many comparable efforts to shorten other scales (Cacioppo et al., 1984; Hensley & Waggenspach, 1986; Leary, 1983; Perri & Wolfgang, 1988; Strube, 1986; Tomaka et al., 1987; Wolfe et al., 1984). Results are essentially the same in all cases. When items are retained on the basis of an internal consistency standard, it is possible to reduce scale length by 50% or more at little apparent expense in terms of reliability or validity (despite the range attenuation disadvantage that necessarily accompanies reduction in number of items). Thus the early returns are promising; when abbreviated scales come into more extensive use and are used to predict a greater variety of criteria, they could compare favorably with their longer counterparts.

Burish's proposal that a small number of items may prove sufficient for measuring certain personality constructs appears to be defensible. The probable cost of relying on small sets of items—though some predictive capacity is apt to be lost—may be tolerable when it is weighed against the advantages of reduced demands on subjects' patience and cooperativeness. Although aggregation across items indisputably offers important advantages (Epstein, 1984), there appear to be some construct–item combinations for which it is less necessary.

Studies in my laboratory (Meyers et al., 1986; Tomaka et al., 1987; Wolfe, 1986) suggest that the case for short scales is most persuasive in precisely those circumstances that are most compatible with the commonsense rationale; namely, where the construct being measured is already familiar to the respondent, is capable of being asked about in very plain language, and has observable behavioral referents. It also seems that items instructing subjects to give what amounts to a self-report of behaviors aggregated across occasions or situations—what Wright and Mischel (1987) call summary constructs—need not be so numerous as other kinds of items.

There are risks as well as benefits associated with the use of very long and very short scales. If investigators are aware of the trade-offs involved, they can consider these in view of the circumstances and aims of their research in deciding which scales to use for personality assessment. Whereas short scales might confer few advantages in work with college students, for example, they could well be decisive in eliciting cooperation from samples of older adults (Hogan et al., 1985).

CONSTRAINTS ON THE KINDS OF CONSTRUCTS THAT CAN BE MEASURED

During the past two decades, students of personality have become increasingly comfortable with a "big five" set of higher-order factors or broad traits: surgency, agreeableness, conscientiousness, emotional stability, and culture. These emerge so dependably that they can be said to fulfill the requirement of critical multiplism (Houts et al., 1986). At last, we are starting to get somewhere!

Why, one may ask, is it these traits and not others that show up time and again? Why are self-deception, self-consciousness, and self-monitoring, for example, not on the list? From the commonsense standpoint, there are three good reasons. The first is that each of the "big five" can be translated directly into everyday language: surgency= energeticness; agreeableness and conscientiousness need no translating; emotional stability=calmness or serenity; and culture=bookishness. Second, each translation is meaningful to the average layperson. Third, each translation has some relatively unequivocal behavioral referents, which makes it possible for people to describe themselves and their acquaintances more or less accurately on each dimension. McCrae and Costa (1987) have documented the capacity of these broad traits, and most of the several facets or dimensions of each, to hold up very well under multitrait–multimethod examination.

The constructs in the alternate list—self-deception and so on—have no simple counterparts in ordinary language, tend to be more difficult for the average layperson to comprehend, and have few obvious or unequivocal behavioral referents. For these reasons, they can be expected to resist measurement technology; it is difficult to imagine that these constructs could yield the required pattern of correlations in a multitrait–multimethod matrix (which is not to say that all the dispositions that matter are subsumed by the "big five").

Results of a study of 142 college students by Meyers and co-workers (1986) demonstrate that convergence between scale scores, self-ratings, and peer ratings varies directly with the construct's observability (and perhaps with how easy it is for the laypersons to comprehend). Here are the convergent correlations found by Meyers and colleagues between scale scores and the average of ratings by between three and six acquaintances: religiosity, .74; alcohol use, .73; physical ability, .60; sociability, .56; boredom susceptibility, .25; concern for appropriateness, .24. This is a pattern with clear implications for an individual-differences approach to personality. It shows that those traits that have unmistakable behavioral referents are most likely to exhibit the convergence required in support of the claim that a construct has real existence or can be dependably measured. The correlations for boredom susceptibility and concern for appropriateness come very close to being nonsignificant (a one-tailed test is required); although these constructs are comprehensible to respondents, they lack the unequivocal behavioral referents that the other constructs possess. By examining scales of different lengths and using different numbers of rating items for their constructs, Meyers and co-workers are also able to show that the number of items needed for adequate measurement of a trait varies inversely with observability of trait-related behaviors and, as Gorsuch (1984) has noted, with the trait's familiarity to respondents.

It follows that there are limits on the kinds of constructs we can hope to measure successfully. The more readily understandable a trait or disposition is to the literate layperson, the greater the likelihood that a useful scale can be devised to assess it. The psychometric excellence of Chapman and Chapman's (1987) measure of handedness, for example, is attributable partly to the fact that everyone is familiar with the construct of handedness. But observability remains the *sine qua non* (Amelang & Borkenau, 1986; Funder & Dobroth, 1987).

Adequate measurement requires the demonstration that at least two traits, when operationalized by two maximally dissimilar methods, exhibit the expected pattern of convergent and discriminant coefficients. In most cases, ratings by acquaintances or other knowledgeable informants will comprise one of the methods against which self-report instruments are validated. Where ratings are used, both subjects and raters must be laypersons if the results are to be taken as representative of what goes on in everyday life (this is another reason why the psychologist should stick to ordinary language when devising constructs and instruments). The implication, of course, is that valid assessment of individual differences in personality can be achieved only, or at least most handily, for those dispositions the layperson is familiar with. This state of affairs not only restricts the range of traits being studied, but in effect reduces trait theory to the status of a merely descriptive endeavor and one limited to cataloguing what, in a sense, nearly everybody already knows anyway at that.

Put this way, the constraints are perhaps overstated [cf., Wright and Mischel (1987, p. 1160) for a slightly more optimistic picture], but the fact remains that psychometric adequacy has its price; we must "acknowledge limits in order to proceed with power and confidence" (Gould, 1987, p. 16).

Without psychometrically adequate measures, we have only speculation and no decisive ways to tell the idle from the valuable. A measuring technique is needed; the one offered here appears most promising. To adopt it, one must also accept the necessary constraints, which, after all, do not rule out the possibility of robust and informative empirical work.

CONCLUSIONS

The trend toward a commonsense approach to personality theory and assessment seems to have gotten its start in the writings of Gordon Allport. In the 1960s, psychologists increased their reliance on personality tests consisting largely or entirely of face-valid items. In 1970, Jackson presented a sequential method for developing such tests. During the past two decades, students of personality have tended more and more to follow commonsense assumptions in measurement, and many tests have been devised in accordance with Jackson's prescription. This trend has enhanced the quality of instrumentation, and improved instruments have in turn led to several replicable demonstrations of consistent patterns of individual differences in personality traits.

Future psychologists will doubtless remain aware of the value of a commonsense approach. Whether they will subscribe to Burisch's view that properly abbreviated scales are in the end more advantageous than full-length scales remains to be seen. I believe the commonsense approach, as embodied in Jackson's 1970 prescription, can ultimately be compatible with Burisch's proposal (despite the slightly ironic fact that Jackson remains one of the stoutest opponents of this proposal).

At present, psychologists are favoring shortness of scales and items. In his 1986 book, for example, Buss describes 37 relatively new personality scales by numerous authors and lists their items. They average eight items in length and for the most part are straightforward, with simple response formats and short, face-valid, clearly stated items. It is encouraging to see this set of instruments; such an array could probably not have been found 20 or 30 years ago, much less presented and recommended for use.

For scientific—as opposed to ceremonial—purposes, the commonsense approach tends to be superior to other techniques of measurement. From a practical standpoint, it minimizes demands on the test taker, and thus, in principle at least, should enlarge the lists of populations and subjects who will provide usable protocols in studies of personality.

It has some limitations as well. It tends to be sheerly descriptive; its advantages over other methods of assessment are probably minimal for traits that lack observable behavioral referents (and perhaps for traits that are not familiar to laypersons); its efficiency is questionable in certain applied settings and with subjects whose reading skills are poor.

The study of personality had progressed to the point where adversarial logic is no longer the order of the day. And psychologists can now avoid deceiving themselves in at least two important respects: mistaking method variance for trait variance and being content to know that a scale works (i.e., exhibits predictive validity) without knowing *why* it works. Multitrait–multimethod analysis enables psychologists to tell the one kind of variance from the other. Devising and using scales that measure one and only one construct (as Briggs & Cheek, 1986, urge) helps to counteract psychologists' willingness to be satisfied when a total score on a factorially complex instrument produces a significant validity coefficient, despite the fact that they have no idea as to whether a particular subset of items is actually doing the explanatory work.

Not long ago, many psychologists were disillusioned about personality measurement (Jackson, 1970, pp. 61–62). Today, its prospects look good; although we are by no means all the way out of the woods, there has been some real progress. The commonsense approach has played an important part in it and now needs to be exploited more fully.

REFERENCES

Ahlawat, K. S. (1985). On the negative valence items in self-report. *Journal of Social Psychology, 112,* 89–99.
Allport, G. W. (1937). *Personality: A psychological interpretation.* New York: Holt.
Allport, G. W. (1953). The trend in motivational theory. *American Journal of Orthopsychiatry, 25,* 107–119.

Allport, G. W., & Allport, F. H. (1928). *The A–S reaction study.* Boston: Houghton Mifflin.

Allport, G. W. (1961). *Pattern and Growth in Personality.* New York: Holt, Rinehart and Winston.

Allport, G. W., & Ross, J. M. (1967). Personal religious orientation and prejudice. *Journal of Personality and Social Psychology, 5,* 432–443.

Allport, G. W., Vernon, P. E., & Lindzey, G. (1960). *Manual for the study of values* (3rd ed.). Boston: Houghton Mifflin.

Amelang, M., & Borkenau, P. (1986). The trait concept: Current theoretical considerations, empirical facts, and implications for personality inventory construction. In A. Angleitner & J. S. Wiggins (Eds.), *Personality assessment via questionnaires: Current theory and measurement* (pp. 7–31). New York: Springer-Verlag.

Anderson, M. L. (1981, August). *Mental Illness and mental retardation. Legitimization for surplus populations.* Paper presented at the meeting of the American Psychological Association, Los Angeles.

Angleitner, A., John, O. P., & Lohr, F. J. (1986). It's *what* you ask and *how* you ask it: An itemmetric analysis of personality questionnaires. In A. Angleitner & J. S. Wiggins (Eds.), *Personality assessment via questionnaires: Current issues in theory and measurement* (pp. 61–107). New York: Springer-Verlag.

Ashton, S. G., & Goldberg, L. R. (1973). In response to Jackson's challenge: The comparative validity of personality scales constructed by the external (empirical) strategy and scales developed by experts, novices, and laymen. *Journal of Research in Personality, 7,* 1–20.

Briggs, S. R., & Cheek, J. M. (1986). The role of factor analysis in the development and evaluation of personality scales. *Journal of Personality, 54,* 106–148.

Burisch, M. (1984a). Approaches to personality inventory construction: A comparison of merits. *American Psychologist, 59,* 214–227.

Burisch, M. (1984b). You don't always get what you pay for: Measuring depression with short and simple versus long and sophisticated scales. *Journal of Research in Personality, 18,* 81–98.

Burisch, M. (1985). I wish it were true: Confessions of a secret deductivist. *Journal of Research in Personality, 19,* 348–353.

Burisch, M. (1986). Methods of personality inventory development—A comparative analysis. In A. Angleitner & J. S. Wiggins (Eds.), *Personality assessment via questionnaires: Current issues in theory and measurement* (pp. 109–120). New York: Springer-Verlag.

Buss, A. 91986). *Social behavior and personality.* Hillsdale, NJ: Erlbaum.

Cacioppo, J. T., Petty, R. E., & Kao, C. F. (1984). The efficient assessment of need for cognition. *Journal of Personality Assessment, 48,* 306–307.

Campbell, D. T., & Fiske, D. W. (1959). Convergent and discriminant validity by the multitrait–multimethod matrix. *Psychological Bulletin, 56,* 81–105.

Chapman, L. J., & Chapman, J. P. (1987). The measurement of handedness. *Brain and Cognition, 6,* 175–183.

Epstein, S. (1984). A procedural note on the measurement of broad dispositions. *Journal of Personality, 52,* 318–325.

Fenigstein, A., Scheier, M. F., & Buss, A. H. (1975). Public and private self-consciousness: Assessment and theory. *Consulting and Clinical Psychology, 43,* 522–527.

Fletcher, G. J. O. (1984). Psychology and common sense. *American Psychologist, 39,* 203–213.

Funder, D. C., & Dobroth, K. M. (1987). Differences between traits: Properties associated with interjudge agreement. *Journal of Personality and Social Psychology, 52,* 409–418.

Gorsuch, R. L. (1984). Measurement: The boon and bane of investigating religion. *American Psychologist, 39,* 228–236.

Gould, S. J. (1987). This view of life: Justice Scalia's misunderstanding. *Natural History, 96,* 14–21.

Hampson, S. E., John, O. P., & Goldberg, L. R. (1986). Category breadth and hierarchical structure in personality: Studies of asymmetries in judgments of trait implications. *Journal of Personality and Social Psychology, 51,* 37–54.

Hensley, W. E., & Waggenspach, B. M. (1986). A brief scale of role-playing. *Journal of Research in Personality, 20,* 62–65.

Hogan, R., Carpenter, B. N., Briggs, S. R., & Hansson, R. O. (1985). Personality assessment and personnel selection. In H. J. Bernardin & D. A. Bownas (Eds.), *Personality assessment in organizations* (pp. 21–52). New York: Praeger.

Holden, R. R., & Fekken, G. C. (1990). Structural psychopathological test item characteristics and validity. *Psychological Assessment: A Journal of Consulting and Clinical Psychology, 2,* 35–40.

Holden, R. R., Fekken, G. C., & Jackson, D. N. (1985). Structured personality test item characteristics and validity. *Journal of Research in Personality, 19,* 386–394.

Houts, A. C., Cook, T. D., & Shadish, W. R., Jr. (1986). The person–situation debate: A critical multiplist perspective. *Journal of Personality, 54,* 52–105.

Irwin, M. E., Lundeen, E. J., & Knowles, E. S. (1988, April). *Effects of retest on the factor structure of two personality tests.* Paper presented at the annual meeting of the Southwestern Psychological Association, Tulsa.

Jackson, D. N. (1967). *Manual for the Personality Research Form.* Goshen, NY: Research Psychologists Press.

Jackson, D. N. (1970). A sequential system for personality scale development. In C. D. Spielberger (Ed.), *Current topics in clinical and community psychology* (Vol. 2, pp. 61–96). New York: Academic Press.

Jessor, R., & Jessor, S. L. (1977). *Problem behavior and psychosocial development: A longitudinal study of youth.* New York: Academic Press.

Knowles, E. S. (1988). Item context effects on personality scales: Measuring changes the measure. *Journal of Personality and Social Psychology, 55,* 312–320.

Leary, M. R. (1983). A brief version of the Fear of Negative Evaluation Scale. *Personality and Social Psychology Bulletin, 9,* 371–375.

Matlin, M. (1983). *Cognition.* New York: Holt, Rinehart, & Winston.

McCrae, R. R., & Costa, P. T., Jr. (1987). Validation of the five-factor model of personality across instruments and observers. *Journal of Personality and Social Psychology, 52,* 81–90.

Meyers, M., Malorzo, L., & Wolfe, R. (1986, April). *MTMM validation of concern for appropriateness.* Paper presented at the annual meeting of the Eastern Psychological Association, New York City.

Murray, H. A. (1938). *Explorations in Personality.* New York: Oxford University Press.

Paunonen, S. V. (1984). Optimizing the validity of personality assessments: The importance of aggregation and item content. *Journal of Research in Personality, 18,* 411–431.

Paunonen, S. V., & Jackson, D. N. (1985). The validity of formal and informal personality assessments. *Journal of Research in Personality, 19,* 331–342.

Perri, M., & Wolfgang, A. P. (1988). A modified measure of need for cognition. *Psychological Reports, 62,* 955–957.

Rocklin, T., & Revelle, W. (1981). The measurement of extraversion: A comparison of the Eysenck Personality Inventory and the Eysenck Personality Questionnaire. *British Journal of Social Psychology, 20,* 279–284.

Scheibe, K. E. (1978). The psychologist's advantage and its nullification: Limits of human predictability. *American Psychologist, 33,* 869–881.

Scott, W. A., & Johnson, R. C. (1972). Comparative validities of direct and indirect personality tests. *Journal of Consulting and Clinical Psychology, 38,* 301–318.

Strube, M. J. (1986). An analysis of the Self-Handicapping Scale. *Basic and Applied Social Psychology, 7,* 211–224.

Szasz, T. S. (1968). Science and public policy: The crime of involuntary mental hospitalization. *Medical Opinion and Review, 4,* 24–35.

Szasz, T. S. (1977). *The manufacture of madness.* New York: Harper.

Szasz, T. S. (1984). *The therapeutic state: Psychiatry in the mirror of current events.* Buffalo, NY: Prometheus Books.

Tomaka, J. W., Lennox, R. D., & Wolfe, R. N. (1987, April). *Social avoidance and distress: Construct evaluation and measurement.* Poster presented at the annual meeting of the Eastern Psychological Association, Arlington, VA.

Wolfe, R. N. (1986). Correlates of scores on the Morningness–Eveningness Questionnaire. Unpublished raw data.

Wolfe, R. N., & Kasmer, J. A. (1988). Type vs. trait: Extraversion, impulsivity, sociability, and preferences for cooperation and competitive activities. *Journal of Personality and Social Psychology, 54,* 864–871.

Wolfe, R. N., Lennox, R. D., Welch, L. K., & Cutler, B. L. (1984, April). *A shortened version of the Fear of Negative Evaluation Scale.* Paper presented at the annual meeting of the Eastern Psychological Association, Baltimore.

Wright, J. C., & Mischel, W. (1987). A conditional approach to dispositional constructs: The local predictability of social behavior. *Journal of Personality and Social Psychology, 53,* 1159–1177.

PART FIVE

EPILOGUE

CHAPTER TWENTY

An Optimistic Forecast

ROBERT HOGAN

This book celebrates 50 years of personality psychology as a formal discipline, the birth of which was announced by the near-simultaneous publication in 1937 of Gordon Allport's and Ross Stagner's textbooks. Allport and Stagner thought they were witnessing (if not engendering) the beginning of a new scientific enterprise. Fifty years later, it might be useful to ask how well we are doing.

Although most people on the street think the subject matter of personality psychology—the nature of human nature—is the core of psychology, academic psychology has a more ambivalent view of the discipline. Two examples of this ambivalence can be quickly cited. First, personality is not a prestigious topic in academic psychology: Federal funding remains scarce and personality psychologists are not invited to join the National Academy of Sciences. Second, personality psychologists make up a small fraction of all psychologists and only about 10% of Division 8 (Personality and Social Psychology) of the American Psychological Association. Despite the popular appeal of personality psychology, it remains something of an acquired taste within academia.

Although personality psychology is not faring as well as some might like after 50 plus years as a discipline, it is nonetheless doing much better than it was a few years ago. The response set controversy, which flared up in the mid-1950s (and which its early proponents still keep alive), was internecine warfare at its worst. The controversy ex-

ROBERT HOGAN • Department of Psychology, University of Tulsa, Tulsa, Oklahoma 74104.

Fifty Years of Personality Psychology, edited by Kenneth H. Craik *et al.* Plenum Press, New York, 1993.

hausted the participants, alienated many nonparticipants, and left the discipline open to attack by unsympathetic critics (advocates of the response set notion argued that the key methodology of the discipline—personality measurement—was deeply flawed and research based on that methodology was uninterpretable).

The response set controversy was followed immediately by a massive behaviorist critique of personality psychology. This critique argued that, not only was the measurement base confounded by artifact (i.e., response sets), but the principle assumption of the discipline—that there is a stable core to personality—was empirically unjustified. This led to the so-called "person–situation" debate, which further diverted attention from substantive issues and further eroded interest in the field.

Since the mid-1980s, however, there has been a resurgence of interest in personality psychology, and I can point to eight trends that are quite encouraging.

First, except for Jones (1990) and Ross and Nisbet (1991), the critics are now largely silent. Block (1965) and Rorer (1965) effectively ended the response set controversy, and Kenrick and Funder (1988) announced the end of the person–situation debate. Not only are the critics relatively silent, but there is a new enthusiasm for personality psychology in the air, and this book is one expression of that enthusiasm.

Second, Allport was consistently critical of nomothetic sciences as a way to study individuals. He would, therefore, be delighted to note that the interpretive model (in which individuals are compared with themselves rather than with group norms) has achieved considerable legitimacy in modern personality psychology, as seen in the writings of Bruner (1986), McAdams (1985), Sarbin (1986), and Runyan (1990).

Third, Allport and Odbert's (1936) psycholexical study of English language trait words provided the textual basis for the development of the Five Factor Model (FFM) (Digman, 1989). The FFM is a well-replicated taxonomy of personality descriptors and provides a very useful springboard for future research as well as a methodology for classifying and understanding the noisome myriad of idiosyncratic personality measures that are introduced into the literature each year. The FFM is a major contribution to the scientific study of personality.

Fourth, for reasons that may be more personal than intellectual, experimental social psychology has been hostile to the notion of individual differences for some years. All that now seems to have changed; a generation of younger social psychologists has discovered the reality of individual differences and has begun to incorporate individual differences measures and concepts systematically into their writing

(Baumeister & Tice, 1988; Cantor & Kihlstrom, 1987; DePaulo et al., 1987; Funder, 1991; Ickes, 1982; Kenrick, 1989; Snyder, 1981).

Fifth, it is encouraging to note the emergence of a group of young personality psychologists in the United States who are seeking to solve some of the fundamental problems identified in the original Allport and Stagner texts (e.g., Buss, 1991; Cheek, 1982; John, 1990; McCrae, 1990; Moskowitz, 1986).

Sixth, Allport's prescriptions for personality research provide the framework for ambitious programs of ongoing work in England (e.g., Emler, 1990; Furnham, 1992) and in Germany (e.g., Angleitner et al., 1990), where Allport traveled in the 1920s and first formulated many of his ideas about personality.

Seventh, clinical psychology was once the traditional ally of personality psychology, but clinical psychology seems to have gone through a paradigm shift; psychodynamics has been replaced by cognitive psychology. Along with this shift, many clinicians seem to have lost interest in personality and personality assessment as traditionally understood. The loss of this important market for personality research has happily been offset by a burgeoning new market in industrial and organizational (I/O) psychology. Over the past six or seven years, I/O psychology has discovered personality and personality measurement (e.g., Barrick & Mount, 1991; Guion, 1987; Hough et al., 1990; Staw & Ross, 1985; Weiss & Adler, 1984). This development is consistent with Stagner's early interest in using personality to understand labor–management problems and other issues in industrial psychology.

Eighth, research on the biological origins of personality is attracting widespread interest in the scientific community. Perhaps the best-known example of this is the research at the University of Minnesota that examines the personality similarities of identical twins reared apart (Tellegen et al., 1988). This research allows us to estimate the heritability of the components of personality with greater precision than before. Using models taken from the study of plant genetics, molecular biologists are beginning to study the genetic origins of personality traits in dogs (e.g., shyness, aggressiveness), and it is only a matter of time before we will be able to use these methods to study the origins of individual differences in human personality.

Finally, well-constructed personality measures often predict occupational performance about as well as cognitive tests do, but they tend not to have adverse impact (i.e., minority groups' scores are usually about the same as those of majority group members). Thoughtful observers of the U. S. Department of Justice note a trend in federal legislation that will soon compel employers to focus more attention on their prospective employees' personality patterns and perhaps increase the use of personality measures in preemployment testing. This trend should further enhance popular interest in personality and lead to a broader acceptance of personality assessment.

REFERENCES

Allport, G. W., & Odbert, H. S. (1936). Trait-names: A psycholexical study. *Psychological Monographs, 47*, (211).
Angleitner, A., Ostendorf, F., & John, O. P. (1990). Towards a taxonomy of personality descriptors in German: A psycholexical study. *European Journal of Personality, 4*, 89–118.
Barrick, M. R., & Mount, M. K. (1991). The Big Five personality dimensions and job performance. *Personnel Psychology, 44*, 1–25.
Baumeister, R. F., & Tice, D. (1988). Metatraits. *Journal of Personality, 56*, 571–598.
Block, J. (1965). *The challenge of response sets.* New York: Appleton-Century-Crofts.
Bruner, J. (1986). *Actual minds, possible worlds.* Cambridge, MA: Harvard University Press.
Buss, D. (1991). Evolutionary personality psychology. *Annual Review of Psychology, 39*, 551–556.
Cantor, N., & Kihlstrom, J. F. (1987). *Personality and social intelligence.* Englewood Cliffs, NJ: Prentice-Hall.
Cheek, J. M. (1982). Aggregation, moderator variables, and the validity of personality tests. *Journal of Personality and Social Psychology, 43*, 1254–1269.
DePaulo, B. M., Kenny, D. A., Hoover, C. W., Webb, W., & Oliver, P. V. (1987). Accuracy of person perception. *Journal of Personality and Social Psychology, 52*, 303–315.
Digman, J. M. (1989). Five robust trait dimensions: Development, stability, and utility. *Journal of Personality, 57*, 195–214.
Emler, N. P. (1990). A social psychology of reputation. *European Review of Social Psychology, 1*, 171–191.
Funder, D. C. (1991). Global traits: A neo-Allportian approach to personality. *Psychological Science, 2*, 31–39.
Furnham, A. (1992). *Personality at Work.* London: Routledge.
Guion, R. (1987). Changing views for personnel selection research. *Personnel Psychology, 40*, 199–213.
Hough, L. M., Eaton, N. K., Dunnette, M. D., Kamp, J. D., & McCloy, R. A. (1990). Criterion-related validities of personality constructs and the effect of response distortion on those validities. *Journal of Applied Psychology, 75*, 581–595.
Ickes, W. (1982). A basic paradigm for studying personality, roles, and social behavior. In W. Ickes & E. S. Knowles (Eds.), *Personality, roles, and social behavior* (pp. 305–341). New York: Springer-Verlag.
John, O. P. (1990). The "Big Five" factor taxonomy. In L. A. Pervin (Ed.), *Handbook of personality* (pp. 66–100). New York: Springer-Verlag.
Jones, E. E. (1990). *Interpersonal perception.* New York: Freeman.
Kenrick, D. T. (1989). A biosocial perspective on mates and traits: Reuniting personality and social psychology. In D. Buss & N. Cantor (Eds.), *Personality psychology* (pp. 308–319). New York: Springer-Verlag.

Kenrick, D. T., & Funder, D. C. (1988). Profiting from controversy: Lessons from the person–situation debate. *American Psychologist, 43,* 23–34.

McAdams, D. P. (1985). Biography, narrative, and lives. *Journal of Personality, 56,* 1–18.

McCrae, R. R. (1990). Traits and trait names. *European Journal of Personality, 4,* 119–129.

Moskowitz, D. S. (1986). Comparison of self-reports, reports by knowledgeable observers, and behavioral observation data. *Journal of Personality, 54,* 294–317.

Rorer, L. G. (1965). The great response style myth. *Psychological Bulletin, 63,* 129–156.

Ross, L., & Nisbet, R. E. (1991). *The person and the situation.* New York: McGraw-Hill.

Runyan, W. M. (1990). Individual lives and the structure of personality psychology. In A. I. Rabin, R. A. Zucker, R. A. Emmons, & S. Frank (Eds.), *Studying persons and lives.* New York: Springer-Verlag.

Sarbin, T. R. (1986). *Narrative psychology.* New York: Praeger.

Snyder, M. (1981). On the influence of individuals on situations. In N. Cantor & J. F. Kihlstrom (Eds.), *Personality, cognition, and social interaction* (pp. 309–329). Hillsdale, NJ: Erlbaum.

Staw, B. M., & Ross, J. (1985). Stability in the midst of change: A dispositional approach to job attitudes. *Journal of Applied Psychology, 70,* 469–480.

Tellegen, A., Lykken, D. T., Wilcox, K. J., Rich, S., & Segal, N. L. (1988). Personality similarity in twins reared together and apart. *Journal of Personality and Social Psychology, 54,* 1031–1039.

Weiss, H. M., & Adler, S. (1984). Personality and organizational behavior. In B. M. Staw & L. L. Cummings (Eds.), *Research in organizational behavior* (Vol. 6, pp. 1–50). Greenwich, CT: JAI Press.

Author Index

Abramson, L.Y. 180, 185
Adelson, J. 187, 193
Adler, S. 295, 297
Adorno, T.W. 30, 37
Ahlawat, K.S 277, 287
Ainlay, S.C. 140, 143
Albright, J.S. 186, 204
Aldrich, D.B. 154
Alexander, I.E. 15, 17,
   126, 127
Alker, H.A. 87, 100
Allen, A. 238, 240–248
Allen, B.P. 218, 232
Alloy, L.B. 180, 185
Allport, F.H. 26, 49–51, 54,
   188, 189, 193, 271, 288
Allport, G.W. 3–19, 23–37,
   39–55, 57–65, 69–73,
   75–82, 83, 86–87, 92,
   100, 112–115, 119–121,
   124, 127, 131–143,
   147–162, 165–174,
   177–185, 187–190, 193,
   197–204, 207, 208, 213,
   215–219, 225, 227–232,
   237–242, 245, 247, 252,
   253, 263, 265, 271,
   286, 287, 288, 293, 296
Allport, R. 45, 54
Alpert-Gillis, L.J. 112–115
Alston, W.P. 193

Amelang, M. 244, 246–248,
   274, 285, 288
Anderson, J.W. 54
Anderson, M.L. 270, 288
Angel, E. 101
Angleitner, A. 215, 218,
   232, 233, 248, 276,
   277, 278, 279, 288,
   295, 296
Anonymous 17, 19, 147,
   162
Argyle, M. 184, 185, 201,
   202, 204
Antonovsky, A. 142, 143
Armstrong, D.M. 263, 265
Aronoff, J. 101, 115, 193,
   194
Aronson, E. 214, 267
Asch, S.E. 75, 83, 209,
   213, 262, 265
Ashton, S.G. 271, 288
Atkinson, J.W. 190, 194
Atkinson, R.C. 214
Atwood, G. 54, 125, 128

Baer, R. 180, 186
Bagby, E. 9, 19, 25, 37
Bailor, E.M. 32
Baldwin, A.L. 148, 151,
   162, 166, 174
Baltes, P. 144
Banaji, M.R. 186

Bandura, A. 112, 141, 143
Barclay, A.M. 101
Bargh, J.A. 257, 264, 266
Barlow, D.H. 124, 128
Barrick, M.R. 223, 233,
   295, 296
Barzun, J. 110, 115
Bates, E. 235
Baumeister, R.F. 15, 17,
   180, 181, 186, 295, 296
Baumgarten, F. 216, 233
Beers, C.W. 168, 174
Bellezza, A.G. 186
Bem, D.J. 87, 92, 100, 137,
   143, 238, 240–248
Berkowitz, L. 186, 204, 214
Berman, H.J. 173, 174
Bernieri, F. 249
Bernstein, M. 268
Bertocci, P.A. 59–60, 63, 64
Betts, G.H. 9, 19
Bhaskar, R. 253, 265
Birch, D. 190, 194
Blalock, H.M. 266
Blamey, K. 145
Blank, A.L. 204
Blankstein, K.R. 258, 266
Block, J. 80, 83, 124, 128,
   213, 221, 223, 227,
   229, 233, 264, 265,
   294, 297

Subject Index